Intoleran

Intolerance
A General Survey

LISE NOËL

Translated by Arnold Bennett

McGill-Queen's University Press
Montreal & Kingston • London • Buffalo

© McGill-Queen's University Press 1994
ISBN 0-7735-1160-1 (cloth)
ISBN 0-7735-1187-3 (pb)

Legal deposit first quarter 1994
Bibliothèque nationale du Québec

Printed in Canada on acid-free paper

This book is a translation of *L'intolérance: Une problématique générale*, published by Boréal, 1989. Translation and publication have been assisted by grants from the Canada Council.

Canadian Cataloguing in Publication Data

Noël, Lise
   Intolerance: a general survey
   Translation of: L'intolérance.
   Includes bibliographical references.
   ISBN 0-7735-1160-1 (BOUND) –
   ISBN 0-7735-1187-3 (PBK.)
   1. Toleration. 2. Discrimination. 3. Social psychology.
I. Title.
HM276.N6313 1994   305   C93-090589-X

This book was typeset by Typo Litho Composition Inc. in 10/12 Palatino.

*To my mother and father,
and to the memory of Aunt Aurore.*

Contents

Introduction 3

PART ONE   THE DOMINATOR

1 A Universal Discourse   11
   Historical Truths   12
   The Laws of Nature   16
   The Will of God   20
   The Imperatives of Knowledge   24
   The Criteria of Art   33
   The Force of Language   38

2 The Language of Objectivity   46
   Religion and Sin   48
   Law and Crime   52
   Science and Anomaly   60
   The Implicit Rules of Discourse   72

PART TWO   THE DOMINATED

3 Alienation   79
   The Body as Object   83
     An Object of Pleasure   85
     An Object of Violence   96
   The Oppressed as Abstraction   109
     A Stigmatized Identity   110
     A Stereotyped Portrait   116
   A Pedagogy of Guilt   123
     "For the Good" of the Dominated   125
     The Burden of Proof   129
     The Oppressor as Victim   132

4 Emancipation 145
   Reconsidering the Dominant Discourse 147
      Relative Identities 149
      Competing Subjectivities 164
   Stages of Emancipation 191
      The Quest for Identity 193
      Toward Autonomy 202
      The Pursuit of Power 211

Conclusion 238

Notes 241

Thematic Bibliography 247

Intolerance

"Truth does not so much do good in the world as the semblance of truth does evil."
La Rochefoucauld

Introduction

Movements of emancipation are not dead. They have simply taken on a form different from the one they had in the 1960s and 1970s. Though the time of vast anti-authoritarian revolt and global critical syntheses may have passed, the struggle for tolerance goes on through patient research and specifically focused action.

Countless organizations are working to improve the lot of communities and individuals who are underprivileged or victims of abuse. Historical and sociological studies of specific oppressed groups or of the general dynamics of domination are also emerging in ever greater number, from both university presses and mainstream publishers as well as from small presses.

Though the aspirations which are the hallmark of these ventures are more modest, they are no less radical, since the combined results of these apparently isolated efforts cannot fail to bring about a profound transformation of society. But this transformation will not come about merely mechanically. Liberation groups everywhere now clearly express a desire to attain not only the power to speak but the power to do things. This quest, the culmination of the liberation process launched in the 1960s, is also made necessary by the need to set in motion resistance to current forms of conservatism.

One of the major paradoxes of the 1980s and 1990s is that progressive aims have endured, even in the midst of the reactionary resurgence which has sought to counter the gains of the emancipation movements. At the same time that a new reliance on argument derived from authority appears to be swaying opinion, there is more freedom to discuss previously taboo subjects. With the beginnings of enforcement of the aptly named charters of rights, we can look forward to far-reaching changes in attitudes and institutions.

However, it is increasingly obvious that these charters are as replete with contradictions as they are with freedom and equality. A mere compendium of rights is no substitute for a philosophy of tolerance and only adds to the splintered appearance presented by emancipation movements in recent years.

Activists and theorists want to find a dialectical unity that will make solidarity in action possible. While this need is being expressed more often, there is nothing new about it. In 1968, Albert Memmi, in the first edition of *L'homme dominé*, wrote of his desire to develop a general study of oppression. In 1981, Angela Davis attempted an initial analysis of three of its parameters in *Women, Race and Class*. Since then, a number of works have appeared to support this line of thinking. But until now, no English-speaking or French-speaking author has discussed *all* the parameters of oppression. The most complete books on the question have been anthologies. Though more exhaustive, these endeavours are weak on synthesis.

It is surprising to see how even those scholars who deal with one specific parameter, like age or health, will most often focus their attention on one aspect of it only (for example, childhood but not youth, much less old age; or mental health but not physical health, and vice versa). The purpose of *Intolerance* is more to broaden our view on the subject than to offer a new theory on any given parameter *per se*.

This was the challenge, then: to propose an all-encompassing analysis, an interdisciplinary study resulting from a single train of thought. The demands of such a project were considerable: apart from the scope of the knowledge required, there was the risk of stumbling over epistemological difficulties unknown to a non-specialist. But this was the price to be paid if one wanted to approach the relationships of domination on a crossover basis rather than in parallel terms, to produce a comprehensive work which finally could serve as a benchmark. Even the criticisms aroused by such a study would open the way to other, more fruitful syntheses.

The methodology, already contained in the objective of systematic exploration, was self-evident. At this initial stage, only comparative analysis would make it possible to arrive at a broad overview of the problem of intolerance.

Although the term "intolerance" is now employed to designate any form of rejection of another person, for a long time its use was more limited. Since the sixteenth century, when the humanists attempted to promote freedom of thought and action to fortify their defence of religious tolerance, intolerance has been defined primarily as the unjustified condemnation of an opinion or behaviour.

The rise of liberation movements in western society in the 1960s extended the notion of intolerance to the dimension of identity. Initially conceived as the rejection of a belief or attitude, this notion was now applied to the rejection of a way of being. Yet while an error of belief is judged in terms of an allegedly absolute truth and dissolute behaviour is assessed in terms of an unshakeable social or moral order, individual inferiority is based on a supposedly objective hierarchy of human beings.

Though awareness of this fact is historically more recent, the oppression of another human being on the basis of what that person is is thus the most radical oppression of all. As such it merits the closest attention. A comparative analysis of the relationships of domination, therefore, must focus on all the parameters of identity, since a person can be perceived through:

- general characteristics arising both from biological categories and from sociological variables (age, gender);
- membership in a socio-economic group (social class) or sociocultural group with or without specific physical traits (in the cases of "race" and ethnicity respectively);
- individual characteristics, most often randomly transmitted, which relate to the individual's sexual orientation, mental or intellectual state, or physical condition, specifically his or her health, integrity, or appearance (shape, size, beauty).

Since recent critical thinking has emphasized the importance of the cognitive aspect in dealing with oppression, this book will approach the comparative analysis of the parameters of identity from the perspective of discourse, that is, the social production of meaning. This discourse may derive as much from "conventional wisdom" as from official or scholarly statements. Understood through a descriptive study of the instances of domination revealed by these sources, the web of *relationships* connecting these aspects will gradually provide the backdrop for a general analysis of oppression. Even though the content of the discourse maintained by the oppressors and the oppressed necessarily varies from one type of identity to another, there are fundamental similarities between their structures.

Although the discourse of intolerance legitimizes relations of domination in all their subtlety, it also gives validity to the most brutal forms of oppression. Intolerance is the theory; domination and oppression are the practice. In that sense, intolerance can be said to be a way of knowing, a means of grasping the complex reality of our dealings with the world and with others by simplifying it. The point of this book is to study the dynamics of oppression in its ideological dimensions more than through the daily exploitation and abuses of power that constitute its more concrete manifestations.

In order to do so, a comparative analysis of the parameters of identity is required, as well as a balanced treatment of these parameters. But contrary to the case when discussing women and homosexuals, many different groups had to be discussed in the case of "racial" and ethnic relations as well as age and social class. Great care was exercised in order to obtain this balance.

A word of caution is necessary.

The previously mentioned similarities in the discourse of intolerance are not only valid from one parameter to the next but are manifested in different countries. At least this is the case in contemporary western society, which will be examined in this book mainly (but not exclusively) through some of its English-speaking and French-speaking components: the United States, Canada and Québec in North America, Great Britain and France in western Europe. In this case, however, a totally balanced overview cannot be the goal as the demographic weight of these different areas varies greatly. And so, although French-speaking cultures are treated fairly, more attention has to be devoted to the English-speaking ones.

Finally, as far as its basic purpose is concerned, this book will not be dealing with "causes," the closest thing in that respect being simple attempts at tracing chains of events. Therefore no argument will be made – within or outside the framework of Freudian or Jungian etiology – pertaining to the psychological profile of the intolerant (or "authoritarian") personality or to the socio-psychological make-up of the "orthodox" (or "closed") mind. Nor will we look for the economic roots of oppression – whether from a liberal or from a Marxist standpoint – or for the political origins of the struggle for power.

We will not delve either into the history of ideas to account for the many facets of cultural domination or try to understand the prevalence of hierarchies in our society in terms of functionalist theories about social control. Obviously, we will stay clear of the philosophical dilemma posed by the relative role played by Nature and Nurture in relations of domination, as well as of the moral dimension that is sometimes invoked in that respect through the mention of "evil."

As a twofold comparative analysis, this demonstration deals with the hows rather than the whys of intolerance. Taking oppression as a given, the intention is to demystify the dominant discourse, to pick apart the logic of the dynamics that intolerance creates. We will show what the various types of dominated groups have in common, as well as what separates them. In addition, we will study the nature of the relations between dominated groups and the Left, and challenge the validity of resorting to a concept like that of "difference" to defend the rights of the oppressed. In all these respects, this volume may serve as both a practical guide and a theoretical work, addressing people involved in concrete action as well as thinkers who influence or mirror its course.

Ultimately, this book concerns everyone. Although the degree of oppression varies greatly from one individual to another, each will have occasion to recognize his or her own words in some of those attributed to both dominators and dominated. Intolerance is not necessarily constant and it does not always strike with equal impact, but there is no field that it leaves untouched. In this sense, intolerance is a radical phenomenon, and any systematic analysis that endeavours to detect it is necessarily just as radical as the logic it dissects. It is possible that this analysis may be criticized for going too far when it is simply trying to get to the bottom of things.

Radicalism is not extremism. Recognizing the collusion that sometimes exists between the fields of law, religion, and science and the established order is not equivalent to contesting the undoubted social progress created by the triumph of law over arbitrary power, or to denying the need that humans feel to give meaning to life through the quest for the Divine; neither does it contest the importance of the benefits contributed to humanity by science over the past two centuries, or scorn the aspiration for knowledge from which stems any critical undertaking. But it is in the very nature of the study of intolerance to approach the major fields of human thought and endeavour from the specific perspective of their possible negative contributions to the dynamics of domination. Always seeking legitimacy, the oppressor does not hesitate to justify his controlling excesses by invoking Justice, Knowledge, or even God.

Indeed, not only does the dominant discourse proclaim the superiority of the oppressor's identity over that of the "other," as well as the objective nature of the expert verdict invoked to defend this principle, but it places responsibility for the inferior position of the oppressed squarely on their own shoulders. Once they embark on the path toward rejection of their alienation, the challenge for the oppressed is to expose the relativity of the various identities and the subjective foundations of the judgments determining social hierarchies. One of the more significant ironies of the phenomenon of oppression is that, when the victims do finally challenge its postulates they themselves are accused of "radicalism."

Several individuals contributed in one way or another to the preparation of this work. Some, like Danielle Juteau, Jean-Marcel Paquette, and François Ricard, provided intellectual input. Others, like Serge Bélanger, Hélène Dion, and Roger Gauthier, supplied moral support. Two people, in particular, were present from the beginning of this endeavour: Debora Resnick and Jacqueline Bouchard. All of these individuals deserve my deepest thanks. I also wish to thank the management of Collège Bois-de-Boulogne, as well as the Fonds pour la formation des chercheurs et l'aide à la recherche (FCAR-ACSAIR), without whose support a major part of the work necessary to write this volume would not have been possible.

I gratefully acknowledge the assistance of Geraldine Rogers, Marilyn van Norman, Lawrence Boyle, June Callwood, Nicole Brossard, Julie Norton, and Michele Landsberg in having this book translated into English.

PART ONE
The Dominator

CHAPTER ONE

A Universal Discourse

The oppressor has no apparent existence. Not only does he not identify himself as such, but he is not even supposed to have his own reality. His presence is so immediate and dense, and his universe coincides so totally with the Universe, that he becomes invisible. Rarely seen, rarely named, he is unique, nonetheless, in having a full existence; as the keeper of the word, he is the supreme programmer who confers various degrees of existence on those who are different from himself.

Stated without apparent reference to any specific group, the oppressor's discourse presents a vision of humanity that espouses the very characteristics of his specificity. As the embodiment of the universal, the dominator is also the only Subject, the Individual who, never being considered to belong to a particular group, can study those impersonal categories of the population who pose a "problem," represent a "question," constitute a "case," or simply have a "condition." Though in liberal democracies all men are proclaimed equal to each other and all citizens equal before the law, not everybody can claim the title of man or citizen. For a long time, only landed property owners had the right to vote; slaves were not even considered men.

The concepts of nation and people are understood with no more unanimity than the individual notions of citizen or person. When "the people" demanded social equality with the upper classes in England or France in the nineteenth or early twentieth centuries, women were not included in this generic appellation. And while the formula "We the People" still sometimes takes on, in the United States, the White Anglo-Saxon Protestant connotations that would define "real" Americans, the "We, the Canadian people" that Pierre Trudeau attempted to enshrine in the preamble to his draft constitution was intended to deny Quebecers the status of nation.

"Minors," as the term implies, or pre-adults, had to wait until the Convention on the Rights of the Child in 1989 before adding the right to choose to their existing right to protection, the 1959 Declaration of the Rights of the Child having enshrined the right to compulsory education. Even today, in some countries, people who reach retirement age are deprived of their adult status, with laws against age discrimination making an explicit exception in their case.

Finally, the denial of legal existence may result in outright repression. A homosexual orientation is not considered to be an offence, but the *behaviour* that it necessarily induces in most of these individuals long rendered them liable to penal sanctions, and still does in some American states. Some of these penalties involved nothing less than the *permanent* loss of voting rights.

Unseen and often unnamed, the oppressor thus is the implicit incarnation of the supreme model, the ideal type, the yardstick that measures the humanity of anyone who does not resemble him. Presented as the standard of perfection, his specificity appears to coincide with the main lines of the universal. The very fact that he exercises the right to examine others confirms his belief and, for a time, the belief of his victim in his intrinsic wholeness.

HISTORICAL TRUTHS

To maintain the oppressed in their alienation, the oppressor must obscure their memory, inducing a collective amnesia that will cut them off from their roots and strip them of their identity. Thus, they will be exiled from the historic time of humanity to the no-man's-land of timeless insignificance. If only the oppressor makes history, he is also alone in having one: whoever masters the present moulds the past.

For generations, History was a series of political events that happened only to "great men": conquerors, kings and prime ministers, or revolutionaries. Most often they were the winners, but sometimes they included individuals judged to be monstrous: Attila, Nero, Hitler, Stalin.

Claiming universality often means aspiring to domination. "It is Austria's destiny to rule the world," said the motto of the Hapsburgs. "Rule, Britannia," sang the English, who during the same era gloried in their domination of the empire of the waves. Oblivious of Canada, Mexico, and the Latin countries of the hemisphere, the United States reserved the name "America" for itself alone. It is easier to determine the fate of populations who have been colonized, peoples "without history," as Lord Durham might have said of the French Canadians in the nineteenth century. During the same period, the names of the African armies and leaders who valiantly resisted the Europeans' colonizing thrust were (with the exception of those in Algeria) swallowed up by the waves of anonymity imposed by the victor (Guillaumin, 1972, 30–1).

Not only is the dominated's history denied, but the oppressor excludes the dominated *per se* from the mainstream of human evolution. Thus, academic disciplines other than history salvage entire oppressed groups as objects of specific observation: such as "primitive" societies (Etienne and Leacock, 1980, 5) for anthropology, and homosexuals (Katz, 1976, 7) and the mentally handicapped for psychology. Sometimes the oppressed are represented instead as creatures of myth: in the Eden-like past for Darkest Africa and the ancient wisdom of the Indians, or through the menacing future held in store by a future expansionist China or world conquest by the "International Jew" (Guillaumin, 1972, 203).

The oppressor monopolizes speech, since the dominated, in the words of Marc Ferro, is "banished from history." There is no category of dominated individuals that has not been reduced to silence, as shown in the titles of activist works which give the impression of a hidden reality or a lost history: *L'histoire sans qualités* (History without Qualities) on women (Dufrancatel et al., 1979), *Familiar Faces Hidden Lives* on homosexuals (Brown, 1976), *Voices from the Shadows* on the handicapped (Matthews, 1983), *Nobody Knows My Name* by James Baldwin on Blacks, and *Gens du silence* (People of Silence) by playwright Marco Micone on Italian immigrants to Québec.

As negligible quantities, the oppressed are chucked into the "common pit" of history (as Georges Brassens said of ordinary people) or into the "outskirts" of time (as Octavio Paz said of the Third World). The dominated may also be ignored even when they are at the heart of the debate: during the famous night of 5 November 1981, when a charter of rights was negotiated for Canadians, the "fathers" of the new constitution forgot to mention women.

Thus, until the 1960s, history was the exclusive preserve of the 5 percent of the population who made up society's upper crust (Shorter, 1975, xiii), and the names of the older men of the dominant class were mentioned only when they exercised power (de Beauvoir, 1970 1: 143). Not until the mid-eighteenth century was old age recognized as a specific age of life in France (Gutton, 1988, 154). Only as part of the history of the *family* were there some indirect insights into women and children, even though women accounted for half the population and children were sometimes just as relatively numerous in traditional society (De Mause, 1974, 2; Walvin, 1982, 11). The same goes for adolescence, "discovered" by psychologists at the turn of the century, and for youth in general, studied in its relationship to the *school*, but never from the perspective of its contribution to change (Gillis, 1974, ix). Finally, the opening of history to include mental handicaps is recent, since madness was regarded as a curse for centuries before it was defined as a form of deviance.

When he is not alone in occupying the historical foreground, the oppressor at least monopolizes the leading role. Since he is the sole agent of history, it speaks only of him and remembers only his name. If the dominated nevertheless manage to assert themselves and emerge from anonymity, their proven virtues will be likened immediately to those of the oppressor, whom they have been able only to "imitate." But more often than not, the oppressed will be faceless, with a role more akin to that of a diffuse force, detectable only in its maleficent effects, an essentially parasitic force existing only in terms of the established order that it seeks to destroy.

The participation of the dominated in history is often clothed in the form of a *conspiracy*. As the repository of a secret power at work down through the ages, the oppressed are perceived as being engaged in a long endeavour to undermine existing institutions. Responsible "for all the sins of Israel," Jews were supposed to be involved in a centuries-old international conspiracy, manifested in our times through a desire to control both Marxist revolutions and capitalist regimes. By the turn of the twentieth century, American Whites also believed that they had to defend themselves against the "Negro peril," represented by the first descendants of the slaves freed by the Civil War. Finally, to justify its occupation of China during the same period, the West invoked the pressing necessity to act against the "yellow peril." A later "peril" was homosexuality, labelled until recently a social "plague" in French law, or a political "menace" by Senator Joseph McCarthy in the post-war United States. Like the Jewish conspiracy, the homosexual peril weighed over every regime, including the USSR, which had to protect itself against this "counter-revolutionary" force.

Perceived as a peril, a plague, or a menace throughout history, the dominated can also appear to be a "social evil." This was the case of the working class in the first half of the nineteenth century; *the working classes are dangerous classes*, wrote historian Louis Chevalier, who, in this famous equation, endorsed the point of view of the propertied classes of that age. Yet it is the pernicious influence of women that would appear to have been manifested over the longest period and with the most persistence. While it is sometimes admitted that "behind every great man, there stands a woman," this backstage role as an *eminence grise* is most often seen to be harmful! "*Cherchez la femme!*" ("Look for the woman!") is the advice given in both French and English when the time comes to find guilty parties. If one believes in the philosophy of historian Arnold Toynbee, "in the heroic age the major catastrophes are usually the mark of women, even if the role of women is allegedly passive. ... More commonly: women are the notorious mischief-makers whose malice drives heroes to kill one another" (cited in Janssen-Jurreit, 1982, 31). Their influence does not seem to have faded with time, at least if one judges by the specific accusation that German women brought Hitler to power.

Instead of historical plots, homosexuals have to answer for periods of excess and *decadence*. Decadence is defined in relation to a Golden Age, of course, most often associated with the exercise of power. Thus, the glorious centuries of the Roman Empire corresponded to those of the systematic military conquest of foreign peoples and the reduction of the vanquished populations to slavery; with the growth of homosexuality, the decline began, explains the medievalist N.F. Cantor in one history textbook.[1]

For other classical historians, such as the American T. Frank, the decadence of Rome arrived with the replacement of the old Latin race at the head of the Empire with Orientals "of a more emotional nature."[2] As a citizen of a country that was about to close its doors to immigrants from eastern and southern Europe in 1921, Frank failed to mention the fact that the *oriental* (Byzantine) part of the Roman Empire would survive its Latin counterpart be exactly ten centuries (until the capture of Constantinople by the Turks in 1453).

Finally, in the view of Theodor Mommsen, winner of the Nobel Prize for literature, the emancipation of women should take primary blame for this decline: by challenging the all-powerful status of the paterfamilias, this emancipation rocked a social order "designed by Nature herself" (in Janssen-Jurreit, 1982, 30).

This same Nature, no doubt, must have prescribed infanticide, since the father of a Roman family had the power of life and death over his children. This practice does not offend historians inordinately, with some even finding it "humane" (in De Mause, 1974, 4–5). Only rare few will bother to express concern about why girls were the prime targets of infanticide, as ethnologists and historians are satisfied to blame this imbalance on vague demographic constraints.

Until the war in the former Yugoslavia, when they became impossible to ignore, diplomats and war correspondents rarely took the trouble to report mass rapes of women during revolutions or armed conflicts, believing that these women were simply victims of the Nature of things. Discreet about these "unfortunate incidents," they preferred to provide day-to-day descriptions of vague shifts in borders or publish the most minor statements made by some of the belligerents (Brownmiller, 1975, 148).

Sometimes the experts display a strange prudishness that prevents them from calling things by their proper names. Either they ignore them, as in the case of rape, or they rechristen them to defuse their shocking nature. Thus, historians speak of "miscegenation" to refer to the right of sexual ownership arrogated for nearly two and a half centuries by White planters over their Black female slaves (Davis, 1983, 25). Scientific detachment here supports the claim to universality by endowing it with an objective character that mitigates, in the tone used to describe it, the very reality of a crying injustice.

Little by little, the point of view of a Manichaean world is imposed, where the right of the strongest is exercised behind the neutral screen of cultural differences, demographic contingencies, or secondary effects of political conflicts. Only the dominated appears as a peril, plague, or menace, while the oppressor is the only true hero of History.

THE LAWS OF NATURE

If the oppressor is alone in being part of history and alone in writing history, this is because he is the only one to change. It is in his very nature to move forward to whatever is more and better. As the sole agent of "progress," he is the bringer of "civilization," the universal model to be imitated by anyone who claims to be a part of "evolution."

On the other hand, the characteristics of the oppressed, determined since time immemorial, are both circumscribed and timeless. They are circumscribed because they reveal his limits, timeless because they derive from a static constitution, an essential disposition. Thus, the oppressed arise in history, invariably and impersonally, as a menace or a plague.

To be capable of progressing to a higher plane of existence, the dominated thus must copy the oppressor, not only because the latter has a superior nature, but in order to give a precise direction to this progress. Though fundamentally static, the dominated's constitution does not exclude variation; however, this would tend more to inconsequential agitation than to the orderly pursuit of an objective. The "inconstant" efforts of certain races or certain classes are well known, according to this view, as are the long-established "fact" of the "unstable" character of gays, the frequent "mood swings" of the embittered handicapped, or the "capricious" temperament of children and the elderly. Being static does not necessarily mean being inert, and the tendency to immoderate and random variability may very well reveal itself to be a deep-rooted disposition: thus the "changeable nature" of women is quite compatible with "the eternal feminine."

While the oppressor embodies the completeness of existence, the identity of the dominated is often defined by what is lacking or by a fault of nature. Nature is posited primarily as an ordering principle, a Physical Order of Things, which escapes human intervention or which is established in opposition to it. In this sense, *Nature* is defined as *what is good* (just as "natural" products can be said to be good).

By this criterion, youth and health would seem to be more "natural" than old age and sickness, even though growing older is an inevitable process and the functional or organic alteration of the human body and mind are part of the very dynamics of life. The condemnation of homosexuality in the name of the (erroneous) belief that animals do not engage in this practice also draws its strength from the implicit association between creatures generally judged to be inferior to man and the entire natural order.

Nature once again is called upon to celebrate the human type most closely matching its perfect ideal. Thus, in his novel *Dukedom*, the British writer John Cowper Powys believed that he could evoke the most primitive emotion of the human race, that triumphant and immemorial joy, the joy that a male child is born into the universe![3] This celebration *by* nature reflects the celebration *of* nature. More respectful of an environment that they do not seek to dominate, North American Natives today appear to be the duty-bound allies of campaigns against pollution, just as their ancestors exemplified the virtues of Nature against the misdeeds of Civilization.

But even more than what is good, Nature represents *what is inevitable*, an inclination that nobody can escape, regardless of their wishes. The same Natives who embodied the superiority of Nature had to be colonized by the White Man nevertheless. The colonizer's discourse is revealing in this regard. If one judges, for example, by the words of a French foreign affairs minister of the late nineteenth century, Gabriel Hanotaux, colonizing other peoples represented a "natural" aspiration of that time, a profound "need of any human society" (in Grimal, 1965, 28).

Nature, the foundation of the oppressor's intrinsic need to dominate others, at the same time dictates all of the innate traits characterizing the oppressed, for it is the difference that betrays the essential inferiority of the dominated. What western scientists believed they had found in the anatomy of Blacks in the early nineteenth century, for example, permitted the maintenance of slavery, which was the focus of an ever-growing moral challenge (Stephan, 1982, xii-xiii). The inferiority of women inspired only contempt, due to "the vices of their sex, principally vanity," as Chamfort wrote (*Maximes et pensées*, n° 381). It was the "natural" garrulousness of women that annoyed Kant (in Lascault, 1977, 171), and, in *Mon coeur mis à nu* (My Heart Laid Bare), Baudelaire wrote that he could not tolerate their vulgarity: "Woman is hungry and wants to eat; she is thirsty and wants to drink. She is in rut and wants to be ravished. Beauty is deserving! Woman is natural, which is to say that she is abominable" (in Bédrines, 1978, 27).

Indeed, what is natural is often perceived as biological. Yet if the biological is not necessarily vulgar and can even give rise to official protestations of respect (the maternal "instinct," for example), it nevertheless confines the dominated to a "specific calling." Thus, for Voltaire, Rousseau, and the Encyclopedists, a woman's "constitution" was reduced to a lack (of strength, health, balance) or to an excess (of hysterical violence, enjoyment, intuition); since her "destiny" was limited to reproduction, she necessarily appeared to be "of no account in society" once she grew older (Diderot, *Essai sur les femmes*).[4]

Women therefore have no right to claim freedom comparable to that of men. Since Nature also constitutes *the ultimate reference to normality*, woman can claim only the status that is "in accordance with her nature." Women are not allowed to be priests, for example: according to John Paul II, this would be contrary to both their humanity and their feminity. Scientific authority confirms religious authority: "Freedom for women means freedom to love. But we cannot go against Nature. Woman is intended for reproduction; she has been appointed to take an active part in the reproduction of the race by pregnancy and child-birth," the psychologist Frank Caprio wrote (1962, 133–4). Enjoying a more limited freedom than that of man, she has no natural right to equality either: "Stop the ERA – You can't fool Mother Nature" was the slogan on some bumper stickers in the United States during the campaign against this constitutional amendment.

While the oppressor perceives certain demands by women as contrary to their nature, it is the very identity of homosexuals that seems to be completely "against nature." Even though 10 percent of the population share this orientation and two out of five men (according to the Kinsey Report) occasionally have engaged in homosexual practices, the oppressor can only consider a feeling or behaviour not reflecting that of the majority to be unnatural.

In the final analysis, nature itself will give the impression that it has gone wrong: an extreme handicap like that of the "Elephant Man" then will be blamed on an "error of nature." Under other circumstances, the oppressor will label this error an "aberration" and will choose to blame it rather than "fate" or the victim, like classical economists for whom the "natural laws" of economics leave no place for unemployment.

The laws of Nature thus dictate the identity of the dominated individual, circumscribing it until it converges with what is good, inevitable, and normal. In so doing, they lay the foundation for the completeness of the oppressor's existence, taken implicitly as a universal model, and the inferiority of the dominated, defined in terms of what they are missing or what constitutes a defect. Apart from the identity of both parties, nature necessarily conditions the relationship between them. It therefore outlines *the roles* that each is called upon to play in the unequal complementarity of the whole and its parts.

For example, there was the "whole" of the nation state, into which European regions "naturally" would be melted (Petrella, 1978, 45); and there was the "whole" of the colonial empire, which grouped together the "countries which (called for) foreign conquest"! "Nature has made a race of workers, the Chinese race; ... a race of tillers of the soil, the Negro; ... a race of masters and soldiers, the European race," said Renan (in Césaire, 1955, 14).

Since the whole, by definition, occupies the field of the universal, its parts can aspire to grow only within the former's territory; it cannot grow beyond the realm of the dominant. When American sociologists of the early twentieth century wanted to explain the socioeconomic success of certain Blacks, they emphasized the assumption that they were mulatto (and thus partially White) (in Ladner, 1973, 122). Some members of the Académie Française who grudgingly accepted Marguerite Yourcenar into their ranks invoked the "androgynous sensitivity" of this female author as justification for this acceptance.

Evaluated in terms of the fraction of "the whole" which it contains, the "part" sometimes is judged solely in the light of what it will become. Initially considered to be little men by medieval society (Ariès, 1973, 12), children, under Calvinism, became wicked creatures to be shaped in the image of better-behaved adults, before being redefined by Locke and Rousseau as virgin wax to be moulded by their elders (Walvin, 1982, 45–6).

When they have no claim to a fragmentary or potential share in the oppressor's identity, the dominated have no role other than to submit to the oppressor and serve him. Submission is one of the vocations of women: "Except in cases which are against nature, man, by nature, is more qualified to command than woman," Aristotle decreed (*Politics*). Borrowing from the Greek philosopher, for whom a woman, all things considered, was a "mutilated man" (*On the Generation of Animals*), Thomas Aquinas considered her to be an example of the necessity of imperfection for the good of the whole (*Summa Theologica*) (in Gallant, 1984, 18 and 24).

Since the dominated have no reason to exist except in relation to the oppressor, the oppressor also finds it inconceivable that they can feel more pleasure in living for their own kind rather than for him. A lesbian's preference to be attached to another woman will often be perceived as a "waste" by heterosexual males, who see themselves as the exclusive and natural beneficiaries of female attention.

Nature, drawing on its own authority, can then be posited as the ultimate criterion of the universal. In this capacity, it will take on the same obviousness in a secular society that the will of God presents to the religious mentality. Until the eighteenth century, secular society was sanctioned by religion; it was only with the powerful scientific undercurrent of the Industrial Revolution that the appeal to natural laws substituted in part for the invocation of divine design as the foundation of the established order. Despite the later rise of Marxist ideology, which claimed the authority of History, the concepts of God and nature are still the vehicles for parallel orthodoxies on the question of relations between races, genders, and social classes.

THE WILL OF GOD

Even when they do not claim to be "universal," most organized religions have pretensions to universal truth, both because this truth would be applicable to all of humanity and because it would shape all existence. Thus, this is total truth, which presumes God's intervention in the lives of individuals and society. According to Judeo-Christian tradition, this intervention at first was direct, with God manifesting his will through revelation. Subsequently, divine activity in the world was mediated by those who declared themselves to be the privileged interpreters of this revelation.

As keepers of the truth, the representatives of ecclesiastical institutions are obliged to make it their duty to spread this truth to every level of society. Thus, for centuries, organized religions were State religions and often ended up confusing their interests with those of the peoples and classes in power. Only during the Enlightenment did the idea of a possible separation of Church and State begin to assert itself in the western mind. Fostered by this evolution, and in the wake of the scientific pretensions of the nineteenth century, secular ideologies came to assert themselves as the official thinking of the next century. Claiming their authority either from Nature (atheistic fascism) or

History (Marxism), these ideologies eliminated religion so as to benefit a particular race or class but aspired, with the same religious zeal, to find a total explanation.

However, the closing years of the twentieth century are witnessing the revival of fundamentalist (Protestant) and integrist ideologies (Catholic, Jewish, or Muslim). Challenging the secular principle of the separation of Church and State, these movements increasingly are demanding that the latter support the aims of the former. While Islam is consolidating its monopoly in the Muslim countries and a political minority holding the balance of power is laying the bases of an Israeli theocracy, the American Christian fundamentalists openly adhere to the principle (unconstitutional in the United States) of the necessary link between politics and religion, and John Paul II is enjoining Catholics to reject the "artificial" separation between religion and secular life.

Competing both for the monopoly of the truth and for recruits, institutional religions often defend similar precepts with regard to relationships of domination. Indeed, in the *concept of God* that they convey, implicit postulates underpin the oppression of certain groups. For if, according to the biblical text, God created man in his own image, man often creates God in his. Thus, in the monotheistic West, God is singular and male. The Judeo-Christian tradition symbolically conceives of God as a "Father," and if Catholicism denies women access to the priesthood, it is in part because Jesus was a man. Although Jesus was a member of the Jewish "race" and the poorer class, the Church does not go so far as to require its priests to share these characteristics. There were even long centuries when the "princes" of the Church almost necessarily belonged to the aristocracy; since the Old Testament, God himself has been presented as "King" and "Lord." Likewise, it was as a blue-eyed, blond-haired man that the Christians of Europe exported the Mediterranean Jesus to other continents; even as they preached his Word to "Indians" and Blacks, Whites were not even sure that these people had souls (Guillaumin, 1972, 15).

A reversal inevitably had to occur, for when a nation claims to serve the will of God, it sometimes happens that the divine will ends up serving the interests of the nation. Between the "In God We Trust" of the United States and the "God is American" of some of its inhabitants, there is only the space of a semantic slip of the tongue. The space is quickly crossed, for example, by some of that country's fundamentalists who oppose the teaching of Spanish as a second language in school: "If English was good enough for Jesus Christ, it is good enough for Texas children," these Americans say.[5]

"God save the Queen," the British still sing, making this their national anthem. *"Gott mitt uns"* (God is with us) the Germans long have shouted. The supreme guarantor of legitimacy, God is often summoned to the rescue of those in power: the power of kings, proclaimed for centuries as monarchs "by divine right"; the power of the people, whose voice is said to be the voice of God (*Vox populi, vox Dei*).

Slavery itself was justified *in the name of God*. Since American colonial planters feared for a time that the baptism of Blacks would give them a right to emancipation, Christian theologians hastened to reassure them by invoking the biblical precedent of peoples whom the Hebrews themselves had taken as slaves (in Ruether and Keller, 1983, II, 233–60). "We did what God wanted us to do," Prime Minister Verwoerd was still saying in 1961 to justify the policy of apartheid in South Africa. The entire colonization movement was supposedly "desired by God." In October 1892, the Belgian Jesuit review praised "this great white race, predestined by God to be the initiator and protector of all others" (Pirotte, 1982, 85). Six years later, when the United States was taking over Puerto Rico and the Philippines, President McKinley explained this policy to a group of Methodist ministers as follows: that he had prayed more than once for Almighty God to enlighten and guide him, and that one night it became apparent to him that the United States had no other solution than to take all of the Philippines, educate the Filipinos, and "uplift, civilize and Christianize" them.[6] This seems to be the same God who, according to Hitler in 1941, told him that he had to declare war on the United States.

For God often "imposes" his designs on those who act in his name. As passive instruments of God's will, the faithful do not appear to have any other choice than to defer. When the fundamentalists condemn homosexuals, for example, they do not so much express their prejudices as they transmit divine precepts. It is also necessary to recognize God's will in torments that, at first glance, appear unjustifiable. "The people who have suffered most are always the most grateful. The room with the wheelchair can become the first step towards Paradise," claims a certain Christian discourse, exalting an image of handicapped people more interested in interceding for humanity than in being treated like everyone else (Enby, 1975, 11).

God would seem to take pleasure in testing people. For some groups, this condition is even an integral part of their identity. In this world-view, the suffering of the handicapped is expiation for the rest of humanity, while the preference of the homosexual is a sign of general corruption among the "non-elect." For French Protestantism, (unlike certain Anglo-Saxon denominations), homosexuality is one of the manifestations of the general sickness of a decadent western society; this conception is akin to that of Catholicism, which sees it as an "intrinsic disorder," and that of Judaism, which judges it to be "against nature."

In general, the Judeo-Christian tradition condemns homosexuality more severely in men than in women. For not only is human nature confused in this view with the male gender, but the downfall appears to be greater for a man who plays the role of a woman or treats another man like a woman than for a woman who acts like a man (McNeill, 1976, 84).

Indeed, if there is one conviction shared by all the "great" religions, it is the belief in female inferiority (Carmody, 1979). The Christian tradition considers man to be made in the direct image of God, while woman is a mere reflection of man. In Hinduism, women are not even eligible for salvation; they must wait for another incarnation. And while, in Islam, the testimony of a woman is worth only half that of a man, the Talmud does not even accept it as valid. Every day, the Jewish male thanks God "for not having made him a woman." Just as Hindu women are denied access to the sacred texts of the Vedas and Chinese women are prohibited from analysing the thought of Confucius, Jewish women are not required to study the Torah, even though this is an essential obligation of their religion. The rabbinate and the priesthood are closed to women in Orthodox Judaism and Catholicism, as is the ministry in some Protestant churches. While Christian women long have been "invited" to keep quiet in church to listen to men, and adult Jewish women have to defer even to a thirteen-year-old boy once he becomes *bar mitzvah* (a "son of the commandment"), Buddhist nuns are obliged to serve even the youngest monk.

Since women are inferior beings, the "universal" religions subject all of them to the husband's authority. Judaism and Islam even leave the initiative of divorce to the man. It was, in part, to maintain this subjugation that countries with Catholic traditions opposed the right of women to vote longer than others: "female political suffrage goes against the unity and hierarchy of the family," declared Cardinal Villeneuve in 1940 (in Boucher and Morel, 1970, 162). It was also in the name of the family hierarchy that the "Moral Majority" managed to defeat a bill in the United States Congress in 1980 that would have granted federal funds to shelters for battered women and children.

The divine authority was invoked in the last century, both in France and in the Anglo-Saxon countries, to require unconditional obedience of children to their parents and teachers. In the schools, submission was demanded especially from those who belonged to the "dangerous" classes (Walvin, 1982, 102–4; Crubellier, 1979, 172).

Thus, through the concept of God conveyed by the "great" religions and through the right arrogated by ecclesiastical institutions to interpret divine will, all kinds of oppressive relationships can be sanctioned in the name of the highest authority. Declaring himself to be the privileged repository of an eternal Truth and a revealed Word, the dominator can impose service to his interests, calling it a response to God's design. Relying on the fundamental need to give meaning to life, which is the foundation of true religious feeling, the oppressor channels the immense collective force generated by the inner aspirations of a multitude of individuals to his benefit. In the divine will, he controls the ultimate axiom, even more decisive and legitimate than those of Nature and History.

THE IMPERATIVES OF KNOWLEDGE

As the supreme form of power, knowledge determines what is said. It thus shapes both consciousness and behaviour. The sum of learning acquired in a given era, it is also the synthesis of this learning, the edifice built on the systematic foundation of principles put forward as postulates. As the product of a coherence that precedes the gathering of information, knowledge anticipates logical conclusions. In this sense, it can be said that research often finds what it had *fore*-seen, and that knowledge is necessarily moulded by the system of thought that presides over its development.

He who speaks controls what is said. Yet only the oppressor is able to speak. Since his perception of the world fills his consciousness, the oppressor inevitably draws the criteria of universality from his own experience. Transmitted from generation to generation, they are further reinforced by the centuries-long silence of the dominated.

Thus, the definition of the other that is conveyed by knowledge is the very one established by the dominator, a definition that inspires and is reproduced by the so-called human sciences. In proposing the dominator as the perfect embodiment of a humanity tailored, from the outset, to his own measure, the various disciplines endorse the intrinsic inferiority of the oppressed, implicitly justifying the latter's dependent condition.

Because he is the original model, the dominator is rarely depicted in his specificity. It is the "other" who is the "object" of observation, and who, because of his or her difference, constitutes the "problem" or "subculture" that the various disciplines endeavour to *analyse*. In sociology, for example, research papers focus more on the workers than on the bourgeoisie, more on youth and the aged than on adults, more on women than on men (Mathieu, 1971). However, whether theoretical or descriptive, general works make apparently universal observations, before briefly mentioning that "we are less well informed about Blacks" or that "it would also be useful to study this question with regard to women."

The gender difference, among others, is often reduced to the biological, the "case" of women being relegated to the sociology of the family or to that of sexuality. However, is questions that primarily concern women, their interests are not even mentioned. Indeed, demography views contraception and abortion as a "population" problem rather than as a women's problem (Morgan, 1984, 6–7). In the final analysis, men continue to be the reference group. While the traditional Marxist school subordinates the domination of women to the capitalist exploitation of their male companions, functionalists establish the class affiliation of women in terms of their marital status: if they are single, their own occupation counts; but if they are married (especially if they are unsalaried), the husband's occupation often prevails (Michard-Marchal, 1982, 13).

For some sociologists, the male gender is also equivalent to an age group. Thus, although women make up the majority of old people, most geriatric studies deal with men (Cohen, 1984, 9). In "La jeunesse n'est qu'un mot" ("Youth Is Just a Word") (*Questions de sociologie*, 1980), Pierre Bourdieu takes boys as his sole model.

Once again, one of the reasons why adolescents of the popular classes want to leave school and go to work very soon is the desire to achieve adult status or the economic capacity associated with it as soon as possible. Having money is very important for asserting oneself with respect to peers *and to girls*, to be able to go out with peers and *with girls*, and thus to be recognized and to recognize oneself *as a man*. (In Michard-Marchal, 1982, 9–10. Emphasis added.)

If they are lesbians as well, women are either ignored by the sociologists or studied in terms of their relationship to "deviance": a prison environment, work as a stripper, prostitution (Ettore, 1980, 8). The very fact of being interested in the question of homosexuality (male or female) for many years presented a danger for researchers, who had to publish their results under a pseudonym.

Although the subject has not been taboo, for a long time American Blacks were treated similarly by White sociologists; when they were not totally ignored, only the most poverty-stricken and the most "deviant" families aroused their interest. It was necessary to wait for

Black sociologists to study their community themselves before the perspective was readjusted. But even then, these researchers often were refused grants when they claimed, in turn, to be studying White society (Ladner, 1973, 474); the dominant group sees itself as the reference point and not as an object of study. From the beginnings of the Chicago School, American sociology took for granted the virtues of the cultural melting pot in which new races and ethnic groups would be blended into the primordial Anglo-Saxon core.

The same postulate of the eventual standardization of differences underlay the study of social groups in the post-war United States; the notion of class inequality, with its potential to generate conflict, was replaced by the concept of a continuous range of occupations and statuses, harmoniously distributed. The tendency of the upper class to fade into the rest of the social structure (by blending with the middle class, for example) was also manifested in Great Britain during the same period (Marwick, 1980, 256–7).

It was not until an official "war on poverty" was declared in the United States that interest in a sociology of poverty developed in academic circles in the early 1960s. But even then, the model of behaviour, for some thinkers, continued to be the one supplied by the dominant group:

> In the chapter that follows, the term *normal* will be used to refer to class culture that is not lower class. The implication that lower class culture is *pathological* seems fully warranted both because of the relatively high incidence of mental illness in the lower class and also because *human nature* seems loath to accept a style of life that is radically *present-oriented*, (Banfield, *The Unheavenly City*, 1970, in Waxman, 1977, 14. Emphasis added.)

Even though it adopts "primitive" societies as its object of study, anthropology has also often obeyed the postulates of the dominant logic. Born out of colonialism,[7] it was marked initially by the desire to resolve the economic and political conflicts raised for imperialist Europe by the use of an indigenous labour force. During the same period, American anthropologists assigned themselves the task of detecting the relative abilities of various immigrants to assimilate into the Anglo-Saxon Protestant mentality (Storper-Perez, 1974, 38–53). In 1916, anthropologist Madison Grant, in *The Passing of the Great Race*, worried about the massive influx of immigrants of "mentally different" races – Slavs, Latins and Jews – which he considered to have a harmful effect on American society. But it was Amerindian societies that would hold the long-term attention of American researchers: perceived statically, they would be described in a wealth of detail that would freeze them out of history (Deloria, 1971).

On the other hand, the adult male is almost always considered to be the true representative of his culture in anthropological studies. "The entire village left in thirty pirogues, leaving us *alone with the women and children* in the *abandoned* homes" Claude Lévi-Strauss could write in 1936 in an article on the Bororo of Brazil (in Michard-Marchal, 1982, 7, emphasis added). Moreover, the share of interest respectively accorded to female and male activities is almost always skewed toward men. Although gathering brings in 70 percent of the community's needs, five times more space will be devoted to describing the ritual of the hunt (Mazey and Lee, 1983, 52). A page and a half will be attributed to circumcision and a half-page to clitoridectomy, or a page and a half to statuary (a male accomplishment) as against three lines to ceramics (made by women) (Michard-Marchal, 1982, 180–1).

Anthropologists and archaeologists who studied the neolithic and historical sites of the Near and Middle East in turn transposed the meaning of the phenomena they observed through reductive translations. Thus they saw an "Earth Mother" (fertility goddess) when, in the original language, this "Queen of Heaven" was the creator and orderer of the world; through their intervention, the "saints" who served her were reduced to "ritual prostitutes." While their pens capitalized the word "God" and the homage paid to him by the faithful was considered a "religion", the term "goddess" was attributed a lower-case spelling in appropriate recognition of the mere "cult" devoted to her (Stone, 1979, 19–22). In museums, statues of goddesses became reproductions of anonymous "divinities," and "complete" dictionaries of mythology gave a name to minor gods (like Baal) while forgetting those of important goddesses (Anat, for example) (Monoghan, 1981, xiii–xiv).

Intersecting with anthropology, to which it provides an analytical framework in certain cases, primatology sometimes endeavours to justify this selective logic. Like ethology and sociobiology, with their objective of the comparative study of animals and humans, primatology seeks universal criteria to evaluate behaviour through observation of the "great" apes. Some researchers in this discipline thus believed that they had to conclude the existence of a hierarchy of *aggressive* males engaged in rivalry for the conquest of *passive* females.

As the pinnacle of nature, man is also the ultimate end point of evolution. "It is generally admitted that with woman the powers of intuition, of rapid perception, perhaps of imitation, are more strongly marked than in man," wrote Charles Darwin, who added, "but some, at least, of these faculties are characteristic of the lower races, and therefore of a past and lower state of civilization" (in Ehrenreich and English, 1979, 19). A disciple of Darwin, considered one of the best biologists of his day, the German naturalist Karl Vogt extended the comparison: "The grown-up Negro partakes, as regards his intellectual faculties, of the nature of the child, the female, the servile White" (*ibid.*, 1979, 117). In short, only the adult male, bourgeois or noble, and white-skinned, could claim to stand at the summit of creation!

But the effects of evolution do not end with the group; it has an impact on the individual as well. Thus, several psychological theories are concerned with the development of the human subject, taking childhood, instead of an earlier period of natural history, as their point of reference. However, the model is still fundamentally the same as for the species as a whole: the dominator.

Any person who strays from the evolutionary path followed by the ideal type will be considered to have a "developmental problem" or to be "falsifying the results" of the research (Gilligan, 1983, 6–164). In the index of Jean Piaget's 1932 study *Le jugement moral chez l'enfant* (Moral Judgment in the Child), there are four references to girls, but none to boys, who are considered implicitly to be "Children"; since girls are more interested in the interpersonal than in the regulatory dimension, they have a "much less developed" legal sense than boys, the author wrote. In 1981, in *The Philosophy of Moral Development*, Lawrence Kohlberg laid down six stages through which moral judgment would develop: based on twenty years of observation of eighty-four children, all of them boys, the study's findings were similar to Piaget's, concluding that girls (as well as other cultural groups) rarely reached the final stages. Even though women are more inclined to create networks, they are still evaluated in terms of how they relate to hierarchies.

Although its generalizations apply to all of humanity, two-thirds of psychological research focuses on men (in Finn and Miles, 1982). Women thus are judged by their "deficiencies": when the *fear* of success is not invoked as a theory, then the *failure* of self-assertion is supposed to explain their behaviour. Even a feminist like Marina Yaguello can be taken in. Observing in boys a "tendency to monopolize speech," she does not so much criticize them for their aggressiveness as she criticizes girls for their "lack of assertiveness" (Yaguello, 1978, 49).

Freudian psychoanalysis, evolutionist to some extent, also takes man as the universal model. Although he noted differences in the eight stages of psychosocial development that he establishes in men and women, Erik Erikson used men's stages in developing his portrait of "life" cycles (*Childhood and Society* in 1950; *Identity: Youth and Crisis* in 1968). "[Thinking] the sexual difference to exist within the sphere of the self" (Irigaray, 1974, 100), Freud, in his 1931 study of femininity, had already defined the sexuality of women in terms of that of men. To the Viennese psychoanalyst, the being in whom Aristotle and Thomas Aquinas saw a "mutilated man" appeared to be afflicted with an "innate sexual inferiority": deprived of the penis (which she envies in the boy), the girl can only hope to alleviate "the defectiveness of [her] genital organs" by making a child (preferably a male) as a substitute. In Jungian psychoanalysis, man and woman seem to play more complementary roles, but it is a complementarity between reason and emotion, between *Logos* and *Eros*. During the inter-war period, Jung even expressed concern about the negative effect that the emancipation of women might have on the institution of marriage and on the spiritual balance between the male and female principles (*Die Frau in Europa*).

While Freudianism attributes "penis envy" to all women, it believes even more strongly that this can be detected in lesbians: instead of "normally" overcoming their "castration complex," they would continue to want to appropriate the penis, thus arresting their development. Some psychoanalysts believe that, without necessarily having this form of mental block, a woman "deprived of heterosexual love" will accept the advances of another woman *"faute de mieux"* (for lack of anything better) (Caprio, 1962, 10). In general, this theory considers homosexuality to be "pathological" by the very fact that it differs from heterosexuality. "We assume that heterosexuality is the *biologic* norm and that unless interfered with all individuals are heterosexual," decreed the Freudian psychoanalyst Bieber, who also advised his colleagues to destroy "the illusion that there is something fascinating in the fact of 'being different' " (Bieber, 1962, 319; 272). Thus, it was possible until the early 1970s to perceive homosexuality as a mental disease.

Yet mental illness itself, in general, was defined as "abnormal behavior" (Alexander and Selesnick, 1966, 12), meaning that it was behaviour different from that of the majority. Since the beginning of the twentieth century, classification systems for various mental illnesses (today the DSM-III and the ICD-9[8]) have been elaborated, claiming to have universal application. Illnesses that did not fit into these classifications were labelled "exotic" or "culturally linked" psychoses: only the Occidental was universal (Marsella and White, 1982, 369). Judged by the European yardstick, some colonized peoples, like the Malagasy, even appeared to deserve their fate. The psychoanalyst Octave Mannoni wrote:

Every European, at one point in his development, discovers in himself the desire ... to break his ties of dependency, to be equal to his father. But not the

Malagasy! He is ignorant of the rivalry with paternal authority, the "virile affirmation," the Adlerian inferiority, trials through which the European must pass and which are analogous to the civilized forms ... of the initiation rites through which manhood is achieved. (In Césaire, 1955, 38)

In the same way that the colonizer continues to be the model for the colonized and the model for woman is man, the child is judged in relation to the adult. For example, Freudian theories concerning childhood were drawn from the interpretation of the personal recollections of adults rather than from systematic observation of children themselves (Janssen-Jurreit, 1982, 207). Even when these children speak directly, often their confidences are believed only selectively, as shown by the recent "discovery" of the phenomenon of sexual abuse after eighty years of existence of a theory supposedly based on childhood sexuality (Miller, 1984).

But children do not really have a say, any more than other dominated individuals. The recognized definer, the thinker who is heeded is the person who has the power to speak. The official truth is laid down by the dominator. Not only does he have the right to decide the content of knowledge, but he controls the means of ensuring its *transmission*.

This explains the long monopoly exercised by the dominator over educational institutions, especially those of "higher" learning. Since the dominator is the one who develops knowledge, he also considers himself best qualified to communicate it and the first in line to receive it. For example, not until the First World War did women obtain the right not only to be admitted to universities but to receive diplomas; they also had to wage a parallel struggle to enter the private preserve of the professions. During the Vietnam War, the president of Harvard University still felt it appropriate to complain that the conflict had left him only "the blind, the infirm and women" as students (Yaguello, 1978, 60). Yet in the United States and Great Britain, it is women (many of whom are returning to school) who enable professors, the majority of them men, to continue to teach; in American Ivy League universities, there are only a few women on the faculty, and these are less well-paid and less often promoted (Pottker and Fishel, 1977, 332; Delamont, 1980, 12).

Neither is there much to envy in the plight of certain "races." While Jewish students were subject to quotas until the Second World War in North American universities, the first Blacks needed the support of the National Guard to enter universities in the American South in the early 1960s. It had long been a "dictionary definition" that the Black race was intrinsically inferior. "Mentally, the Negro is inferior to the

White," said the *Encyclopedia Britannica* in 1911 (in Hoffman, 1973, 6). He belongs to a race "which has never played more than a secondary role on this planet," Bescherelle's *Dictionnaire national de la langue française* pontificated at the end of the nineteenth century, and the 1896 edition of the *Larousse complet illustré* described the Black race as "inferior in intelligence to the White race" (in Pirotte, 1982, 83–5).

Neither are the dominated a good source of witticisms, at least if one judges by the standard reference works. Women account for only 0.5 percent of the quotations in the fourteenth edition of *Bartlett's Familiar Quotations* and only 1 percent of the second edition of *The Oxford Dictionary of Quotations*. Yet in *The Quotable Woman* (1985), American author Elaine Portnow managed to find no fewer than 9,000 *bons mots* pronounced by 1,500 women down through the ages. Similarly, in an earlier work, Québec writer Madeleine Hébert compiled 1,000 thoughts of 470 women of various nationalities and all historical periods.[9] But if one believes the 1984 edition of the *World Book Encyclopedia*, it is not even certain that women belong to the human species; indeed, while there is an entry for "woman," the entry for "man" also gives a reference to another entry: "human being."[10]

The dominator is also almost alone in "making the news" ... and in reporting or analysing it, as revealed by the data available since the 1970s. Women who produce and comment on the news in the media are rare, since the press is run by and for men in the thirty to sixty age bracket (Beauchamp, 1987, 106). Although their numbers may have increased since 1975, only 7.7 percent of the persons interviewed in England in that year were women (Kramarae, 1981, 73). Whether in the electronic media or the press, women in western Europe and North America generally do not hold management positions, their role being limited to supporting the news as researchers, assistants, and freelancers (Ceulemans and Fauconnier, 1979; Beauchamp, 1987, 224–32). A study conducted in 1986 for the Canadian Radio and Telecommunications Commission (CRTC), *Sex-Role Stereotyping in the Broadcast Media*, further revealed not only that women made up only 21 percent of the persons interviewed on the television news, and then as non-specialists, but that the number of women journalists had declined proportionally since 1982. This latter phenomenon, combined with the false impression that there are now too many women in the media, is also true of the United States, where the media continue to hire more male journalism school graduates, even though two-thirds of the students, and those with the best marks in these schools, are women (Faludi, 1991, 370–8).

Moreover, in the mid-1980s, while members of cultural minorities in the United States accounted for only 4 percent of print journalists and 1 percent of editors-in-chief of daily newspapers, only 8 percent of the news correspondents of the three major television networks belonged to ethnic minorities and were assigned in priority to covering these communities. Information thus is controlled by White Anglo-Saxon Protestant men from the middle and upper classes.[11] In the United Kingdom, as the United States, most of the attention of the print and audiovisual media goes to celebrities, with the dominated receiving only a fraction of this when they make themselves noticed by "negative" behaviour, such as strikes, demonstrations, riots, or crime (Halloran, 1977, 11–5).

The problem confronting the handicapped is not much different. Though the challenge met by handicapped athletes is much greater than for "normal" participants in sports, the media are scarcely inclined to report the results of the Special Olympics.

The selective handling of the news also reveals how curiosity about the plight of the dominated is mitigated. It was only after a young White woman fell victim to the Boston Strangler that a local daily decided to run a series on the subject. The murderer had already killed five White women between the ages of fifty-five and seventy-five and a young Black woman without attracting any of this unusual attention (Brownmiller, 1975, 223). The reaction is similar in the case of social classes, since the way the news is reported depends primarily on the public's ability to identify with middle-class values. The National Council on Welfare thus observed the propensity of the Canadian media to use "we" when reporting the departure of vacationers for more pleasant climes and the pronoun "they" when referring to unemployed people waiting for their government benefits (*La presse et la pauvreté*, 1973, 4, 23). In general, the western press also tends to portray youth either as victims (of violence or accidents) or as the authors of criminal acts (Claes, 1992).

Through the content of learning and the transmission of information, the dominator imposes a privileged image of himself – privileged because it is presented as superior, and also because it is the image most frequently invoked. Thus, the oppressed most often is depicted as a "problem," the focus of the specialized scientific disciplines of "Man," someone whose negative behaviour occasionally attracts media attention.

If need be, the oppressed will be conceded the right to have direct access to learning and even to contribute to the acquisition of knowledge. But often they will be invited to focus on their own plight, their competence still being limited, in the view of the dominator, to the elucidation of their own "case." With all the more reason, any attempt by the oppressed to study the dominator in the perspective of his "condition" of oppressor will be contested as lacking objectivity.

Just as power is reinforced by the full weight of generations of accumulated knowledge, the authority of experts grows with the status conferred by the dominator. With one legitimacy supporting the other, the established order will appear to derive its validity from the very exigencies of Truth. Sometimes this is the Truth of Revelation, as transmitted by God himself. But it can also be the Truth of Reason, as acquired by Science, through the quest for correspondence between mind and reality.

THE CRITERIA OF ART

Power has often shaped the imagination. If artists have been able to continue to appeal to creative freedom, just as researchers have held to their independence of mind, it is because they have often shared (apart from occasional political repression against them) the same fundamental belief in the dominant criteria of universality.

Thus, not only do art and literature favour a representation of the oppressed that strips them of any heroic character, but they have relegated their production to the ghetto of specific genres or emphasized their qualities of "imitation," when they did not exclude them outright from the world of *creation*.

Taken to the extreme, the dominated cannot really claim to be the author of an original work. In the same way that the standard works on art history had no place for Black artists in the United States (Peterson and Wilson, 1976, 7), there were no references to women painters or sculptors in the classics of this field for most of the twentieth century. Contemporary art critics and museums have scarcely been interested in their work either: while important American magazines like *Art Forum* or *Art in America* respectively devoted 88 percent and 92 percent of their articles to male artists between August 1970 and August 1971 (Parker and Pollock, 1981, 3–7), only 29 artists of 713 group exhibitors in the major New York museums and 1 out of 53 with an individual exhibition were women, between 1960 and 1970 (Lascault, 1977, 55).

In any case, when they attempted creation, women would cease to be feminine. This, at least, was the opinion of sculptor Reg Butler in 1962:

I am quite sure that the vitality of many female students derives from frustrated maternity, and most of these, on finding the opportunity to settle down and produce children, will no longer experience the passionate discontent sufficient to drive them constantly towards the labours of creation in other ways. Can a woman become a vital creative artist without ceasing to be a woman? (In Parker and Pollock, 1981, 7)

The consensus seems to be based on the perception of woman as reproducer, and of man as producer, in the natural order. In the nineteenth century, the most eminent British critic of his age, John Ruskin, affirmed that man "is eminently the doer, the creator, the discoverer," while woman's "great function is praise" (ibid., 9).

Women would be poor architects or composers of music according to art historian Kenneth Clark, who, in the mid–1970s, believed them to be devoid of "the architectonic sense" of construction (Petersen and Wilson, 1976, 6). No doubt this is why the history of music remembered the names of Johann Sebastian Bach and four of his sons, but not that of his daughter Elisabeth, who also composed, nor that of his second wife, Anna Magdalena Wülken, who some today think may have written the "Anna Magdalena Bachbuch," several cantatas, and certain parts of the *Passions* (Morgan, 1984, 239). No doubt this is why the parents of Fanny Mendelssohn opposed their daughter's career, publishing her first songs under the name of her brother Felix (Neuls-Bates, 1982, 143), and why Gustav Mahler forbade his wife Anna, who nevertheless produced orchestrations for him, to continue to compose after their marriage, and why the psychoanalyst of Thomas Mann's daughter, Elizabeth, recommended that she choose between music and family life (Russ, 1984, 50; 37).

But in any case, what could all these woman have done but copy men? Even though she had met Edgar Degas only once during an exhibition *of her own works*, didn't one critic say that the American painter Mary Cassatt was Degas's *student* (Russ, 1984, 50)? For Charles Beaudelaire, Eugénie Gauthier painted "like a man" (Parker and Pollock, 1981, 8). This remark, however, can sometimes be intended as a compliment. In the exhibition catalogue of the works of Suzanne Valadon at the Musée national d'art moderne in Paris in 1967, Bernard Dorival claimed to see in her "the most virile – and the greatest – of all women painters" (ibid., 122). A critique of the opera *Der Wald*, by Englishwoman Ethel Smyth, which played at the Metropolitan Opera in 1903, concluded that she had "successfully emancipated herself from her sex," due to her extensive use of the brass section (Neuls-Bates, 1982, 226). The same praise was addressed to writer Mary McCarthy for her "masculine mind" (Russ, 1984, 22).

When women are not seen as mere imitators of men, the authenticity of their works is questioned. For example, some critics assumed that Branwell Brontë had written the novels of his sisters Charlotte and Emily, while others affirmed that *Jane Eyre* would be a masterpiece if the author were a man but a shocking work if it were written by a woman (Russ, 1984, 22–7). Similarly, Margaret Cavendish, Duchess of Newcastle, would be accused of hiring a man to write her books, while it is La Rochefoucauld, rather than Madame de La Fayette, to whom *The Princess of Cleves* would sometimes be attributed.

Homosexuals were also supposed to display barely any originality. According to psychoanalyst Edmund Bergler, Oscar Wilde was only an "imitator" and Somerset Maugham a "superficial" writer (Bergler, 1967, 92; 160). Relying on such "scientific" studies, G.-M. Sarotte judged that the works of gay authors reflected their neuroses and self-hatred, as in the cases of playwrights Tennessee Williams and William Inge (Sarotte, 1976, 156). Indeed, when critics did not simply ignore the theme of homosexuality, or prefer the symbolism practised by other novelists (Mann, Musil, Proust, Forster) to the "bad taste" of authors who described it explicitly (Burroughs, Genet, Selby) (Meyers, 1977), they reduced the contribution of gay creators to "homosexual art." This art would be judged to be all the more homosexual in that these writers and artists, in the same breath, would be required to stick to the sole theme of their sexual preference.

In the eyes of the dominator, the works of the dominated belong to "specific genres." While the dominator himself produces Art and Literature, a gay writes a "homosexual" novel, an Inuit carves an "Eskimo" sculpture, and a woman produces a "woman's" film. Even in 1978, the London critic John McEwan felt compelled to deplore the "taste for detail" displayed by women when "left to their own devices" (Parker and Pollock, 1981, 7). "She paints pictures like she would make hats," Edgar Degas said of Berthe Morisot (Lascault, 1977, 137).

To the extent that it agrees with the dominator's image of the dominated, the latter may be recognized as having a specific talent. Evocative of the sexual immorality and animal vitality that Whites attributed to Blacks, jazz was readily exalted as their specific territory. Blacks, considered to be good singers and dancers, were given a place in musical comedy films (Leab, 1975, 57, 123). But Black artists long were unable to express themselves in the "higher" genres of classical dance or opera, either because they were "the wrong sort" or because it was felt necessary to deplore their lack of finesse. It was only in 1955 that Marian Anderson could first appear at the New York Metropolitan Opera, after having been expelled, a few years earlier, from Constitution Hall by the Daughters of the American Revolution. For racists, opera remained an essentially White art form, in which ambiguous make-up had to disfigure some blonde Aïda.

The dominant art and literature also reserve the right to deal with all themes, while the dominated are sometimes prevented from discussing their own. Of the thirty writers who evoked the subject of lesbianism in the nineteenth century, five-sixths were men, who further had the objective of condemning it (Foster, 1975, 116). In the 1950s, publishers in the United States chose to put out the trashy paperbacks of male authors rather than the realistic works of the woman primarily concerned. Where these women erred was in avoiding the automatic tragic ending or the inevitable conversion to heterosexuality that constituted the expected conclusion (Martin and Lyon, 1980, 18).

If the oppressed were sometimes refused the possibility of speaking positively about themselves, there was even more reason for opposing them when they sought to talk about the dominator. Thus, a number of theatre critics challenged the universal nature of Tennessee Williams's plays, on the pretext that the author's morals (homosexuality) had too great an influence on his conception of life (Sarotte, 1976, 157). Others accused Edward Albee's portrayal of the couple in *Who's Afraid of Virginia Woolf?* of being too tough to be applicable to heterosexuals (Russo, 1981, 85). Referring to the great English female novelist of the nineteenth century, George Eliot, Leslie Stephen (the father of Virginia Woolf) believed that he detected "a certain feminine incapacity for drawing really masculine heroes" (Russ, 1984, 12). American critics claimed that the work of Willa Cather, who came from the Midwest, was "regionalist," while that of William Faulkner, a Southerner, passed for universal (ibid., 52–3).

What is less universal, indeed, than a regional art or literature? This is the criticism often directed at the French-Canadian novel by French publishers, for whom only Parisian literature is universal. Circumscribed in space, the art of "small" countries is also limited in time. "Fashions pass! Québec will only be a fad," asserted writer Michel Brandeau in an interview reprinted by *Le Devoir* on May 3, 1986, seeking to explain the lack of interest shown by Paris critics in Québec literature. The reaction is similar in the cinematographic field. "There are fads. There has been Swiss, Québec and Brazilian cinema. ... Québec films exploded world-wide at one point in time. Its authors had to digest their success," the director of the Cannes Film Festival confided to *Le Devoir* during the 1984 Montreal World Film Festival.

In his film *La mémoire*, the Egyptian director Youssef Chahine portrays the total detachment with which a festival like Cannes can treat a cinema that is not yet "in fashion." If one judges by the proportion of English translations of works other than those from western Europe (less than 1 percent of the contemporary literature published in the United States, and less than 2 percent in the United Kingdom, according to UNESCO), all Third World literature is "regional."

As the sole truly universal creator, the oppressor is the only artist who can portray others accurately. Not only does he monopolize the right to speak about himself, he also claims to be more competent to depict the dominated than they are themselves. Under the oppressor's pen or gaze, the dominated are most often stripped of heroic qualities and embody only the impersonal image of the group to which they belong.

This is particularly true of women. Painting already tends to constitute an "ideal" woman by representing her as a set of individually perfect "parts" (Lascault, 1977, 123–5). Erotic literature and film push this to its limits, breaking down the female body even further, describing it through a mirror or a keyhole, or focusing on only a single part (a thigh, a breast, a buttock, a knee, even a walk) (Dardigna, 1980, 261–2; Carrière, 1983, 68). As for the elderly, most of the time they will be considered either as poor subjects for a novel or solely as a pathetic theme (Fischer, 1977, 120, n.17). A gay character, who certainly will be found in a screenplay on homosexuality (Russo, 1981, 23), will reappear only in a comedy or a horror film for the mass market (Dyer, 1980, 30). With the exception of the popular *Dances with Wolves*, all "Indians" in the movies tend to resemble each other, since the seventh art does not bother to distinguish between the different nations (Berkhofer, 1978, 103). Initially played by genuine Natives, these roles were quickly monopolized by White actors more skilled in "playing Indian" as producers understood it (Bataille and Silet, 1980). A similar type of indifference is exhibited on another level: while nine out of ten French citizens live in the "provinces," these play only a background role in French films; except for Brittany or Provence, whose specific nature is given more respect, the regions are never more than "elsewhere," places where detectives conduct investigations or people go on vacation (*Cinéma des régions*, 1980, 6–10).

Like the regions, the colonies long served only as the background for the dominator's exploits. An entire literature in French (Pierre Loti, Guy de Maupassant) and English (Edgar Rice Burroughs, Rudyard Kipling) used it for local colour or as a lower point of reference on the scale of creation (Astier Loutfi, 1971, 57–9; Street, 1975, 6–10). The dominated are stripped of heroic traits because they exist solely in terms of the dominator. Whether good or bad, the "savage" appears in literature not so much through a description of the Amerindian experience as in the guise of an alternate symbol of harmony with nature or of rejection of order and Christianity (Monkman, 1981, 3–5).

When they do not portray heroes confronting the challenges of a hostile world (the colonies, for example), the dominant art and literature represent the universe controlled by these heroes as a place where harmony prevails. For British novelists of the nineteenth century (George Eliot, Charles Dickens, Charlotte Brontë), and for the

American filmmakers of the Depression (Frank Capra, George Cukor, Preston Sturges), conflicts between social classes were portrayed most often as the doing of irresponsible agitators and were concluded with a happy ending (often a wedding) thanks to the good will of *individuals* (Eagleton and Pierce, 1979, 12–9; Marwick, 1980, 143–55).

If the oppressed succeed in "raising themselves" above the common lot of mortals, the dominator will not hesitate to assimilate them. This attempt at co-optation will often skirt the edges of the most flagrant shamelessness. Thus, in "La jeune fille aux joues roses," published in *Le Figaro* in 1946, Julien Green chose to interview an Auschwitz survivor ... who had converted to Christianity before her deportation. Writing a preface to the French edition of *The Diary of Anne Frank* for Calmann-Lévy in 1950, Daniel-Rops postulated the same ultimate conversion of the young Dutch girl who died in an extermination camp (Wardi, 1973, 256). An admirable Jew could only be a Christian!

Through all the modes of expression of beauty (literature, fine arts, music, film), the dominator, therefore, constantly reproduces his own image. As the only universal image, it seeks to encompass all others, which can never approach it other than imperfectly. The oppressor not only occupies the field of creation, he imposes his own standards of representation, reserving the right to deal with everything. Stripped of genuinely heroic qualities, the oppressed are depicted primarily as dependent: seen through the oppressor's eyes, they are represented only in his terms.

Through the criteria of beauty and the imperatives of truth, the dominator controls what is said. In the name of what is beautiful and true, he can set himself up as the perfect embodiment of humanity, and the oppressed can only hope to attain art and knowledge through him. Imagination and reason, sensibility and logic appear to give their universal sanction to the established order, further endorsed by the verdict of experts.

THE FORCE OF LANGUAGE

While common language transmits a view of the world that reproduces the dominator's image, even the dominator's style of *elocution* is imposed on society as the first sign of competence. Deemed to be more convincing and more intelligent, this speech stands out clearly from the uncertain *tone* of the dominated (Edgerton, 1967, 163).

It is the general lot of all dominated people who remain in a state of alienation that the oppressor quickly freezes their linguistic characteristics into stereotypes that give them their identity. Thus, "feminine" language will be associted intrinsically with timorous speech, chatter, and even the purism that is then defined as non-creativity. In his book *Language, its Nature, Origin and Development*, published in 1922, Otto Jespersen accuses women of not thinking before they speak (in Yaguello, 1978, 56–9). Québec history textbooks[12] have portrayed the languages of the indigenous peoples as suffering from a fundamental lack of vocabulary (Vincent and Arcand, 1979, 148–9). French novelists very often have put a sort of "pidgin" speech into the mouths of their colonized characters (*"Toi pas savoir,"* for example, which translates as "You no know"), and the Chinese were represented in caricature and comic strips of the inter-war period as incapable of conjugating their verbs (Astier Loutfi, 1971, 111; in Pirotte, 1982, 68).

But the power relationship between the dominated and the dominator shows through particularly in the different treatment they receive in cases of equal competence. An American who adopts a Southern drawl, the immigrant "allophone" or francophone who does not have an English-Canadian intonation, or the person from Wales or northern England who does not speak with the standard Oxbridge accent will all be judged less fit to fill an important position, just by the sound of their voices (Gardner and Kalin, 1981, 142–5; in McConnell-Ginet, 1980, 151), because they are "less clear" and "less independent," even though it often will be conceded that they are more amiable and generous!

The ethnic and regional line of demarcation of competence has long followed social divisions as well. For example, members of the French provincial upper class often refrained from speaking the regional patois among themselves, and English notables preferred to adopt the "regional middle-class accent." Even in the United States, a few privileged accents (those of Boston, Philadelphia, and New York) were imposed during the inter-war period as the accents of the upper-middle class (Marwick, 1980, 200). In the American films of that time, actors were obliged to use a mid-Atlantic accent when they played characters high in the social pecking order. Though independent for a century and a half, the United States continued to be subject to the fascination of the great British Empire.

More often than not, the language of competence is that of the conqueror. The French spoken in Canada by the descendants of the people conquered in 1760 is a case in point. The contemptuous or condescending reaction that it aroused in others reflected the inferior status of those who used it. The insistence of English Canadians on learning Parisian French is one example of this, as is the tendency of the French to mock not only the anglicisms but the local accent, the imprecision of the language, and the slackness of the pronunciation. Although the Spanish spoken in the Americas exhibits similar characteristics in relation to Castilian, as does American English in relation to the English of the Home Counties, the demographic weight of the United States and the Latin American countries, as well as their political and economic importance, have contributed to winning international respect for a way of speaking that is not entirely that of the metropolitan cultures of Europe.

The Québec situation is different. Abandoned by a mother country that did not give it time to emancipate itself, it was subordinated to a foreign power (Great Britain) and then put under the tutelage of one of its colonies (English Canada) before slipping into gilded dependence on a world power (the United States), which would end up influencing all of them. Its speech thus inspired no more respect than that of the people of the southern United States, who had also lost a war.

Even in Europe, certain ways of expressing oneself, in "regions" which often were unified against their will, have been discredited. Defined geographically and socially by the end of the eighteenth century, the various patois of France were held responsible for children's poor performance in the classroom (Richard, 1982, 133–4). Similarly, the nineteenth-century English believed that Welsh and Gaelic were hostile to rational effort. In addition to standing as a barrier to commercial prosperity, "the Welsh language distorts the truth, favours fraud and abets perjury" a British parliamentary committee concluded in 1846 (Hechter, 1977, 74–7).

The handicapped also had to suffer the effects of a dominant culture which said that there was only one legitimate way of speaking. Despite the remarkable social progress that sign language had allowed deaf persons to achieve since the beginning of the nineteenth century, the ban on its use, imposed by American schools for the deaf in the 1880s, compromised the education of the deaf for seventy-five years and confirmed the prejudice that they had to settle for "modest" jobs.[13]

The dominator seeks a biological basis for *accent* and language (Guillaumin, 1972, 67). Studies in comparative philology even attempted, in the United States and England of the nineteenth century, to establish profound correspondences between race and language (Gossett, 1963, 123). Since physical characteristics, according to the dominator, are signs of an inferior identity, the elocution problems of the physically or mentally handicapped, the supposed lisping of the homosexual, or the halting delivery of the Amerindian are perceived as summing up the entire personality of the dominated.

Even *intonation* is supposed to reflect the "nature" of the oppressed. Western novels often attributed a "nasal" tone to Jews, for example. Blacks were supposed to have a "supplicatory, whining intonation." "A White addressing a Negro behaves exactly like an adult with a street urchin, and the latter responds by simpering, mumbling, sweet-talking, wheedling," deplored Franz Fanon (1952, 44). Their very constitution was supposed to make homosexuals speak with their characteristic affectation: when Richard Burton was to play a gay character in Stanley Donen's film *Staircase*, an American journalist (no doubt oblivious of the sexual preferences of some great actors of the English stage) asked him if he would "disguise his magnificent voice to make it homosexual" (Russo, 1981, 213).

There also seems to have been a lesbian manner of expression: after being conquered sexually by James Bond in *Goldfinger*, his former adversary, Pussy Galore, is supposed to have begun speaking "not in a lesbian voice, but in a girl's voice" (Russo, 1981, 156) – a simpering voice, no doubt, or a shriller one. Indeed, feminity sometimes has been associated with a high-pitched voice (Yaguello, 1978, 56). Although this connection is not made as much nowadays, use of the upper vocal register still gives the impression that an elderly woman is speaking; for example, producers of television commercials will ask an actress playing a grandmother to speak in a high voice (Cohen, 1984, 203).

To the dominator's ears, accent and intonation reveal membership in an inferior group. Since he considers his own intonation to be normal, he will not notice it, any more than he will consider that he has an accent compared to other people. Whether it is real or merely attributed to them, the tone adopted by the dominated in their speech will also serve as a measure of their competence.

While elocution is supposed to indicate a person's ability, the *structures of language* already reflect the oppressor's claims to universal inclusion. Use of the pronoun "one" or the passive voice will often designate the dominant group, for example, established as an implicit point of reference ("it is believed by highly placed sources" or "it is now known that" or "one knows that"). The eternal "Man" is also white-skinned most of the time; he is relatively young, his sexual tastes are orthodox; he is middle or upper class; he has produced the Industrial Revolution and invented democracy. In short, he is a westerner, an Occidental. But above all, he is a male.

The tendency to make the oppressor equivalent to the human race is manifested in the rule, common to several languages, that the masculine takes precedence over the feminine (regardless of the number of persons considered). "He" (or in some languages, the male plural), "man", or "the men," or even "the guys," may include all women in certain cases, while the opposite does not apply: "the women" (or the female plural) refers only to themselves – exclusively.

This precedence is expressed even in exercising the right to speak. Contrary to the widespread opinion that women abuse conversational etiquette, men in fact are responsible for interruptions in 98 percent of cases (Yaguello, 1978, 48–51). Women mainly have private discussions, so their comments are treated as "gossip"; since men instead discuss public affairs, they are said to be talking about "news."

In addition to the oppressor's pretensions to universality, language reflects the hierarchical relationships that stem from it in society. The dominator will almost always be mentioned first in any series of names or terms: Adam and Eve, Romeo and Juliet, Pelleas and Melisande, Tristan and Isolde (Michard-Marchal, 1982, 177). Common usage also refers to men and women, parents and children, teachers and students, Whites and Blacks, bosses and workers ...

Not only does the *form of designation* give an advantage to the oppressor by granting him automatic precedence, it also emphasizes his personal characteristics while treating the oppressed as a category (Guillaumin, 1972, 163–94). In the French media, among others, while adults are attributed a specific age and are never identified as such (no news report will say "An adult died of cold"), children, adolescents, and the elderly receive specific mention. As in the case of many minorities, a woman's first name will also be cited, while a man will be designated by his surname alone. The opposite may happen as well, but the treatment in most cases will be different ("Mr. Brezhnev and Mrs. Indira Gandhi"). When an individual from the lower classes is mentioned (especially in the crime news), the French media will indicate the person's social affiliation first ("Butcher's clerk Louis Lapierre entered the pharmacy ..."). However, if the person mentioned belongs to the bourgeoisie, his or her occupation will serve as a modifier in French news-writing and follow the name ("Mr. Roger Bédard, member of Parliament for the riding of ..."). In the case of a foreigner, French reporters mention the nationality first ("A Moroccan taxi driver is suspected of having ..."). Finally, in the case of someone who is mentally ill, the reference to his or her condition is direct ("After killing his wife and children, the madman fled ...").

Only the oppressor, therefore, is portrayed as having personal qualities. The oppressed seem to exist only on the oppressor's terms. This is particularly true in the case of women, even when they "make a name for themselves" (Michard-Marchal, 1982, 10). "Cellist Mstislav Rostropovitch and his wife are deprived of Soviet citizenship," *Le*

Monde reported on March 17, 1978; yet "his wife" was the internationally renowned singer Galina Vichnevskaya. Even in 1987, *Le Petit Larousse* did not consider it necessary to devote an entry to Marie Curie, who was mentioned only indirectly in the entry for her husband:

CURIE (Pierre), French physicist, born in Paris (1959–1906). He discovered piezoelectricity and studied symmetries in physics. With his wife, Marie Sklodowska, born in Warsaw (1867–1934), he discovered radium (Nobel Prize, 1903 and 1911).

Yet Marie Sklodowska won the second Nobel Prize without her husband in 1911, since he had already been dead for five years. Two Nobel Prizes to her credit were not enough for her to merit a personal entry in a well-known dictionary.

This unequal treatment extends to many semantic asymmetries (Yaguello, 1978, 141–51): "*un homme public*" translates in English as "a public man," but "*une femme publique*" is a prostitute. A "*galant*" is a "ladies' man," but a "*femme galante*" is a "woman of loose morals." An "honest" man is just that (and if he is "*honnête*" he is deemed to be cultivated), but to say that someone is an "honest" woman ("*une honnête femme*") is a comment on her sexual morals in both English and French. A man is a Don Juan; a woman is a nymphomaniac. In the French language, a man can be a "*gars*" (guy), a "*compère*" (crony), a "*patron*" (boss), or a "*maître*" (master, teacher, or lawyer), but a woman is a "*garce*" (slut or bitch), a "*commère*" (gossip), a "*matrone*" (matron, midwife, or hag), or a "*maîtresse*" (mistress). At worst, a man will behave like a peacock, a bantam rooster, or a bear with a sore head (the French words "*paon*," "*coq*," and "*ours mal léché*" have about the same meaning). But a woman most often will be considered as some form of chicken ("chick," "cackling hen," and "mother hen" are common in English, while a "*poule*" in French is a "tart," a *poule mouillée*" is a "drip," a "*poule de luxe*" is a "high-class hooker," and a "*poule pondeuse*" is a "good layer," a very fertile woman). A woman can also be another unflattering type of bird – "*une bécasse*" (birdbrain), "*une oie*" (silly goose), "*une dinde*" (also a silly goose, but literally a turkey), or "*une pie*" (a chattering magpie). A man will be learned, discreet, ambitious, or critical, while a woman will be a bluestocking, a hypocrite, an intriguer, or hysterical.

Insults can also be given a feminine tilt, the better to injure the other party ("*salaud*" – roughly equivalent to "swine" or "bastard" – becomes "*salope*," "dirty bitch," even when addressed to a man). Or a female relative of the target is attacked ("son of a bitch," "yo' mama," or the French *"cocu"* – cuckold) (Yaguello, 1978, 155; 120, 162).

This type of hierarchical division, reproduced in language, can also be found between social classes. For centuries, the Russian aristocracy spoke German or French among themselves, and only an outburst of patriotism during the Napoleonic invasion forced that country's nobility to study the language of the peasants.

While semantic slips also occur in the oppressor's relations with other dominated groups (some signs in the United States before desegregation were addressed to "White *Ladies*," while others referred to "Black *Women*"), use of offensive comparisons is even more frequent. "No Jews or dogs allowed" was a lawn sign displayed by certain affluent North American clubs and resorts for quite some time. And some British restaurants still ask their customers to leave children under fourteen and dogs at home (Greer, 1984, 3). Signs in some public places in France at the turn of the century forbade people to spit or speak Breton, There are also two-edged compliments that seem to imply that the exception proves the rule: "We have a Senegalese history teacher. He is very intelligent," said the colonizer of the colonized, or "Our doctor is Black. He is very nice" (Fanon, 1952, 114). The colour black itself represents evil, emptiness, or death in several languages. Historians refer to the most unenlightened period of the Middle Ages as the Dark Ages. Very little that is positive can come out of a black mood, the black market, a blacklist, the black sheep of the family, or the blackening of somebody's name. On the other hand, in French, *"blanchir"* means to prove someone innocent. Automatically associated with purity, whiteness is also a sign of superiority: Canadian anglophones used to tell francophones to "Speak White," even though there was no difference in their skin colour.

The conception of the dominated developed by the dominator therefore conditions the choice of words the latter uses to refer to the former. This applies even to pronouns not used to confirm the relationship of inequality. The impersonal and all-encompassing "they" refers to "others" as the essential embodiment of difference ("*They* control the economy," "*They* molest children"). The elderly and the handicapped are objectified and diminished when they are referred to as "they" in their own presence. But when a servant addresses his master in the third person, he is distancing himself and showing a form of respect; only the master can cross the divide that separates them, going so far as to speak familiarly to the servant and call him by his first name (Memmi, 1973, 188, 193). The familiar second-person pronoun (*"tu"* in French), common to some Indo-European languages, is used automatically when talking to a younger person or a member of the lower class. In these cultures, men also speak familiarly to women or call them by their first names more quickly than women would wish or would permit themselves to do with men (Mazey and Lee, 1983, 39). The tendency is often the same when Whites address Blacks (Fanon, 1952, 45) or when a citizen of "the old stock" speaks to immigrant workers (Granotier, 1979, 10). Unless the interlocutor's social status was high enough, Europeans for a long time spoke familiarly to the colonized in their contacts with them. Even recently in Québec, it was not rare for White police officers to address Native women as "*tu*," even when they were married women in perfectly good standing with the law (André, 1976, 133, 149).

Sometimes the oppressed will be tempted to regard themselves as being less important. They will mitigate the personal nature of a success by passing it off as the result of a collective effort. This phenomenon is particularly frequent among women. But just as use of the third person may alternately reveal inferiority or be a sign of respect, the "we" of modesty harks back to the "royal we." Although in less common usage today, this "we" continues to be employed by judges or religious leaders whose power is thus strengthened by the higher authority of the Law or of God.

Whatever the field of thought or the activity considered, the established discourse puts the dominator forward as the ideal model of humanity and thereby justifies the subordinate relationship that the dominated is called upon to maintain with him. These dynamics are at work in learning, art, and language and derive from the official interpretation of the constraints imposed by History, Nature, and even God.

The claims of the dominator to embody the universal human type depend on the legitimacy conferred by the experts. These experts do not so much claim to speak in their own name as to serve bodies of authority beyond them. There are supposed to be universal criteria outside and above everyone, and their sole task is to discover these criteria so that they can invite society to join them in humble submission.

In most cases, however, the experts belong to the dominant group, from which they also derive their authority. Their verdict will unfailingly justify the established social order. The oppressor thus believes he is entitled not only to maintain a universal discourse but to speak the language of objectivity.

CHAPTER TWO

The Language of Objectivity

An expert is a person who possesses in-depth technical knowledge in a specific field. He may even have devoted years to the study of a single question. Thus, an expert is a specialist. Since an expert will often know more than ordinary mortals about a subject, there will very likely be a widespread conviction that he knows everything about it, and he will have the last word in response to criticism. The expert is a person of influence. The respect imposed by his intellectual training and disinterest also gives him, in the eyes of many, the right to make pronouncements on matters outside his field. The expert is sometimes seen as an original thinker. As the privileged agent and interpreter of knowledge, he commands acquiescence to his opinions solely by virtue of his competence. The expert is always an *authority*.

Ordinary mortals thus are invited to suspend their judgment and defer to the expert. Like a revealed truth, his verdict is applied generally, with no explanation of how it was developed: *Magister dixit* – the master has spoken. Only another expert can invalidate an expert's opinion, since lay people have not been initiated into the arcana of advanced knowledge. And who more than the dominated risk losing their impartiality in the defence of their own cause? Who, more than the dominated, are inclined, through the intensity of their emotion, to compensate for the inadequacy of their knowledge? As the ultimate non-initiates, the dominated have less authority to speak than anyone else.

"The male ... tends by nature to expertness and specialization," the influential American psychologist G. Stanley Hall wrote at the beginning of the twentieth century (in Ehrenreich and English, 1979, 119).[1] "Women ... always remain subjective," affirmed Schopenhauer, who, while granting that they sometimes had talent, did not allow that they have genius.[2] Historian Gustave Welter, author of a history of Russia

(*Histoire de Russie*) considered to be a "classic" by *La Petite Bibliothèque Payot*, believed, on the contrary, that women sometimes have genius. "Catherine II had ... a brain and – a very special case in the history of women – this organ functioned in absolute independence of the weaknesses of the flesh. ... She was only a member of the weaker sex by night. By day, she was a man, and a great man."[3]

For who judges competence if not the dominator? It was precisely because they considered themselves to be of superior intelligence that the White colonizers, for example, believed they were entitled to impose their tutelage on the peoples of Asia and Africa: "We cannot admit that the essential principles of our civilization ... are not the essential principles of *all civilization*, whatever it may be; that the fundamental bases of our morality are not right to govern the morality *of all men*," wrote a Belgian colonizer in a book appropriately entitled *Dominer pour servir* (Dominate to Serve) (Ryckmans, 1931, 98, emphasis added).

The dominator has not only the power to interpret the difference but also the power to create it. It is the dominator, for example, who will define deviance and mental illness in a given society. Thus, he need only designate some form of identity or behaviour as falling into one of these categories to remove from the persons who possess them the right to speak for themselves.

It is becoming "increasingly evident not only that psychiatry has come of age but also that our civilization may have entered an age of psychiatry," the historians of this field, Alexander and Selesnick (1966, 6), observed with pleasure. Once mental illnesses were grouped in "international" classifications and treated by pharmaceutical therapies, the definition of them established by the specialists would seem to exhibit all the guarantees of objectivity and scientific rigour (Marsella and White, 1982, 6). Thus, according to the prevailing opinion at a given time, homosexuality might or might not be considered a disease.

The more a "patient" protests his sanity and insists on declaring himself to be healthy, the more obvious it will become to the expert that he is neither. "Since she is insane, she does not understand that she needs treatment" is the attitude of the next-of-kin and the professional attending the mentally "afflicted" person (Szasz, 1970, xvi; Santos, 1977, 43). Science and the law thus allow these people to be treated against their will.

Others will simply be excluded from active life once they have reached a stage of their existence in which the experts judge that their competence has diminished. This applies to physical and intellectual competence,which would decline biologically over the years, and professional competence as well, which necessarily would go quickly out of date in a technocratic society in which age suggests disqualification rather than accumulated experience (de Beauvoir, 1970, I, 334).

When experts conclude that the dominated are "naturally" unfit, they often claim to do so with great reluctance. But the expert serves only the truth, not his desires. He relies on the *facts*, to which he must submit. Thus, the expert's writings may express regret ("we must admit," "it must be said") at having to admit the inferiority of the dominated in a certain matter.

Indeed, what is more immediate, more irreducible than a fact? If there are two sides to an issue, can there be more than one side to a fact? A fact does not stem from emotion and is free from the hazards of ideology: it belongs to the realm of reality. One must bend to its logic. The fact seizes the expert's attention; the expert does not choose it. What adds to the self-evident nature of a fact is that it often appears to have received unanimous acknowledgment for a long time. It sometimes is enough for the specialist simply to call it back to mind ("everybody knows that ..." or "it is generally admitted that ...").

It is thus in his capacity as an objective observer of the facts that the religious, legal, or scientific expert rules on what constitutes a sin, offence, or anomaly. And it is often from the expert's opinion that the dominator derives the right to keep the dominated under his control. The dominated will sometimes have to be purified, punished, or treated. One operation does not exclude another. Since the expert's authority derives from the same established order, sometimes the definitions of illness, moral transgression, and crime will coincide.

The opinion of the theorists and functionaries of Religion, Law, and Science thus has the effect of legitimizing the relationships of domination by accrediting the thesis of the dominator as the ideal model for humanity. Taking their cue from the very inferiority that they have to attribute to the oppressed, theologians and ministers of religion, legislators and magistrates, researchers and scholars believe they may claim the exclusive right to determine the fate of the oppressed.

RELIGION AND SIN

As a system of beliefs and practices presiding over a society's relations with a higher principle, religion automatically claims to derive from the highest authority. Since the religious faiths prevailing in the West posit the direct intervention of God, among other beliefs, they accept Revelation as a fact. This fact is fundamental, because it is both the foundation of an essential reality and the starting point of a universal belief. It is also indisputable, not subject to reconsideration, and the basis of incontestable arguments derived from authority. Thus, the claims of the interpreters of the Revealed Word that they are God's privileged instruments on earth cannot be questioned, nor can there be any doubt as to their ultimate objectivity.

Although writings concerning the divine message extend over a period of fifteen hundred years and were written by different men in various styles, they are presented as a timeless whole from which coded and numbered excerpts can then be cited, independent of the historical context. Taken all together, these "sacred" texts, these "holy writings," constitute the pre-eminent "Book" (the Bible, on the same basis that the Koran literally is the "Reading" of the Word). The commentaries to which it gives rise, propounded by "fathers" and doctors (of the Jewish Law or of the Church), themselves form a whole (the Talmud or the Tradition) which in turn becomes the bearer of orthodoxy.

The Jewish people, guided by the rabbis, became God's "chosen," while the popes and ayatollahs who pronounce in the name of the Most High claim to be "infallible." It is always God who "speaks through the mouths" of fundamentalist ministers.

The faithful are first required to accept the authority of the leaders before adhering to the content of the doctrine. The chief rabbinate of Israel reserves the right to determine who is a "true" Jew. Liberation theologists have been subject to distancing by Rome as much for their criticisms of the hierarchy as for their attraction to Marxism.

The various religious orthodoxies, all speaking in the name of Truth, invest themselves with the right to silence those who propagate "error." While the Catholic hierarchy advised silence on the question of women in the priesthood and imposed it on the Jesuit John McNeill in his research on homosexuality, American fundamentalist preachers have launched a "crusade" against gays and lesbians and censor school textbooks that do not present a traditional image of women. At the same time, rabbis declared the war waged by Israel in Lebanon to be "holy," and the mullahs perceived Iran's war against Iraq to be "holy" as well.

Not only do God's designs seem to be identified with the will of those who claim to speak in his name, while his very image reflects the characteristics of the dominant group, but Heaven is called upon to legitimize the dominator's definition of sin. Curiously, this definition, by a sort of symmetry, reflects the mirror image of the dominated.

"Sin came into the world through woman," some "fathers" of the Church decreed. Sometimes idealized, woman most often represents the symbol of evil in the "great" religions (Carmody, 1979, 17–18). A temptress, she is considered to be sexually insatiable and dangerous to men (especially to saints), who, as we have seen, remain the universal norm in the divine order. "When women have reflected, studied, and prayed as much as men, then the discussion will resume [on their access to the priesthood]," declared Auxiliary Bishop of Montreal Cimichella on the occasion of the papal visit to Canada.

However, like Orthodox Judaism, which reserves the study of the Torah to men, the Catholic Church has scarcely encouraged the education of women. In the nineteenth century, the clergy opposed secondary-school education for girls (Aubert, 1975, 208). The male hierarchy often made the connection between the condition of women as sinners and the necessity to maintain them in a dependent state. "In addition to many pains and sufferings, God imposed upon Eve that she be subjected to her husband," Pius XII declared in his address of 10 September 1941, adding that "equality in studies, schools, sciences, sports, and competitions causes feelings of pride to rise in the hearts of many women."

The Injunction to cover their hair and even veil their faces, long imposed on women by a number of "universal" religions, attests both to a will to dominate women and the suspicion felt in their regard. The very functions dictated by a woman's identity, in addition to barring her almost everywhere from divine ministry, place her in a position of ritual impurity. Thus, in Orthodox Judaism, she must *purify herself* after menstruation or childbirth (doubly so if the child brought into the world is a girl).

Entire races have been made guilty of collective crimes for which they must be punished and held up as examples. Accused of deicide, the Jews are said to have brought upon themselves centuries of persecution, which Christians felt entitled to inflict upon them. Held responsible for the lack of respect exhibited by their common ancestor Ham towards his father Noah,[4] Blacks felt the weight of the divine curse that delivered them into slavery.

Like the Hebrews and the Muslims, Christians long sanctioned the reduction to servitude of human beings who did not belong to their religion (Kaké, 1977, 12–15). The Apostle Paul, who hoped to alleviate the rigours of slavery, nevertheless did not call for its abolition; Augustine and Thomas Aquinas even saw, in this institution, a form of expiation for sin desired by *God*, with Thomas Aquinas also declaring slavery to be part of the *natural* order. This practice would not be condemned definitively until the nineteenth century.

Apart from the enslavement of the Blacks in the modern era, the exegesis of Ham, applied on a larger scale, served to justify colonization (and later segregation). For while Ham was cursed, the descendants of Shem were given the Law, and those of Japhet (the Nordic peoples) were endowed with the technical knowledge that would allow them to establish their control of the planet (Memmi, 1982, 79).

On the other hand, the tendency to discourage any rebellious impulses in the dominated classes moulded the discourse of the Christian churches, which preferred to dangle the prospect of a reward in the hereafter before their eyes. More concerned with inducing charity in a few than in demanding justice for the greatest number, the churches invited the rich to be "generous" in the same breath that they preached resignation to the have-nots. Thus, *"right-minded"* individuals could choose to maintain "their" poor, who served as a means of salvation for masters whose material fortune they had already ensured. In the modern age, the Puritan tradition of Calvinism even provided a theological foundation for the power of the dominant class. Interpreting the miserable condition of the unfortunate as the sign of possible predestination to eternal damnation, it endorsed the economic methods of the rising bourgeoisie, which could claim to be God's "elect." In the Anglo-Saxon countries, until the nineteenth century, this same tradition would spread the thesis of the innate "perversion" of the child, a perversion inherited from original sin (De Mause, 1974, 10). Protestant fundamentalists, who reject women's right to abortion in the name of the child, represent the modern renewal of this current, agitating for a return to corporal punishment of the very young.

The notion of sin has perhaps been associated more with homosexuals than with any other dominated group. Although it has been well-known since the nineteenth century that homophilia is a sensibility more than a form of behaviour, most western religions continue to condemn "sodomy" as a transgression. Believing that gay individuals are not responsible for their "social maladjustment," the Roman Congregation for the Doctrine of the Faith (in its December 1975 declaration, and then in the 1992 *Official Catechism*) nevertheless prohibited them from *living* their sexual preference: this "anomaly" would go against the "objective moral order." In addition to finding homosexuality to be against nature, the Torah and the Talmud condemned it as a "crime." The combined opposition of Catholic, fundamentalist, and Judaic institutions to the extension of civil rights to gays (Carmody, 1979, 135; d'Emilio, 1983, 146) and even the simple decriminalization of homosexuality reflects a larger will to punish moral misconduct through the judicial process.

Conversely, secular legislators will often invoke divine precepts to establish the rules of the temporal community. Confusing the designs of Providence with the public interest, the established order may wish to impose civil punishment on behaviour from which religion has already sought to purify the sinner. Thus, for the same action, a dominated individual who is found guilty of a transgression against God also risks having to atone for a crime against Society.

LAW AND CRIME

Law, the sum of the rules governing human relations in a given society, draws from a group's established values to determine the conventions that will modulate the conduct of its members. Developed by legislators in the name of a few great divine, natural, or historical principles, all of the standards to which society is subject are posited as coming from beyond, or even above it. Whether sanctioned by simple longevity or by a founding assembly, legislation takes on the value of unshakeable fact (*Dura lex, sed lex* – "the law is hard, but it is the law"), which impartial magistrates will be required to apply.

The legal codes governing social relations often follow the lines established by the dominant ideology. Even when they are chosen directly by the population or, as was shown dramatically in the elevation of Judge Clarence Thomas to the United States Supreme Court in 1991, when they are appointed by people who themselves have been elected, lawmakers and magistrates most often come from an established group. Thus, this group possesses the first of all powers, the one that conditions all the others, the *power of definition*.

It is up to the definer to decide who is entitled to claim the *status* of man or of citizen. In various periods, a Black could be valued at three-fifths of a man and a Jew considered generally as "subhuman." Likewise, one need only note the frustration of many Canadian Natives in having to wait for a Parliament, foreign to their values, to decide who is a "true" Indian to grasp the full importance of the power of definition. Thus, even though the practice of matrilineal succession has prevailed in certain tribes (among the Iroquois, for example), Native women who married Whites lost their right of access to the reservation, territories, and special payments granted by certain treaties, while men of their race who married a White woman retained their status.

But there are other ways for the dominator to maintain his power. He may establish *specific laws* to govern dominated individuals and groups whose "differences" he deems to be too far from the ideal norm. This is the principle behind all legislation that sanctions discrimination, whether it be discrimination in employment and income, housing and education, or the more general discrimination that takes the form of segregation by prohibiting access to certain places or specific types of contact (for example, sexual relations) between groups. This segregation can be overt, as in the case of Jews in Nazi Germany or Blacks in the United States after the Civil War, or take the insidious form of institutional seclusion, experienced until recently by the physically or mentally handicapped, or even by the elderly. Discrimination sometimes will be general, like the discrimination long practised against women who systematically were paid less than their male colleagues. It can also be more specific, as in a measure like Clause 28 in Thatcherite England, which prohibited positive references to homosexuality at the local council level, or as in the proposed 1992 amendment to the Oregon state constitution, prohibiting any legislation promoting the civil equality of gays and lesbians.

Even when it does not endorse it officially, the law sanctions discrimination in refusing to prohibit it by name. The dominated are well aware that they must fight today to obtain recognition of their right to equality just as they had to fight in the past to be "granted" the right to vote.

While liberal democracy intends citizens to be equal before the law, it is first essential for the law to be equal before citizens. Yet not only is the dominator capable of legislating in various ways depending on whether or not a group is different from him, he is also allowed to establish contrary laws for comparable categories of the dominated. Thus, the oppressor modulates discrimination both vertically (from himself to the oppressed) and transversely (between various dominated groups).

Already perceived as inferior to men due to their gender alone, wives long had a different status from that of their unmarried sisters. "My wife and I are one and I am he," went one British saying. True in Great Britain, this principle also shaped the law of other western countries in the nineteenth century and into the twentieth (Branca, 1978, 160–70; Callu, 1978; in Boucher and Morel, 1970, 203–5). Civilly incapacitated during marriage, women were effectively denied the right to enter into contracts, testify in court, or sue in a civil action without the authorization of their husbands or a judge. Until 1893, women in England were forbidden to own property, and Frenchwomen had to wait until 1907 before they could dispose freely of their wages. While the Civil Code of 1866 allowed married Québec women who were "separate as to property" or "separate as to bed and board" to administer their assets, it did not give them the right to dispose of them. It was only in 1964 that a women in Québec could practise a profession distinct from that of her husband. For a long time, Québec fathers also enjoyed exclusive or preponderant authority over the children, until Bill 16 (1964), which established the principle of joint direction of the family's moral and material affairs. In France, it took until 1970 for the concept of paternal authority to give way to that of parental authority.

Unlike the unmarried woman, the wife thus had to repay her husband with her obedience for the protection he promised to give her. While the law guaranteed the single woman's sexual integrity, it purposely suppressed that of the wife (Brownmiller, 1975, 412). Following the example of legislation in the United States, Canadian law until recently protected the husband from the accusation of raping his wife.

The legal lot reserved by the oppressor for minority groups of equivalent size betrays a similar double standard. Depending on which group is dominated and which is dominant, not only will the oppressor's law not be identical for both, but the mode of application of the *same* law also may differ.

Asymmetrical federalism, which has dictated the contrary evolution of Franco-Canadians and Anglo-Quebecers since 1867, is an example of this type of inequality of the law before citizens. From the beginning of Canadian Confederation, Québec was endowed with special status: not only did the founding law grant protected provincial ridings to the British minority (which could not be altered without its consent), but this minority had the benefit of legislative and judicial bilingualism, which was denied to the French minorities in the other provinces. In addition, the legal guarantees granted by the Act of 1867 both to French Canadians and to English Canadians did not prove to be as effective *in their application* for the former as they were for the latter. While "confessional" or denominational schooling was protected by the constitution, this very soon proved to be a fragile promise for the schools of the French-Catholic minorities of New Brunswick (1871) and the newly established province of Manitoba (1890 and 1916). Ontario practised linguistic discrimination (1912), and the provinces created thereafter (such as Saskatchewan and Alberta) were exempted from the obligation to supply their citizens of French origin with Catholic schools.

Founded in 1870, Manitoba, like Québec, was supposed to be officially subject to legislative and judicial bilingualism. Starting in 1890, however, the government of that province took the initiative to escape this obligation. It would take eighty-nine years for a Supreme Court judgment to reverse this decision. Even then, Franco-Manitobans had to wait patiently for this ruling to be translated into concrete measures, and were subjected to pressure from the highest political authorities to accept a "compromise."

But it is not only the constitutional guarantees granted to ethnic groups that result in different modes of application of law. Depending on whether or not a criminal belongs to the dominant group, the judicial apparatus is not always equally severe in imposing penalties for violations. In the United States, for example, Blacks often received much tougher sentences than Whites for raping a White woman, but the sentence was lighter if they sexually assaulted a Black woman (Brownmiller, 1975, 237). The same goes for adults who molest children: in Great Britain, among other countries, men who attacked boys were sometimes subject to harsher sentences than those who attacked girls (Schofield, 1965, 154).

Even if a male homosexual is the *victim* of an assault, the mere fact of his identity is seen automatically as a mitigating circumstance. According to writer Dominique Fernandez, *"casser du pédé"* ("gay-bashing") is considered inconsequential by some French magistrates. Judged by an entirely White and middle-class jury, the murderer of homosexual Harvey Milk, a San Francisco city councillor, was given a sentence of only five years' imprisonment for a crime that had also caused the death of the city's mayor.

As both judge and litigant in the formulation of the laws and the way they are applied, the dominator puts forward his specific *values* as coinciding with divine, natural, or historical laws. This is precisely what happens in the case of "sodomy."

For a long time, the civil authorities believed that they were entitled to legislate on the practice of anal sex. Regardless of whether it was committed by a heterosexual or homosexual couple, it was prohibited by law, at least in the Anglo-Saxon countries (Craft, 1978, 66; Hoffman, 1969, 78–9). However, since it was associated more often with homophilia, for many years it carried the death penalty; though it was abolished in France during the Revolution, this would continue to apply in the United States and Great Britain until the mid-nineteenth century (Marmor, 1980, 19 and 50; d'Emilio, 1983, 14). While homosexuality was soon permitted by the Napoleonic Code (as long as it was between consenting adults in private), it still ranked as a felony in the United States in 1950, comparable to kidnapping, rape, and murder.

It would take until 1967, in England, and 1968, in Canada, for homosexuality between consenting adults in private to escape legal penalties. In Bill 88, Québec, eventually followed by other provinces and one territory, would go even further by guaranteeing the equality of gays in its Charter of Rights. It was only in the 1970s that half the states in the United States followed in the footsteps of Canada and England. France, which had fired the first shot of liberation in the early nineteenth century, nevertheless introduced the notion of an offence "against nature" in the Penal Code, under the Pétain regime, for cases of homosexuality with individuals under twenty-one years of age. In 1960, homosexuality in France was declared to be a "social plague" similar to alcoholism and prostitution. These discriminatory laws were not repealed until 1978 and 1980 respectively.

The dominator also arrogates the right to guide all of the dominated's life. Wishing to establish a power that he considers his automatic right, he will harbour resentment against the dominated, not only for seeking to escape his control, but for aspiring to a freedom equal to his own.

Thus, the laws governing adultery long held the wife to be more guilty than the husband. It was only in 1923 that England established the equality of spousal rights in this matter. Until recently, both in Québec and in France, the husband was not even subject to penalty unless he kept his concubine under the conjugal roof. There was even a time when a French husband benefited from extenuating circumstances if he killed his wife when he caught her in the act of adultery (Callu, 1978, 51), a right obviously not extended to the wife. As a member of the Dorion Commission on the civil rights of women in Québec said in 1929:

Whatever one may say, it is well-known that the injury inflicted on the heart of a wife is generally not as keenly felt as the one suffered by a husband deceived by his wife.... Forgiveness naturally comes more easily to a woman's heart ...; his wife's infidelity also exposes him to the gnawing of ridicule.... Are the children he is raising his?... No doubt the husband can have children out of wedlock; his wife does not raise them. (Collectif Clio, 1982, 342)

The right of guardianship also extends to children. Not only was family violence considered, until very recently, a private matter, but the power to exercise it was granted to anybody acting as an extension of parental authority. In the nineteenth century, the practice of corporal punishment against children was very widespread (Walvin, 1982, 47; Crubellier, 1979, 148). The Criminal Code of Canada (as well as the Québec Civil Code) still allows a teacher, a parent, or a person acting in place of a parent to use force to correct a child, provided that this force does not exceed what is "reasonable" under the circumstances.

However, what is deemed reasonable may vary in different eras. The death penalty applied to nearly 230 types of offences in England at the turn of the nineteenth century, and children were often condemned to it. The vast majority (90 percent) of those hanged in that period were minors, and this punishment was not abolished in their case until 1833 (Chesnais, 1981, 148; Walvin, 1982, 158).

The favourable prejudice automatically enjoyed by adults also accounts for the lack of credence that judges long granted to children's testimony when the latter were victims of a form of violence duly condemned by law. Influenced by the medical authorities of the age, the courts considered such testimony to lack credibility or to be null and void. Rape charges filed by young girls were often dismissed as the result of a whim or an overfertile imagination, when the accusers were not flatly accused of mutilating themselves intentionally to support their parents' alleged blackmail operations (in Rafter and Stanko, 1982, 38). Drawing upon the authority of psychiatrists and psychoanalysts, an American law professor explained, in a review devoted to the problems of the 1960s (*Law and Contemporary Problems*), why the judicial system generally had to be suspicious of children's testimony:

The psychiatrist or the psychoanalyst would have a field day were he to examine all complaints of rape, sexual tampering with children, incest, homosexual behaviour with young boys, deviant sex behaviour, etc., in any given community. He would find that complaints are too often made of sexual misbehaviour that has occurred only in the overripe fantasies of the socalled victims. Frequently, the more or less unconscious wish for the sexual experience is converted into the experience itself. (In Schofield, 1965, 153)

Homosexual witnesses sometimes have experienced similar treatment, with American courts categorizing them as liars (in Marmor, 1980, 207). The same unfavourable prejudice is still the basis of the judicial reluctance to entrust homophilic parents with responsibility for their children. Thus, mothers have often lost custody of their little ones and fathers have been denied their visitation rights. In general, gays are not permitted to adopt children (ibid., 214).

This type of dictate also affects the mentally handicapped. As many as thirty American states prohibit them from marrying, and more than fifteen extend this ban to epileptics (Bowe, 1978, 185–6). Always influenced by scientific experts, the courts have even sanctioned the principle that the authorities have the right to treat the bodies of the mentally handicapped without their consent by allowing them to be subjected to sterilization. In 1927, the United States Supreme Court declared this measure constitutional; thus, without the necessity of informing the patients, unwed mothers, prostitutes, and children deemed to be too undisciplined were sterilized after being categorized as feeble-minded (Gould, 1981, 335–6). In Great Britain at the turn of the century, poor women living on State support after having an illegitimate child were also sterilized as mentally ill (Craft 1978, 1–2). In the early 1970s it was still legal, in certain parts of Canada, to use this method of treatment on women with psychological problems (Matthews, 1983, 16).

The rights conceded to the dominated by the dominator, who modulates how they are formulated and applied, are also *conditional*. In the same way that specific protection will be refused to the most vulnerable people, so will the exceptional clauses contained in these laws be invoked just when this protection is most necessary.

For example, European and American conventions, be they international or regional, authorize the suspension of certain rights and freedoms at times when they deem public order and the *security of the nation* to be threatened. In other words, international law takes up the concept of "legitimate self-defence" granted by criminal law to individuals and extends it to the benefit of the State. Thus, in the name of the state of emergency, the War Measures Act was invoked in Canada in 1970, allowing the police to arrest hippies in Vancouver as well as the Québec separatists against whom the move was initially directed. The 120,000 Americans and 20,000 Canadians of Japanese origin who were herded into internment camps by the government and stripped of their property during the Second World War also saw their rights sacrificed on the altar of national security (in Lecomte and Thomas, 1983, 62).

Even homosexuals represent a high risk to the security of the State, according to the military machine and the civil service: witness the resistance of certain military leaders to accepting the principle, set forth in 1992, of the official integration of gays and lesbians into the Canadian and American armed forces. In the 1950s, at the height of the influence of Senator Joe McCarthy, who went so far as to associate homosexuals with Communism, the FBI and local police departments wove a vast net throughout the United States to track them down. Even the Post Office was recruited for this purpose (d'Emilio, 1983, 47). In Canada, a witch-hunt was launched by the Royal Canadian Mounted Police for similar reasons in the 1960s, investigating not only civil servants but any person suspected of being homosexual.

Apart from national security, there are other limits to the protection provided to the rights and freedoms of citizens in a country's constitution. These limits are related to *the particular values of a society*. The Canadian Charter of Rights and Freedoms, for example, opens the door to judicial interpretation when it accepts restrictions "subject only to such reasonable limits prescribed by law as can be demonstrably justified in a free and democratic society." It even contains a "notwithstanding" clause, which allows the legislator (federal or provincial) to declare explicitly that a law or provision will apply independently of the Charter.

Contrary to widespread belief, the Soviet constitution granted its citizens all possible individual freedom, but the constitutional text clearly stipulated that the exercise of these freedoms should "conform to the interests of the workers and support the socialist regime." One need only recall that this fundamental law was adopted in 1936, just at the time of the great Stalinist show trials, to understand the sometimes disproportionate role played by the exception in relation to the rule in the application of the most progressive legal texts.

With the same apparent good conscience, the USSR stifled groups of political, religious, nationalist, and feminist dissidents after signing the Helsinki Accord of 1975. In response to those who criticized these violations, the Soviet government invoked the principle of *State sovereignty*. This principle is another escape hatch used by governments to maintain their full flexibility in the interpretation of rights and freedoms. In denying any outside organization the authority to verify how these texts are applied, these governments reserve the sole right to ensure the protection of the same groups that they might threaten.

Since classical international law is averse to recognizing the individual as the subject of law (Torelli and Beaudoin, 1972, xx) and only rarely commits itself on fundamental freedoms (the Universal Declaration of Human Rights has no compulsory value), those oppressed who do not already have some clout of their own in international law must count on the sole moral authority of the great international texts to obtain protection.

By the nature of the rights, conditional in form and relative in time, that he concedes to the oppressed, the dominator can consolidate the power he holds and define the type of legal status possessed by each party in their social relations. Often established in the name of the moral order, this status also receives the frequent endorsement of scientific experts. Psychiatrists and psychoanalysts, among others, have often been called upon to advise legislators and judges. Even more than the jurist or the theologian, the scientist claims objective detachment. This detachment initially results from his relation to the object of observation, which is external to the scientist, but it is also understood to be the normal disposition of a rigorously trained mind. As a product of the division of labour that developed with the Industrial Revolution, the specialist benefits from the two-centuries-old favourable prejudice of a technological society still fascinated by the discipline of facts.

SCIENCE AND ANOMALY

As the sum of the knowledge acquired by reason about nature, society, and human beings, science claims to be based on objectively observed facts. All the discipline of the researcher and all the training of the scholar are intended to ensure that they heed only the constraints of scientific truth.

Automatically taken for granted in the case of the "pure" or "exact" sciences, which have nature as their object, the impartiality of the expert will sometimes be questionable in the study of society or of human beings. Here it appears to be more difficult to ensure the observer's independence of his own values, and it is harder to grasp, just as definitively, a more changeable object. Thus, there will be a frequent tendency in the social sciences to model themselves on the physical sciences in seeking an equivalent capacity for prediction and control in the human field. With all the more reason, the biological sciences will be inclined to reify complex phenomena (intelligence, for example), the better to measure and classify them (Gould, 1981, 24). Thus the adherents of unconditional positivism will come to judge only quantifiable realities as important.

Quite often, this approach will require a postulated point of reference in relation to which the calculation will be possible. Thus, the notion of difference will be implicitly posited in the methodology followed by the human sciences. This difference will have been considered an anomaly by various disciplines, depending on the era. Whole dominated groups have been observed as abnormal cases because of the scientist's impression that they were far from the dominant norm. Although the jargon has changed to justify it and science has replaced a certain idea of God in this regard, this norm always had to be the same as the one embodied by the oppressor. This transition from one privileged source of authority to another occurred at the beginning of the nineteenth century, as illustrated by the case of women, among others.

In defining the concept of "feminine nature," beginning in 1760, the philosophy of the Enlightenment gave a scientific formulation to the ideas received from religion: from the sinner she had been, woman became reproductive (Knibiehler, 1983, 8–115). Reductionism therefore endured. Not only was the role of her ovaries deemed to determine her beauty, her fidelity, and even her intellectual place in society, but the normal condition of women would be completely likened to sickness by the turn of the twentieth century: when menstruating, she had "the disease of women"; when pregnant, she was "indisposed"; when menopausal, she was experiencing "the death of the woman within the woman"; even childbirth was considered pathological (Ehrenreich and English, 1979, 110–20). Curiously, richer women appeared to be most vulnerable in the view of physicians. In a treatise published in New York in 1874, one of them wrote:

The African Negress, who toils beside her husband in the fields of the south, and Bridget who washes and scrubs and toils in our homes of the north, enjoy for the most part good health, with comparative immunity from uterine disease. (Ibid., 114)

This extreme fragility of White, middle-class women also explains the position of medical experts of that era on education for women. While the clergy denounced the "pride" that study could inspire in women, scientists expressed fear of women's potential deterioration. One British specialist observed:

For a time all seems to go well with her studies; she triumphs over male and female competitors, gains the front rank, is stimulated to continued exertions in order to hold it. But in the long run nature, which cannot be ignored or defied with impunity, asserts its power; excessive losses occur; health fails, she becomes the victim of aches and pains, is unable to go on with her work, and compelled to seek medical advice. (In Murray, 1982, 222)

If she decided to remain single, the better to be able to learn, this, according to the eminent American psychologist G. Stanley Hall, was "the very apotheosis of selfishness from the standpoint of every biological ethics" (in Enrenreich and English, 1979, 129).

Thus, confined to the home and completely explained by her reproductive function, woman (at least in countries dominated by a Victorian ethic) did not have the right to aspire to the sexual pleasure that might have resulted from this function. "When she thinks of this at all, it is with shrinking, or even with horror, rather than with desire," wrote the physicians of that time (in Masters and Johnson, 1979, v). Sexual desire was considered to be an almost exclusively masculine feature.

The experts' obsession with pleasure did not manifest itself only in relation to women. The struggle against masturbation, for example, would mark the entire nineteenth century, with medical experts again taking over from the religious authorities. Appliances were invented to contain the practice, and doctors did not hesitate to resort to surgical intervention to suppress it. These methods endured, although in more limited fashion, into the twentieth century. The last clitoridectomy in the United States was performed on a five-year-old girl in 1948 (Ehrenreich and English, 1979, 123).

The medical profession had begun to express its fear of masturbation in the eighteenth century. In 1760, Professor Tissot published a treatise in Lausanne on the diseases caused by this activity. This work was followed by numerous contributions from other researchers, who all emphasized the physical risks, including madness and death, that this practice could cause in the young. The apprehension proved to be especially keenly felt in the wealthy classes, which believed in the harmful influence of servants or children from inferior social backgrounds (in Mead and Wolfenstein, 1955, 157–8). A British sexologist of that era described the effects of masturbation on the body and intellect as follows:

The frame is stunted and weak, the muscles underdeveloped, the eye is sunken and heavy, the complexion is sallow, pasty or covered with spots of acne, the hands are damp and cold, and the skin moist.... His intellect has become sluggish and enfeebled and if his evil habits are persisted in, he may end in becoming a drivelling idiot or a peevish valetudinarian. (In Walvin, 1982, 137–8).

Nineteenth-century science was pleased to postulate a physical punishment for moral profligacy, even if this profligacy was attributable to a person other than the victim. In his *Livre des mères ou instructions pratiques sur les principes fondamentaux de la propagation de la race humaine* (Book of Mothers, or Practical Instructions on the Fundamental Principles of the Propagation of the Human Race), the French-Canadian doctor Elzéar Paquin declared, in 1850, that illegitimate children had an "inferior constitution."

This biological theory did not disappear completely in the twentieth century. Even in 1957, an American physician believed the following description of a lesbian to be valid:

The homosexual female is characterized by deficient fat in the shoulders and at the girdle, firm muscles, excess hair on the chest, back and legs, a tendency to over-development of the clitoris. There is also a tendency toward a shorter trunk, a contracted pelvis, under-development of the breasts, excess hair on the face and a low-pitched voice. (In Martin and Lyon, 1980, 15)

In short, the lesbian resembled a man. Conversely, other medical authorities believed that the male homosexual was similar to a woman. One doctor maintained, in 1951, that the intensity of desire in gay men followed the rhythm of the menstrual cycle (in Katz, 1976, 61). Testifying on behalf of the American government in 1967, another authority (Dr. Socaridès) caused the dismissal of a homosexual employee of the Defence Department, asserting that the homophile "is frightened of his own body.... He does not know the boundary of his own body.... He will believe that parts of his body are missing" (in d'Emilio, 1983, 216).

In nineteenth-century Britain and the United States, homophilia was already associated with masturbation by medical experts (Weeks, 1983, 25), since homosexuality and masturbation, in their view, had common roots in immorality and pathology.

Automatically denied to respectable women, refused to children through masturbation, and condemned in homophiles, sexual pleasure thus was the dominator's prerogative for a long time. Even today, the condition of the physically handicapped is often considered to deny them access to this pleasure. Perceived solely as an object of treatment, with a condition imposing special rules of decency, the handicapped ceases to be a sexual person. The intellectually handicapped have a similar, though more ambiguous, problem. Insofar as institutional authorities fear the consequences of sexual activity in a person who most often remains physically intact, they tend to deny the presence of desire, and even of need, in this person (Craft and Craft, 1978).

The questions raised by the practice and theoretical approach of psychotherapy go beyond the bounds of mere intellectual deficiency to encompass mental illness. In this matter, treatment varies, depending on whether or not the client belongs to the dominant group. In 1960, in the United States, psychiatric patients from the upper social classes benefited from private therapy, for example, while the poor were hospitalized and treated with pharmaceuticals (Myers and Bean, 1968).[5] The same gap exists between Whites and Blacks. Not only do mental-health specialists favour a personal approach (cognitive or psychoanalytical) in therapy, but their textbooks and publications are silent on the reality of racism and persecution (Goffman, 1961, 377). Black militant Eldridge Cleaver (1968, 11) observed that his psychiatrist "had heard me denouncing the Whites, yet each time he interviewed me he deliberately guided the conversation back to my family life. ... His conclusion was that I hated my mother."

In the late 1960s, 99 percent of clients seeing psychoanalysts in the United States were White (Thomas and Sillen, 1972, 135). However, more Blacks were admitted to State hospitals. Since the conditions of race and class were ignored in assessing the patient's mental state, diagnoses of schizophrenia therefore were more frequent among this population (Chesler, 1983, 323). Particularly flagrant in race relations, the difference in the treatment of mental handicaps also arises in the context of inter-ethnic tensions. For example, more Acadians than English-Canadians are inmates of mental institutions in New Brunswick (Saint-Amand, 1986, 185).

Differences in diagnosis still show through in the assessment of different genders, with women being declared mentally ill when men would be considered to have behavioural problems (Guyon-Bourbonnais, 1981, 58). At least until the 1970s, experts deemed women to be more "disturbed" than men in countries as varied as England, Sweden,the United States, and Canada (Chesler, 1983, 115). Women stayed longer in hospital, were given more drugs, and were subjected to more radical treatment (electro-shock, for example). Most "patients" over age sixty-five in asylums were also women (ibid., xxii). In the late 1970s in the United States, professors of medicine tended to use the pronoun "he" to designate the fictim of a physical disease and the pronoun "she" to refer to a mental patient (Guyon-Bourbonnais, 1981, 90). Since one implicit postulate was that "real" women were not violent, psychiatrists and criminologists more often perceived a murderess than a murderer to be mentally ill, and qualified an infanticide as schizophrenic, though this diagnosis was not applied to the male author of an identical crime (in Rafter and Stanko, 1982, 173).

Unlike Freud, who did not condemn it as such, many psychoanalysts also acted as militants of orthodox morality on matters of sexual orientation. "Psychoanalysis should morally counsel homosexuals," wrote Dr. Eyck (1966, 272). After proclaiming his intention to examine the homosexual "fact" with "objectivity" and without "value judgment" (ibid., 10), the French psychoanalyst stated that he approved of the lawmaker's intention to classify this preference as a "social plague" (ibid., 278–91). Thus, law and science were made to serve religion.

The contribution of psychoanalyst Edmund Bergler was even better known. Published at least six times, his work *Homosexuality, Disease or Way of Life?* was long considered to be a classic. Intending to stick to the medical "facts" (1967, 8) and counter the influence of Kinsey-style "pseudo-scientific" studies (ibid., 174), Dr. Bergler portrayed the homosexual as a *totally* sick personality. Jealousy, masochism, spitefulness, and narcissism were seen as universal characteristics of homosexuals (ibid., 44). Those who did not openly display these traits would have them at least "potentially" (ibid., 145). Since homophilia was a "dangerous poison" (ibid., 30), a "cancer" (ibid., 80), and even a form of "pollution" (ibid., 165), it was necesary, according to

Bergler, to "fight" it on all "fronts": morality (although, in his view, the homosexual takes malicious pleasure in violating its precepts), the law (although, as a masochist, the gay male also would seek to provoke repression), and especially medicine, since psychoanalysis alone could prove to be effective when all was said and done (ibid., 281–82).

If one believes another psychoanalyst, Dr. Frank Caprio, the case of the lesbian would be comparable in gravity to that of the male homosexual. Thus, his painstaking observations forced him to conclude that "many" lesbians suffer from obsessive compulsive neurosis (1962, 303), that "the vast majority" are unstable (ibid., 304), that "many" lack scruples (ibid., 39), that, "in all," homosexual relationships are tinged with infantilism (ibid., 45), and that "[many] lack incentive to further their education, show no desire to take up a hobby, and live a life of dissipation" (ibid., 170). They are also narcissistic, sadistic, and masochistic. In the fourth part of his book on female homosexuality, the part devoted to "clinical" data, Dr. Caprio reports lesbian "confessions" in support of his thesis. The psychoanalyst is also happy to point out that some of them ended up "join[ing] a church" and renouncing their "neurotic values" (ibid., 80) to get back on the "right track" of "normality" (ibid., 294).

The confidence of psychiatrists in their own competence to understand their patients better than the latter understand themselves also accounts for the indifference with which they received the confidences of abused children until very recently. The lack of seriousness with which pediatricians treated the problems of battered children (Van Stolk, 1979, 130) was displayed for decades by psychoanalysts regarding young victims of sexual abuse.

Following in the footsteps of Freud, who in 1905 renounced the theory of the seduction of children by their parents and laid the foundations of psychoanalysis by postulating, on the contrary, the desire of the former for the latter, psychoanalysts, to all intents and purposes, denied the very existence of incest. "Many of our patients report that they have tried again and again to tell social workers and psychiatrists about their incest history but are cut off and obviously not believed," a male pediatrician and a female psychoanalyst wrote recently, admitting that they themselves had ignored this reality for years (Kempe and Kempe, 1984, 5–6).

A relatively young discipline, psychoanalysis has often seen its epistemological foundations challenged and its theses brushed aside as impressionistic by the fervent adherents of more exact sciences. Sometimes emanating from the dominant group, these critiques did not so much challenge the conclusions of theories that, in the final analysis, justified the established order as they contested the method used to arrive at them. Very early in the nineteenth century, even before the advent of Freudianism, there was a fascination with measurement as a criterion of scientific rigour. For example, craniometricians endeavoured to measure the volume of the human brain. Thus, according to the French surgeon Paul Broca and the German anatomist Karl Vogt, cerebral volume was larger in a man than in a woman, in a mature adult than in an old man, in an individual of a superior race than in another of a lesser race, and in an eminent man than in a person of mediocre talent (Gould, 1981, 89–109). On this scale, an adult Black male would be equivalent to a White woman, who would be comparable to an elderly White man. According to Broca's disciple, Gustave Le Bon, one of the founders of social psychology, the intelligence of a woman was also akin to that of a "savage": she therefore should be relegated to the inferior tasks that "nature" had reserved for her, and one should avoid educating her.

Only Léonce Manouvrier would oppose Broca, correcting his calculations of female skulls. Manouvrier introduced such criteria as weight, age (the older women observed by Broca bore more risk of degenerative diseases), and height (to which brain size, but not intelligence, is proportional).[6] Arguing that "everyone knew" that women were inferior, Broca would not take these reservations into account, even though he had endorsed them previously to counter the conclusions of a researcher across the Rhine who had found that German brains weighed an average of 100 grams more than French brains. Postulating a link between the level of intelligence and the volume of the brain, Broca also believed that each of these factors increased with historical evolution. Since analysis of the dimensions of skulls of different periods found in Parisian cemeteries revealed degrees of variation incompatible with his theory, Broca decided to attribute the largest brain-pans to aristocrats and the smallest to members of the popular class. Thus, by the virtues of tautological proof, postulated conclusions were summoned to the rescue of an undemonstrated proposition.

In addition to measuring skulls and brains, nineteenth-century scientists were interested in the human body as a whole. Anatomists like Cuvier, for example, compared the races, after deriving their descent from the sons of Noah – Shem, Ham, and Japhet (Berry and Tischler, 1978, 34). Anthropometricians also developed theories that led to the same conclusions as those reached by the specialists in craniometry (Gould, 1981, 115–19). One of these, known as the recapitulation theory, postulated that the adult Black male, the White female, and the White child all represent a previous stage in the evolution of the White *male*. A hierarchy was also supposed to exist among White men. In the view of the American paleontologist E. D. Cope, for example, southern European men, because of their emotionalism, were more akin to women than to men of the north. Having abandoned this characteristic in their youth in favour of reason, northern males fully embodied the ideal norm. In the name of this thesis, Cope opposed the vote for women.

Around 1920, however, the recapitulation theory had to give way to the contrary thesis of neoteny (Gould, 1981, 120–1). According to the Dutch anatomist Louis Bolk, superiority derived from slower development and the retention of childhood traits in adulthood. Forgetting seventy years of opposing theory, and heedless of the fact that women and Orientals, for example, are more neotenic than White men, scientists sought to "prove" that the same groups declared inferior in the name of recapitulation were still inferior, but for diametrically opposite reasons.

Criminology was strongly marked by anthropometric postulates (Rafter and Stenko, 1982, 3; Gould, 1981, 124–38). Thus, the theses of the physician Cesare Lombroso posited the existence of an atavistic criminal who would reproduce, in his person, the physical and moral characteristics of primitive humanity: jutting jawbone, prominent cheekbones, pronounced brow ridges, large hands ... and a love of evil for its own sake. Lombroso also portrayed female criminals as being both worse than men and masculine in character.

As Lombroso's theses show, researchers at the turn of the twentieth century were influenced deeply by evolutionist doctrine. Taking up the theory developed by Charles Darwin to account for the evolution of species, some applied the principle of natural selection (dictating the survival of the fittest) to human communities. Thus, the English philosopher Herbert Spencer recommended that natural selection be given free rein in society by eliminating assistance to the poor, the chronically ill, and the mentally handicapped. Social Darwinism also required young men to combat racial degeneration by submitting to military service: the Victorian mentality henceforth expected of physical discipline what it previously asked of religious training (Gillis, 1974, 142; 156–7).

Racial purity obsessed several adherents of evolutionist theory. Not only did the apostles of eugenics believe in the superiority of certain peoples over others (for example, Joseph Gobineau in that of the Aryans, or Houston Chamberlain in that of the Germans), but they also militated, like the physiologist Francis Galton, against the multiplication of the unfit and for the reproduction of more robust individuals.

In the United States, eugenics soon led to the establishment of sterilization programs for individuals deemed to bear hereditary taints: the mentally defective, the mentally ill, epileptics, syphilitics, moral "perverts" (such as alcoholics), and sexual "perverts" – in short, all those who constituted, or who eventually *could* constitute, a "threat" to society (Kittrie, 1971, 313–15). In the mid–1960s, twenty-six states still had laws on sterilization, and twenty-one of them even authorized it without the consent of the persons concerned.

In addition to the sterilization measures gradually taken against "degenerates," a law on immigration quotas for "inferior" ethnic groups was introduced in 1924. Thus, declared to be "feeble-minded" by the experts, a great number of Jews, Latins, and Slavs henceforth would be prohibited from entering the United States. Under this law, many German Jews fleeing Nazism would be refused entry in the 1930s. Even French Canadians received the attention of specialists. In 1926, an American psychologist made the following observation:

From Canada ... we are getting ... the less intelligent of working-class people.... The increase in the number of French Canadians is alarming. Whole New England villages and towns are filled with them. The average intelligence of the French Canadian group in our data approached the level of the average Negro intelligence. (In Block and Dworkin, 1976, 380)

Eugenic theses on heredity were most often linked to the calculation of the *intelligence quotient* (IQ). Psychologists thus made their own contribution to giving scientific credit to the belief in the innate mental inferiority of certain races or social classes. Intelligence tests were the basis on which academics Lewis Terman (of Stanford), Robert Yerkes (of Harvard), and Henry Goddard (of Vineland, later Princeton) founded their conclusions on the "feeble-mindedness" of ethnic groups that were to be targeted by the immigration quotas.

Calculation of the intelligence quotient was also extended to the social classes with the implicit objective of distinguishing between them. Long geared to the values of the middle class (White and professionally oriented), intelligence tests ended up standardizing the American nation to such an extent that the Supreme Court had to require, in 1971, that a real link exist between the job to be performed and the obligation of taking a test.

But it was in England that the effects of intelligence tests on social classes were most immediate. Under the influence of the British psychometrician Cyril Burt, an Education Act was adopted in 1944 that allowed this technique to be used to determine which students would go to university and which would not. It would take nearly thirty years (until 1972) for it to be proved that Burt (knighted in the meantime) had resorted to fraudulent methods to obtain his results.

Based on Burt's studies, the American Arthur Jensen, in 1969, again raised the thesis of the genetic inferiority of Blacks. Although psychometricians have never succeeded in agreeing on the notion of general intelligence, Jensen claimed, on the basis of this criterion, to trace a hierarchical evolutionary line of human beings (Block and Dworkin, 1976, 413–65; Gould, 1981, 317–18), along which some categories would be classified as inferior to others. Blacks would fall into this inferior category, along with social groups whose income did not increase from one generation to the next.

While Jensen's work tied in with the evolutionist movement, another adherent of psychometry, William Shockley, winner of the Nobel Prize in the completely unrelated field of physics, resubscribed to eugenics by calling, in 1972, for the sterilization of low-IQ individuals who were a burden on society (Block and Dworkin, 1976, 413). This call resembled a certain discourse of the Depression years in Great Britain which proposed that the same "remedy" be used against the unemployed (Rose and Rose, 1977, 94).

But the will to justify the hierarchical relations established between groups in society is revealed not only through the measurement of degrees of intelligence; psychologists also consolidate the instituted forms of domination by aspiring to shape *behaviour*. For some behaviourists, among others, since everything is a matter of conditioning, it is possible to change deep-rooted tendencies and induce reflexes that better conform to society's norms. For example, in the case of homosexuals subjected to this adjustment process, experts sought to provoke disgust with their own gender (aversion therapy) by resorting to emetics and electric shocks.

Although they place a greater emphasis on instinct than on conditioning, ethologists also liken the state of social relations to an irreducible order of things; the passive "masses" would be acted upon by people whose responsibility, finally, would be diluted in larger determinisms (Archard *et al.*, 1977, 279). This postulate is revealed, for example, in the writings of Konrad Lorenz: "A sexual or mass murderer does indeed elicit horror and amazement, just like any *impersonal natural* catastrophe," he wrote in his *Studies in Animal and Human Behaviour*.[7] The analysis of human customs believes that the study can be enriched by systematic comparison with animal habits. This, at least, is the wager made by sociobiologists. As the heirs of evolutionist biology and genetics, they not only give greater importance to the influence of heredity in human behaviour but also postulate the tendency of each gene to seek maximum reproduction. This tendency would explain rape, for example, at least if one believes the American David Barash, for whom a man who assaults a woman simply chooses this specific strategy to respond to a vital necessity.[8]

Launched by the entomologist Edward O. Wilson in 1975, sociobiology proposes biological bases for objects of study hitherto devolving upon the humanities. Furthermore, its founder also considers biology to be the ultimate arbiter of morality and social norms.

Only by interpreting the activity of the emotive centers as a biological adaptation can the meaning of the canons (of morality) be deciphered (...). The question that science is now in a position to answer is the very origin and meaning of human values, from which all ethical pronouncements and much of political practice flow. (In Montagu, 1980, 102).

Morality, therefore, is linked to the principle of natural selection, of which all behaviour is the product. Thus, aggression should be considered innate behaviour in man. Drawing analogies with animals. sociobiologists justify the exercise of male domination of women or deduce the propensity of human groups to xenophobia from the practice of territorial monopoly in certain species. Aggression and territoriality would not prevent manifestations of altruism, but these would primarily be the effect of deliberate calculation, with the individual seeking to ensure the survival of his genes.

Although more refined than in the last century, the theses of the experts who today justify the social relations of domination find their foundations in the same syntheses that then favoured explanations of an evolutionist and hereditary nature. Likewise, there is still a keen fascination with everything that concerns the brain as the seat of intelligence.

In the middle of the last century, neurologists situated intelligence in the frontal lobes, before identifying it with the parietal lobes at the turn of the twentieth century. This difference would have curious consequences for the determination, by scientists, of the relative volume of various lobes, depending on gender. In each of these two periods, the woman's lobes were deemed to be smaller, though the female frontal lobes began to appear proportionally more developed than those of men at the very time (the end of the century) when this difference could, in contrast, show male parietal superiority (in Miller, 1982, 192).

History is now repeating itself with studies on the hemispheric asymmetry of the brain, the left hemisphere being considered the seat of verbal and logical activities while the right hemisphere would modulate spatial and intuitive faculties. Despite the still very limited character of the research, conclusions were drawn in the early 1970s emphasizing an eventual gender difference in the organization of the brain. According to certain researchers, the male brain would be "better lateralized" and "more specialized," with the hemispheres functioning more separately in men than in women.

Thus, man remains the standard to which woman is compared. Assuming that gender differences really exist in the brain, the question is why one chooses to think of cerebral organization in terms of lateralization or specialization ("better" in men), rather than in terms of bilaterality, homogeneity, integration, or balance (which would give women the advantage).

Another paradox is that, despite a theory that the male brain is more specialized, the right hemisphere has been associated with men and the left hemisphere with women. Thus, intituition, which long was considered a female characteristic, now becomes a synonym of creativity in men, while logic is given up, without a shot fired, to women and labelled "linear" thinking.

In the same way that theories on gender differences in the brain began to spread, a new clinical concept appeared in the early 1970s. Used to describe the adoption of socially condemned behaviour, the notion of "minimal brain damage," or MBD, *postulated* the existence in the brain of a lesion which, nonetheless, was physiologically undetectable. An extension of the concept of hyperkinesis (excess physical energy), MBD initially designated a childhood "disease" before being applied, in the United States, to poor students or undisciplined children. According to one American researcher, elements of this syndrome would be manifested, for example, through social aggression or by playing with younger children or, for a boy, by playing with girls (in Rose and Rose, 1977, 174).

Sometimes subsidized by the judicial and penal system, medical research on behavioural adjustment even occasionally took the form of surgical intervention (Rose and Rose, 1977, 176-7). In their book *Violence and the Brain*, published in 1970, the specialists Mark and Ervin went so far as to propose removing part of the brain (the amygdala) of the 5 or 10 percent of ghetto-dwellers likely to cause race riots. Similarly, French physicians had already attempted, during the colonial period, to explain the then very high crime rate among Algerians in terms of the non-integration of their frontal lobes in their brain function (Fanon, 1974, 223). Twenty years later, other experts would qualify this "non-integration" as "greater specialization" when it appeared to be more pronounced in men than in women!

Thus, there is a very clear propensity in the work of certain neurologists to look for the origin of the dominated individual's behavioural "problems" in his or her brain, rather than in the social conditions that created them. With all the more reason, psychosurgeons allowed themselves to intervene in the case of individuals who automatically were categorized as mentally ill. Thus (particularly in the 1940s), lobotomies were performed on these individuals (Alexander and

Selesnick, 1966, 285) and electro-shock was administered to them, even before neurologists knew its biological working (Fréminville, 1977, 138). Often likened to the mentally handicapped, homosexuals were also subjected to these two types of "treatment," when specialists did not simply prefer to resort to genital surgery (Kronemayer, 1980, 81–7). This is the context of the theory set forth in 1991 by a neurobiologist of the Salk Institute, who argued a link between male homosexuality and the smaller volume of the hypothalamus.

By the very fact of the sustained interest they display in a question, and the data they patiently accumulate to explore it, experts claim the right not only to privileged decision-making power but to make decisions *in the place of* the persons concerned. Most often, this right will be granted officially and sanctioned both by a document (a diploma or licence) and by affiliation to a professional body, duly mandated to control the recruitment of its members. Often drawing upon the same system of moral values, the legal and scientific orders mutually support each other in a common defence of the dominant ideology.

Thus, to the benefit of "professionals," the oppressed lose the right to a say in the very decisions that affect them most closely!

THE IMPLICIT RULES OF DISCOURSE

Measurement, so dear to the western mind, first manifests itself in its *tone* of delivery. Only statements formulated with detachment are truly worthy of belief. When expressed with too much emotion, the most genuine truths risk provoking incredulity. Lies, however, when communicated with the utmost calm, can be received attentively and sway their audience for a time.

Yet it is precisely characteristic of the victim to "bemoan his fate, which is often annoying" (Memmi, 1992, 82). Defending its refusal to publish a report that it had commissioned, in 1981, on the special *problems* of handicapped women, the Nova Scotia government invoked the "too depressing" nature of its content, as well as the overfrequent references to sexuality (Matthews, 1983, 9). Between reality and "objectivity," it was reality that had to give way. "We preferred the testimony of Jean-Charles Pagé to any other because of his balance and his obvious good faith," wrote the publisher of the well-known book *Les fous crient au secours* (The Crazies Are Crying for Help), while making the following admission: "Other mental patients suffered more than he and could give an even more incredible testimony which perhaps would be a more faithful illustration of the intolerable scandal of our alleged psychiatric hospitals (Pagé, 1961, 7)." However, though "more faithful," this testimony was not sufficiently "balanced."

Respect for cold objectivity, strongly recommended to the victim, will be required, with all the more reason, from the researcher. But rarely will the dominator believe he has found this in a scientist who does not confirm his own opinion of the dominated. If, for example, the psychoanalyst Edmund Bergler felt he had the authority to reject the positive conclusions of sexologist Alfred Kinsey and of sociologist Donald Webster Cory (Edward Sagarin) on homosexuality, it was because, in his view, they had been "emotional" in their defence of the phenomenon (Bergler, 1967, 170 and 278). During the 1960s, when he was seeking to alert his colleagues to the plight of battered children, Dr. Vincent Fontana was criticized for being overemotional; it was also believed that he surely had "exaggerated" the gravity of the problem, assuming that this problem "really" existed (Fontana, 1983, 30–1).

Christiane Rochefort was more than just emotional – she was alleged to be "hysterical" in her book *Les enfants d'abord* (Children First). This, at least, was the opinion of one critic, who preferred to write a very sober study of childhood in western literature, rather than a "diatribe" on their condition (Kuhn, 1982, 230). A discourse conveying demands is always judged to be too "committed" in relation to the "objective" considerations of the dominator, who benefits from the situation that created these problems. More than being merely committed, a denunciatory work will sometimes be considered "polemical" and even labelled "pamphleteering." This was the fate reserved for *The Second Sex* by Simone de Beauvoir and *The Wretched of the Earth* by Franz Fanon, among others, before they became classics on the status of women and of colonized peoples.

Often, the charges of emotionalism and partiality will focus on the personalities of those who challenge the dominant ideology. In the view of some current neo-liberals, the partisans of equality between social classes, for example, display "emotional immaturity" and "Oedipal narcissism" in criticizing free enterprise: suffering from a "fragile ego," they necessarily fear comparison with others (Harouel, 1984, 270–1).

When the dominated display some inclination to emancipate themselves, the dominator has the impression that they are acting arbitrarily and even capriciously. No longer understanding the dominated, he will require an explanation and want to know what justifies this "sudden" desire for change. "What does Québec want?" English Canadians wondered as the nationalist movement developed. "But what do women want?" some men now ask, exasperated by the current plurality of feminist tendencies. "The following great question remains unanswered, one which I myself have never been able to answer despite my thirty years of studying the female soul: 'What does woman want?' " Sigmund Freud declared to Marie Bonaparte, to some extent reproaching the object of his study for the incomprehension he himself felt.[9]

Projecting onto the dominated his own state of mind, which is the detachment provided by the defence of great principles supported from a position of strength, the dominator is often concerned that his counterpart displays so little sense of humour. If there is *one* emotion that the oppressed are criticized for not knowing how to display, this is it. Having become incapable of humour, the dominated will appear to be "obsessed" by the cause they defend and unable to "speak of anything else." Above all, they will seem incapable of speaking of it with anything other than seriousness, and often even with rebellion.

"It is always said that someone is exaggerating when he describes an injustice to people who do not want to hear about it," Albert Memmi oberved (1973, 27). For apart from its balanced *tone*, the discourse, to be credible to the dominator, must obey the *logic* of measurement. Indeed, no rule would be a better guarantee of objectivity than that of the "happy medium." Starting from the implicit postulate that two opposing points of view are necessarily *extremes*, the happy medium is defined as the ideal dialectical position, equidistant from the contrary positions demanded by the balance of opposing forces in a given period. A militant's statement of the problem will then always, necessarily, be considered extreme.

Thus, the most humanitarian approach may be rejected "objectively" as radical. In the recent edition of a *History of the United States* published under the direction of Carl Degler, a Princeton academic endeavours to demonstrate the stakes of the Civil War by portraying as back-to-back "extremists" the champions of slavery *and* the partisans of its abolition. Although he was one of the opponents of the extension of this institution to the newly created states of the American West, Abraham Lincoln supposedly showed "moderation" by siding, at the same time, with the maintenance of slavery where it already existed in the South.[10] While more than 170 countries have already achieved independence on this planet, the sovereignty of Québec is presented as an "extreme" position by the adherents of "renewed" federalism, who propose their option as the happy medium between independence and "unconditional" federalism.

Moreover, there is no need to oppose comparable realities in the dynamics of the happy medium. When the French psychoanalyst Christiane Olivier, in *Les enfants de Jocaste* (The Children of Jocasta), wrote that she aspired to "speak the language of the middle," she claimed to seek it between the two "extremisms" of the Freudian discourse and the feminist discourse (Olivier, 1980, 5).

Because the geometric constraint that modulates the dominant discourse on the happy medium is also exercised through time, the power to define the reference period will be a major stake in the calculation of the relative distances separating the contrary points of view from the ideal centre. In 1973, when the ABC television network presented the first feature film sympathetic to gays (*That Certain Summer*), psychiatrists employed by the network required the screenwriters to include negative dialogue on homosexuality, dialogue that automatically served as a "counterweight" to the basic position adopted by the film (Russo, 1981, 222). The fact that the very subject of homophilia had been ignored or treated with contempt for forty years in film and twenty-five years on television was not enough, it seems, to establish balance.

Supported by the conventional "wisdom" ("You have to present both sides of the issue," "You have to mention the pros and the cons"), the concept of fairness is implicit in the rule of the happy medium. Also implicit is the principle that everyone is entitled to his or her opinion. For many, this very quickly leads to the conclusion that all opinions are valid. This was the point of view supported by a contributor to *La Presse* when he expressed surprise that a Jewish association was filing a defamation suit for systematic Holocaust denial against Ernst Zündel, a Toronto resident of German origin.[11] A Laval academic, who wondered whether the Armenian genocide should be interpreted as a mere deportation carried out by the Turks in legitimate self-defence, also concluded democratically "that it would be wise to leave this debate to the historians and to the intelligence and moral judgment of each individual."[12]

As one vector among others in the force field of the established discourse, an idea will command attention more readily if its promoters first appear to compromise in adopting it, or if adversaries have arisen who have the good taste to fight on both sides at the same time. For in the dialectics of the relationships of domination, it is not as important to defend a just cause as to pass for the defender of the happy medium.

However, it is ultimately up to the dominated to alter the rules of the game in their favour and undermine the discourse of the objective fact through the politics of the *fait accompli*. By pushing back the limits of the "extremes" through fundamental challenges, this policy will shift a "happy medium" in the direction of the dominated, away from a centre that until then had propped up the established order.

But the road to emancipation is long, and the oppressed first will have to become conscious of their condition of inferiority. Imbued with the dominant discourse, which keeps them in subjection, they must relearn how to think for themselves, at the same time that they have to demand the right to speak.

PART TWO

The Dominated

CHAPTER THREE

Alienation

Alienation is to the oppressed what self-righteousness is to the oppressor. Each really believes that their unequal relationship is part of the natural order of things or desired by some higher power. The dominator does not feel that he is exercising unjust power, and the dominated do not feel the need to withdraw from his tutelage. The dominator will even believe, in all good faith, that he is looking out for the good of the dominated, while the latter will insist that they want an authority more enlightened than their own to determine their fate.

The very meaning of alienation is that it estranges people from themselves. Adopting the image created by the oppressor, the dominated see themselves through others' eyes. Like the mentally ill, to whom the term was initially applied, the alienated cease to belong to themselves. As Emma Santos says, in her *Itinéraire psychiatrique* (Psychiatric Journey), alienation means "being dispossessed of one's self" (1977, 27).

Before being stripped of their property or rights, the oppressed are robbed of their identity. The dominator defines this identity in their stead, reducing it to a difference that is then labelled inferior. The oppressed become "alien" in their own eyes, unable to recognize themselves in the image presented to them. Every day, the world around them and the discourse that supports it confirm their inadequacy and the negative reflection of their singularity. Living in an environment that they do not control, the dominated are also inhabited by an alien way of thinking. Unlike the vanquished, who continue to deny the legitimacy of the power to which they must succumb, alienated individuals inwardly endorse the validity of their required submission and help lay the foundations of the relationships of domination that entrench their subjugation.

As objects of external action, the dominated are a negligible quantity, receiving their value from others. When their own sensibility is not ignored (as in the case of the aged, whose diseases are automatically "normal"), the very legitimacy of their feelings may be unappreciated (such as the pain of the lesbian or male homosexual who loses a longtime companion). Alienation *from* something also means alienation *within* something, since the internalized domination is based as much on the absence of participatory ties as on the existence of a dependent relationship (Pellerin, 1983, 31). Subjugation thus is a form of poverty, the comprehensive type of poverty defined by Michel Mollat:

A position ... of weakness, dependence and humility, characterized by deprivation, changing with different historical periods and societies, of the means of power and social consideration: money, power, science or technical qualifications, honourable birth, physical vigour, intellectual capacity, freedom and personal dignity. (In Brébant, 1984, 107–8)

In this sense, even the physically or mentally handicapped are impoverished. In this sense, as well, workers continue to be poor, despite their increased standard of living. For although the arduous nature of labour is being eased by automation and computerization, wage-earning manual labourers still remain dependent (Memmi, 1973, 121–9). This dependence, apart from the little control it allows them over their own destiny, is reinforced by the servility it engenders. As the following testimony of a Canadian aboriginal shows, the reflex is so deep-rooted that it continues to operate even when the victim is aware of it:

I was extremely fearful of white bosses. They terrified me. I always found them arrogant and cruel. Psychologically, their superiority practically crippled me. As soon as the boss gave me orders, I would become obedient and subservient, thankful for every small favour, no matter how insignificant. (Adams, 1975, 4)

Relationships among the oppressed are affected as well. Mothers are often reproached for transmitting a tradition of passivity and subordination to their daughters, fuelling the more general condition suffered by their gender as a whole. Anger and mistrust mar the relationship between generations, with children perceiving fear in the very people who should be able to protect them. The Black American writer James Baldwin did not observe anything else in his father, and it took him years to understand the latter's submissive attitude

(Baldwin, 1963, 34–5). The rift between parents and children deepens even further when young people decide for fight actively against oppression.

It is possible for people to be conscious of their oppression, even when they are resigned to not having the means to fulfil their desire for liberation. For Black slaves of the early nineteenth century, trapped in a foreign and hostile land, individual revolt could not yet lead to organized resistance with outside support. But even when emancipation is possible, consciousness of oppression is almost always accompanied by the fear of failure or the dread of success in those who have experienced centuries of servitude. The fear of failure confirms the intimate conviction of real inferiority induced by the oppressor. The dread of success is the result of a long tutelage which, by definition, did not instill the oppressed with the habit of responsibility.

Thus, as in the case of certain victims of extreme poverty, alienation risks becoming a way of life to which individuals eventually become anchored:

The development of shame can be a defence mechanism and, from then on, shame no longer has the dialectical character which initiates change and begins to support the work of redemption. The desire to achieve dignity first requires self-love. (In Brébant, 1984, 12)

While some are born into a condition of alienation and experience it all their lives, others enter this condition suddenly and unforeseeably, like the totally assimilated German Jews converted overnight into second-class citizens by Hitler's Nuremberg laws, or like individuals afflicted by a physical handicap late in life. In the words of one polio victim, "something happened and I became a stranger. I was a greater stranger to myself than to anyone. Even my dreams did not know me" (in Goffman, 1963, 35).

Even when this is foreseeable, it sometimes may be a novel feeling to learn alienating domination. This is the case of the latent homosexual who discovers his preferences, or the person who, having decided to assimilate into another ethnic group, finds himself in direct contact with xenophobia. This is not an experience unique to individuals. A refugee community that was part of a homogeneous society in its country of origin will endure the hard experience of minority status once it settles in a foreign land; the middle classes, guaranteed a certain degree of social consideration by their position in times of prosperity, will find it difficult to accept the proletarianization that results from an economic crisis. Even more insistently, unemployment will deprive individuals or groups of their self-esteem by rendering them dependent on the aid of others or of the State.

The reminder of their dominated status may be brutal, even for those whose daily lives are full of humiliation. By making them *suddenly* visible, certain situations will revive the stigma to which they are commonly subject. Treated with respect on the telephone or by mail, persons of colour or "different" features will find themselves refused housing or work after face-to-face contact has been established.

But even when it is completely foreseeable or inevitable, the alienating condition is most often felt as the effect of external circumstances and a more or less gratuitous curse. Thus, while some have the impression that they are "slipping" inexorably into old age, others feel that they have aged "overnight." In both cases, old age is an alienating experience. Simone de Beauvoir, who defined it as "a reality which is indisputably ourselves even when it affects us from outside" (1970, II, 24), gives a good description of this dialectic of ambiguity:

Old age is especially difficult to bear because we always had considered it to be an alien species: have I become someone else while remaining myself? (Ibid., 14)

No doubt the reality or perspective of old age triggers understandable apprehension in an individual who feels his or her vital forces declining and an awakening awareness of death. But the experience of old age is also conditioned by the judgment imposed by society. Even though, unlike other forms of "difference," age affects *everyone*, the western mentality continues to idolize youth. "I am proud to have *stayed young*," an active and healthy senior citizen will say. The ideal proposed by the surrounding culture with regard to age is not so much to integrate the different components of the life cycle as to preserve the characteristics of the initial stage of existence at any price, to the bitter end. Gerontophobia begins as contempt for something found in other people and ends up as contempt for something that eventually will be manifested in oneself (Fisher, 1977, 134).

Alienation invades a person's entire being. Trapped by this logic of dehumanization, the dominated are perceived and treated both as the embodiment of reality in its most immediate and compact form and as an abstract category into which all individualities are merged. An entire pedagogy of guilt is articulated around this static reductionism, making the oppressed bear the primary responsibility for their condition and categorizing any impulses toward liberation as an act of aggression against the oppressor-victim.

THE BODY AS OBJECT

The bodies of the oppressed do not belong to them. When they are not called upon to sacrifice them on the altar of Race, History, or some other divinity, they simply belong to the person on whom they depend.

Thus, a woman's body long has been the property of her husband, or, more broadly, of her family. Eating after and, if necessary, less than the rest, her work is free and appropriated by her family. Long reduced to a solely reproductive function, she has never definitively obtained the power to control the number of her pregnancies. As a member of a nation defeated in an armed struggle, she will be considered by the victor as part of the booty, upon which he can exercise his "rights."

Due to their relative bodily weakness, children also, to some extent, are the property of their parents, on whom they depend for survival. The law even recognizes that parents have the right to use physical coercion against them. At the mercy of adults, who hold authority over them, children are not strong enough to oppose the abuse to which they may be subject. In an era of declining birth rates and rising divorce, a child is even a resource, kidnapped for the clandestine adoption market, or a disputed piece of property in the conflict between former spouses.

Physical strength is also a value to be sold, as evidenced by the century-long struggle waged by unions to contain its use. There was even a time when bodily subservience was total, through the enslavement of entire races declared inferior for this purpose. If exploitation in today's western world no longer comes in the extreme guises it assumed in past centuries, it nevertheless continues to weigh upon foreign workers, who are not yet officially protected from the market's abuses.

Reduced to the status of object, the bodies of the oppressed can no longer be perceived as completely their own. "I feel boxed in," a North African immigrant in France confided to Tahar Ben Jelloun (1977, 31). Industrial accidents are frequent among Arab workers in France, evidence of their frustration and of the sexual impotence which they did not experience in their country of origin (ibid., 62). "Boxed into" their own skins, victims of racism feel the existence of new barriers that shut them in. For an individual of colour living in the White world, "knowledge of one's body is a uniquely negative activity ... a knowledge in the third person," Franz Fanon wrote, describing the mirror image produced by a homogeneous society upon a contrary identity (1952, 109).

Rape victims have an opposite and even more alienating feeling that they are exposed to the elements, having lost, to some extent, the sense of an indestructible barrier that their bodies had set up against the outside world.

But there is no greater alienation than that of the physically handicapped, an alienation born out of an invasion of one's entire being by an "autonomous" body "which gains ground, spreads, annexes and alienates" (*L'écran handicapé*, 1983, 86). In this case, the disoriented impression felt by the victim of racism or rape in the development of his or her bodily structure becomes a feeling of imbalance, as the overpresent body finally vanishes, reduced to a head. In the words of Anne-Marie Alonzo:

My body is not mine. The background is motionless. Reduced to the head, tension mounts ... . All that remains is the dream, legs restored to sight and corrected, arms shooting out, shoulders. I am surprised at the desire for my hidden body. I am nostalgic for myself as if for another, already known.[1]

This inner malaise is compounded by the effects of the other's gaze. Discomfort, a singular phenomenon at first, is compounded by the embarrassment that wells up when the difference is made visible. The presence of the handicap gives "normal" people the impression that, without any other preliminaries, they can speak freely to the victim about his or her infirmity, asking what caused it and telling this person about similar cases of which they have heard (Goffman, 1963, 16).

The established order also exposes the body, watching for differences when they are not automatically displayed. In the case of homosexuals, for example, the therapist who defines permitted loves or the political inquisitor of a regime where "these things do not exist" will measure the physical reactions that might betray the subject's real tastes. Therapists or inquisitors will then try to "correct" these unorthodox penchants by conditioning the body, through doses of pain, to prefer the nude body of the other gender.

No doubt the demands of constant self-control weigh most heavily upon transsexuals. Confined to a body that they do not perceive as their own, they experience the ultimate alienation: a sensibility alien to the material shell that supports it. They can only make these coincide through a mutilating operation. The very lengthy process leading to the final transformation will expose them, for awhile, to the ridicule and rude stares of the people around them.

The oppressed do not belong to themselves. This even includes the pleasure that their oppressors can claim from them. There is the ambiguous pleasure of beauty, which sometimes will be reserved for the oppressed, only to be otherwise denied. There is also the pleasure of sex, which can be taken without qualms only from those who are already objects of social contempt.

An Object of Pleasure

Unlike sexuality, which is an area of comprehensive inferiorization for the oppressed, *beauty* is considered to be solely the prerogative of the dominator, except in women, for whom it serves as a pedestal. While it is a mode of *confinement* in the case of women, it is mainly a means of *exclusion* for the dominated as a whole.

Associated with youth in western culture, beauty automatically is denied to elderly people. "Age before beauty," the conventional "wisdom" pithily decrees, marking the irreducible nature of their opposition. Thus, one should not be surprised at the reaction of one old woman who, fearing that her young female friends would perceive her aging, was reluctant to leave them for a prolonged period (Macdonald and Rich, 1984, 58). The "ugliness" of the old has been mocked in the West for hundreds of years, especially in women (de Beauvoir, 1970, I, 196–237). This double standard is apparent in the French proverb that a man should have the age of his feelings and a woman that of her appearance.

If it is imperative that women are the fair sex, this is because they should not claim the prerogatives of the "stronger sex." "*Sois belle et tais-toi*" ("Shut up and be beautiful") they are told in French. Maximum beauty in a woman is equated with minimal intelligence. If, indeed, "gentlemen prefer blondes," they also know they are "dumb." Though not the least interested in evaluating a woman's IQ, men will readily compute her measurements. Contests oppose women to each other on the basis of their figures rather than their intellect. A woman must aspire to please primarily through her physique, even if this means resorting to plastic surgery to correct the "ravages" of time or subjecting herself to a diet that may take her to the brink of anorexia.

The "beauty myth" creates an obstacle course for women. The current idealization of youth means that physically more handsome individuals are automatically considered more competent (in Miller, 1982, 275), implying that women have to be both young and beautiful. Not long ago, both an American television network and Radio-Canada, the French network of the Canadian Broadcasting Corporation, considered it appropriate to take female personalities off the air when they turned forty. But outside of trades like television, which depend heavily on image, the old impediments still prevail. Women who are too beautiful will be refused positions of responsibility, their intrinsic incompetence implicitly taken for granted (ibid., 276).

Women thus lose out either way. Their beauty, sometimes associated with intellectual unfitness, will also be seen as a sign of moral deficiency. According to the conventional "wisdom," pretty women are also "the most dangerous." On the other hand, they may be guilty simply because they are not beautiful. Juries will be less inclined to believe a physically unattractive rape victim, for example, on the grounds that she probably was "looking" for what happened to her (in Miller, 1982, 277).

The same goes for lesbians, who will often be seen to have been "left on the shelf." Not seductive enough for a man, they will "settle" for another woman. Ugliness and homosexuality most often go hand in hand. Female lesbian characters are portrayed as repulsive in the novels and short stories of Zola, Daudet, and de Maupassant (Faderman, 1981, 282).[2] Even taking lesbianism as a literary theme will have unpleasant implications for an author. In 1964, a literary critic at the *Ottawa Citizen* expressed surprise, in reviewing Jane Rule's novel *Desert of the Heart*, at "how such a nice-looking woman could even have chosen so distasteful a subject" (Rule, 1975, 1). There are certainly beautiful homosexual women in literature, but a compensating logic demands that they be flawed by unscrupulousness. Literature and film thus portray them as sophisticated women, often rich and in positions of authority (teachers, for example), "weaving their web" around a young, innocent girl.[3]

Leaving aside the noteworthy cases in which beauty is portrayed as dangerous in women, public opinion generally associates beauty with goodness (in Miller, 1982, 260–2). Fairy tales have always countenanced this link, almost unfailingly depicting unsympathetic characters as ugly. One need only think of Cinderella's step-sisters and the plethora of misshapen (and old) witches pervading this type of "children's" literature. The innumerable criminals who have made a fortune for the comic book industry are most often ugly as well.

The implicit postulates associating moral virtue with beauty can only add to the difficulties of social integration encountered by the physically handicapped. An aesthetic hierarchy will even be established within the range of infirmities. The more deformed the body or the closer to the face the injury is located, the more difficult it will seem to bear the handicap: it is better to lose an arm, for example, than to be disfigured (in Miller, 1982, 259). Psychotherapists even partially assess the adaptation of the mentally ill on their physical appearance, or base their prognosis on this criterion, (ibid., 277).

The same goes for unruly children, whose teachers more often tend to postulate the existence of psychological problems if the child is ugly, but ascribe misbehaviour to "a bad day" if the child is good-looking (in Miller, 1982, 272–3). If they are pleasing to the eye, they will be judged more intelligent by their teachers. Their employers will have the same impression (unless the applicant is a woman) when the time comes to fill a responsible position or evaluate the competence of their personnel.

Physical beauty thus is the key to social mobility. The upper crust are sometimes referred to as "the beautiful people" ("*le beau monde*" in French). In the nineteenth century, public opinion viewed the aristocracy as being distinguished by delicate features, slim waists, and fine hands (Van den Berghe, 1978, 23; Marwick, 1980, 20). In contrast, peasants were supposed to be coarser-looking, with stockier builds and larger, "peasant" hands. Workers also seemed to be relatively ugly compared to the entrepreneur, who was well fed, well dressed, and well rested (Memmi, 1973, 126).

Beauty was supposed to be the attribute not only of one class but of one race. Buffon and Benjamin Franklin already saw Whites as its supreme embodiment in the eighteenth century (Gould, 1982, 32, 40). Two centuries later, Oliver Wendell Holmes believed that he should rejoice at the virtual elimination of the Redskins to the benefit of a human group (the White race) whose image was a little closer to "the image of God."

Some twentieth century French literature represented the Jew as being small in size, with frizzy red or black hair, a prominent nose, and protruding ears (Wardi, 1973, 264). Even today, some continue to see a "Jewish nose" as a kind of handicap, with certain women, and young people of both genders, resorting to plastic surgery to "correct" it. Similarly, a recent fashion trend required Asians to westernize the appearance of their eyes by removing the epicanthic fold. Though sometimes arising from individual choice, the desire to model oneself on the physical features of the dominator may emanate from an entire group. A whole generation of African-Americans decided a quarter of a century ago to lighten their skins and straighten their hair: Black did not yet mean "beautiful."

Suppressing or reducing visible differences is one way to try to integrate with the dominant group. However, this method is fundamentally alienating in that it ultimately leads to personal physical transformation, in addition to a dependence on inward adherence to criteria of beauty that deny one's own bodily structure. This is an alienating approach, especially for a woman who, in her primary obligation to please the male, risks becoming a pale reproduction, even a caricature, of an image that will never really be hers. Thus, she will continue to be available to the dominator as one of the dominated, without really managing to counter the competition represented by the dominator's woman in the eyes of the males of her own group.

The logic behind the definition of aesthetic standards in a given society is inevitably linked to *sexuality*. For the dominated male, being loved by a woman of the dominant group represents not only a way to obtain a share of this beauty, but the ultimate revenge. "In loving me, [the White woman] proves to me that I am worthy of White love," Franz Fanon wrote (1952, 71). By the very fact that she is White, a woman necessarily will appear to be beautiful in the eyes of a Native or a Black (ibid., Cleaver, 1968, 159). "Ain't no such a thing as an ugly white woman," an old Black man confided to Eldridge Cleaver. This woman will be all the more beautiful if she is blonde, and thus part of the dominant ethnic group within the White race (Adams, 163; Memmi, 1972, 112).

Through projection, the dominated male will even come to believe that women of his own race prefer his rival from the dominant group and hold him in secret contempt (Adams, 1975, 165). Cleaver's confidant acknowledge this: "There is no love left between a black man and a black woman. I'd jump over ten nigger bitches just to get to one white woman" (1968, 159).

What is true for men of colour or for colonized males is also true for Jewish men, even though they are white-skinned. When they do not idealize the Jewish woman who has remained faithful to a patriarchal tradition, literature and films by American Jewish authors tell the story of a "Jewish Ugly Duckling" or a "Jewish American Princess," with the men willingly sacrificing themselves to the charms of a blonde Christian woman (a *shiksa*) (Erens, 1984; Savona, 1974, 205–16).[4]

The contempt felt by the dominated male for the female of his group is linked to his fascinated attraction to the female of the dominant group. Yet this fascination does not focus so much on the White woman (or the blonde) as *a White woman*, as it does on the White woman as *the White man's* woman. This White man had long denied him access to his own women, while permitting himself to enjoy women of the dominated group. An entire system of rules was elaborated to contain this *taboo sexuality*. There were many laws condemning not only mixed marriages but sexual contact between the races. More often than not, violations of the latter prohibition resulted in punishment only when they involved a dominated male with a woman of the dominant group. Several American states, for example, banned intimate relations between Whites, on the one hand, and Blacks or Orientals, on the other, just as the Nazi regime in Germany prohibited such relations between "Aryans" and Jews.

Foreign workers, to whom labour-starved western countries had only wished to open their doors for a limited period (long enough to build a railway, for example) were also objects of suspicion due to their single male status. From the Chinese in North America at the end of the nineteenth century to the Arabs in France in recent years, these immigrants have been ascribed unacknowledgeable needs while at the same time they were deprived of the right to bring their families with them.

Sexuality was also forbidden to homophiles, who were only permitted the majoritarian way of loving sanctioned by law and morality. The Puritan and Jansenist mentality also prohibited "impurity" in children, obsessing about masturbation and then going on to find fault with the awakening of natural curiosity.

In others, sexuality is simply ignored. The condition of the handicapped supposedly renders them insensitive as well as disabled. For the elderly, joys previously permitted become "dirty" simply because of their greater years.

In women of "good family," sexuality was more than ignored – it was denied. They had to wait until the 1960s for a revolution in morals to recognize their "right to pleasure."

One of the more paradoxical aspects of domination is that the sexuality of the oppressed is given exaggerated importance while, in the same breath, it is relegated to silence. Since the dominated are considered to be inferior, the oppressor will often believe that he is permitted greater sexual liberty with them. Even though the dominator necessarily has the power of subjugation, he is more likely to take advantage of the *de facto* delivery of an already submissive victim than to take satisfaction from the possibility of personally reducing her to submission. Similarly, while the control he exerts may be mingled with physical violence, he will prefer to pay for her consent rather than break her resistance. This arouses him by attaching a greater price to the eventual abandonment; he does not see it as an opportunity to inflict additional humiliation.

In an osmosis of contempt involving human groups of inferior status, sexual pleasure becomes confused and enveloped, like them, in the aura of murky excitation aroused by the forbidden. In the dominator's view, sexual pleasure thus becomes the *privileged domain of the oppressed*. This is the source of the dominated's fascination for the dominator, as well as the threat that the dominated represent.

Thus, for English Canadians like the Mayor of Vancouver, a few years ago, the *"joie de vivre"* of French Quebecers went hand in hand with the deplorable laxity represented by the behaviour and laws of their Liberal representatives in Ottawa (with regard to abortion and homosexuality, among other matters).

In his *Reflections on the Jewish Question*, Jean-Paul Sartre clearly demonstrated the mixture of sexual repulsion and attraction that the Jews inspired in anti-Semites. An example of this phenomenon can be found in the following text: "French Canadian female workers had to choose between two forms of exploitation by the Jews," wrote Robert Rumilly in his *Histoire de la province de Québec* (in Tebour, 1977, 301), thus endorsing the myth of the "animal magnetism" given off by the men of this group. As for the woman of this "race," she would be the target of an even murkier emotion. The French expression *"une belle Juive"* ("a beautiful Jewess") has an odour of rape and, in the eyes of the dominator, evokes the image of the "docile servant girl" subject to the whims of Christian men who nevertheless will marry "Aryans" (Sartre, 1954, 57). One need only read *Gilles* by Drieu La Rochelle, or *Narcisse and Goldmund* by Herman Hesse, to sense the potential danger in the desire of the oppressor for his object. The oppressor uses the pretext of the very violence that is exercised against his victim to impose on her an availability from which he can profit.

Gypsies, who are associated with music and drinking, also are supposed to have a propensity for lechery. This is particularly attributed to Gypsy *women*, who are considered to be sensual and seductive (in Pirotte, 1982, 34–5). To judge by a comment frequently made by some Whites, Blacks also "only think about sex." The novelist Paul Morand took up the association between Black sexuality and other forms of physical pleasure. "There is certainly something of the Negro in all of us: shouting, dancing, rejoicing, expressing oneself is being Black," he wrote in *Paris Tombouctou*, going on to define Blacks in terms of rhythm and copulation (*"tam-tam coït"*) (in Kimoni, 1980, 49).

The belief in the greater sexual potency of Blacks is so widespread that White racists sometimes believed they had the right to castrate them. These Whites even feared competition during the time of slavery, when the masters of Southern plantations, with impunity, could demand carnal services of their Black female slaves that they could not ask of their well-bred White wives. If one judges by their growing presence in today's multi-billion dollar pornography industry (Lederer, 1982, 3), women of colour continue to be perceived as easy objects of enjoyment.

When the French novels of the colonial period dealt with North African cities or Asian countries, their primary focus was on prostitution: apart from the frequent recurrence of the word *"petit"* ("little"), titles like *Thi-Sen, la petite amie érotique* (Thi-Sen, The Little Erotic Friend), *Petite Mousmé* (Little Mousmé), or *Les petites épouses* (Little Wives) reveal the same reduction of entire groups of foreign women to a solely sexual function (Astier Loutfi, 1971, 60-1). The colonies were also considered a choice preserve by Europeans who found it difficult to satisfy their unorthodox tastes on their own continent. Pedophiles and pederasts, both heterosexual and homosexual, found "little" girls or young boys in the West Indies, North Africa, or elsewhere who appeared to be immediately accessible to them (Weeks, 1983, 41). Like André Gide or Oscar Wilde, following in the footsteps of Guy de Maupassant (in *Châli*), they sang the praises of the erotic arts practised by these children, when they did not personally take advantage of them. At the end of the twentieth century, this trade still exists in the Third World, where erotic tours give Japanese or western businessmen access to children and women made specially available to them by prostitution networks established in South Korea, Thailand, Senegal, or Kenya. Since AIDS is ravaging prostitutes, even those between twelve and fifteen years of age, virgin children are especially in demand, and customers are offered six-year-old girls in "baby brothels."

In America itself, a flourishing industry, using children as sex objects, has developed since the 1970s. By the end of the decade, one and a half million children were employed in the United States as prostitutes or pornographic models, and more than 250 publications were devoted to descriptions of sexual activities with young children between three and five years of age (Rush, 1980, 169). Such relations between adults and children are not limited to the realm of fantasy; in addition to prostitution, incest is now being "discovered" as a reality of which girls are the primary victims. According to the logic behind sexual domination, some fathers even believe that their children "like it."

This logic is reinforced by the vulnerability that the oppressor detects in the victim. Apart from the vulnerability inherent in children of "tender" age, there is also the obvious weakness of the handicapped. The attraction of certain men to crippled women is well known, for example. A specific type of voyeur will even take rare pleasure in the spectacle of certain physical anomalies. One sector of the pornography industry specializes in the depiction of deformed or exceedingly obese women (Lederer, 1982, 47).

Since the dominated category may change depending on the community or historical period, the sexual tastes of the dominator will be modulated by the context. In colonized or segregated societies, they will be conditioned by a racist logic; in others, social barriers will orient them toward women of a lower class.

Thus, the European nobility and bourgeoisie of the nineteenth century were accustomed to take their pleasure, often described as hygienic, from a female factory worker, a *demi-mondaine*, or a showgirl, after having had their first sexual experience with the family's maidservant. Caricatures of the *"Belle Époque"* frequently depicted a Breton peasant girl "knocked up" by a vacationing Parisian (Lebesque, 1970, 118). But the young maid or provincial rarely could count on the support of the son of the family when she became pregnant; instead, she would lose her position. No commitments were owed to a woman of the dominated group, nor to the domestic, the working girl, or the Jewish mistress (Wardi, 1973, 136), nor to the devoted mulatto of the colonies (Fanon, 1952, 53–71).

This did not prevent the colonizer from regarding the sexuality of the colonized as primitive, or the bourgeois from seeing that of the proletarian as animal (Dufrancatel, 1979, 167); this seemed to be the ideal excuse for taking advantage of it. Thus, upper-class English homosexuals, like Oscar Wilde or E. M. Forster, felt a particular fascination for young working men.

The dominator will be all the more inclined to attribute greater sexual freedom or potency to the members of the dominated group if he belongs to a society that scorns its manifestations. Ashamed of his own needs, he can think of really satisfying them only with someone whose judgment he can disregard. Not only would the dominator be embarrassed to ask his own wife to share some of his pleasures, he would be indignant to know that the mother of his children was capable of it. The murky joys of prohibited relations are specifically refused to women of the dominant group. Lady Chatterley's passion for her gamekeeper caused a scandal. And a racist's ultimate argument against a liberal is to confront him with the possibility that his *daughter* will marry a Black. The fantasies of respectable women, tempted by the imagined prowess of a delivery man or a man of colour, reveal the sexual barriers erected by the culture that moulded them. This same culture, which readily accepts that an older man marries a teenage girl, considers it inappropriate for a mature woman to do likewise with a man several years her junior.

Long forbidden physical pleasure, or perceived as having less need of it by nature, women have also paid the price of a western tradition that judged their sexual appetite to be insatiable. This tradition, initially religious, confirmed the verdict of the conventional "wisdom" ("The only chaste woman is one who has not found a lover," "Ugliness is the only guardian of women"). Women were able to escape the choice between sainthood and whoredom, only to be confronted with the insoluble dilemma imposed by those who wanted them to be both virgin and mother.

If contempt for women does not necessarily imply disdain for sexuality, suspicion of sexuality goes hand in hand with suspicion of women. As we have seen, this equation clearly emerges from the special treatment reserved for women by the oppressor in the sexual power relationship he maintains with all dominated groups. This is just as true for the parameters of handicap or age as for those of race or social class. This observation also applies to homosexuality.

For example, the ancient Greeks could exalt love between men without their women seeing any improvement in their own status; but the infamy to which homophilia is consigned in Judeo-Christian civilization derives from the conception of this preference as a man's desire to be a woman. Thus, forced to reveal his past to the Zionist militants whose ranks he is seeking to join, the young survivor of the death camps, played by Sal Mineo in the film *Exodus*, is more ready to admit that he stripped the dead for the Nazis than his shame that they used him "like a woman."

Gays will often be criticized as well for their high frequency of intimate sexual relations with different partners ("They only think about sex"). Because it implicitly confuses sexual orientation with sexual activity, the popular mind retains more of an impression of the manifestations of behaviour than of all the components of a sensibility. As the tendency of the majority, heterosexuality is thus imposed as the ideal norm which automatically guarantees greater monogamy. Therefore, homosexuality and heterosexuality seem to call for *intrinsically* opposing attitudes, one of which, in the final analysis, is an aberration in relation to the other.

However, important variables are disregarded in such a clearcut statement of the issue. Unrecognized, or automatically associated with that of gay men, lesbian behaviour does not appear to be taken into account in this approach. Nor is the behaviour of women within heterosexual couples distinguished from that of men. Ignored once again are such parameters as the impact of social judgment on an amorous relationship, the existence or absence of models allowing people to position themselves in these relationships, or the possible variations in heterosexual unions, depending on whether they are free or sanctioned by marriage.

Once these factors are taken into account, tendencies would seem to emerge reflecting differences *between genders* rather than between the two types of *sexual orientation*. Thus, in intimate relations, gay and heterosexual men exhibit somewhat similar behaviour: both more frequently establish relations based on domination and easily separate sex from love. Conversely, women of both orientations attach greater symbolic value to monogamy, with lesbians having even fewer sexual relationships than other groups (whether these be married heterosexuals, common-law heterosexuals, or especially homosexual men, who have more relationships than all the others).

Thus, when demonstrated in their "pure" state, tendencies specific to women and men (regardless of origin) increase in gays and lesbians, with the greater frequency of undifferentiated sexual relationships being more a *male* than a specifically homophilic phenomenon, for example.[5] The judgment rendered by society regarding the same behaviour, however, will reinforce the erroneous belief in the intrinsic superiority of one orientation over the other, a belief that sees a manifestation of "Don Juanism" in the accumulated conquests of the heterosexual male while the multiple relationships of the homophile are interpreted as a form of pathology or immorality. The same double standard also means that a heterosexual woman who is very sexually active is labelled a "nymphomaniac" or a "slut."

One of the more ironic popular misconceptions about homosexuality lies in the perception that lesbians are physically available to all comers and endowed with a polymorphous sexuality that would render them indifferent, not only to emotional considerations, but to the very sexual identity of their partner. This is not because the dominator associates their morals with those of male homosexuals, but because he refuses to believe that a woman has an irreducible form of sensibility that would exclude him. He also prefers to amuse himself with the idea of a sexuality that he ultimately defines in his own terms. He perceives the lesbian as a faithful auxiliary, who will "prepare the ground" for him with another woman, and share her pleasures with him: "Every man and every woman, if they wish, can be pleasured by her" (Jacques, 1981).

Already defined as inferior as members of the second sex, homosexual women thus appear as suitable pleasure objects for oppressors seduced by the possibility of the ultimate ecstasy through a sexual transgression within sexuality itself. There is no pornographic magazine that does not tell of the feats of such a woman, the victorious rival of her heterosexual sister, in her acquiescence to the insatiable desires of men coveted by both the lesbian and the straight woman.

The male of the dominant group thus monopolizes the right to all transgressions. While society does not necessarily encourage these offences, it leaves them to the male, on condition that they are not permanent, since anyone who would claim to mix the pure and the impure by going so far as to legitimize his liaison with a woman of a forbidden race or class would lose status. However, a woman of the dominant group who, without going this far, merely dares to engage in a sexual relationship of this kind, would incur the anathema reserved for someone who has intrinsically demeaned herself. Only the homosexual man, more specifically one who is "feminized" through sodomy, risks being so personally soiled in the eyes of society.

As a reserved field of symbolic space, sexuality plays a role both as the private preserve of the oppressor and as a place of confinement for the dominated. When it is prohibited or perceived as humiliating, sexuality will be experienced, by preference, with a person deemed to be inferior or in a distant physical or metaphorical universe.

For if sexuality is something that is experienced with "other people," it also happens *elsewhere*. Sexuality is frequently associated with foreign places in the dominant discourse, especially when the phenomenon being considered assumes an automatically negative connotation. The Romans held the Greeks responsible for homosexuality, while the latter attributed it to the Persians and the peoples of the Near East; in the Middle Ages, westerners blamed the Muslims (in Marmor, 1980, 86). Depending on the period and the context, love between men would also be denounced as the "Indochinese vice" or the "Arab vice" (by the colonizers) (Astier Loutfi, 1971, 37–8), and the "English vice" (by the French) or the "French vice" (by the English) ... when everyone did not agree that it was a "German vice" (Kronemeyer, 1980, 50). The origin of syphilis also seems to have posed a problem, with the French perceiving it as an "Italian disease" and the English as a "French disease"; for the Russians, the disease, of course, was "Polish" (in Marmor, 1980, 86).

The diagnoses of conventional "wisdom" were often taken up by art and literature. Thus, the homosexual tendencies of certain characters in American novels were described as something that could find release only in "another country" (Sarotte, 1976, 306). In Québec films of the 1960s, the link with a foreign land was symbolized by the character of the English lesbian (in *Valérie*) or the homosexual engaged to an anglophone (in *Trouble-fête*).

More orthodox forms of sexuality did not escape this equation with the symbolic elsewhere. Québec films of the 1960s and 1970s linked sexual emancipation either with the image of the "foreign woman" (*À tout prendre, Le chat dans le sac, Les corps célestes*) or of a Québécois who had travelled widely (*L'initiation, Après-ski, Pile ou face*) (Carrière, 1983, 62, 67). In French-Canadian "novels of the soil" in the 1930s, the seducer came from another country, when the rare scenes of free love did not take place in a far-off land (Boynard-Frot, 1982, 147–8).

When the Motion Picture Production Code came into force in 1934, female characters in American movies who dared to display obvious sexual desire were depicted as abnormal, dangerous ... or European (Haskell, 1974, 91).

The French language itself conveys the implicit postulate that sexuality is primarily the doing of foreign women. By an inevitable semantic slippage, words designating foreign women become synonymous with women of "easy virtue," as in words like *hétaïre, mousmé,* or *odalisque,* the etymological meaning of which was not initially negative (Yaguello, 1978, 154).

There is no doubt the sexual dimension of oppression. It is the desire to commit aggression through sex. It is also the pleasure extorted from the weak by those for whose benefit the established order was created. Finally, it is the power to demand satisfactions, too shameful to share with one's peers, from victims who are already objects of scorn. This last form of sexual exploitation is especially alienating since, in a perverse feedback, it is both the effect and cause of oppression.

Indeed, the dominator cannot fail to be tempted to justify his power over the dominated by the need to control the very sexual energy that he exploits. He will claim that he has to contain it, to civilize it. As the humiliated outlets of their masters' secret impulses, members of the dominated group, on the other hand, have to pay the price of the remorse kindled by the very pleasure that has been demanded of them.

An Object of Violence

There is no aspect of the oppressed's person over which the dominator does not claim some rights, at some time, or which the dominator does not feel authorized to dispose of in some way to his advantage. The method used by the dominator may be subtle or brutal, and the discourse justifying it may be open or implicit. But in concrete terms, the effect is the same: the body always ends up as the object of oppression.

The privileged access that the dominator allows himself to the *sexuality* of the oppressed is already a form of implicit violence. Indeed, "pleasure" is for the dominator more than for the dominated, and the victim's consent is obtained by the power relationship that immediately places him or her in an inferior position to the oppressor.

Not only may the dominator eventually seek to punish the victims for the very need that he has forced them to satisfy, but he will even see sex as an immediate way to inform the oppressed of their subjugation. Thus, sexual pleasure experienced as humiliation will be transformed into the pleasure of humiliation through sex.

By imposing oral or anal practices on the victim, sexual *abuse,* in most cases, will have the objective of adding to a pre-existing condition of inferiority. The pedagogical intent of heterosexuals who rape a lesbian "to teach her a lesson" betrays their determination to break her resistance, which is intolerable to them. Young hoodlums who rape an old woman in revenge because she has nothing worth stealing do not obey an irresistible sexual need either.

Indeed, rape is being perceived less and less as the unfortunate result of uncontrollable passion and is now defined as the act of aggression it really is. The insults often accompanying the act and the rapist's frequent claims that his victim "likes it" are more than a symptom of his self-contempt as an object of female desire; they are obvious proof of his punitive intent.

The incidence of rape has been staggeringly high since the 1970s, particularly in countries like Sweden, West Germany, and the United States. In the latter case, the number of rapes increased fivefold in fifteen years (Chesnais, 1981, 475), a larger statistical increase than for murder, assault, or robbery (Brownmiller, 1975, 190). This continues to hold true at the beginning of the 1990s, while complaints, both of acquaintance rape and rape by strangers, continue to be less numerous than the real incidence of this crime. After accounting for racial tensions in the case of the United States, the common factor for the three countries mentioned (apart from their shared Protestant tradition) has been the relatively early development of movements for women's emancipation.

In the documentary *Not a Love Story*, a pornographic magazine publisher openly admits the link between violence against women and the success of feminism when he notes the special satisfaction that men may feel in seeing a woman on her knees. On her knees or in chains, mutilated, whipped, and even burned, if not urinated or defecated upon (Lederer, 1982, 2–10).

Even when stripped of any coercive intent, coitus itself, in erotic literature, is considered to be the metaphorical representation of all action affecting the world, and sexuality is compared to ritual sacrifice or war (Dardigna, 1980, 81–3). By osmosis, the military symbolism of male sexuality (a conquest, a siege, a cavalry charge) and the designation of power relationships in sexual vocabulary (screwing, skewering, penetrating, poking, or the French *"enfiler,"* with its connotations of running someone through with a sword) correspond to each other (Guillaumin, 1978, 2, 26). The same goes for American porno shops that sport Nazi insignia (Dardigna, 1980, 316).

Though women are the preferred victims, they are not alone in suffering the harmful effect of the connection the dominator has created between violence and sexuality. In addition to the literal application of this warrior logic on the battlefield, scenes of sexual violence are played out in prisons every day. A younger, more sensitive, less athletic, or more handsome prisoner may be forced to serve as a "woman" for his cellmates (Brownmiller, 1975, 294–5). The "men" who demand this submission will often be heterosexual prisoners who confirm their belief in their virility by playing the *active* role in their relations with the weaker party.

However, when children are involved, weakness is inherent in the victim's very identity. While family members will teach children to beware of "strangers," most often a close relative (in 80 to 90 percent of the cases) will commit the assault; in almost all cases this will be a man, the victim being a young girl seven to nine times out of ten (Rush, 1980, 2 and 175; Brownmiller, 1975, 308).

Shaken by the unexpected identity of the assailant and trapped by the love or respect she has been taught to feel for him, the child has no defence against the threats or blackmail of the adult's sexual advances. Up to one million children are the victims of such unwanted relations each year in North America. Sexual compulsion becomes physical abuse for those who suffer as a result from vaginal or rectal fissures or perforations, amygdalitis with blennorhagia, and even death by asphyxiation (Rush, 1980, 2, 6). One out of every four or five women and one out of ten men will have experienced coercive sexual contact in their childhood.

But the violence exercised under the guise of sexuality is not solely the abuse of a weaker person's body. On the contrary, it may seek to deprive the oppressed of a part of his or her sexual life, *a deprivation* that will take the brutal form of genital mutilation, for example. Such a tradition was created with the consent of the Catholic Church, which allowed removal of the testicles of male children to preserve their soprano voices (Kempe, 1984, 4). First used in the papal chapel in the sixteenth century, these "castrati" became the stars of European opera. And what could be done in the name of art has also been done in the name of religion or initiation rites. Circumcision, practised on the newborn (in Judaism) or on children of three, five, or seven years of age (in Islam), has its philosophical roots in sacrifice. Sometimes justified after the fact as a hygienic measure, it also came to be perceived as a sign of virility or as a means of increasing sexual pleasure.

Such considerations do not apply in the practices of excision and infibulation to subjugate young girls to their future husbands. Not only must the virginity and then the chastity of the woman be ensured at any price against the assaults of other men, but the woman herself must be protected against her own desires, since females are deemed to be "hypersexual"[6] by nature.

Certain less brutal procedures have nevertheless been used in the West to deprive specific categories of people of part of their sexuality. These procedures were not so much intended to prevent access to sexual pleasure as to eliminate their ability to reproduce. In Great Britain (Craft, 1978, 1–2), Canada (Matthews, 1982, 16), and the United States, the mentally handicapped, more than any other group, bore the brunt of laws and medical diagnoses that allowed them to be sterilized. In 1986, the Supreme Court prohibited this practice in Canada.

"Mentally handicapped," moreover, should be understood here in the broader sense of individuals who, being poor or belonging to "inferior" ethnic and racial groups, sometimes were sterilized without their knowledge. Theoretical explanations were even proposed to justify this method, especially in the United States, where sterilization was recommended in the cases of a large variety of other persons. In the view of geneticist H.H. Laughlin, for example, who expressed these views in the early 1920s, 10 percent of the population were carriers of "bad seed," including the deaf, mutes, and epileptics, as well as orphans, vagrants, and, of course, the mentally handicapped. A few years earlier, psychometrician Lewis Terman declared that "all feeble-minded are at least potential criminals" and "that every feeble-minded woman is a potential prostitute would hardly be disputed by anyone" (in Block and Dworkin, 1976, 345–6).

In the late 1960s, mildly retarded individuals still had to agree to be sterilized to obtain release from certain American psychiatric hospitals, which greatly complicated their subsequent attempts to marry and live normally (Edgerton, 1967, 154–6).

Even more radical have been the attempts to erase the difference by causing the disappearance of the very entity that sustained it. Whether applied systematically against a group or targeting a community through some of its members, policies were established with the effect of depriving the oppressed of *life* itself. There are many historical examples of such policies, and the modern western era is far from exempt. The Inquisition, among others, burned tens of thousands of women at the stake for witchcraft, along with Spanish and Portuguese Jews in the culmination of the wave of anti-Semitism born in the eleventh century with the Crusades. It also burned "sodomites," whose moral transgressions began to be confused with the sin of heresy by a triumphant Christianity in the Low Middle Ages.[7]

Just as the witch-hunts led to the execution of hundreds of women in the same city or region, and whole villages were sometimes emptied of their female population,[8] the Jews of Europe continued, until the twentieth century, to be the target of pogroms that eventually caused them to emigrate to America. As for homosexuals, laws allowed them to be condemned to death until the end of the eighteenth century (in France) or until the mid-nineteenth century (in Great Britain, Canada, and the United States) (Marmor, 1980, 18–9; Kinsman, 1987, 76; d'Emilio, 1983, 14).

Beginning in 1880 and until well into the twentieth century (1940 or even after), Black Americans, like European Jews, became victims designated for summary execution. Thousands of them were lynched without any form of trial (Chesnais, 1981, 167). Some, after being hanged, were even burned in public, to the great satisfaction of the White population assembled for the spectacle. In half the cases, the victims were forced to atone for crimes (or more precisely, accusations) of rape or attempted rape. The number of *legal* executions for these offences reflected the penchant for sexual transgression that Whites projected on Blacks: between 1900 and 1950, forty Blacks, for example, were condemned to death in Louisiana, compared to only two Whites, both of whom were immigrants (in Lederer, 1982, 99–100).

Even more systematic was the brutal treatment reserved for the indigenous peoples by the Europeans who landed in America, a treatment akin to genocide. From a population of approximately eighty million before the arrival of the Whites, the Native peoples of Central and South America were reduced to ten million by the middle of the sixteenth century. Massacres, forced labour, epidemics (due, among other reasons, to the extreme fatigue engendered by mistreatment and the Spaniards' refusal to care for peoples marked, in their view, by divine punishment), and the resulting refusal of the vanquished to procreate under these conditions led to an ethnocide that, even today, is ignored in official history books (Todorov, 1982, 138–41). This ethnocide has long continued in Central America, where dictatorships of the extreme right have made the "Indians" of Guatemala their special target.

Decimated by centuries of warfare against the White invaders, by the uprooting of sedentary tribes (such as the Cherokee) imposed by the Europeans, and by diseases (smallpox, tuberculosis) deliberately spread to them by the Whites, the indigenous peoples of the northern half of the continent have fewer members today than they did five centuries ago. From a population of one million in the American colonial period, they fell to 250,000 in 1900, climbing back to the initial figure of one million in 1970 in the United States (Olson, 1979, 5; Butcher, 1977, 17 and 24). The same phenomenon occurred in Canada, where the indigenous population (apart from Métis and "non-status" Indians) stood at 300,000, both in 1970 and in 1600 (in Gardner and Kalin, 1981, 22–3).

But the fastest and most far-reaching genocides, in demographic terms, undoubtedly were those committed in the twentieth century (a consequence of technological progress!). Starting in 1915, one and a half million Armenians (60 percent of the population) were eliminated by the Turkish government during the First World War. Twenty-five years later, the Nazi death machine, with industrial efficiency, managed to crush almost entire peoples – tens of thousands of Gypsies and nearly six million Jews. Other extermination plans targeted the Slavs as the next victims, millions of Poles and Russians having already perished in massacres perpetrated by Hitler's troops against the civilians of the East.

There have also been innumerable historical conflicts based on the hostility between different peoples that did not have genocide as their objective. Of the approximately 164 altercations between states in the period from 1958 to 1966, all except fifteen had an ethnic, racial, or tribal origin (Saïd and Simmons, 1976, 16). With the collapse of the Communist empire, centuries-old tensions re-emerged at the beginning of the 1990s, specifically in the former Soviet Union and in the particularly tragic example of Yugoslavia.

A secular version of the wars of religion, ideological struggles also result in civil or class wars no less atrocious than inter-ethnic clashes (nearly one million deaths in Spain in 1939). At the height of absurdity and horror, there was even one case, that of Cambodia, in which a doctrine (what is more, an *egalitarian* doctrine) required that one-third of a nation (more than two million people) be liquidated by their own government.

Extermination is not reserved only for specific classes or ethnic groups. Though contrived in the name of a social or national ideology, systematic massacres targeting individuals of another identity have been committed. Between 200,000 and 400,000 homosexuals, for example, perished in the Nazi death camps, the second-largest category of victims after the Jews (McNeill, 1976, 82; Marmor, 1980, 19). During the same period of the war, a number of Soviet homophiles were deported to Siberia, under the pretext of their presumed complicity with the Nazi regime (Chesnais, 1981, 189)! Similarly, the mentally handicapped, already victims of sterilization policies, were subjected to "euthanasia" under Hitler. To "preserve the purity of the race," 70,000 people were killed in this way, some of whom suffered only from nervous depression.[9]

Whether designated handicapped or identified as members of a people or class marked for persecution, children do not escape death any more than adults. There has even been a constant tendency in history to target them specifically as victims. In antiquity, for example, infanticide was an accepted measure, practised against both the legitimate newborn and those born out of wedlock (Ariès, 1973, 15). With the exception of the Greeks and Romans, the civilizations of the ancient world all engaged in religious sacrifice of young victims on some scale (De Mause, 1974, 28).

Fantasies of killing and actual executions were frequent in several ancient cultures: Chronos devouring his children, Agamemnon preparing to immolate Iphigenia, Abraham raising the knife over his son Isaac, Pharaoh (and later Herod) massacring the firstborn, Christ offering himself for humanity at the request of his Father (Memmi, 1982, 36).

Though severely punished starting in the Middle Ages, infanticide nevertheless continued to occur "accidentally" until the nineteenth century, especially in the case of illegitimate children, rejected by a society that at the same time harshly judged their mothers (Ariès, 1973, 15; Chesnais, 1982, 168; De Mause, 1974, 25).

Apart from the physically or mentally handicapped newborn, girls were the most frequent victims of infanticide. To achieve this result, there was no need to deliberately eliminate children of the female gender. It was sufficient, as is still done in poorer parts of the planet, to feed girls less well than boys.

Although the victim's degree of physical powerlessness is not the same, the term "deferred infanticide" has been used in the case of young males sent to war by their elders' generation.[10] Through the relatively recent practice of compulsory military service and systematic conscription of the nation's best and brightest in times of armed conflict, the youngest and healthiest men are forced to go to war. Countries like France, for example, experienced a wholesale slaughter that mowed down almost an entire generation in 1914–1918. More then ten million soldiers perished during the First World War, and seven million others were severely disabled. Even in the case of a less murderous conflict like the Vietnam War, the proportion of military personnel killed is higher among the very young: half the American soldiers who lost their lives in this Asian country were under twenty-one years of age (Wilson, 1978, 22). Regimes as fanatical as those of Hitler, in Germany, or Khomeini, in Iran, also have not hesitated to send adolescents, barely past their childhood, into battle against seasoned foreign troops. In 1990, ten million children were used as soldiers in various guerrilla wars.

While the young, from newborns to young adults, are readily sacrificed in certain circumstances, it is old people who, in other cases, will be called upon to give up their lives. The "voluntary" suicide of the aged is the counterpart of infanticide in some so-called primitive societies. Whether agricultural or nomadic, what these cultures have in common is an acute scarcity of resources (de Beauvoir, 1970, I, 131). They choose to solve this by simply neglecting to feed the aged or condemning them to certain death by expulsion from the group.

Almost as severe as the deliberate attempts on the lives of the oppressed, and often with comparable effects, another form of violence has been used by the oppressor: the radical deprivation of *freedom*. This deprivation is sometimes aimed at an entire group, with its postulated inferiority or the dominator's need for its labour being alone sufficient to justify compulsion. Such an attack on the *collective* freedom of a human community is most often explained by a desire for total economic exploitation. This is the whole meaning of an institution like slavery, which has been officially prohibited only since the nineteenth century.

The slave was considered to be nothing more than an object. From the legal point of view, he had the value of a "chattel," which could be bought, sold, and marked. All of the civilizations of antiquity engaged in the trade in human beings to a greater or lesser degree, with the Greeks and Romans resorting to it on the vastest scale. Apart from individual victims of abduction or piracy, whole populations, after the defeat of their armies, automatically became the property of the conqueror.

Although slavery faded away when the age of conquest ended, it endured in the West until the Carolingian period, before being legitimately re-established in the sixteenth century in the wake of the great period of global exploration and discovery. The methods employed remained those of antiquity. Thus, while it acknowledged slaves to be "God's creatures," Colbert's Black Code (promulgated in 1687) still defined them as "chattels" and even gave masters the right to counter escapes by mutilating fugitive Blacks (by cropping their ears or amputating a limb).

After decimating the "Indians" of South America in attempting to use them as slave labour, the Whites began rounding up the peoples of Africa to transport them by force to the new continent. Between the sixteenth and nineteenth centuries, fifteen to twenty million Blacks (the sturdiest) were deported to the Americas in this way. If one includes those who perished aboard the slave ships during the crossing, or during battles in Africa to escape the European slavers, nearly sixty million people were removed from the African continent (Kaké, 1977, 74–5).

The oppressor reduced the dominated to slavery so as to derive sole benefit from all of their labour. The logic presiding over this institution, therefore, was primarily economic, with the physical strength of a human being serving as a source of energy. It was no mere coincidence that slavery was finally abolished in the nineteenth century, when the Industrial Revolution was well under way. Having an immense pool of cheap White labour, made up of peasants driven from the countryside into the cities by a parallel revolution in methods of agricultural production, the new entrepreneurs no longer had to spare human resources, which seemed inexhaustible.

The human cost of the Industrial Revolution was enormous. Thousands of working men and women died in the factories and mines (4 out of every 1,000), with labour killing more people (except in the United States) than criminal violence (Chesnais, 1981, 423–5). Although paid, the proletariat initially received a wage deliberately calculated to sustain life only minimally. Working at piece rates and high-speed production, they were also liable to fines for distractions or the least breakage. Working conditions were abysmal: workers were deprived of adequate ventilation and lighting, and they were all the more vulnerable to industrial accidents due to their chronic lack of sleep. For example, young girls employed in the silk industry got up at five in the morning and finished their labour at ten or eleven at night. After two years of this drudgery, they lost both their health and their beauty. If they were reduced to unemployment or fell victim to exhaustion or to an accident on the job, workers did not benefit from any form of protection to preserve them from misery.

Children were not spared any more than adults. Working up to seventy-two hours a week from nine years of age, some were also victims of brutality or sexual abuse in the factory or in the mine. To be able to survive and feed themselves better, twelve-year-old girls even resorted to prostitution (Walvin, 1982, 51–144). Children four or five years of age had to work sixteen hours a day, and even at night, in certain American cigar factories and in the cotton mills of the South (Ehrenreich and English, 1979, 186). Although schooling become compulsory and various parliaments gradually raised the legal working age, children continued to be used in industry until the First World War.

Fairly rare now in the contemporary western world, child labour is still common in Third World countries. In 1993, a decade after the International Year of the Child (1979), between 100 and 200 million children were being employed in the same types of jobs as adults, compelled to work because of exploitation or the economic difficulties of the southern hemisphere. Despite this, 40,000 Third World children die of hunger every day (Rémy, 1984). As for those who survive, their physical and mental development is compromised by precarious living conditions (Rimbaud, 1980, 7). While one and a half billion human beings are starving or undernourished in the southern hemisphere, this region benefits from only 5 percent of the health care spending and 25 percent of the doctors on the planet (Simon, 1985, 19–20).

While more privileged overall, western children do not escape economic misery. In general, children from underprivileged backgrounds (often including Black and Native populations) are more frequent victims of accident and disease than children of well-to-do families, in addition to having a mortality rate twice as high. As shown by the recessions of 1981 and 1991, periods of economic difficulty increase the number of children thus affected (for example, to 20 percent in Canada, in both cases).

In addition to the threat posed by precarious economic conditions, children bear the burden of acts of violence. Between 1972 and 1978, about six million children were neglected or mistreated in the United States and Canada (van Stolk, 1979, viii). In France, in 1979, one out of a hundred and fifty children suffered the same fate (Straus, 1982, 44). Although children are beaten at all ages, babies under three years old are the prime targets (Fontana, 1983, 25). A February 1989 study by Johns Hopkins University in Baltimore showed that murder is the leading cause of infant mortality. Young children are victims of lacerations, burns, abdominal and eye injuries, and bone fractures, and some die from this abuse (ibid., 227; Gelles and Cornell, 1983, 47). Children are even mistreated by their parents *because* they are mentally or physically handicapped, since less humane treatment appears to be tolerated more in such cases (*Les sévices institutionnels*, 1982, 117–21).

Beating a child can be perceived or presented as a way of administering corporal punishment, and thus as a legitimate measure. The principle of resorting to coercion to train children was endorsed, until the eighteenth century, by almost all western thinkers with an opinion on education, humanists included (De Mause, 1974, 40–3). Even in the nineteenth century, the whip, the pillory, and confinement in the dark were employed regularly in French or British schools (Walvin, 1982, 49–50; Crubellier, 1979, 148).

But the violence between generations is not only exercised by adults against the young. It is increasingly evident that adults also mistreat their aged parents. In the same way that the children least able to defend themselves seem to be the most frequent targets of violence, so are the frail elderly (between eighty and eighty-four years of age) the adult group most threatened (Cohen, 1984, 97–8). Because women live longer than men, they are the main victims of neglect, theft, and even physical assault; robbed of their pensions and deprived of food or care, they are deliberately isolated and battered as well.

Younger women can be battered too, by their husbands, instead of by their children. This is probably the most common form of violence in the world (in Price and Sokoloff, 1982, 187). In Canada, one woman in ten is mistreated in this way and, according to the Statistics Canada figures for 1991, nearly half of murdered women are killed by husbands or ex-husbands. In half these cases, the violence began when she was pregnant. Furthermore, 25 percent of Québec women who attempt suicide are victims of brutality by their spouses.

But the aggression threatening the health and physical integrity of the oppressed is not always the effect of a close family member's spontaneous and uncontrollable anger. Although initially subtle or difficult to identify, some forms of violence can be masked by systematic practices. With the sanction of the experts, these are supposed to be "for the victim's own good" and sometimes involve the victim's consent.

It is appropriate at this point to duscuss the whole problem of so-called "shock" therapies. Methods have been used in the treatment of mental illness, without those who applied them even knowing how they worked (Fréminville, 1977, 122–38; Alexander and Selesnick, 1966, 280–5). Apart from electro-shock, cardiazol or insulin injections were administered to schizophrenics, causing epileptic seizures or comatose states; some patients were even subjected to lobotomies. In the nineteenth century, psychiatrists were already resorting to coercion in the guise of therapy: whips, chains, application of caustic products or red-hot irons to the skin, inoculation with scabies (to stop inactivity), and incisions were a few of the methods employed by certain experts against their patients (Fréminville, 1977, 65–115).

The confusion of medical practices with disciplinary measures continued into the twentieth century. Patients who were not docile enough were subjected to electro-shock, and those who were most stubbornly undisciplined were even lobotomized; others had all their teeth pulled because they tended to bite, and women underwent hysterectomies in the guise of "treatment" for their sexual "promiscuity" (Goffman, 1961, 382; Solidarité-psychiatrie, 1984, 130).

Gays and lesbians did not escape these radical therapies. When they were not confined to an asylum or "treated" with hormones, emetics, or electro-shock, they were subjected to lobotomies or genital surgery (castration, vasectomy, clitoridectomy, ovariectomy) (Kronemeyer, 1980, 81–7).

But violence also has indirect manifestations. In such cases, it is inherent to the living conditions imposed on a group or the environment in which that group evolves, and its presence is constant. Foreign workers, for example, are more vulnerable than others to accidents in the workplace: holding difficult jobs which do not attract local nationals, and often unable to count on any form of income security, they must take more risks to earn their bread (Labelle et al., 1980, 40).

Better protected than immigrant labourers, local workers nevertheless are at more risk of industrial accidents than individuals from a higher social class. In England and France, for example, the risk is seven or eight times greater (Chesnais, 1981, 426–7). This disproportion persists in the case of violence in general. Whether accidental, criminal, or suicidal, violence has the most massive effect on the popular classes, even in the case of children; thus, in England, the risk of violent death is ten times hither among children in working-class communities (ibid., 405). In general, manual labourers and the unemployed age faster and die earlier than university graduates and professionals (Ariès and Duby, 1987, V, 338). In 1991, the Community Health Department of one Montreal hospital (Verdun) reported that the gap between the life expectancy of affluent and underprivileged individuals could exceed ten years.

The dynamics are the same in societies where different "racial" groups coexist. While it is true that in France, for example, immigrants die sooner than the native population, a February 1990 study in the *Journal of the American Medical Association* tended to show that while adult Blacks and Whites in the thirty-five to fifty-four age bracket often died of similar diseases, Black deaths came twice as early. The homicide gap is even more spectacular. In the United States, in particular, while Whites are victims of violence six times more often than Europeans, Blacks are affected seven times as often as Whites; violence is the leading cause of death among young African-Americans between the ages of twenty-five and thirty-five (Chesnais, 1981, 91–4). Accounting for 43 percent of homicide victims at the beginning of the 1980s, this group represented 50 percent ten years later. More violent, Blacks are also the primary target of violence.

When exercised against the human body, the power of the oppressor is revealed as direct and immediate. It expresses the oppressor's supremacy in all its force, while reminding the dominated of their own powerlessness.

Initially incapable of directing their anger and frustration effectively against the oppressor, the victims turn against each other. Ultimately, this violence may lead to self-destruction, since the feeling of being inextricably trapped becomes obvious to the oppressed.

Thus, it is an almost universal law that suicide increases with age (Chesnais, 1981, 205). While old people account for 10 percent of the population of the United States, they represent one-quarter of the suicide victims (Butler and Lewis, 1977, 67). Suicide is also more frequent among the depressed, with the suicide rate among the mentally ill twenty to a hundred times higher than for the rest of the population (Chesnais, 1981, 209–10).

A more recent phenomenon is the increase in youth suicides in the past few years. According to Statistics Canada, the suicide rate in the fifteen to twenty-four age group rose from 15.5 per 100,000 in 1960 to 70 per 100,000 in 1985. In Québec, suicide became the second leading cause of death among boys in that age group, after car accidents, and third after car accidents and cancer among teenage girls in the same age bracket. In the United States, there are 400,000 suicide attempts by young people each year, 10,000 of them successful.

Problems other than those related to age may add to the causes of youth suicides. For example, there is an overrepresentation of Muslim girls among French adolescents who try to take their own lives. For some of them, the tension during puberty between the culture of their fathers and European values may have seemed intolerable (Davidson et al., 1981, 47). The same goes for young Natives in Canada, who kill themselves seven times more often than other young people in this country.[11] Thus, the suicide rate is generally higher among migrants once they have settled in their host country than when they lived in their own homeland (Chesnais, 1981, 210). The same trend applies to Natives, whose suicide rate is twice as high as that of Whites (Dupuis, 1991, 65).

Suicide is also more frequent in low-income communities, since the power elites (both in the East and in the West) are much less inclined to resort to it (Chesnais, 1981, 284). Just as unemployment generates pathological reactions and an increase in the rate of psychoses, the number of suicides also rises in periods of economic crisis (ibid., 213; Thouez, 1988, 15).

Becoming conscious of one's homosexuality, especially if this comes later in life, may also upset the individuals involved to such an extent that they see suicide as the lesser evil. Suicide attempts are twice as numerous, for the same age group, during this crucial period; subsequently, however, they become much rarer (Ariès and Duby, 1987, V, 372).

Physical violence, whether exercised against them by the dominator or used by the dominated against themselves, is a frequent component of the oppression suffered by the dominated. This violence can assume the most brutal forms and even claim to be exercised for the victim's own benefit.

But in attacking the body, the oppressor also alters the self-image of the oppressed and moulds them to his thinking. Alienation is thus the result of a much more insidious process than the mere learning of powerlessness. Ultimately, the oppressor no longer even needs to resort to force. One stare will suffice to put the dominated in their place, a stare directed at a difference instantly betrayed by their bodies' visible features.

THE OPPRESSED AS ABSTRACTION

One of the more paradoxical aspects of the dynamics of alienation is that it is experienced in the body at the same time that it transforms the dominated into a disembodied being. Perceived both as a sexual outlet for his or her master and as raw material against which physical power can be exercised, the oppressed is also seized upon as an abstract symbol of an entire group's identity. He or she is both an immediately accessible carnal object and the allegorical representation of "difference."

Having stripped his victims of any individuality of their own, summing them up in a few general characteristics, the oppressor has an even better claim to relegate them to intellectual confines if he believes that he has defined the boundaries of their essence. The definition of the dominated proposed by the dominator will always be simple and reductive. It is intended as an instrument of power as well as a means of knowledge. A too-complex victim risks escaping the oppressor's hold. Victims must be made to correspond to their imposed character sketch, whether they like it or not.

Once this venture has succeeded, that is, once the process of alienation has begun, the dominator will believe even more strongly that he has truly understood the specific nature of the oppressed, since he recognizes the very characteristics he himself has induced. Whence his very clear impression that he possesses an intimate knowledge of the dominated ("I know these people") and his certainty that such knowledge is shared by his peers ("Everybody knows that ...").

The oppressor's vision of the oppressed depends less on experience than on a predetermined conception of social relations, a conception this vision attempts to justify by permitting the dominator to see what he *wants* to see. Knowledge of the individual or group in question is postulated even before contact is established.

The dominated do not have to be present for an opinion to be formed concerning them, and the obviousness of the received idea of them will be reinforced by constant transmission within a given society. This is the source of the stereotyped generalizations that circulate about the oppressed. As a rigid mental category claiming to depict an entire group, a stereotype does not so much convey a negative image as it ignores complex traits, the better to highlight the difference that distinguishes this group from the dominator (Martin, 1964, 12). Thus, the part is represented as the whole, and diversity is sacrificed to the imperatives of unity. Although sometimes based on an accurate foundation (especially when it is flattering), the stereotype most often will be unfavourable (Helmreich, 1982, 244).

Prejudice, like a stereotype, not only proposes a distorted and incomplete *vision* of the victim, but even more harmfully, also involves an *attitude* that conveys scorn and hostility (in Pirotte, 1982, 4; Levin, 1975, 35–6). The reducing mechanism used by simple minds seeking an easy grasp of reality is compounded by a negative emotion, with the risk of eventual exclusion.

Thus, it is through another's eyes that the dominated receive their identity and, therefore, their relative worth and place in society. The dominator looks right through the oppressed without seeing them, to mark their social insignificance and relegate them to anonymity, or else focuses on them, to emphasize their visibility and stigmatize them.

A Stigmatized Identity

Intolerance is always fuelled by physical differences, which it views as signs of intrinsic otherness. Nowadays it is considered unimportant to have red hair or be left-handed, but in other times (not so long ago), these traits were thought to punish or exclude those in whom they appeared. At best, left-handed children were accused of impoliteness and women with "fiery" hair were deemed to be more lascivious.

Ignorance spared the human race a number of public burnings. What would have happened if such characteristics as rare blood type had been visible in certain individuals, or if people had known of such embryonic anomalies as a liver on the left and a heart on the right? A long list could be drawn up of all the anatomical, genetic, or hormonal differences whose invisibility allowed blissfully unaware minorities to escape persecution.

The progress of hygiene and medicine also removed from public view some of the infirmities and handicaps that rendered their victims vulnerable to ridicule or exclusion (in *Les âges de la vie*, 1982, 14). The disappearance of infantile rickets and osteoarticular tuberculosis, for example, have reduced the number of deformed or hunchbacked bodies. There are also fewer deaf people and amputees, just as, in the

West, there are fewer individuals who are toothless or whose faces are disfigured by skin cancers.

But there are still many difference around which the desire to exclude can be crystallized. Skin colour, among other factors, continues to separate entire human groups, and even accented speech will sometimes instantly trigger an intolerant reaction. As we have seen, otherness can just as easily be perceived through the sense of hearing as through its visible manifestations, and inferiority can be postulated from the way a person speaks as much as from his or her facial features.

The first challenge that must be faced by individuals bearing a *visible difference* is in their contact with other people (Goffman, 1963, 42). As soon as they are seen, they are seen not only as "other" but as beings of lesser value. The greater the difference, the more it will be discredited in the dominator's view: having become a stigma, a mark of shame, this difference will be perceived as revealing an identity that is itself stained and compromised (ibid, 2–3).

Thus, for some people, the simple act of leaving one's home is a constantly repeated test, a genuine ordeal. This is the case for people afflicted with particularly pronounced deformities, such as those caused by neurofibromatosis ("Elephant Man" disease). Simply mingling with a crowd to run their errands will subject them to stares, and even to the cruellest remarks.

Stigmatization is manifested not only in spectacular cases; it often takes on subtler forms. Individuals obviously suffering from a mental illness, for example, are arrested as crime suspects 20 percent more often than so-called normal people.[12] Nor do police forces seem to look favourably on young people, whose guilt they more often take for granted.[13]

There is no possible respite for those who bear the mark of their difference on their bodies. The choice of assimilating into the dominant group, which less visible minorities sometimes may resolve to do, will always be closed to them. Franz Fanon gave a moving description of the despair felt by someone who is hopelessly trapped:

> [The Jew] can pass unnoticed. ... The Jew is only disliked once he is detected. But in my case, I need a new face. I am not given a chance. I am overdetermined from the outside. I am not a slave of the "idea" that others have of me, but of the way I look.... I keep silent, I aspire to anonymity and oblivion. I will accept everything, as long as I am no longer noticed! (Fanon, 1952, 113)

The problem of *invisibility* is completely different from that of visibility. Although the latter, at first, is more difficult to bear for an *individual* who has no option, the former, in the longer term, is particularly harmful to the oppressed *as a whole*.

Undoubtedly, no dominated group has experienced the benefits and disadvantages of invisibility as much as homosexuals. Unlike members of other oppressed groups, it is possible for almost all homophiles to pass for members of the majority: their physical appearance (if not their behaviour) does not betray them automatically, and their identity is very little defined by their affiliation with a group. However, they have had to pay for this possibility of choice with total isolation, and no dimension of their environment has seemed to reflect their sensibility. To some extent, gays are the only minority whose existence the oppressor has managed to deny.

For centuries, homosexuality was considered a vice or an "unmentionable" crime, or as the love "that dare not speak its name." That which had no name ended up having no reality, either. Whether openly or implicitly, a consensus was established in society that one did not speak of "that." Especially in North America, "these things" were not spoken of, whether in the most innocuous dimensions of daily life or in the various forms of art and thought. For example, until the late 1960s, Bell Telephone refused to list associations whose name contained the word "homosexual" in the phone book (Bullough, 1979, 67). Only a few years ago, newspapers like *Le Devoir* also refused to publish advertisements announcing gay activities.

For years it was forbidden in the United States to speak of homosexuality on the stage or in film. Between 1927 and 1967, plays presented in New York State could not mention the subject (Katz, 1976, 14). Established in 1934, the Motion Picture Production Code cited "divine, natural and human laws" to forbid treatment of homosexuality in American films (Russo, 1981, 44, 122).

In truth, it was permitted to refer to homosexuality in film on the condition that contemptuous words like "faggot" were used, or that this lifestyle was described as horrible, or that homophilic characters were portrayed as clearly unsympathetic (Russo, 1981, 116–29). Biographical films reinvented an orthodox love life for such famous individuals as Cole Porter, General Charles Gordon (*Khartoum*), or Rudolf Valentino (ibid., 66), while critics (like that of the *New York Times*) did not hesitate to label moviegoers homosexuals if they had the bad taste to appreciate foreign films that dared to deal with the issue (ibid., 58, 131). Such practices were maintained long after the Code's revision (in 1961) allowed films to speak of homosexuality. Fans of *La Cage aux folles* were still accused of homophilia by one commentator, and the special tastes of certain famous men (Lawrence of Arabia, Clyde Barrow of *Bonnie and Clyde*) were subjected to appropriate "retouching" (ibid., 132–5).

Understandable to some extent in a medium like film, which is aimed at an audience long influenced by Puritanism, the tendency to charge the defender of an unpopular position with guilt by association or to falsify reality to make it correspond to one's personal wishes is much less comprehensible when such acts are committed by researchers who pride themselves on their intellectual rigour.

The academic community has not been exempt from recourse to such methods. Merely displaying interest in the phenomenon of homosexuality has long appeared suspect to the authorities, and even to colleagues. The risks of being ostracized and even losing one's job thus remained high until the 1970s in the social science and history departments of American universities (Berger, 1982, 9; Katz, 1976, 8).

The very reality of homosexuality was ignored in works that dealt with what seemed to be "safer" themes. Most histories of Greece written before 1950, for example, do not mention the homosexuality accepted in certain circles (Bullough, 1979, 53). Revealing passages have been expurgated from the correspondence of famous individuals (the American poet Emily Dickinson or the British essayist Mary Wollstonecraft, among others), often by members of their own families (Faderman, 1981, 140, 174–6).

When serious authors (doing pioneering work in the field) published in-depth analyses of homosexuality, their work was disregarded by other researchers and critics. This was the case for the documentary study by Jonathan Katz, *Gay American History* (1976), and the literary and historical work by Jeannette H. Foster, *Sex Variant Women in Literature* (1956), which was rejected by a university publisher despite a prior commitment to publish it. Aside from British or American researchers such as Michael Schofield and Edward Sagarin, even those who used alternative publishers, like the American Barbara Grier, were obliged to resort to pseudonyms when they wanted to discuss the question.

One of the greater ironies of history is that at the same time that efforts are made to deny the existence of invisible minorities, they are attributed vast (and negative) influence on society. The first of these attitudes probably leads to the latter: "plots" can only be hatched by people who are unseen. Thus, evoking Marcel Proust and André Gide as examples, psychoanalyst Edmund Bergler believed he had to warn the public against the "invisible" role of homophiles: "The influence of homosexuals in certain professions is great; in the theatre and the entertainment world in general, in fashion and interior decoration, in the academic world, among writers, and to a lesser extent among critics" (Bergler, 1967, 273–4).

This homophobic belief in the omnipresence of a maleficent homosexual is the same as that of anti-Semites who attribute an "international conspiracy" to the Jews. Unlike a member of another "race" (a Black, for example), Jews can often pass unnoticed. Thus, anti-Semites will object primarily to the "idea" of the Jew, the presence of their victims not being absolutely necessary for them to be the targets of their hostility. Hatred of Jews thus persisted in Spain, long after the Jewish population had been expelled from its territory by the Inquisition, and still survives today in Central Europe, after the massacre of nearly all that region's Jews during the Second World War.

The specific stigmatization suffered by invisible minorities still has very weighty collective consequences. Not only does the dominator deny their presence (when he does not seek to eliminate them physically) but he attributes a fictitious existence to them, which later will justify acts of repression against them. Trapped by the invisibility that assures them of relative immunity from stigmatization, the victims remain powerless to deny the lying theories circulated by the oppressor.

The insoluble dilemma posed for the group will eventually have a highly negative impact on the individual. Invisible to the dominator, the dominated will be just as invisible to their peers, thus giving them the long and agonizing impression that they are the only ones of their kind in the world. Conditioned to hear only the discourse that denounces them, they will fluctuate perpetually between self-contempt and the conviction that they nonetheless are not monsters.

In addition to confusion and isolation, the psychological cost of invisibility involves countless other frustrations. While some allow themselves to be trapped in a double life, others prefer to deny an entire part of their identity for years. To "pass" for normal, they often must feign participation in demonstrations of contempt (jokes, for examples) that target members of their own group, and must avoid the company of those who might be like them (Goffman, 1963, 76–88). Even the most innocuous details of everyday life call for constant calculation. A person who suffers from a nervous disorder will arrange with his therapist not to phone him at home or at work. Publishers of homosexual magazines will do likewise, mailing their publication in a "plain brown wrapper" and omitting the sender's name.

Even more dramatic are the cases of those individuals who, solely because of their identity, are placed in situations of direct threat.

The British and American laws that condemned homosexuality, for example, made a fortune for master blackmailers rather than helping to defend morality: 90 percent of the blackmail cases in England in the early 1960s concerned homosexuals, and full-scale national blackmail rings existed in the United States in the 1950s, targeting gays and lesbians (Russo, 1981, 129; d'Emilio, 1983, 51).

In the final analysis, violence is the logical outcome of stigmatization. This violence is primarily linked to the implicit conviction that there is nothing really wrong is causing suffering for someone considered inferior by the majority, and that the very fact that this person is the object of opprobrium justifies the "punishment" inflicted. On an even more fundamental level, violence is inherent in the very dynamics of stigmatization, which essentially consist of identifying the minority as being "other." Once members of a minority have been categorized in this way, it is possible to distinguish them, and then exclude them. Ultimately, the majority may even decide to eliminate them.

There are extreme cases where this *elimination* has been physical. But more often than not, the desire to suppress the other manifests itself *symbolically*. The underlying violence will be no less real, since the mere hypothesis of the existence of a different type of being will be deemed repugnant and the radical character of the imaginary means employed to deny this existence will be maintained with disturbing consistency. Thus, when American films, after thirty years of silence, began to speak of homophilia, it was to "kill" the gay protagonists. In twenty-two of the twenty-eight films dealing with the subject between 1962 and 1978, the script required that the central characters commit suicide or experience some other form of violent death (Russo, 1981, 52). The same thing occurred in the literature of the nineteenth century and the first half of the twentieth century (in Zola and Balzac, for example), with lesbians frequently killing themselves, when they were not themselves murderesses (Foster 1975, 114 and 239; Faderman, 1981, 267–83).

Neither does the oppressor seem disposed to tolerate a certain type of relationship with the other. For example, an individual who transgresses the sexual barriers erected by the established order between groups of unequal status will experience the same symbolic fate as would be reserved for a same-sex love. Thus, in American literature, love stories between people of different races or ethnic backgrounds often end tragically; in the adventure novels of James Fenimore Cooper, romantic relationships between Indians and Whites were doomed to failure (Butcher, 1977, 15). The dynamics have been the same in film where, at least until the 1950s, the minority partner (Black, Asian, Chicano) in the rare mixed couples depicted on screen would always meet a distressing end (Miller, 1982, 13).

The dominator also harshly judges the crossing of age barriers, especially when they are transgressed by older women with young men. Whether the more mature partner is portrayed as a mere initiator for her companion (in European cinema) or whether she is automatically an object of ridicule (in American films), this type of amorous relationship never seems to be able to last (Haskell, 1974, 275). Even a film as daring as *Harold and Maude* ends in the suicide (utterly gratuitous) of the old woman, a suicide that occurs shortly after the couple make love.

Thus, there are types of relationships and forms of sensibility that the dominator refuses to accept, even in the realm of imagination. This refusal is the negation of the other, and this negation often takes the form of symbolic elimination. The desire to cause the difference to disappear presupposes that the oppressor first becomes aware of the other's existence as a real person, before hastening to deny it all over again. But more often than not, he will prefer to ignore this reality, as his works of art and the established order provide him with the reassuring reflection of his own image.

Certainly, the dominator is not always able to ignore the other's existence completely. While he may refuse even to imagine the possibility of certain types of relations with the other, he cannot claim to be constantly unaware of the latter's *presence*. He will then endeavour to control this echo by shaping a tailor-made idea of the dominated that corresponds to his needs.

Stereotypes are reassuring. They simplify things that otherwise would be complex and give people the impression that they have a grasp of reality. Exposed to the raw light of stereotypes, the "other" is reduced to a few brush strokes that can serve as a definitive portrait.

A Stereotyped Portrait

Often sanctioned by expert authority, stereotypes permeate even the most minor aspects of public opinion. Acquired when language and culture are learned, they are structured by the official education that children receive from adults, and even school textbooks convey them systematically.

Once again, repetition reinforces what seems obvious. Warned that the dominated have a particular character trait resulting from their "difference," the dominator will not be surprised to observe its frequent manifestations. Having taken note of all those who adopt the behaviour he expects of them, he will feel entitled to conclude, in all impartiality, that the entire group to which they belong do the same thing.

By virtue of circular reasoning, he will take it as proven fact that *all* women drive uncertainly, that *all* Blacks act as if they own the whole road, that *all* lower-class people are rude to other drivers, that *all* teenagers drive too fast, and that *all* senior citizens drive too slowly. Certainly, he will often curse at a middle-aged, middle-class White man who commits any of these faults, but he will see this as the effect of the personality of a specific individual. At worst, he will retain a disagreeable memory of the incident, but he will not use it to add another dab of paint to the portrait of an abstract category of "typical" beings.

In the same way that the behaviour of one individual may tar an entire social group, the characteristics attributed to a group are often called upon to account for the personality of an individual. Thus, one person's impatience will be seen as a tendency "specific" to the handicapped, while another's trenchant wit will be perceived as the effect of his homosexual orientation.

Simple postulates will be invoked by serious thinkers to explain aspects of contemporary society or major historical events. Thus, assured of an automatic echo in public opinion, the "mentality" argument may serve as an all-purpose proof. The "Slavic soul" will be used to explain a thousand years of Russian autocracy, while the "warlike spirit" of the Germans will account for the numerous conflicts in which they have engaged. Depending on the moment, French-Canadian reactions will be written off as *"Latin* emotionalism" or attributed to *"Norman* prudence."

Sometimes, women of certain ethnic or social groups will appear to have specific attributes. For a long time, the "Black mammy" has been seen as comical and amply proportioned, while the "Jewish mother" and the "Italian mamma" were overprotective and long-suffering. Finally, there was the "classic" case of the mother of a homosexual, who was either too domineering or smothered her son with too much attention.

American public opinion, which preferred to attribute President Reagan's disastrous performance in his television debate with Walter Mondale on the eve of the 1984 election to the effects of age rather than to his personal incompetence, also shows that old age, in the public's view, embodies the ultimate form of intellectual stagnation.

However, there is no need for the mentality or symbolic characteristics attributed to the dominated to be negative. For example, today's adults like to believe in the primordial "innocence" of the child, and the rich will readily acquiesce to the idea of the essential "dignity" of the poor.

But, in general, a stereotype is less designed to present a flattering picture of the dominated than to reassure the dominator. More often than not, it will be based on the implicit postulate of the intrinsic inferiority of the group it claims to depict. This inferiority will be intellectual and psychological, of course, but it will also take on physical attributes.

The oppressor's mental impressions of the dominated's *body* have an immediate and very blunt impact. The image of *dirt* provides one example. Over the centuries, many ethnic or social groups, from Natives to Gypsies to Blacks, have been accused of uncleanliness. The English deplored the filth of the Irish, while the Jews were seen as dirty by the Poles, and the latter, in turn, were accused of the same fault by the Americans (Helmreich, 1982, 71). The poor and the unemployed have also been reproached for this by the well-to-do, particularly during the Industrial Revolution (Garraty, 1978, 91–2).

As a metaphor for an essential failing, dirtiness is sometimes independent of a person's actual physical condition: expressions such as "dirty faggot" or "dirty wog" are primarily intended as an insult to the very identity of the minority individual. Although initially insults directed at the body, calling someone an "old bag" or an "old fart" (or in French a *"vieille peau"* – an old skin) betrays a more symbolic rejection of the other, just as the accusation of being a "dirty old man" (*"vieux dégoûtant"* in French) conveys a denunciation of supposedly shameful sexual morals. Sometimes condemned as "filthy sluts," women are undoubtedly the object of the most radical marginalization, being attributed an essential ritual "impurity" by several "great" religions.

Labelled as unclean, the dominated are also associated with a related condition – *disease*. Their harmful impact on the "tissue" of society is perceived as insidious. The oppressed "undermine" and "sap" the established order; they operate discreetly, as the beneficiaries of government payments, acting as "parasites" on the vital forces of the nation. Invisible minorities arouse particular suspicion of subversive activities. The Turkish government wanted to uproot a "cancer" when it sent the Armenians on their long death marches in 1915; the Nazis sought to exterminate the Jewish "vermin" twenty-five years later. Even more invisible, homosexuals are depicted as a social "plague," mere contact with whom can "contaminate" adolescents and adults.

The dominator also arrogates the right to "purge" the environment, by removing the "gangrene" eating away at the collective "fibre." In this sense, intolerance takes on an almost immunological form, with the healthy antibodies of society violently rejecting what it perceives as "foreign" elements.

Having become less elusive, the oppressed will be identified with an *animal*. Except in the case of children, where images are most often tender ("teddy bear," "kitten," "pussycat," "bunny rabbit," or, in French usage, *"ourson," "chaton," "petit poussin"*), these metaphors tend to express contempt. For examples, women frequently are referred to as "chicks" in America, "birds" in England, and *"poules"* in France. Reflecting the impression of uncleanliness, the allegorical image of the "pig" has also been applied to members of specific races (such as Jews and Blacks) or of a lower social class ("They live like pigs"). In the case of the elderly, the pig metaphor is used in French to stigmatize the persistence of "indecent" sexual vitality (*"C'est un vieux cochon"*), while calling someone an "old goat" has a similar meaning in English. In western folklore, an old woman has been compared to a "spider," weaving a malevolent web of witchcraft (Weigle, 1982).

A sophisticated lesbian, in French usage, is also a "spider" (*"araignée"*), weaving her web in the shadows to trap an innocent young girl. Likened automatically to a woman, a gay man will be noticed for his "bitchiness" (the French equivalent, *"vache,"* means "cow") and his "viper" tongue.

To designate the primitive side of beings he considers primarily as brutes, the dominator will compare them to "apes." Europeans referred to colonized Africans as "monkeys" (*"macaque"* in French) (Komoni, 1980, 46), while the Oriental's face appeared to be a "simian" mask.

The established discourse follows an opposite dialectical line in the case of social classes and races deemed to be inferior. This time, the oppressor exalts the athletic prowess of the "other," the better to deny him the possibility of aspiring to intellectual accomplishment. For example, boxing is the pedestal readily acceded by the dominator to Blacks or to ambitious young men from tough neighbourhoods. Physical strength, to men of the dominated class or race, is what beauty is to women as a whole: a trap.

More than any other attribute, the oppressor claims the superiority of *intelligence*. His century-long preoccupation with IQ and with the weight or configuration of the brain in individuals of a different race, class, gender, or even age is abundant evidence of his desire to take himself as the measure in this matter. More often than not, expert opinion has coincided with popular opinion. For example, there was no need for in-depth research to know that women were "illogical" and even "silly" on occasion; at best they were conceded some "intuition." While the "weaker sex" was often accused of silliness, certain "inferior" races were reproached for their "stupidity." The former charge evoked the light-headedness of a bird, while the latter implied the denseness of a brute. In European eyes, the colonized thus appeared to be "feeble-minded" (in Grimal, 1965, 28) as well as "superstitious" and "left behind by progress." Even today, western Blacks continue to be the target of attacks on their intelligence, while Africans appear to be the victims of dictators as "naïve" as they are cruel.

Nations seem to take pleasure in identifying ethnic groups who will serve as the butt of their jokes about stupidity. The Boeotians played this role for the Ancient Greeks. Today, the Poles fulfil this function for Americans, the Belgians for the French, and the Newfoundlanders (Newfies) for Canadians. Inhabitants of another region will do just as well as foreigners to embody ineptitude; in France, for example, the provincial is generally labelled "narrow-minded."

This can apply to the provincial, or the peasant. Though sometimes considered wily, the peasant is used as a symbol of intellectual slowness. "Uncouth" of manner, the "country bumpkin" is supposed to have the naïvety required by life in a limited world. The image of the working class is scarcely more enviable. In the novels of Agatha Christie, among others, the few rare characters of working-class origin always have an "innate" honesty, as well as an almost physical inability to express themselves (Bill, for example, in *Three Blind Mice*).

There are certainly dominated individuals in whom the dominator recognizes a significant degree of intelligence, the better to turn the "type" of intelligence with which they are endowed against them. Thus, Jews will never be so much brilliant as they are "crafty" or "cunning," and their business success will frequently be attributed to a lack of scruples. Declared to be educated and "wise," Japanese and Chinese, in the same breath, will be judged "inscrutable" and "sly." Finally, though homosexuals are generally acknowledged to have good taste and a penchant for art, their form of humour will be labelled caustic and their refinement portrayed as a symbol of decadence.

The judgment rendered on the intellectual capacity of individuals based on their age is not devoid of ambiguity either. For a long time, the aged have been perceived as both endowed with superior wisdom and vulnerable to mental regression. "There is a wicked inclination in most people to suppose an old man decayed in his intellects," Samuel Johnson said. The faster pace of modern technology has accentuated this equivocal attitude, as the virtues of experience seem to give way to those of greater intellectual means. In short, there is no real example in which a characteristic attributed to the dominated is flattering from all points of view. Alternatively, naïvety or cunning can serve to discredit their intelligence.

The same principle applies to *character* traits. Rarely are the dominated conceded to have definitively positive qualities. One of the most common propensities in the various dominated groups seems to be their fundamental *inertia*. Blacks, Natives, and even foreign workers who are deemed to be taking undue advantage of the welfare and unemployment insurance benefits extended to them by the generosity of western countries are often accused of "laziness." Neither do the local "jobless" escape these accusations of shirking; they are suspected of living deliberately at the taxpayers' expense.

Contrary to his attitude to other categories of dominated, the dominator often wants women to be dependent. This dependence was attributed to a fundamental "passivity." Literature and film, among other art forms, long represented women as solely concerned with obtaining the protection of a husband and the security of a home. Schoolbook after schoolbook reproduced this image of women as housewives, and the rare women who worked outside the home were depicted as unmarried. Even children's literature left a virtual monopoly on action to the male protagonists (Guyon-Bourbonnais, 1981, 64).

A woman's civil status alone, therefore, dictated the roles she could play: as a fiancée, wife, or mother, she lived in terms of a man. Even in the latter's absence, her existence was still defined by him: as a spinster, she was frustrated and ridiculous; as a widow, she was noticeably embittered; as a lesbian, she had been ignored by men.

Whether imposed or merely wished for on the part of the oppressor, the oppressed's tendency to inertia and their resulting dependence are reflected on the moral plane. If the dominated have no real control over their own fate, this is because of some deep-rooted fault on their part. The dominator doubts their steadfastness in meeting the challenge. Whether lazy of their own accord or passive by nature, the oppressed always give the impression of being more or less *cowardly*.

"Everybody knows," for example, that women are fearful and easily inclined to attacks of nerves or tears. Precisely because they are considered effeminate, homosexuals do not inspire much confidence in those with whom they might have to face a common danger; thus, the police and the military prefer to dispense with their services.

The reputation for bravery of the men of certain races or ethnic groups also leaves something to be desired. Public opinion, for example, remembers the successive defeats of Mussolini's troops by the Allies but not the exploits of Italian partisans against the Germans. Until the creation of Israel, Jews also seemed little inclined to displays of physical courage, and even during the Holocaust, they were sometimes accused of an innate inability to resist. Ignoring the heroism of freed slaves during the Civil War, American films imposed the image of fearful Blacks, always ready to roll their eyes at the slightest danger (Leab, 1975, 43). For centuries, the nobility, which had arrogated the privilege of a martial career, also claimed to have a monopoly on honour and daring. Peasants and artisans had the less edifying role of being massacred regularly, to allow the nobles to prove their virtues. Neither did courage ever seem to be a prerogative of old age. Often lauded for their wisdom, elders at the same time were reproached for overcaution. Finally, persons temporarily afflicted with mental illness, or even nervous depression, often suffer the effects of a popular judgment that considers them permanently vulnerable to psychic "collapse." Those who are not worried that they eventually will "crack" under the pressure of excessively heavy burdens will instead criticize them for complaining about an "imaginary illness." In either case, their ability to overcome challenges will be called into question.

The process of inferiorization thus follows the same logic from one victim to another, in that it seeks to define differences in body, intelligence, and character. Factors such as intellectual capacity or degree of activity serve as parameters whose calculation invariably leads to the conclusion that the oppressed do not measure up to the dominator. Regardless of the results of the evaluation, the oppressed will always come out the loser in the dominator's eyes, and whatever might seem to be a manifestation of the oppressed's superiority will be perceived as evidence of their incompetence.

Ambiguity is thus at the very heart of the victim's condition. Above all, this ambiguity reveals the dual role of immediately available object and automatically impersonal abstraction that the victims are forced to play to the oppressor's benefit.

Confronted with control that the dominator claims is for their own good, the oppressed are trapped in total alienation. Apparently gaining in security what they lose in autonomy, they can no longer imagine any other type of relationship than one that renders them subordinate. They end up "consenting" to their condition and to the way they are portrayed by the dominator.

A PEDAGOGY OF GUILT

Before it becomes a psychosocial phenomenon, the shame felt in being a victim is psychological. "Why me?" asks the stunned airline passenger taken hostage by a terrorist group. "There must be a reason for this," a resident tells herself after her community is devastated by a tornado.

For there *must* be an explanation for suffering. The more evil seems to strike arbitrarily, or the more aggression appears to be beyond measure, the more necessary it is to find a plausible reason. One frequent reaction is to find scapegoats responsible for a given catastrophe; thus, the Jews were accused in the Middle Ages of causing the terrible epidemics that ravaged Europe. But individuals and communities, when struck by disaster, also tend to seek "repentance" for the errors they are sure they have committed to deserve such cruel treatment.

In a society based on the work ethic, for example, individuals "reduced" to unemployment can only wonder about their own competence. They will be inclined to do this even if millions of workers are affected by the impersonal repercussions of international economic pressures. During the Depression of the 1930s, the victims tended to feel not only resignation but a strong sense of shame and impotent rage against themselves (Lazarsfeld *et al.*, 1981). Having, in addition to this, to accept the modest material help provided by "relief" in Canada was seen as a humiliation (Broadfoot, 1978, 155-67).

Although they occurred on a more limited scale and safety mechanisms dampened their effects slightly, the 1982 and 1990 recessions triggered similar attitudes in people who lost their jobs. Some who had granted spontaneous interviews to newspapers tried to withdraw them, suddenly fearing that they would be "recognized" and thus compromise their chances of finding work. Others expressed their intense humiliation at ending up in the ranks of the unemployed and considered it a supreme degradation to eventually have to "live off" welfare.

The tendency to feel guilty for an unjust fate is even stronger when the victim is personally affected. Even the most gratuitous physical assault is experienced as a defilement. This can be seen in the reaction of female rape victims, who say they feel "soiled" and keep trying to wash away an invisible stain. Others, beaten by their husbands, believe they "deserved" it, and that they deserved it all the more if they were hit more often. So they try to mend their ways and avoid "provoking" their spouses.

The feeling of guilt is comparable among children brutalized by their relatives or drawn into an incestuous relationship against their will. Not only do they feel guilty for having "attracted" such treatment, but they are concerned about creating problems for their parents by seeking outside help, or have the impression that they are betraying their family in some way when they are placed in another home (*Les sévices institutionnels*, 1982, 56).

Children are particularly vulnerable to the shame generated by victimization. As the only student of Native origin in a Trois-Rivières school, young Alanis Obomsawin preferred not to tell her parents that she was beaten frequently by her schoolmates.[14] Physically handicapped children will feel guilty for disappointing their parents and for representing a source of conflict in their family by their very existence (Chicaud, 1979, 24).

People suffering from a physical ailment frequently react by looking for the cause in themselves, and their families, too, question their own responsibility in the matter. Even widespread diseases that "strike" later in life are perceived by the victims as a form of punishment. This is the case, for example, with certain women who are told they have breast cancer.

The same goes for some mental patients. Confined to the Louis-Hippolyte-Lafontaine psychiatric hospital, a sixty-five-year-old mother wondered why she deserved this fate:

If I'm here, I tell myself it's because I must be sick. Yes. So maybe I deserve it. That may be it. Who says that I wasn't wicked in another life? Who says that I didn't cause people to suffer in another life?... I don't remember, but that must be it. (Provencher, 1982, 63)

The impression of guilt is sometimes so closely intertwined with the feeling of shame that both persist for decades, even when it is obvious that a real injustice has been committed against the person. Thus, more than forty years later, there are still Canadians and Americans of Japanese origin who, "ashamed" of having been ostracized and stripped of their property during the war, still hesitate to demand any compensation from the government of their country. Similarly, German homosexuals waited until 1969 before they dared to ask the government, on behalf of gay people who had survived the Nazi concentration camps, for the same compensation it had agreed to pay to other victims.

Already stigmatized and stereotyped, an individual involved in a relationship of domination will have to cope with an even heavier social handicap since the oppressor, strengthened by his winning position, will endeavour to maintain it through an entire pedagogy of guilt. Relying on the very alienation that renders the victim susceptible to his discourse, the dominator will seek to make the latter an accomplice to his or her own subjugation.

"For the Good" of the Dominated

Far from aspiring to wrong the dominated, the oppressor assures them that he is doing these things for their own good. If he subjects the dominated to his control, it is precisely with this objective in mind. Can human beings who, by nature, are not always aware of their own interests be left to their own devices? In short, subjugation is also a form of *protection*, since the dominator knows better than the dominated what is good for them.

Far from finding satisfaction in the power he holds over the oppressed, the dominator feels it to be a burden, an additional responsibility weighing on his shoulders. He therefore sees the control he exercises as a duty more than a privilege.

This attitude was evident among slaveholders. Thus, the planters of the southern United States could claim a kinship between the tutelage they maintained over their slaves and that which they claimed over their own women and children. Although both groups were at the mercy of the plantation owner, their very weakness was supposed to induce a desire to protect them rather than to treat them harshly.[15] To the slaveholders, the justification for the roles of master, husband, and father stemmed from the same paternalistic source.

The logic that presided over the colonization of the African and Asian countries was scarcely different, with the Whites claiming "the right of the strong to help the weak" (Grimal, 1965, 28). This conviction of fulfilling a duty and discharging a heavy responsibility is found in the words of a Belgian colonialist who appears to have been momentarily perturbed by a bad conscience:

Dominating to serve .... This is the only excuse for colonial conquest; it is also its full justification. Serving Africa means civilizing it. Not only to give birth to new needs and supply the means to satisfy them; not only to exploit, not only to enrich, but to make the people better, happier, more like men. (Ryckmans, 1931, 5).

The very concept of a "protectorate," which an international law framed by the Europeans applied to certain countries undergoing colonization, depended on a belief in the intrinsic deficiency of these countries, a deficiency that "called for" some kind of assistance, and thus for a sharing of their sovereignty. North Americans proceeded similarly with "their" indigenous peoples, on whom they imposed the "protection" supposedly guaranteed by special treaties, reservations, and even policing (Adams, 1975, 171).

Since the colonized were considered to be "big children," it should be no surprise that they were often treated as such. After all, who more than a child needs to be protected, often "against himself"? Therefore, it will be necessary to teach children things they do not yet know and that adults, by definition, know better than they. "Spare the rod and spoil the child" is one folk precept clearly endorsed by legal theorists and practitioners. Commenting on Section 43 of the Criminal Code of Canada, which allows parents to use force, Supreme Court justices justified this type of recourse by invoking "the good of the child's education."[16]

Even the public institutions that deal with children are called child "protection" agencies. Since the State then acts as the substitute for the parent, and the generosity of the host structure cannot be suspected, the violence sometimes exercised against an institutionalized child long appeared to be more tolerable than the violence that occurred in his or her natural family (*Les sévices institutionnels*, 1982, 8–9).

Other types of institutions have also imposed constraints on vulnerable people whom they gave themselves the mission to help. This was particularly the case for mental patients, who were taken away in the nineteenth century from the bestial conditions in which they lived and placed in the more serene environment of the asylum. But even though a regime of gentleness was initially substituted for chains and brutality, alienists (the precursors of psychiatrists) came to recommend the use of more draconian methods: "A single chord still vibrates in [the insane] – that of pain. Have the courage to touch it," advised one of these savants (in Fréminville, 1977, 102).

Of course, it is the expert and not the patient who must display courage in these circumstances. This conviction seems to have endured into the twentieth century, if we can judge by the statement made by two psychiatrists specializing in shock therapy:

Today, with the use of massive cardiazol and insulin injections, the agony belongs to the physician, who tremblingly watches for all the signs of alarm so that he can ward them off. It does not belong to the patient, who is ignorant of the dangers and is no longer conscious. (In Fréminville, 1977, 119)

Thus, it is possible for the dominator to believe that he is vested with the power to establish controls, resort to physical force, and even mould consciousness, always invoking the welfare of the individuals and groups on whom he imposes his will as justification. In claiming to obey the imperatives of a responsibility that weighs more heavily upon him than anything else, he exonerates himself of any blame, when he does not simply create his own heroic reputation. How can one doubt the purity of the motives of someone who suffers from the very discipline to which he subjects others?

As the main beneficiary of all these efforts, the oppressed should be the last to question the dominator's sincerity. They know that the dominator does not wish to harm them in any way; they know that attitudes that, at first glance, may seem fairly harsh are really inspired by the best intentions. Thus, the oppressor will often believe that he can congratulate himself on the reaction of the dominated, who validate his actions by seeming *to wish to remain under his guardianship*. "I feel that the majority of francophones would like things to continue like they and their ancestors have known them for the past 113 years," an Anglo-Manitoban said in 1984, opposing the legislative and judicial bilingualism that the anglophone provincial government itself had blocked for nearly a century.[17]

In short, the dominated would agree with the dominator about their fate. To know the opinion of the former, it would almost be sufficient to ask the latter. Not only does the oppressor know what the oppressed thinks, but he knows that the latter thinks like him. There is no need for more than a single discourse, a simple reminder from the benefactor being occasionally necessary for those in his debt to remember that they still share the established opinion.

Thus, western law long maintained that the husband was the "protector" of his wife as well as the head of the family. The initial challenges to their subordinate status by these women were dismissed by the magistrates, who feared that they would "do them a disservice" by endorsing them. In 1929, the first report of the Commission on the Civil Rights of Women reminded Québec women of the implicit consent they were supposed to have given to the prevailing legal code:

This law only introduced rules of social hygiene, the beneficial value of which women are well aware, into the household. To tell the truth, what it protects are not the rights of the man to the detriment of the woman but rather the conjugal and family partnership ... in recognizing the husband's title of family head which he already drew from natural law. (Boucher and Morel, 1970, 162)

It was again with the intention of protecting women that various legal systems long prohibited them from serving on a jury (Rafter and

Stanko, 1982, 7) and that medical bodies excluded them from their profession and excluded midwives from their bedside (Ehrenreich and English, 1979, 64). How could a being of such a delicate "nature" bear confrontation with morally sordid or physically repugnant realities? In the name of the same concern for "the genuine betterment of her condition," access to higher responsibilities has been closed to women. In denying women the right to be priests, for example, the Auxiliary Bishop of Montreal invited them "to surpass the inferior education which society, and not the Church, has bequeathed to them."[18] In short, women *would not want* power or, at least, should not desire it. This is the true constant in the dominant discourse, which refuses them certain roles but also claims to obligate them to perform other functions.

Thus, a plethora of pornographic works, which dwell on descriptions of rape, imply that the victim *wants* to be forced to submit; she supposedly wants it so much that she congratulates herself on a "richer" sexual life and a "now-awakened" potential in this regard (in Lederer, 1982, 210–11). Often sanctioned by the authority of psychologists, such postulates leave their mark on the general mentality, starting with that of the magistrates required to judge the secret desires of very real victims.

The right to *choose* one's pleasure does not seem to be taken into account, since it appears to be the way of women to want others to make decisions on their behalf. One of the great strengths of the dominant discourse is its flexibility, allowing the oppressor to find justifications for the most contradictory needs. Thus, the dominator will say of a woman on whom he has no claim that he merely dared to force her "to reveal her true potential," or that the fact that she was already sexually active proved that she was available to any man.

But the ambitions that the dominator cherishes for the dominated are not always so crude. Sometimes they stem from a declared desire to *elevate their conduct*. There are a thousand ways to make people happy: one can impose unsought sexual pleasure or deny them the right to enjoy sex in the way they want. But in both cases, the constraint will be imposed "for their own good."

"Society is cruel," the dominator thus tells the homosexual. Forgetting that he himself sets the tone for society, it is almost with resignation that he demands that homosexuals conform to the practices of the majority. While claiming to have a high opinion of the homophile, he aspires to prevent him from choosing "the easy path."

The preoccupation with breaking the dominated to the practice of healthy values sometimes shaped the orientation of whole societies, with the elite endeavouring, for example, to stigmatize the "immorality" of the lower classes, when they were not claiming to mould their behaviour. The following edifying instructions, dated from about 1870, were addressed by an American furniture factory to its employees:

Any employee who smokes Spanish cigars, drinks alcohol in any form, is shaved by a barber or frequents gambling halls and public dances will give his employer every reason to suspect his integrity, his good intentions and his honesty in general. Each employee must tithe 10% of his annual income to the Church.... Men will have one evening off per week, two if they are regular church-goers.... After working 13 hours in the shop, every employee shall use his leisure time to read good books and think of the glories and the building of the Kingdom of God.[19]

Thus, in the final analysis, the burden of proof always rests with the oppressed. It is up to them to show that what the dominator says of them *is not really true* and that an injustice is being committed against them. Based on a presumption of guilt, this is a negative proof, and thus particularly difficult to demonstrate.

The Burden of Proof

Albert Memmi describes the attitude of every dominator when he says that a racist "does not punish his victim because he deserves punishment, but declares him guilty because he is *already* punished" (1973, 217).

The dynamics of domination demand that the cause of the subjugation which is the victim's lot be sought *in the victim*. Regardless of whether the emphasis is placed on the intrinsic nature of an inferiority inherited at birth, or on the influence of an environment that has left its mark, it is the victim who bears the blame (Ryan, 1976, 7).

This logic seems so obvious that it prevails even in the judicial system. The insistence of certain criminologists on establishing a typology of victims reveals this approach. Taking the vulnerability of young people, the mentally handicapped, or women as their starting point, theories claim that "the victim shapes and moulds the criminal" (in Rafter and Stenko, 1982, 4). Thus, an act of assault, like rape, for example, is labelled a "victim-precipitated crime," leading the system to fear primarily a false accusation against the assailant.

Sometimes attempts are made to attribute the situation of entire communities to a disposition specific to the dominated. To explain the conditions of Blacks in the United States, White sociologists resorted to theses of "cultural deprivation," the "tangle of pathology," or "innate inferiority" (Ladner, 1973, xxi). Mixing history with genetics, psychometricians did not hesitate to decree that Blacks were descended from Africans who were clearly less intelligent in that they were stupid enough to allow themselves to be taken as slaves, or not to get killed in revolts upon their arrival in America (in Berry and Tischler, 1978, 74).

Colonization also was "explained" by the psyche of the conquered populations. Regarding the inhabitants of Madagascar, the psychoanalyst Mannoni wrote:

When [the Malagasy] succeeds in establishing such relations [of dependency] with his superiors, his inferiority no longer bothers him; everything is fine. When he does not succeed, and when his insecure position is not regularized in this manner, he feels a sense of failure. (In Fanon, 1952, 95)

Thus, phenomena of civilization as far-reaching as slavery and colonization were attributed to the personalities of those who paid their price. But it was not only foreign peoples who were given the curious power of shaping history through subjection to it. Even in the West, it was the working class that seemed to cause unemployment: in the nineteenth century, investigators frequently concluded that improvident, alcoholic, and uneducated proletarians were responsible for triggering economic crises, despite the increasing obviousness of their cyclical nature (Garraty, 1978, 91–117). Even today, unemployment is still perceived as an anomaly of the system, or as the effect of a blemish in the victim, in a society that continues to value production without being capable of providing jobs to everyone.

Public opinion also continues to believe that poverty generally is due to a "lack of effort" or some other form of character flaw. In North America, where the myth of equal opportunity is particularly prevalent, this reaction was lent credence by social workers in the early twentieth century, who held to the traditional belief that the poor suffer from "emotional immaturity" and "deepseated conflicts within the personality" (Waxman, 1977, 87). After being accused of immorality in the nineteenth century, the unemployed and the poor would be declared sick in the twentieth.

Young adults also serve, on another level, as scapegoats for the errors of an entire society. Forced to fight a terrible war in Vietnam in the 1960s, Americans barely past adolescence, once they returned home, were included in the condemnation of this war by public opinion, which had changed in the meantime. Many preferred to conceal the fact that they had seen action, including nurses who, for the first time in United States military history, were accused of having been sexually promiscuous with the troops. Twenty years earlier, the parents of young French veterans who returned wounded from the war in Indochina had to pick up their sons at night and in secret, fearing that mobs exasperated by the continuation of this unpopular conflict might do them harm.[20]

In the case of imposed physical relations, the burden of proof often falls on the victim. This happens not only to children but also to men who are forcibly sodomized, who must have been homosexuals for such a thing to happen to them, and to women, who undoubtedly must have "asked for it" when they were raped.

Using psychiatric opinion as its authority, a classical treatise on evidence (Wigmore) reminded American judges in the 1970s of the impressive number of "complexes" with which women and young girls who file rape charges are afflicted: "inherent defects," "abnormal instincts," harmful influence of their "social environment," and "temporary physiological or emotional conditions" (in Brownmiller, 1975, 414).

Even more revealing are the reactions to the tribulations of battered women. While these may have provoked outright laughter in Canadian members of Parliament at one time, they gave rise to more subtle comments on the part of psychomedical experts. One psychiatrist, contributing the only study on this question in a collective work entirely devoted to the theme of family violence, chose to approach the subject by setting forth a typology of victims. According to the British psychiatrist J.J. Gayford, these victims would be either "inadequate" or "highly competent." A competent woman was defined as "aggressive," this aggression being exhibited, for example, in cases where she "forces" her husband to depend on her (in other words, when she supports a jobless spouse). But there are other types of battered women, according to this analysis: those who provoke mistreatment; those who drink, take drugs, or have psychological problems; and those who themselves are "violent," meaning those who "try to hit back." In short, if one is to believe the learned psychiatrist, "the problem of violence starts when a man with a low frustration tolerance is paired with a highly provocative woman"![21]

Beyond the individual dynamics of relationships of domination, whole stretches of western, and even world history have been explained by the reaction of the oppressed to their oppressor. Races inclined to submit allowed slavery and colonization; irresponsible workers who did not know how to save money caused unemployment; young people who often did not wish to fight bore the responsibility for wars that their country no longer wanted.

In its final stage, the pedagogy of guilt developed by the dominator results in a spectacular role reversal. As the high point and culmination of the established discourse, the postulate that poses the oppressor as victim is the sign of the definitive alienation of the oppressed. Not only must the dominated bear the burden of the passive guilt dictated by their inferior status, but they henceforth appear as the *agents* of premeditated crimes and subversive intents planned long in advance.

The Oppressor as Victim

To justify his radical control of his victims, the dominator must be able to accuse them of an absolute crime (Memmi, 1982, 114). Stereotyped discourse already portrayed them in the disturbing light of their innate ambiguity, when the traits of their intelligence, character, or body did not betray clearly pernicious features. Even History appears to have transmitted a long tradition of suspicion of the various ills engendered by "Jewish conspiracies," Black or yellow "perils," homosexual "plagues," and women as "powers behind the throne."

Different age groups also supposedly represented a danger. Even the most vulnerable human beings sometimes seemed to be a threat to society. For example, Christian reformers of the late seventeenth century wished to bring children "to their sense" as part of a general effort to raise individual moral standards (Ariès, 1973, 7–8). Some simply wanted to "knock sense" into these children, but others (of the Calvinist tendency) sought to combat the "evil disposition" and the "pollution of sin", that marked them (ibid., 185; De Mause, 1974, 10–12).

There is growing awareness of the progressive increase in the number of elderly citizens, yet popular opinion is scarcely more flattering to them than it was in the past. For centuries, old women were malevolent figures. In the fairy tales of the Brothers Grimm (Snow White, Hansel and Gretel), 80 percent of the evil characters were women (ogresses, wicked stepmothers, witches), and the only ones who did good were really young beauties in disguise (de Beauvoir, 1970, I, 218–19; Guyon-Bourbonnais, 1981, 66). More numerous today than old men, women of advanced age are still the first to pay the price of a trend that began to emerge in the late nineteenth century in the western world, whereby old age is considered to be as taboo as the death it prefigures (Ariès, 1976, 375–81). It is no surprise that two-thirds of contemporary jokes about the aged have a negative content (Levin and Levin, 1980, 75–6).

While old age is the annunciation of physical death, a handicap, or even a disease, evokes images of some moral blemish in the popular mind. This is particularly the case for sexually transmitted diseases, as evidenced by the example of AIDS, whose prime victims, in western countries, were at first also homosexuals, long condemned by the judgment of "right-thinking" people.

Like the more general "decline" resulting from the passage of time, "failing" health is perceived as a downfall from a standard of perfection. Forgetting that human beings are mortal, the New Age movement, too, often posits health as an original state of harmony, any deviation from which would be due to the negative "attitude" of the afflicted individual. Some alternative therapies, though otherwise quite praiseworthy, go so far as to add the feeling of failure to an already difficult condition by offering sick individuals the model of "exceptional patients," the number of whom must, by definition, be limited.

"A sound mind in a sound body," the conventional wisdom long ago affirmed. "Ugly as the seven deadly sins," it also decreed in French, making beauty equivalent to goodness. In film and in literature, dwarves, hunchbacks, or cripples often embody the forces of evil or represent signs of divine punishment brought down upon an individual or a community (Richard III, Dr. Frankenstein's hunchback servant). Just as the Christian Middle Ages stigmatized Jewish "error" by depicting the synagogue as a blindfolded figure, films like those of Buñuel, for example, used the blind as symbols of repressive forces (*L'écran handicapé*, 1983 427). Physical and mental handicaps thus are confounded into the same condemnation.

Mad scientists, vampires, perverted doctors, and fanatical assistants have all been depicted in film as bearing the signs of their cherished demonic aims upon their bodies (*L'écran handicapé*, 1983, 67)! Since madness is associated with violence, ordinary mental patients are often deemed to be potentially dangerous.

In the Middle Ages, mental illness was already seen as a punishment, both the cure and the cause of which were supernatural (Feder, 1980, 101). During the Renaissance, the Inquisition would even classify madness in the same category as witchcraft and heresy. The Classical Age made no small contribution to the halo of guilt already surrounding madness when it confined victims of mental handicaps in common places of internment, together with sex-offenders (debauchees, prostitutes, homophiles), violators of religious prohibitions (blasphemers, desecrators), and practitioners of free-thinking (alchemists, fortune-tellers) (Foucault, 1984, 106–21).

But handicaps can also have very specific physical connotations, causing the dominator to draw away immediately *in the presence of* the oppressed. This was the case for madness, already perceived by "normal" people as a harbinger of violence; it is also the case for physical infirmity, in dread of the discomfort it is likely to cause. Thus, a handicap results in rejection more for its visibility than for its severity. Regulations adopted by certain towns or corporations in the United States, for example, prohibited access to public places or to mass transit for individuals who, because they were sick, mutilated, or deformed, could be a "disgusting object" for other people (Bowe, 1978, 186).

A similar type of physical repugnance caused the United States Civil Service Commission to bar homosexuals from government departments. According to its chairman, the "revulsion" and "apprehension" caused to other employees by the solicitations or "assaults" of homophiles constituted sufficient cause for their dismissal (in Marmor, 1980, 208). One must believe that women knew better how to defend themselves than men, since it took more than fifteen years until heterosexuals themselves could be the object of harassment complaints. This double standard still applied in 1992–93 when, in both the U.S. and Canadian military, resistance to the official integration of gays arose at the very time that cases of harassment against women were being brought to public attention in ever greater numbers.

If they are dangerous to adults, homosexuals must be an even greater menace to children. Anita Bryant's entire crusade against them in Florida in 1977, and the whole campaign in support of Proposition 6, which sought to ban them from teaching in California the following year, were based on the widespread belief that gays would primarily target the young. This was also the theme of the homophobic movement that developed in France in the 1960s.

From a danger to individuals, homosexuals very soon became a social "plague." In the past, they had already been associated, depending on the requirements of the context, with idolatry, paganism, or heresy. In 1986, the Vatican decreed (without specifying how) that homosexuality represented "a serious threat to the life and welfare of a great number of people" and that it caused a growth in "irrational and violent reactions." The secular ideologies of the twentieth century did not lag behind in their judgments on homophilia, even going so far as to confuse it with totalitarianism – Communist totalitarianism, if one judges by the McCarthyites, or fascist totalitarianism, according to certain partisans of the Left.[22] In the view of Dr. Edmund Bergler, the homosexual was the accomplice of *both* types of regimes at once. "It is also well known," the psychoanalyst wrote, that the *kapos* of Nazi concentration camps were "too frequently" homosexuals;[23] also, despite the absence of testimony, he deemed that there was "good reason for the assumption" that there was identical participation by homosexuals in maintaining discipline in modern Soviet labour camps (1967, 279).

The same attachment to the "facts" can be found in Dr. Frank Caprio's argument on the relationship between lesbianism and crime. After observing, in the introduction to his book, that gay women rarely have problems with the police (1962, xv–xvi), the psychiatrist made the following assertion in the conclusion: "Crime is intimately associated with female sexual inversion. Many crimes committed by women, upon investigation, reveal that the women were either confirmed lesbians who killed because of jealousy or were latent homosexuals with a strong aggressive masculine drive" (ibid., 302).

Although the murderous criminality of the cities did not surpass that of the countryside until the very end of the nineteenth century, the French and English bourgeoisies who profited from the Industrial Revolution also likened the working classes to "dangerous" classes (Chesnais, 1981, 78). Workers in that period thus were accused not only of destabilizing the economic system by inducing unemployment but of arousing agitation and threatening public safety. And today, European and North American labour are accused of causing economic recessions, no longer by some fundamental laziness but by deliberate action.

Thus, in the depths of the 1982 crisis, the bankers of the International Monetary Fund (IMF) chided workers for demanding wages deemed by them too high for an acceptable return on investment. In their view, the repercussions of these wages on the state of the economy were more serious than those of constant technological upheavals, successive energy crunches (1973 and 1979), and errors in management by corporations obliged to seek billions of dollars in government aid (Chrysler, Dome Petroleum).

As would be shown by the stock-market crash of 1987, by the "recession" that began in the early 1990s, and by financial scandals both international (BCCI) and national (commercial frauds in Great Britain, dubious practices by Japanese brokerage firms, the collapse of the American savings and loan associations that would cost the taxpayers $ 600 billion), particular errors in judgment, fuelled by the greed that would set the tone for the "Decade of Greed," persisted throughout the 1980s. Companies and financial institutions (including certain banks that had already made risky loans to the Third World) profited from easy money, made available by financial deregulation, to overinvest in real estate or take control of previously healthy companies. They did so by using junk bonds, whose subsequent drop in value would lead to overindebtedness, remedied only by the dismantling of these companies and the sale of their assets. These various manoeuvres undermined the economy, resulting in massive job losses and a trend toward moonlighting and short-term employment, which successive cuts in the capital gains tax, the solution demanded by the affluent, would do nothing to stop.

The thesis of the collective responsibility of the dominated is all the easier to sustain if they owe their identity to their affiliation with a group. Members of a social class are automatically considered to be *all-inclusively* suspect of dubious acts. This applies not only to members of a social class but to those of an ethnic group or race. Since their identity has the twofold characteristic of invisibility and affiliation with a group, Jews have been particularly called to account for the masterminding of "international conspiracies." Already accused of deicide, poisoning wells, and murdering children in the Middle Ages, ambitions of "world conquest" were further attributed to them by a forged document written in Czarist Russia (*The Protocols of the Elders of Zion*) at the beginning of the twentieth century.

Members of certain other peoples have been attributed a reputation for criminal violence. This accusation is made against Blacks and Hispanics, among others, since their "nature" seems to incline them to aggression. As for Italians, "everybody knows" that most of them belong to the Mafia, and even the Democratic candidate for vice-president of the United States, Geraldine Ferraro, was obliged to prove that she had no connection with organized crime. Other races are called before the bar of History and their danger to others is put forward as evidence. Thus, Amerindians were supposed to be bloodthirsty because they were savages, and Asiatics cruel and hypocritical because they were too civilized.

The logic behind the colonizing thrust of western countries was scarcely different. After reducing Blacks to slavery in the seventeenth century, Whites demanded that Asia and Africa, in the nineteenth century, deliver up the wealth in their possession. While some justified these conquests by invoking the deaths that these continents had cost to Europe, others urged the vanquished populations to "share the common treasure of humanity" to "*make life easier*" for the temperate countries that needed it (in Astier Loutfi, 1971, 84; in Grimal, 1965, 93–4).

When the resistance of the colonized peoples was expressed openly, the colonizers immediately felt themselves persecuted. Thus, Europeans saw themselves as the "forces of order" dealing with "rebels," forces of order whose acts of "courage" against "fanatical" adversaries were reported by western media and history books. The impression of victimization felt by the White peoples in taking over foreign continents was manifested all the more intently when the security of their own territory was in question. Encouraged a century earlier by the westerners to share the resources of their own continents, the "heritage of the human species" as a whole, Africans and Asians now found themselves barred from White countries. Arabs, for example, were now accused of "colonizing" France and behaving as if they were in "a conquered country."[24]

A veteran of the Algerian War and a former active participant in France's colonial empire, Jean-Marie Le Pen, who along with the members of his National Front now calls for immigrants and their children to be sent back to North Africa, claims to be part of those who are *really* being attacked. "Extremists? We ourselves are victims of violence," he said after the June 1984 European election, claiming that adherents of his movement were treated as "subhuman." A senior Canadian civil servant, who declared himself sympathetic to the Ku Klux Klan, did not express himself any differently when he justified his support by invoking the fact that the Klan is a "minority" and that it therefore suffers from "discrimination."[25]

Even the authors of genocides now deem themselves to be victims of unjust intrigues by the peoples they had previously sought to "resettle." Taking advantage of the resurgence of anti-Semitism and the rise of revisionist writings on the nature of the Nazi extermination camps, one western school of opinion, influenced by positivist psychology ("The past is the past") is increasingly sensitive to the idea that there should be clemency for the "defenceless old men" that Nazi criminals have supposedly become.

Thus, a racial minority that was once perceived as the persecuted group comes to be considered the aggressor against those previously recognized by public opinion as its executioners. What is true for the Jews, whose oppressed status has nevertheless been established officially, is all the more true for the Armenians, whose tribulations have never entitled them to be acknowledged as victims by the international community. This is why their complaints against the Turkish government are not only rejected but labelled a form of harassment. In this case, the roles have even been completely reversed. In a pamphlet published in 1982, the Assembly of Turkish-American Associations called upon the Armenians to renounce hatred, to "instead adopt the attitude held by hundreds of thousands of Turks living today, whose parents and grandparents perished at the hands of Armenian bands during the First World War."[26]

Thus, the different dominated groups have not only borne the burden of proof with regard to a dominator who was only looking out "for their own good," but they have had to withstand criticism for allegedly oppressing those of whom they believed themselves to be victims. They are criticized for oppressing them individually, sometimes threatening the physical safety of individuals, as well as for endangering entire continents, by undermining the established order or by conspiring to take control of the planet. But they are not accused only of crimes, political or judicial; they have also been charged with moral offences, with no less severe repercussions.

Sin, like crime, has represented a form of aggression against the person of the dominator or against the society that he has built. Children have inherited it, the handicapped have symbolized it, homosexuals have embodied it, and races or social classes have committed it or had to expiate it. But it is *woman* who is considered to be the primary cause of sin, and it is through her that sin is supposed to have entered the world. In the eyes of men, Eve bears the principal responsibility for an offence that she committed with Adam. Millennia later, as revealed in society's attitude toward prostitution, women are still charged with an act that, by definition, they cannot commit alone.

Women have also been portrayed as dangerous, as the feminine names long given to hurricanes demonstrate: "*Femme en colère, mer déchaînée*," goes the old French proverb ("Angry woman, wild sea"). Folklore has condemned her even longer as a "snare" for men: "*Trois filles et leur mère, quatre démons pour le père*" ("Three daughters and their mother are four demons for the father"); "*Si tu veux te venger d'un homme, envoie-lui une jolie femme*" ("If you want revenge on a man, send him a pretty woman"); "*Bats ta femme tous les matins: si tu ne sais pas pourquoi, elle le sait*" ("Beat your wife every morning: if you don't know why, she does"); "*Un homme en paille vaut une femme en or*" ("A man of straw is worth a woman of gold"), etc. The opinion of women expressed in English proverbs is the same ("A bad woman is worse than a bad man"), and there are countless examples of vituperation against dominating wives ("He that has a wife has a master"). The recommended treatment is the same as in French ("A woman, a dog, and a walnut tree, the more you beat them, the better they be").[27]

"*Cherchez la femme*" both languages advise to identify the origin of a catastrophe, often one of a historical nature. According to one type of reasoning in England, for example, British women caused the loss of Britain's Indian Empire.[28] The Pétainists saw the defeat of 1940 as the result of the selfishness of Frenchwomen, who "killed" their country by refusing to bear large numbers of children.[29] German women, who had given birth to more children, were accused of having sent their sons to the slaughter (Janssen-Jurreit, 1982, 317). More than women, it has been mothers who, since the advent of Freudianism, have been held responsible for "all the sins of the world." There do not seem to be any fields where a mother's influence, open or hidden, is not felt, and no mischief of which she is not capable. In the West, the mother has become a *universal scapegoat*. "*Cherchez la femme*" in the twentieth century almost inevitably means finding the mother.

The mother is supposed to be primarily responsible for the fate of the individual. Depending on whether she is overprotective of her child, or rejects him, or does both at the same time, she risks marking him forever by directing "unconscious hostilities" against him (in Ehrenreich and English, 1979, 277–33). Thus, extreme indulgence on her part may betray repressed aggression, as does extreme authoritarianism. For every mother, in the depths of her soul, allegedly would refuse motherhood, and thus feminity. As Dr. Joseph Rheingold wrote in 1964: "It is kill or be killed. Most mothers do not murder or totally reject their children, but death pervades the relationship between mother and child" (ibid., 235).

If not the child's life, it is the child's health that the mother "unconsciously" puts in danger. There is the mother of asthmatic children who, according to some, conceals her hostility behind a mask of excessive care, and the "schizophrenogenic" mother who induces a psychosis in her little one (in Guyon-Bourbonnais, 1981, 78). In short, she is an all-inclusively "pathogenic" or "death-dealing" mother, whom experts, responsible for treating young autistic or handicapped children, sometimes take as the *cause* of their patients' condition (Zucman, 1982, 32–100).

Beyond the burden she carries for the life or physical and psychological health of the individual, the mother is held responsible for the success of the latter's sex life. While some psychiatrists, for example, blame both parents almost equally if they happen to have a homophilic child (Caprio, 1970, 337), others accuse the mother of being *solely* responsible for "causing" both lesbianism in girls and homosexuality in boys (Kronemeyer, 1980, 13–15).

Furthermore, she is also supposedly responsible for any pedophilic tendencies that her husband might display, or for his incestuous relations with their daughter. In the first case, the woman's "dominant-dependent" behaviour must be blamed, according to these authorities (Kempe, 1984, 30–1); in the second case, the problem would stem from *either* a passive *or* an aggressive attitude on her part (ibid., 52).

In cases of incest, the severity of the consequences for the child is also supposed to vary depending on the sexual identity of the partners involved. Thus, according to some authors, father/daughter incest "is not always the act of a pervert" (the experts emphasize the role of the *wife* in this case), while mother/son incest "is generally considered more pathological" (the role of the husband is not mentioned). As for homosexual relations between children and parents, mother/daughter incestuous relations "undoubtedly would be less traumatic" (than between mother and son), while father/son relations are "more disturbing than a heterosexual relationship," since there is a risk that "passive" homosexual behaviour will be induced in the child (Straus, 1982, 95–6).

In the view of these psychoanalysts, the daughter is less of a victim than the son, and the mother more guilty than the father, even guilty *for* the father. While pronouncing categorically on the condition of men, the specialists' verdict is satisfied with postulating the condition of women. In this regard, there is noticeable use of the conditional tense in cases where the daughter is involved in a relationship with her mother. As for the mother/son relationship, Dr. Kempe admits that "we don't know why" it is more damaging than father/daughter incest. Kempe is quite willing to concede that a young girl will be marked by the experience of incest with her father, but maintains that she will mainly be angry at her mother who, "above all others," should have been able to protect her (1984, 157) – apparently even more than her father, who seems to have only been an accidental participant in the whole story.

The mother bears the primary burden of guilt for the incest committed by her husband. For example, she might be deemed guilty of having "abandoned" her household, as when she "absents herself" by going out, visiting friends, working outside the home, or even falling ill ... or becoming pregnant. One specialist even congratulates himself that an incestuous father was able to "verbalize openly his anger towards his dead wife for abandoning him" (in Ward, 1984, 166–7). Found guilty of leaving her family unprotected, the woman is also held responsible by psychoanalysts for the failure of sexual relations with her husband. Frustrated by this failure in which *he never seems to be responsible for anything*, he appears to have no other choice than to turn to their daughter. Furthermore, the wife supposedly feels relieved that her child is taking her place, or is glad to be able to experience, through her daughter, her Oedipal desire for her own father (ibid., 168, 174).

In the realm of sexual behaviour, the Mother represents an ideal universal scapegoat. When the mother of the female child is not incriminated, the mother of the father himself, or the mother of his wife, will bear the blame. In the last two cases, experts will judge her to be overpossessive. One of them even believed that he could trace such a tendency back to the "maternal grandmother" of the man in question (in Ward, 1984, 172–3).

The dynamics would be no different in cases of rape, where the attacker is only a chance factor in a matter taking place primarily between women: the victim and a female relative of the rapist. In the view of the specialists, this relative would be either the rapist's mother or his wife; sometimes they are both accused jointly. Based on a study of *eight* wives of rapists, one American criminologist and psychoanalyst concluded:

... the wives of the sex offenders *on the surface* behaved toward men in a submissive masochistic way but *latently* denied their femininity and showed an aggressive masculine orientation; they *unconsciously* invited sexual aggression, only to respond to it with coolness and rejection. They stimulated their husbands into attempts to prove themselves, attempts which necessarily ended in frustration and increased their husbands' own doubts about their masculinity. In doing so, the wives *unknowingly* continued the type of relationship the offender had with his mother. *There can be no doubt* that the sexual fraustration *which the wives caused* is one of the factors motivating rape. (In Brownmiller, 1979, 194–5. Emphasis added.)

Once the responsibility of a woman, and more specifically that of a mother, is established definitively with regard to the life, health, and sexuality of individuals, her influence over their fate cannot fail to spill over onto the entire community. The role played by mothers in handicaps, homosexuality, incest, and rape has obvious social repercussions, but other fields, more immediately collective in nature, have also been identified by the specialists as their sphere of action.

So-called scientific studies and official reports, for example, have targeted mothers as the cause of the inferior status of certain races or social classes. Thus, according to some sociologists, the higher crime rate characteristic of underprivileged environments would be due to the "toughness" of human relations imprinting the "subculture" produced by these environments, this "toughness" itself being linked to the lack of male role models suffered by boys raised solely by a mother (in Waxman, 1977, 9). The father being absent, "matriarchy" would be to blame for delinquency in subproletarian families. One socio-economist quoted the following testimony of a delinquent as proof of this hypothesis:

I prefer banging the walls to beating my wife. It reminds me too much of my father ... . We had iron bunk beds and when my father was drunk he'd put my mother's head between the bars of the bed and he'd hit her ... . My mother had breakdowns. Sometimes she'd go to the hospital the next morning, because she'd been hit too much or she was having a breakdown. It made me crazy to see my mother cracking up. (Brébant, 1984, 75)

Trying to find the deeper meaning behind the young man's revelations, the author drew the following conclusions:

The testimony of this delinquent not only reflects the determining *presence* of the mother in moments of violence but perhaps, even more, the quest for a positive image of the father. ... The *most striking* element of this conversation is not the condemnation of the violence of which *the son* was *the victim* but rather the suffering resulting from the intense desire to be able to have a father and to recognize himself in his father. (Ibid, 75–6. Emphasis added.)

It would thus seem that the mother can only be guilty. She will be guilty without even having to be "present" at the scene of the action (in the case of incest, among others) and may be the first to receive the blows without earning the status of victim. But whether he is absent or violent, the father remains idealized. At least he is idealized by the experts, who often will find mitigating circumstances for his behaviour, or will be more "struck" by the *unexpressed* desire of the son to recognize himself in his father than by the *real* compassion he displays for his mother.

Often presented in this light, "matriarchy" can only be inherently bad. Its consequences will be considered so grave that they can be detected on the level of entire communities – such as underprivileged classes, where the one-parent family structure supposedly causes delinquency – as well as in the particularly disadvantaged members of certain racial groups. Thus, in a famous 1965 study, the Moynihan Report, the entire phenomenon of the economic inferiority of Blacks in the United States was explained by the harmful effect on *boys* of that group of being raised by their mothers.

In the same period that Moynihan, a sociologist, was blaming Black mothers for the violence of their sons, psychoanalyst Erik H. Erikson held their Native counterparts responsible for rapes that their own sons might eventually commit. Since it was the custom of Sioux women to breast-feed their children long after they began teething, Erikson concluded that the mothers could only frustrate their children by refusing to let them bite, and that these frustrations would encourage some of their boys to take sexual revenge on girls later in life (in Janssen-Jurreit, 1982, 214–15).

There thus seems to be no doubt: the mother's influence on individuals and groups is decisive and universal. It is decisive because it often determines the harmful course of their evolution, and universal because there is no single parameter of identity on which this influence is not exercised.

The mother is also guilty in every way – guilty of being passive *or* aggressive, guilty of being dependent *and* dominant. Is the father of her children absent? Then she is "matriarchal." Is he too insistent with their daughter? Then she is deemed to be an "accomplice" or the "cause" of incest. Never a victim herself, she "provokes" her husband when he batters her, and it is *her son* who really suffers the blows that she receives. When her children are affected directly, it is still the plight of her son that receives the most attention. Although men are the *agents* of most, if not all, cases of incest, rape, delinquency, and murder, the experts will begin with her in seeking the cause. Not only is her guilt heavier than that of the man when, perchance, she commits an act like incest, but her "complicity" appears to be even graver than the assault itself when the man instigates the violence.

A perpetual excuse for the behaviour of her husband or son, only rarely can she invoke the harmful role of a husband or father as a mitigating circumstance. In the final analysis, men even seem to suffer the most for aggressive acts. Just as the son was deemed to be the first to pay for the blows received by his mother, so do certain criminologists sometimes perceive rapists as the "victims of a disease from which many of them suffer more than their victims" (in Brownmiller, 1975, 193).

It is also striking to observe the extent to which the mother's mischief occurs "latently" and "unconsciously." She *does not know*, for example, that she wants to push her daughter into the arms of her husband, or sleep by proxy with her father, or incite her son to rape and murder, or even personally kill her handicapped child. Only her psychoanalyst knows for sure.

It has long become a habit to put forward (or endorse) the thesis of female guilt. Giving a scientific veneer to the conventional "wisdom," Freudianism subscribed to the centuries-old response *"cherchez la femme."* Where historians had suspected the influence of the "power behind the throne" and churchmen the work of the "daughters of Eve," psychoanalysts simply chose to see the role of the mother.

While the willingness to blame women for everything is particularly deep-rooted and spectacular in western tradition, the tendency to reverse the roles of oppressor and oppressed underlies all relationships of domination. This is one of the rare cases, if not the only one, where the dominator tries to "pass" for something he is not.

There is no *flagrante delicto* situation (a great power attacking a small country), no inhuman institution (such as slavery), no form of persecution (genocide included) for which the oppressor cannot eventually place the responsibility on the shoulders of the victim. There is no human being who is so vulnerable (a handicapped person, a child, an old woman), so devoted (a mother), or so terrorized (a homosexual in a period of mass hysteria) that he or she cannot be accused of possessing some pernicious power.

The established order must be justified and the explanation supplied for this purpose endorsed by the oppressed themselves. Their submission will be ensured most efficiently by the feeling, instilled by the dominator, of their own guilt – not only the passive guilt of someone who pays for an inferior *identity* with an inferior *status*, but the active guilt that must be shouldered by the symbolic or postulated real author of an act of aggression.

In accepting the discourse that depicts them as the oppressors, the dominated plumb the depths of their alienation. Imbued with a dialectic that isolates them from their peers and puts them at the mercy of the dominator, they will often collaborate in subjugating other oppressed people to the dominator's will. They will even seek to stifle any emancipatory impulses that might be displayed by some of their own people or to undermine their first emerging ties of solidarity.

The pedagogy of guilt is applied even more forcefully when the established order is challenged. Already under the impression that the oppressed is the aggressor in periods of dominant harmony, the oppressor will be even more convinced that he is the victim of the oppressed when the foundations of their long relationship begin to be challenged.

For a time will come, not always sustained or definitive, when the oppressed will break free of the established logic and claim the right to speak. A time will come when the oppressed will give words their true meaning and see reality as it is. In short, a time will come when the oppressed will perceive that they are the real victims.

This is when the long process of liberation will begin, a process in which the oppressed must advance without the aid of established models and must reinvent discourse, a process in which the oppressed must discover a long-hidden history and rethink both the universal and the objective. In short, a process will begin in which the oppressed will be called upon to relinquish received ideas for the insecurity of doubt and to renounce the comforts of dependence for the risks of autonomy.

CHAPTER FOUR

Emancipation

To emancipate themselves from the oppression to which they have often been subjected for centuries, individuals and groups have to escape their places of confinement and take their turn at occupying the field of the universal. These places of confinement have been both physical and symbolic, taking the form of concrete ghettoes and subtle exiles disguised as pedestals. By imposing his own specific characteristics on the universal, the dominator had occupied this field alone. The desire of the dominated to "come out" of the imposed limits will be accompanied by a determination to "reintegrate" themselves into society.

Rejoining the field of the universal does not mean merely *sharing* a predetermined field of thought and action with the oppressor. It also involves *creating* new currents of freedom that flow in different directions or overturn the old way of thinking.

Before taking their place in the sun, however, and even before taking power, the dominated must speak out. They must break the silence about the real nature of their condition, or the very fact that it exists; they must reinvent discourse, and develop new syntheses.

In addition to its cathartic effect on the oppressed, speaking out makes it possible to create networks of solidarity with counterparts who recognize themselves in the narrative of this evolution. The success experienced by different consciousness-raising groups, bringing together people of the same common affiliation, cannot be explained otherwise. Particularly developed in the United States in the 1970s, these groups reflected the need felt by women or homosexuals, for example, to share their experiences, after long being unaware of their common nature.

Today the trend is to publish works that are more theoretical, many of them collective efforts. The first major syntheses to break the silence or unanimity and launch the debate have been succeeded by analyses which, though sometimes covering vast areas of research, are more limited in their ambitions.

While they do not necessarily accept their content, these analyses do not deny the heritage of long-established classics like the writings of Karl Marx on the working class, or more recent studies like those of Simone de Beauvoir on *The Second Sex* (1949), Betty Friedan on *The Feminine Mystique* (1963), Kate Millett on *Sexual Politics* (1969), and Germaine Greer on *The Female Eunuch* (1970), or those of Jean-Paul Sartre in his *Reflections on the Jewish Question* (1947), Franz Fanon in *Black Skin, White Masks* (1952) and *The Wretched of the Earth* (1961), or Albert Memmi in *Portrait du colonisé* (1957). They also continue to benefit from the critical reflections of Erving Goffman in *Asylums* (1961) and Michel Foucault in his *Histoire de la folie à l'âge classique* (1961). Although they differ greatly in the way they approach the question of age, *L'enfant et la vie familiale sous l'Ancien Régime* (1960) by Philippe Ariès and *Old Age* (1970) by Simone de Beauvoir are indispensable references. While no comparable study exists on homosexuality, surveys like those reported by Alfred Kinsey in *Sexual Behaviour in the Human Male* (1948) and *Sexual Behaviour in the Human Female* (1953) at least breached the wall of silence before Michel Foucault launched a more general synthesis in his *Histoire de la sexualité* (1976).

But after years, even decades of activism often nourished by these authoritative studies, and after the numerous publications that followed them, attempting to develop even more comprehensive analyses, works have emerged in recent years that, while no less critical, have sought to reinvent knowledge one piece at a time: by rediscovering a historical heritage, by exploring unknown fields, by taking a new look at older areas, by compiling anthologies of new or recently discovered "classics," or by presenting a balance sheet of acquired knowledge.

The authors of these works, often collective efforts, have chosen to limit their objectives to a specific area of research or reflection. Thus, they frequently focus on countries, periods, or themes (stereotypes, violence, discrimination) or on fields of thought or action (law, religion, philosophy, the various arts and sciences; media, politics, business). They approach questions in the light of a specific science (sociology, anthropology, social psychology, history, linguistics) or from a multidisciplinary perspective. Finally, as an ultimate sign of this diversification, the schools to which they belong (liberal humanist, functionalist, radical, socialist, Marxist, separatist) are just as varied as their methodologies (comparative, phenomenological, relativist, universalist, "interactionist").

However, this explosion of research does not mean that the number and diversity of publications have reflected all the different parameters of identity as it relates to oppression. While many works of research and theoretical analysis have been devoted to social class since the nineteenth century, and to race or ethnicity since the Second World War, far fewer have dealt with questions of handicap and age. However, there has been a proliferation of publications on gender (since the early 1970s) and sexual orientation (since the mid-1970s); specialized journals and mass-circulation magazines have been founded, and publishing houses have been born to alleviate the effects of the subtle exclusion of minority authors. Mainstream publishers gradually have begun to publish the works of women and homosexuals, and university presses are producing a multitude of theses and scientific works by or about women or gays.

In addition to the social questions they already discuss, university curricula are making more room for gerontology, the study of ethnic communities, the status of women, and the situation of gays and lesbians, and even have programs entirely devoted to these issues. Taking their demographic importance into account, the variety and number of works authored by women (Americans in particular) indicate how much progress still has to be made in the case of dominated groups hitherto more neglected by researchers and theorists.

Regardless of how far their work has advanced or the approach they have adopted, thinkers and activists have the same objective: to speak out and thus retake possession of themselves. Dealienation requires reconsideration of the dominant discourse so that language can be reinvented. This reconsideration most often will be gradual, since emancipation is a laborious process, initially expressed in the logic of the oppressor.

RECONSIDERING THE
DOMINANT DISCOURSE

In "Orphée Noir" ("Black Orpheus"), his 1948 introduction to Léopold Senghor's Black poetry anthology, *Anthologie de la poésie noire*, Jean-Paul Sartre noted the existence of an "iron law which denied the oppressed all weapons which he did not personally steal from the oppressor." Not only does the oppressor initially hold the monopoly on power, which sometimes must be snatched from him piece by piece, but the dominated depend on him for the production of discourse. The dominated thus are beholden to the dominator even in the need to give meaning to their condition. They may reject or accept this meaning, but for a long time they will continue to define themselves in its terms.

The reinvention of language requires a challenge to a dominant discourse that has come first chronologically – chronologically and *logically*, since without an oppressor there is no victim, and tolerance requires no definition when it appears to be the normal state of affairs. There is no "problem" other than the one raised by the domination of the weaker by the stronger, and, in reality, the Black, homosexual, or female "question" is only the White, heterosexual, or male question. If it became universal, tolerance, like oppression, may be exercised for centuries without having a name. Its very predominance in the relation between individuals and between groups would presume a fundamental equality which no tensions would endanger.

In a non-egalitarian society, however, the dominator sets the tone, imposing his discourse and summoning a reaction to his power. In this sense, the dominator is his own destabilizing agent. As the lowest common denominator in a society built on shaky grounds, force, exercised openly or implicitly, ultimately gives those who initially bowed to the will of the strongest the desire to revolt, thereby rocking the very foundations of the hierarchy it is designed to protect.

One of the not inconsiderable effects of oppression is that the dominator succeeds in imposing his logic even on the process adopted by the dominated to escape his control. This logic is double-edged, supplying both the victim with weapons and the oppressor with pride in having produced them. For example, some westerners have boasted of having taught Africans and Asians the principles of a revolutionary and liberal heritage after these were invoked to launch decolonization.

Before they can turn his logic against the dominator and even reinvent it completely, the dominated must free themselves from the snares and pitfalls pervading the discourse that has moulded their thinking, a discourse that they did not initially recognize as alien because it presented itself as all-encompassing and impartial. They must recognize this discourse for what it is by demonstrating that special interests and partial knowledge lie concealed behind its claim to universality and rigour. This critical undertaking will allow them to determine which part of the dominant discourse they endorse by *choice* and the extent of the new meaning they will have to produce on their own.

The first thing that will have to be called into question will be the principle of an ideal model of humanity or of complete objectivity. In seeking emancipation, the oppressed, sometimes vulnerable to the temptation of establishing an ideologically orthodox social order to their own advantage, would do best to renew the prevailing discourse by emphasizing the relative nature of differences in identity and recognizing the inevitability of competing subjectivities in the development of knowledge.

Relative Identities

To present himself as the ideal human type, the dominator often invoked irreducible laws sanctioned by Nature, God, or History. In his view, the power he exercised over the oppressed was not so much the result of undue reliance on force as the effect of uncontrollable imperatives, if not of a Higher Will. In relation to the universal model that the oppressor seemed to represent, the dominated always appeared to be afflicted with some defect or intrinsic failing.

After long endorsing the logic of a discourse taught to them as the only one that was valid, the dominated began to feel doubts. At first vague and fleeting, these doubts were aroused by the oppressor's own failings in living up to his idealized model of humanity. As the oppressed became more actively aware of their own worth, their doubts grew more insistent.

Gradually, the dominated ceased to see the oppressor's defence of his special interests as the inevitable tribute owed to a superior being. Divine, natural, or historical laws that espoused such narrow designs became suspect. It eventually came to mind that these laws were pure creations of a group wishing to legitimize its privileges.

In power relationships, the identity of the individual or the group can only be relative. Since each is distinct from the others, society is made up of a cluster of often overlapping differences. The dominated not only have to demand the "right to be different," they must also show that the dominator himself is always somebody's "other," that he neither holds the top ranks in a hierarchy of human beings nor totally represents a version of humanity that happens to match him perfectly – he is the embodiment of a relative otherness, just like any minority.

Emancipation does not so much consist of exchanging the roles of oppressed and oppressor as fundamentally changing the ways in which the definition of identity is understood. Thus, age can be restored to the context of the life cycle, and a handicap can be gauged in terms of individual abilities, rather than being perceived solely in relation to fleeting youth or an ideal physical condition that reflects abstract standards. Within this perspective, homosexuality itself becomes one case, among others, of the diversity of sensibilities rather than a "deviation" from a single way of loving, and the relationship between woman and man becomes one between partners rather than the domination of the "weaker" by the "stronger" gender. And far from being signs of an intrinsic inequality of abilities that separates them, the differences between races or social classes become just so many examples of the variety of strategies adopted by human groups to meet the challenges of their environment.

As renewed by the dominated, the discourse will be based on such notions as diversity, complementarity, and flexibility rather than on the more exclusive concepts of superiority or totality. Not only did these concepts work to the disadvantage of the oppressed, even the oppressor could not live up to them. By basing his power on the supposed obviousness of his own wholeness, the oppressor denied himself the right to fail; by hoping to be the ideal Man, he condemned himself to eternal perfection. Just as the all-too-human designs he attributed to God, Nature, or History ultimately caused the victim to doubt the real foundations of their alleged laws, the increasingly obvious limits of the superman would undermine the model's prestigious image.

For example, instead of being unconditional, the "protection" promised to women and children in exchange for their obedience to the "head of the family" was not always assured, since he did not necessarily have the means or the will to play his role as provider or defend their home against outside threats. In many cases, husbands or fathers themselves were the main source of violence against their kin.

There has been similar disillusionment in social relations. As members of the less affluent classes eventually realized, the successive economic crises that occurred until the Second World War, as well as the recessions of varying severity afflicting the West in the past decade, often highlighted the improvidence or error-ridden management of business executives whose competence had seemed undoubted.

One major historical event, more concentrated in time, also hastened the emancipation process: the Second World War made no small contribution to the liberation of the colonized peoples of Africa and Asia. The defeat experienced in 1940 by the previously invincible European "powers" to which they had been subjugated (France, England and the Netherlands) gave them the opportunity to take the true measure of their colonial masters.

The myth of the dominator as superman was exposed even in cases of individual oppression. For example, homosexuals became aware that the morals of a majority that claimed to stigmatize their lifestyle were not necessarily beyond criticism just because they were less marginal. As a person, the dominator is no more invulnerable than his power is infallible, irreproachable, or invincible. Not only can nobody be assured of permanently escaping physical disability or mental illness, but, inevitably, the simple degree of health or strength available to function will vary during any individual's lifetime.

Thus, there are limits to the oppressor's competence and power, and even to his morality. In short, after claiming to be perfect, the dominator will be shown to be just as human as the dominated who he had complained were too human ... or not human enough. In their growing doubts about the oppressor's intrinsic superiority, the oppressed have to reconsider the parallel principle of their own inferiority. Once the victim's alienation, hitherto maintained by stigmatization and the artful pedagogy of guilt, has been shattered, there is no longer any "definitive" truth that cannot be retought, nor any new frontiers that cannot be explored.

"Axioms" thought to be patently obvious since time immemorial have to undergo radical reconsideration. Thus, the very notion of a "maternal" instinct deeply rooted in a woman's nature is being reinterpreted in the light of history. Reinserted into a cultural context, a mother's love for her child has been expressed differently down through the ages: less apparent in the seventeenth and eighteenth centuries, it reached its heights with the beginnings of the nuclear family and the exclusion of women from the family economy in the nineteenth century, but began to change direction in the 1960s with the ebbing of traditional maternal sentiment and the joint manifestation of the father's greater interest in child-rearing (Badinter, 1980, 469–70; Shorter, 1975, 5–17). Likewise, the criteria that distinguished certain widely condemned forms of conduct from a single orthodox mode of behaviour ceased to appear aniversal. The definition of what is good, inevitable, or normal in a culture – in short, the definition of what is natural – does not necessarily coincide with what another culture proposes. Thus, homophilia, deemed to be "against nature" in one place, is accepted elsewhere as self-evident, and that which was a perversion yesterday becomes a question of taste tomorrow (d'Emilio, 1983, 145). For example, in nearly two-thirds of non-western societies, homosexual activities are perceived as normal or acceptable, at least for certain members of the community; in the other one-third of these societies, where such activities are condemned, they nonetheless are pursued in secret.[1] Both to Kinsey (1948, 666) and to Freud,[2] homophilia seemed to be a universal human tendency: Kinsey defined it as one of the end points of a continuous scale of preferences ranging from 0 (for exclusive heterosexuality) to 6 (for total homosexuality), while Freud considered a primordial disposition to bisexuality to be deeply rooted in human beings. The American sexologists Masters and Johnson even noted the existence of sexual fantasies with homophilic content in subjects who sometimes were openly homophobic and in those who were classified at 0 on the Kinsey scale (1979, 186-7).

Nature thus does not always impose the imperatives that the dominator would have wished to attribute to it, and culture often plays a very great role in the so-called "determinisms" seen by biologists or in supposedly "constitutional" attitudes. When examined with a more critical eye, "natural laws" often end up being exposed for what they really are: theoretical constructs, sanctioned by the very groups whose privileges they serve.

Since the verities of Nature have often been deemed by the established discourse to coincide with Divine Will, any challenge to them could only raise questions about the real demands of the Sacred. Realizing that God's image corresponds as closely to the features of the dominator as heavenly designs appear to coincide with the latter's interests, the oppressed begin to rethink their entire relationship with religion. The notion of the oppressor as the reflection of God meets with an entire dialectic equating the oppressed with sin, the mirror image of the divine.

The end of alienation thus occurs on two levels – the reappropriation of the Sacred and the removal of the dominated's own sense of guilt. Ready to break, if necessary, with the mediating power represented by ecclesiastical institutions, the dominated aspire to a spirituality in which they finally can play their full part, and refuse to consider themselves the prime repository of moral transgression. The approach may vary, but the effect will always be the same: the challenging of a God perceived both as an upper-class White male and as the supreme guardian of the only sexual practices that the dominator accepts. In some cases, the challenge will be radical and will result in a complete break. Thus, despairing of ever finding a non-subordinate place in Christianity, some Black Americans began to convert to Islam in the 1930s. Altering Mohammed's doctrine, these "Black Muslims" turned the dominant discourse completely on its head, casting Whites as devils and Blacks as the superior race in the divine order. However, a majority of African-Americans opted for integration. Demanding that the principle of "equality for all before God" be transposed into social relations, Black Christians, during the 1960s, called for an end to segregation in churches and other public places.

Renewing acquaintance with lunar cults or those devoted to the Mother Goddess, some feminists followed a similar path in separating from Christianity. But many women, disenchanted by an excessively male-oriented theology and sexist church practices, chose to put forward the concept of a gender-free God rather than one who was feminized. Far from endorsing the thesis that the daughters of Eve are the primary source of evil for man, these new activists recalled that, in the Catholic Church at least, two thirds of the practitioners were women. Thus, collectives like "*l'Autre parole*" in Québec offer a spiritual alternative to women through militant work within the institution. Sometimes these aspirations are satisfied, at least if one judges by the decision of the Anglican Church in 1992 to accept the ordination of women.

If has often been said that while the Catholic hierarchy alienated itself from women in the late twentieth century, it had already lost the working class in the nineteenth century. Not only did Rome champion the privileges of the nobility by condemning the liberalism of the Enlightenment and the revolutionary heritage of 1789, thus benefitting the Ancien Régime, but it then took decades before it was moved by the often extreme misery to which the Industrial Revolution, conducted without consideration for social costs, had reduced a great many proletarian families.[3]

The more or less circumscribed suspicion now displayed by the Vatican regarding liberation theologians and Third World Christians whose social involvement seeks to improve the plight of underprivileged populations and victims of dictatorship is reminiscent of Rome's reaction to the problems of workers a century ago. But instead of leaving the Church, modern Catholic activists, like many women, simply choose to disregard the Vatican's directives.

The situation is very similar for homosexuals. While many resign themselves to leaving the ranks of "universal" religions, which give them no other choice than to "live in sin" or submit to perpetual abstinence, others have tried to remain, hoping that their patience will be rewarded by wresting a few concessions. Thus, like Franciscan liberation theologian Leonardo Boff, who left the priesthood after twenty-five years, Jesuit John J. McNeill long endeavoured to advance the reflection on the condition of homophiles in the Church, despite Vatican censure, before resolving the contradiction by leaving. This reflection has largely involved the application of historical exegesis to the Scriptures. Taking up the questions asked thirty years ago by the Anglican D.S. Bailey (1955), contemporary researchers are casting doubt on the condemnatory interpretation given to certain biblical passages. Thus, the transgression of which Sodom and Gomorrah were accused was only classified as homosexuality later in the Judaic tradition (in the last century before Christ, during the period when the Jews were in contact with the Greeks); in earlier centuries, the inhabitants of the two destroyed cities had been charged with excessive arrogance and inhospitality (McNeill, 1976, 72–4). As for the major texts of the Apostle Paul that were supposed to deal with the question,[4] there is obvious confusion over their interpretation, if one judges by the number of different versions or translations (at least nine) that have been proposed (Ménard, 1982, 80).

Whatever the distortions that may have affected certain passages of the Old and New Testaments concerning sodomy, the awareness that homosexuality is a way of thinking and feeling more than a way of behaving is relatively recent in history (dating from the nineteenth century). Thus, taking into account the knowledge acquired in the past several years with regard to sexual preferences, and strengthened by the fact that God himself created them the way they are, gays decided to join the ranks of religious groups that opened their doors to them (the Quakers and the United Church, among others) or to continue to be part of mainstream traditions while creating parallel communities. In North America these include Dignity for Catholics, Integrity for Episcopalians, and Naches for Jews.

Regardless of the group to which they belong, dominated individuals who remain believers demand more meaningful participation in religions whose universalism was often limited to propagating the concept of a God to whom the dominator always lent his features. Though some established hierarchies are increasingly resistant to change, the rampart of ancient certainties has been breached, and it has become more difficult for the official authorities to impose the belief that the path to perfection must be steeper for some categories of people than for others.

As demonstrated regarding the discourse on maternal "instinct" or the religious condemnation of homosexuality, the centuries-old constraints imposed on the oppressed, when placed in a historical context, often lose the character of irreducible "laws." By the yardstick of time, theories, even when defended in the name of God or Nature, are quickly exposed for what they really are: the product of a specific culture legitimized by allegedly indisputable authorities.

For this mystification to be possible, however, it was necessary that the dominator put forward History itself as the ordering principle, on the same basis as God or Nature, and seize control of the historical discourse for a long time. In the discourse presented *in the name of* History, the oppressed were portrayed as *anonymous* forces of evil or decadence, at work throughout Time. On the other hand, in the discourse *on* History, the only *agent* whose name and exploits were worth reporting was the dominator himself. The discourse on history and the discourse in the name of history go hand in hand. The absence of the dominated as subject, and the parallel, hidden influence attributed to them by the dominant hero, make it possible to exclude victims from power while holding them responsible for the disasters that have occurred. Thus, even if he exercises sole control over society, the oppressor can exempt himself from any guilt. Not only is the fiction of the malevolent role of the dominated constantly maintained, but the positive contribution that they have provided, against all odds, is itself ignored.

Exiled by universal evolution to a timeless limbo, the groups in whom such historical amnesia has been induced must depend on the dominator to obtain the meaning of their condition. Those who have no history cannot claim to "make" history; without a past, it is difficult to shape the present and the future. One of the primary concerns of the oppressed as they move toward emancipation is to restore their presence in the framework of time.

For nearly all dominated groups, this approach is the inevitable condition of ending alienation, since knowledge of their history is the sole guarantee for reappropriation of their identity. Only youth, perhaps, escapes this logic, since it is characteristic of this age group to believe that history begins with them and that they can remake the world without the embarrassing burden of tradition (Silverstein, 1973, 6). Youth is also special in that it is the basis of a temporary identity. Because youth comes at the beginning of life, it creates an overall impression that the universe is new and original; but because it is also ephemeral, the only forms of solidarity it creates are immediate.

Thus, with the exception of youth, dominated groups see the development of their collective memory as a necessary condition of their liberation. However, a major challenge must be met, since they sometimes have to find and even identify the sources of their history. These sources, by definition, are rarely official or, having initially nourished the dominant saga, do not automatically come to mind as the possible basic material of a more critical narrative. To reconstruct the historical discourse, the dominated must often, at the same time, reinvent methodology.

This task, the product of long and patient effort, does not accommodate readily to the victims' pressing needs to blaze the still shadowy trail of their emancipation. Therefore, one of the first quests will often be to seek out the names of important figures in their affinity group, in whom they can find heroes.

The case of homosexuals is particularly illustrative of this need. Public opinion often categorizes them as effeminate men, and thus as cowards. Disregarding the prejudice that this equation reveals regarding the character of women, homophiles will be glad to reclaim warriors as "virile" as Alexander the Great, Julius Caesar, Richard the Lion-hearted, or the Prince de Condé. They will compile whole biographical dictionaries to highlight the rich contribution of gay women and men in the fields of art, literature, and philosophy.[5]

Persons coping with mental illness will derive some comfort in finding themselves in the company of Robert Schumann, Gérard de Nerval, Vincent Van Gogh, Friedrich Nietzsche, and Gustav Mahler. The physically handicapped will take pride at the achievements, against all odds, of an epileptic Julius Caesar, a deaf Ludwig Von Beethoven, or a Franklin D. Roosevelt afflicted with poliomyelitis. Others will question the very notion of handicap. Who is more infirm, after all: the quadriplegic who paints with his mouth and the blind man who has no trouble finding his way in the dark, or the tennis player who is already "finished" at age thirty and the smoker who is out of breath after merely climbing a flight of stairs?

Despite its inoffensive and sometimes even slightly ridiculous nature, the quest for heroes is laden with challenges to the established view of things. It is a challenge to the dominator's pretensions to unique superiority, of course, but it is also a challenge to the very concept of a model. Why, for example, should a one-legged amputee emulate one of his peers who hurtles down a mountain on a single ski, when an individual benefiting from all his limbs does not necessarily feel like practising this sport? Is it imperative that a septuagenarian who wants to stay active and alert become a long-distance runner or an artist of genius? Not everyone is Pablo Picasso, Nadia Boulanger, or Pablo Casals, and if a person of thirty is not asked to demonstrate his or her strength or speed, why should people of seventy have to prove their endurance? The right to equality means the right to be average.

As they hesitantly reappropriate their identity, the oppressed, by the mistakes they make, will be drawn into reinventing the concept of universality or reconstructing the past. Founded on an ever-broadening knowledge, the logic of their own cause will gradually give rise to the need to go beyond the search for a few famous names and join the official mainstream of history. New sections will be added to the traditional accounts of long-known events as established authors finally make room in their reflections for groups whose very existence had always been ignored.

This small place in the official histories will most often remain marginal. A "cultural" chapter, for example, will be added or juxtaposed to the "real" history, which, for the majority, will continue to be the unfolding of political and economic facts. This cultural chapter will also serve as a grab bag, along with some information on the intellectual and artistic works of a period, for brief comments on social groups, ethnic or racial minorities, regions of a country, women, and youth.[6]

This is why the dominated will have no other choice than to write their own history. Having taken a wide lead over other oppressed groups in the struggle against oppression, theorists and practitioners interested in social classes began, in the nineteenth century, to propose a new historical approach. First undertaken in the context of Marxist analysis, this reappraisal continued in the twentieth century with the "new history," more concerned, for example, with the plight of the twenty million people who lived in seventeenth-century France than with the life of Louis XIV alone.

Having begun their work more recently, researchers of other dominated groups have endeavoured, for some time, either to explore specific historical lines of approach (by theme, by country, by period) or to propose the beginnings of a synthesis of the comprehensive evolution of their particular community. There is an awareness that, apart from long-term intellectual enterprises, there is a need to create practical channels for the reflections of non-academics and other thinkers. Pioneering works of this kind also have the merit of countering, to some extent, the traditional ideas that official "science" continues to convey about the victims of history. The twofold objective set by Bernard Assiniwi in his history of the Native Peoples of Upper and Lower Canada, *Histoire des Indiens du Haut et du Bas Canada*, is valid for all oppressed groups:

To the readers of this book. Whether you are an Indian like me by blood or by choice, that which follows concerns you directly, because it is very important that *you know what you are*! If you are of European descent, this also concerns you directly because it is high time that *you know who I am*! (1973, I, 7)

The farther research advances, the more critical it will become. By endeavouring to rediscover an ignored past and correct the prevailing errors of perception about various oppressed groups, researchers ultimately challenge the very processes that allowed *their history* to be destroyed or falsified, and the structures responsible for their exclusion *from history*.

The relative absence of the dominated from the field of art, for example, is more a measure of their oppression than of their alleged inferiority. The fact that the agents of a tradition that excluded them can now blame the victims for the invisibility that these very agents maintained indicates the efficiency of an oppressive machinery that is still intact. Thus, while women gain from discovering the names of their sisters who wrote, painted, or composed music in centuries past, it is no less crucial that they know the reasons invoked by male critics for relegating these female artists to obscurity, and identity the practices that have had the effect, when this was not their declared purpose, of denying these women access to creative outlets.

The bias of the critic is especially obvious in the double standard applied in the evaluation of certain paintings. Works initially praised when they were attributed to men suddenly met with reservations once their female origin was known. This was the case for one portrait (of Marco di Vescovi) originally believed to be the work of Tintoretto, before it was discovered that his daughter Marietta had painted it (Hess and Baker, 1973, 45–6). A similar fate was reserved for the paintings of Judith Leyster and Constance Charpentier, originally attributed to Frans Hals and David respectively. After being judged "perfect" and "unforgettable," the "Portrait of Charlotte du Val-d'Ognes" suddenly betrayed its "cleverly concealed weaknesses" and the "subtle artifices" of a "feminine spirit" when it appeared, after 1951, that Constance Charpentier had painted it rather than David himself (Parker and Pollock, 1981, 8, 106).

The same phenomenon occurred in literature and music. Books by Rosamund Lehman, Elizabeth Bowen, or Anaïs Nin were qualified by male critics as "thin," "insignificant," or "futile," when they were not accused of being "hysterical" (Foster, 1975, 351). The psychoanalyst Otto Rank summed up this type of thinking when he told Anaïs Nin that "when the neurotic woman gets cured, she becomes a woman. When the neurotic man becomes cured, he becomes an artist" (in Russ, 1984, 14). Forgetting (or ignoring) the works of Anna Magdalena Wülken-Bach, Fanny Mendelssohn-Hensel, and Clara Wieck-Schumann, one critic, who believed that the "absence" of women from the field of musical composition should be attributed to their over-emotionalism, proposed as definitive proof of their inability the fact that no woman has ever succeeded in joining the ranks of the best male composers "when she has had the opportunity" (in Neuls-Bates, 1982, 207–9).

By studying the institutional machinery of cultural life, researchers have shown that access to official channels of artistic production was most often closed, even prohibited, to women. Thus, not having the symbolic tools provided by instruction in Latin (reserved for men) in the age of Shakespeare, Englishwomen had to wait until non-traditional literary genres (such as the novel) developed in the nineteenth century for their writings to be published (in McConnell-Ginet et al., 1980, 208–18). Similarly, in the fine arts, women did not have the right for three centuries (starting in the Renaissance) to paint nudes. Until the nineteenth century, their portraits, landscapes, and still lifes figured as minor genres in relation to the historical tableaux prized by the modern age. French and English women were even openly excluded from art academies in the eighteenth century (Parker and Pollock, 1981, 27–35).

Similar constraints existed in music. Women were forbidden to sing in church choirs, and those who worked in the secular field were required, from the time of the Counter-Reformation, to give way to the castrati of the Italian opera. They also had to wait until the late-nineteenth century to obtain the right to use "non-feminine" instruments (because these "deformed" their bodies or facial expressions) (Neuls-Bates, 1982, xi–xv). On the other hand, their being barred from positions as orchestra conductors and opera directors, or as choirmasters in the courts and churches, made it impossible for them to compose elaborate works, not to speak of the fact that access to conservatories and orchestras as ordinary students and performers was closed to them, sometimes into the twentieth century.

The explicit marginalization suffered by women in the creative field, and the unjust fate often reserved for the works of those who did manage to break in, are revealing in terms of the general fate of most dominated groups. By controlling the production of works of art, the dominator also ensured that an ideal image of himself and a stereotyped portrait of the oppressed were presented. He remained both the sole *creator* and the prime *model*.

Little by little, new historical investigation has undermined the foundations of this claim to universal superiority. In dismantling the machinery of this long mystification, the oppressed are shedding light on some of the remote causes of their current inferior status. Gradually the pieces of an immense jigsaw puzzle are being assembled, their arrangement corresponding ever less to the unbalanced unity of official history. Under the pressure of progress in more serious critical research, the hitherto accepted meaning of society's evolution is being reconsidered, and new patterns of force are being mapped to orient future syntheses.

If the criteria of artistic creation or representation have been strongly dependent on the established powers in a given period, there is reason to assume that the questions and answers of researchers in the search for truth have been modulated in turn by the influence of their environment.

Not only do the various disciplines of Learning have a history, but they also take place *in* history. The discoveries of scientists and the theories they develop to account for the natural universe are almost all presented as absolutes, with knowledge seeming to progress *logically* from truth to truth, rather than heeding concerns that arise from the context. The oppressed who have had to suffer the conclusions of the researchers of the dominant group will gain from restoring them to their proper place in *chronological* Time.

This is the only way that the oppressed will be able to follow the meanderings of certain branches of science, which, like craniometry, have sometimes disappeared after being discredited. In following the thread of history, the oppressed will also perceive the permanence of the desire to justify domination, a permanence manifested through the use of existing sciences (genetics, psychometry) or the creation of new sciences (sociobiology).

It is no accident, for example, that racial science was born in the nineteenth century. The century of imperialism, the rise of national rivalries in Europe itself, and the opposition to slavery in the New World (Stepan, 1982, x) required a foundation for the idea of the superiority of the ascendant powers, that of Whites in general, and of the Nordic or Germanic populations in particular.

After the American Civil War, it was the principle of segregation, rather than that of a henceforth impossible slavery, to which the "research" of that era endeavoured to give substance. Largely on the basis of this research, the American courts decided to declare compulsory separation of the races to be constitutional in the United States (Newby, 1967, 19–61).

Between 1850 and 1950, the fundamental outlook of racial science would remain the same, based on the conviction acquired, even before the results of the research were obtained, that there was an innate inequality of human "types" dating back to prehistory (Stepan, 1982, xx–xxi, 171–8). The policy of extermination of "inferior" types, to which this conviction would lead under the Nazi regime, had the effect of discrediting racial science, however. A new and more critical science, population genetics, succeeded it, placing greater emphasis on the genetically unique character of the *individual*, as well as on the sharing of a specific genotypical distribution by certain *statistical* (and not racial) categories of subjects.

But in the wake of the challenge hurled at the established order in recent decades by certain dominated groups, and in the context of an economic instability that has persisted since the mid-1970s, a reaction is emerging in the established power structure, seeking to legitimize its latest denial of equality by again basing it on science. Thus, the New Right in France and the National Front in England draw upon the postulates of sociobiology to justify their theories about the differences between the races. Sociobiology is also invoked by some

American adherents of traditional values with regard to marriage and the family. Created in 1975 in the United States, this science uses animal analogies to interpret human behaviour (sometimes making connections with a behaviour as specifically human as adultery, for example), endeavouring, as if by chance, to justify the old division of labour between the genders at the very time when American feminism is at its most militant. Psychoanalysis, which itself sought to root the traditional roles of women and men in scientific criteria, made its appearance at the turn of the twentieth century, a particularly tumultuous period for women's demands. The fact that this wave of the women's movement faded away in the 1920s was probably not unconnected to Freudianism's incipient success in public opinion.

Already recruited in the past century to sanction the hierarchical nature of the relations between races and between genders, science has also been used by those who aspired to maintain a none-egalitarian class system. Again in this case, the historical context inspired a supposedly "objective" concern. Thus, in mid-twentieth-century England, the vogue for Cyril Burt's psychometrical work on the innate character of intelligence was linked, in part, to the vigorous opposition in that country to a particularly rigid social hierarchy. Then, while technological upheavals followed in rapid succession, the Americans Jansen and Hernstein believed that they should link the (nonetheless widespread) fact of unemployment to a hereditary tendency in families (in Block and Dworkin, 1976, 505).

Reconsidered in a historical perspective, scientific theories arguing inequality between groups most often appear to be the product of the dominator's concern with legitimizing a type of relationship that is to his advantage. He benefits from this relationship, not only by preserving his power over the weak, but by maintaining intact the fiction of his arrogated right to pretend to be the universal model. Relative in time, the content and mode of his defense of this fiction may also vary in a given period, depending on the authors and schools of thought involved, both within the same discipline and from one discipline to another.

Thus, although animal behaviour serves as a criterion for sociobiologists and certain primatologists in evaluating human conduct, the conclusions will differ depending on whether or not they confirm the implicit postulate of the dominator's superiority. Because it appears that the male is more aggressive and the female remains more attached to the group *among the primates*, women are supposed to accept man's domination *in human society*. On the other hand, when it seems that human beings are *different* from animals, as in their stronger sexual desire[7] or in the possibility that the female orgasm is exclusively human,[8] some scientists will still conclude that women exist to serve men's pleasure. Apart from its being contested that only human females have orgasms, it is increasingly apparent that the degree of dominance varies from one primate species to another, and the distinction between the genders of the same species is primarily one of strategy rather than of essence. There is also reason to ask what principle requires that the habits of "our animal friends" (themselves vulnerable to the influence of the environment) should dictate the behaviour of human beings, at any price. If it is so important to find "natural" reasons for one gender to necessarily serve the other, why not find them among humans themselves, and require men "limited" to a single orgasm to make themselves available to a woman "capable of several" (Masters and Johnson, 1979, 207)?

The same double standard applies in the case of homophiles. Indeed, it is surprising that examples of frequent homosexual activity observed in several species of mammals are not emphasized as strongly to counter the oppression of gays as the supposed evidence of primate gender inequality is used to justify the oppression of women.

The paradigmatic value assigned (with the fluctuations we have seen) to animal behaviour by sociobiologists and certain primatologists is scarcely more obvious than that which anthropologists attribute to prehistoric human society. The apparent fascination with the myth of origins stems mainly from the thesis that man's domination of woman originated in the control exercised over primitive groups by the male Hunter of large animals. Apart from the fact that this theory is just as unprovable as that of the feminists, who believe they can detect the signs of an initial matriarchy centred on the female Gatherer of plants (Rosaldo and Lamphere, 1974, 2–7), one wonders what relevance such a type of social organization can have to modern civilization.

Though recognizing the hypothetical nature of the factors on which he based his theories, Freud himself postulated the existence of fatherhood as a primordial social institution.[9] Psychoanalysis also posited man as the universal model. Thus, the Oedipus complex and penis envy in women were supposed to be found in all populations on the planet. Developed within the context of Viennese society at the turn of the twentieth century, the foundations of Freudian theory posited that every woman in the world envied the male penis and sought to compensate for this "deprivation" through childbearing. But just as the multi-orgasmic capacity of woman was hidden by the dominant male culture to the profit of the myth of male technical superiority, so might the impression that a woman was deficient without a phallus betray the fear of someone who had one that he could lose. Some feminists, themselves interested in psychoanalysis, began to wonder whether the problem was not completely reversed. Instead of the woman envying the male penis, perhaps the man covets the female womb and breasts. Since the womb and the breasts allow the woman to *have the child*, the man might well resent the enormous symbolic value of this "unshareable female enjoyment" (Olivier, 1980, 180).[10] He then would minimize the importance of childbirth, postulating instead that the *woman* desires to possess what *he* has. In this way, he would ward off his own discomfort at being excluded from pregnancy and his fundamental fear of castration. In attributing the intention to the woman of wanting to take his penis, the man would assure himself that he really has one, because *she* wants it (Irigaray, 1974, 58–61). His own image would be reflected through the "defect" from which she allegedly suffers, and ultimately he could project *his own* narcissistic tendencies onto her. (Indeed, Freud attributed a more highly developed narcissism to women than to men!)

Finally, Freudianism shared a propensity with many other western psychiatric theories to isolate mental illness from environmental conditioning and see its etiology and symptoms as universal constants. Yet such an approach itself is specific to the White, western middle classes (Marsella and White, 1982). If major psychoses actually have a universal character, their diagnosis and treatment, and even the behaviour they induce in their subjects, vary in different cultures. The basic philosophy surrounding mental illness is fundamentally different in the Orient and in the West. Since western culture is focused on the individual rather than on society, a profound dichotomy exists between the body and the environment, between the body and the mind, and between emotion and cognition, a dichotomy revealed, in part, by the separation of the sciences that study these elements (neurology, psychiatry, medicine). In the same way, mental balance is perceived in the West as a *state* or a *conclusion* rather than as the *process* understood by Oriental thought. Even in the West, concepts of mental illness differ from one country to another. Thus, the viewpoint of American professionals is closer to that of their compatriots than to that of their German colleagues, for example. While Americans, in general, often see the resolution of illness as a matter of will, most Germans distinguish emotional problems, which can be cured, from madness, which is supposed to be incurable (Townsend, 1978, 9–11).

The "objective" facts of mental illness are difficult to separate from the values prevalent in a society. Indeed, it is rather important to know which suffers from the greater affliction: the individual, or the environment in which this person lives. Very critical of the establishment, the psychiatrist R.D. Laing observed, for example, that a man who declares that human beings are machines will be considered a great scholar, while an individual who says that he *is* a machine will be judged "depersonalized"; a girl who fears that she has an atomic bomb inside her will be treated for "hallucination," but politicians who threaten to blow up thousands of people on the planet will appear to be reasonable (1965, 12). So what is the real nature of the illness to be treated: the false identity acquired by an individual or the false realities to which this person is often asked to adapt?

Once the dominator's criteria for his ideal type of humanity are known, scarcely any foundation remains to his pretense to embody the universal model. Invoked frequently for centuries, the "laws" dictated by God, Nature, or History in support of these claims are exposed as much less irreducible when they are studied relative to time and space. And the imperatives of Art and Science seem to have a strange tendency to fluctuate.

To rejoin the realm of the universal, the dominated must not only rediscover the path to their identity and a sense of their own capabilities; at the same time, they must put the dominator in his proper place as one specificity among others in the vast array of human diversity. But to end a specific group's claim to represent the entirety of an ideal humanity or to stand at the apex of a pyramid of unequal identities, the victims must not only expose the character of the difference between human beings, which is relative by definition, they must also shatter the immense illusion (if not the imposture) that these absolute distinctions can be based on *objective facts*.

The verdict of the experts, subject to modulation by the interests of the powers it implicitly serves or by the prejudices of the dominant discourse that has shaped it, may seek, at best, to be honest and lucid, but it must never be accepted as objective. To the extent that it is possible to apprehend the truth, knowledge is acquired not so much by accumulating verified facts as by the continual shifts in the perception of a polymorphous reality. Since this is especially true of social relations, where the object is in constant motion, expert subjectivities will be shown to be as varied as group identities proved to be relative.

Competing Subjectivities

The disciplines seeking to give meaning to human relations cannot in every case invoke an impossible scientific absolute to impose definitive conclusions. Between the questions they ask and the theories they develop in response, researchers reveal the outside influences to which they are vulnerable, even in the type of facts they choose to observe.

In this sense, there is reason to say that a "science of the moment" exists (Achard *et al.*, 1977, 281), and that a fact is always "someone's fact." A fact has no intrinsic value. Just as one can doubt the reality of a sound if nobody is there to hear it, so is a fact relevant only to the extent that an observer has taken the trouble to note it.

It is not enough that a fact be true for it to stand as evidence or example. Its relationship with *all* other facts must be clearly established. This is why a fact is never neutral, because, as true as it may be intrinsically, it must have been *meaningful* to someone first. It may have meaning to one person but not necessarily to another, or to both but not necessarily in the same way.

Thus, the competing judgments of various specialists can only be subjective, especially since they vary within the same field of production of meaning (law, science, religion), from one period to another, or from one milieu to another.

Those who, solely due to their identity, have been accused of crime, disease, and moral transgression for centuries will have to emancipate themselves from this fiction of absolute objectivity. If the imposture of the universal model dictates the notion of the intrinsic inferiority of the dominated and their necessary subordination to the oppressor, the illusion of impartiality allows the dominator to monopolize the discourse and thus maintain the conditions of both inferiority and subordination indefinitely.

Victims on the road to liberation must break out of this vicious circle and see this "objectivity" as merely the name given to the dominator's own subjectivity. But just as it might seem preferable for victims to counter the oppressor's aspirations to universality by revealing the diversity of interdependent identifies rather than trying to take over the oppressor's claims, it may also be more advisable to recognize subjectivity in knowledge as inevitable, rather than claiming that they, in turn, are the only group capable of abiding by the facts.

A number of theorists from dominated groups have understood this and quickly have given up the illusion of objectivity. Although they remain fully committed to fairness and rigour, they show their colours from the outset: "I did my best to present fairly all the evidence for and against each thesis I dealt with. I never deliberately omitted or distorted any evidence, even though it was contrary to my convictions," wrote theologian John J. McNeill in his book on homosexuality (1976, 23). But for those who might accuse him of *pro*-gay "partisanship," he added:

However, even if there is an element of truth in this criticism, I would still feel justified in my approach. For too long all we have seen is writing and counselling biased in the other direction. One of my goals is to open up a new dialogue by pushing the dialogical pendulum a bit in the opposite direction. (Ibid.)

This reliance on the *fait accompli*, which shifts the "happy medium" by pushing back the "extremes," has been adopted by other spokespersons of dominated groups. In the preface to *Asylums*, his famous analysis of psychiatric hospitals, sociologist Erving Goffman proposed to reestablish a long-shattered balance by immediately declaring that he tended to favour the patient's approach: "For this last bias I partly excuse myself by arguing that the imbalance is at least on the right side of the scale, since almost all professional literature on mental patients is written from the point of view of the psychiatrist" (1961, x).

Anti-establishment thinkers have a keen sense of the oppressor's false objectivity, and sometimes deliberately demand the defence of the victim. In the words of one Canadian historian of Native origin, for example: "Why should I, an *Indian*, be objective, when historians belonging to other ethnic groups have never been objective?" (Assiniwi, 1973, I, 11). The Tunisian writer Tahar Ben Jelloun, who worked as a psychological counsellor to North African workers in France, even claimed "the right to subjectivity" as a form of the right to be different (1977, 9). Feminist Dale Spender, who made no secret that she was defending a cause, took a similar line: "As women's resources are appropriated by men ... then all I am prepared to 'supply' is a positive portrayal of women – a commodity not much in 'demand' in a patriarchal society" (1983, 19). She went even further in putting forward the following principle: "My 'criticisms' [of other women] are in private until the view of a woman carries the same weight as a man's" (ibid., 738).

Most of the time such positions are set forth in the preface, though sometimes they appear right in the title. Thus, to mark the futility of claims to consider all facts *objectively*, an article on women by Québec sociologist Danielle Juteau was entitled *"Visions partielles, visions partiales"* (Partial Visions, in both senses of the term) (in *Les femmes dans la sociologie*, 1981). The partisans of the dominant discourse proceed no differently, larding their prefaces with references to the "facts," "objectivity," and "scientific rigour."

The preoccupation of theorists from dominated groups with the inevitable nature of subjectivity is reflected in the way language is employed. Systematic use of the first person is recommended to individuals and groups as a means of affirming their identity. In addition, especially for feminists, a constant shifting between "I" or "we," on the one hand, and "they," on the other, is proposed as a way of reducing the distance between the author-subject and the community to which this person continues to belong at the very time that this community is being studied.[11]

The subjective positions set forth in the oppressed's discourse are also intended to be relative. As analysis matures and as research goes into greater depth, the pluralism of viewpoints within the emancipation movement becomes increasingly evident. Anxious to avoid the false security of total and absolute truths, a number of thinkers endeavour to emphasize not only the multiplicity of ways of living the same identity but the many modes of thought and action that can be used to defend them.

Several different Lefts (Communist, socialist, social democratic) aspire to do battle for the interests of the underprivileged classes, and there are also various ways (pro-sovereignty, autonomist, regionalist) to serve a national cause. In the same way, there is no more uniformity in homosexuality and the ways it is asserted (if only because of the differences between gays and lesbians) than in the types of female sensibilities or the practices adopted by militant women to make their views prevail. Just as it is more accurate to talk of *feminisms*, one can evoke the multiple reality of *homosexualities*.

The title of one Québec work on youth reveals this tendency to avoid the trap of essentialist generalization. *Jeunesses: des illusions tranquilles* (1986) (Varieties of Youth: Quiet Illusions) shows that even the category of age now escapes monolithic definition. Finally, although the diversity of their conditions should be immediately obvious, a growing number of handicapped people are demanding that they no longer be perceived as a homogeneous group.

A movement may have many diverse tendencies without being labelled "divided." The oppressed thus have reason to hope that they will not be confined to a new identity ghetto, barely after emerging from the old one.

Once the victim's subjectivity is assertd as a means of liberation, and once it is recognized that there are a variety of ways of being or of taking militant action, the victim's task has only just begun. Because the oppressor's discourse will continue to claim impartiality, the dominated may appear all the more to admit the scope of their own biases by attacking this objectivity as a myth. Theorists and practitioners of contestation must target the examples of subjectivity that are central to the dominant logic and expose the various ambiguities or contradictions between principle and practice to which they give rise.

What is special about the dominant discourse is that it has an answer for everything, because it constantly changes its level of coherence. What is true today will not necessarily be true tomorrow, and the same argument used to prove the superiority of one group will also serve to emphasize that of another. This extreme versatility in the production of meaning is the doing both of experts and of the lay public, as the verdicts of authority and the dictates of folk "wisdom" often reinforce each other.

There is one constant, however, that can be detected immediately in the established discourse: its dynamics always favour the dominator. Regardless of the method or process, proof of the oppressor's superiority inevitably bursts forth. This does not require deliberate intent, but the scale always tips in the same direction.

These changes in the level of coherence can operate in various ways in the established discourse. For example, they may arise within the same strategy, or the same logical element may float between different strategies without alteration. Michel Foucault attempted to take this type of artifice into account by invoking the concept of the *tactical flexibility of the discourse* (1976, I, 132–5).

For example, awareness of an impossible dilemma can be seen in the following testimony of a hospital worker, sympathetic to the cause of psychiatric patients:

The patient no longer knows how to behave: if he doesn't communicate, he is said to be suspicious, but if he asks questions or exerts pressure, he's a rebel. If he asks to sign a refusal of treatment, he will be persuaded that he has problems. (*Solidarité-psychiatrie*, 1984, 146)

The position of the mentally ill appears to be innately ambiguous. Often accused of "imagining their illness" by non-professionals, their depressive state nonetheless will be sufficient reason to deny them certain responsibilities. Though considered an illness by experts, their handicap sometimes will be "treated" with punitive methods, or their reluctance to accept therapy will be perceived as evidence of bad intentions on their part.

There are even cases, such as homosexuality, in which the "illness" is categorized as an offence,[12] and the patient and the criminal end up being confused in the eyes of the authorities. While law declares homophilia to be "against nature," medicine is disturbed by its "contagious" influence. Yet can something that is against nature be contagious at the same time? A crime and an anomaly to legal and scientific experts, homosexuality is also defined as a sin. Thus, God, like Nature, is called upon to sanction homophobia. But those who invoke Leviticus to condemn homosexuals are indifferent to other passages of the same book of the Bible prescribing ritual sacrifices and adherence to certain dietary practices (Marmor, 1980, 18).[13] The abandonment of these observances is readily attributed to historical evolution, but, in the view of the censors, the prohibition of sodomy must remain intact.

Every level of the discourse on homosexuality is a minefield. Like Jews, who constitute an invisible minority, lesbians and gays are accused of "being everywhere." But if they dare to come out of the closet and present themselves as they really are, they are accused of "making an exhibition of themselves." The authorities spared no effort to catch them when the were forced into hiding. Before various laws adopted in the 1960s allowed consenting adults to have homosexual relations in private, the same police forces that hesitated to "violate" the privacy of the home in coming to the aid of battered women had no scruples about catching homosexuals in their homes.

The text of a law like the one long maintained by England concerning sodomy is very revealing of the tactical flexibility of the legal discourse. Except between 1781 and 1826 (a period marked by a decline in the number of guilty verdicts), this law did not required proof of penetration and the emission of semen to bring about a conviction (Weeks, 1983, 12–14). Assaulted women had a heavier burden of proof in situations of this kind, since legislators and magistrates were more zealous against sodomites than against rapists.

Though more ignored, lesbians also paid the price of the tactical flexibility of the dominant discourse. This holds true particularly for the medical discourse. More than their heterosexual sisters, they were accused of *both* narcissism and penis envy, since psychoanalysts seemed to find no contradiction in claiming that they wanted to resemble a man *and* to seek their own image through the body of another woman. Popular opinion is just as quick to make such judgments. Indeed, a curious myth circulates that lesbians are "great in bed" and "the only thing they need is a good screw" (by a man). If a lesbian is raped, the same conventional "wisdom" will judge that "she needed it." If her heterosexual sister has suffered a similar fate without "needing it," she was probably "looking for it." And if this woman wasn't "looking for it," then obviously she was trying to play "hard to get."

The double standard applied to a woman when she figures as a victim will be even more detrimental when Divine or human justice sees her as the *author* of a sin or a crime. The example of abortion is particularly revealing. Apart from the fact that a long history of involuntary sterilization of poor, handicapped, or racial minority women in North America has never aroused the authorities' eloquent indignation, there is good reason to wonder what logic drives a President of the United States, whose advisers calculated the chances of a "limited" nuclear victory with twenty million dead, or "pro-life" activists, who set fire to clinics, make death threats against female patients, and kill doctors to oppose abortion in the name of the right to life.

The position of the Catholic Church – which maintained excommunication for abortion after the Canon Law reform of 1983 and in its *Official Catechism* in 1992 – is even more incomprehensible if one recalls that such radical condemnations were not applied in the past against Nazi war criminals (Hitler and Himmler were of Catholic origin) or today against Mafia killers, IRA terrorists, or Latin American death squads that kill street children.

Moreover, the entire Catholic viewpoint on women places them in an insurmountable dilemma. In November 1980, John Paul II said he saw the role of wife and mother as the "specific vocation" of women. However, he later stated (in a December 1983 speech to American bishops) that "virginity in the name of the Kingdom of Heaven better expresses the gift of Christ to the Father in our name." Yet since motherhood, the *specific* vocation of women, necessarily requires sexual activity, should it be concluded that the aspiration to virginity is contrary to the nature of women? This contradiction finds its perfect expression in the model of Mary,[14] whom the Church has put forward for centuries as a woman who is *both* virgin and mother. This model is all the more unattainable in that dogma maintains that Mary not only bore a child without first experiencing sexual relations, but that she herself was born without the taint of original sin. Nevertheless, this is the privileged ideal to which the Church wishes women to submit. On the eve of Jean Paul II's trip to Canada, in order to refute the demands of certain practising Catholic women for access to the priesthood, Paul-Emile Cardinal Léger affirmed: "When a woman tells me she would like to be a priest, I tell her that I would like to be the Immaculate Conception." The only problem is that while a man can become a priest, there is no way that a woman can aspire to an immaculate conception. Thus, a woman loses on both counts: she can neither be a priest nor without sin; she can be a virgin, of course, but this to some extent will be against her nature, or she can be a mother, thereby accepting inferior status.

Women long have been mothers without the Church encouraging them to seek sexual pleasure. Conjugal relations were imposed on them as a duty to be fulfilled in order to have children or to allow their husbands to "satiate the lusts of the flesh." But the performance of this duty, necessarily bound to women's specific vocation, was stained with venial sin, and their confessors often advised them not to take communion the next morning (Aubert, 1975, 63).

The same type of contradictory approach prevails in Orthodox Judaism, which considers women's menstrual blood to be impure because it is the sign that fertilization has not occurred, while refusing the mother the merit of fulfilling the commandment (*mitzvah*)[15] of conception because this might put her life in danger! Deriving more from specious argument than from the tactical flexibility of the discourse, another interpretation is that women have it better than men, since they have fewer responsibilities in the Jewish religion. This begs the question of whether the same logic dictates that the absolute ideal is simply to be a non-Jew.

In another example of the tactical flexibility of the dominant discourse on women, the female gender, considered to be the outstanding locus of "natural" determinisms, also embodied the misdeeds of Culture in the view of manly men of the nineteenth century, who were disgusted with civilization. Refined and delicate, women were also likened to the decadence of France, the metropolis, by the writers of the colonial school (Astier Loutfi, 1971, 110), while authors like Mark Twain and James Fenimore Cooper described male characters wholly committed to the conquest of the primitive "nature" of the American West, who were fleeing the softening influence of "society," as well as that of women (Pearson and Pope, 1981, 19).

Sometimes applied to the imaginary or symbolic order, the double standard has a very concrete reflection in the everyday experiences of women. The legal framework imposed on women's relationship with motherhood forced them to do the impossible. The same western society that, in the nineteenth century, exalted the role of the mother as an "angel of the hearth" refused her any real power over the child, reserving it for the father. But the same principle did not apply to responsiblity. In France, the Napoleonic Code, which considered a woman to be a minor and legally incompetent, nevertheless prescribed suits to determine the identity of the mother while prohibiting paternity suits (Dufrancatel, 1979, 169). Until late in the twentieth century, a woman could be convicted in France for abandoning her family (Callu, 1978, 262). In Québec, despite the respect officially professed for women's "innate" ability to care for young children, it was not until the late 1920s that a woman could be the legal guardian of a minor (Collectif Clio, 1982, 334).

Just as the nineteenth century put mothers on a pedestal while depriving them of power in the family, so women were encouraged to stay home, while at the same time society continued to adjust to their role as factory workers. This low-paid work profited bourgeois employers, who would have been offended to see it performed by "respectable" women (Murray, 1982, 5). Considered too frail to walk alone in the street when she belonged to "good society," a woman seemed strong enough to haul ore cars in the mines when she came from a working-class background.

In the treatment of the social question, as in others, the dominant discourse has learned to be versatile. "It is not [my opinion] which I have presented to the readers of this book, but the facts," wrote a French jurist in his work entitled *Essai sur l'inégalité* (Harouel, 1984, 10) (Essay on Inequality). According to the "facts" in question, the aristocracy of the Ancien Régime was forced to exploit the people's labour so that, freed of any material care, they could devote themselves to development of the intellectual and artistic works in which the West takes pride. "Culturally, inequality was thus infinitely more fertile than equality," the author concluded, claiming that "a small contingent of exceptionally intelligent or gifted children" from the popular classes (generally little inclined to matters of the mind) succeeded, in any case, in rising to the level of the powerful (ibid., 51–3).

This brief synthesis of social history, however, serves only to introduce the real thesis of *Essai sur l'inégalité*, which is to exalt economic neo-liberalism as the best *current* means of developing wealth. The "real question" should be very clear for the West: "Will we remain rich, or will we become poor again?" In addition to the problem of relations between classes, the book claims to settle the issue of relations between *countries*: industrialized countries and the Third World. After expressing his concern for presenting an "objective" analysis (ibid., 239) of the subject, the author endeavours not only to recall the previous benefits of colonization (medical progress, idea of an international order founded on justice), but to point out the dangers of *wealth* for the benefit of a hemisphere that supposedly has demanded western aid for too long: "While still having to seek it, the Third World should be well aware that raising the standard of living does not bring happiness" (ibid., 250).

Whether posed openly and shamelessly, or only revealed implicitly, the "only" question, the "real" question, almost always triggers a readjustment of the tactical presentation of the discourse by the property-owning classes. Thus, remedies that appeared unacceptable when they benefited one group will become very reasonable when another group benefits. The financial institutions and major corporations that today deplore the "excessive" generosity of the "welfare state" to the general public will find it very legitimate, for example, for Chrysler, Dome Petroleum, banks in western Canada, and American savings and loan associations to be kept afloat at the taxpayers' expense when they are in difficulty.

Even some religious authorities sanction the dual discourse in social matters. "The service of the priest is not the same as that of a doctor or social worker, nor of a politician or a trade unionist," declared John Paul II in an address to liberation theologians during his July 1980 trip to Brazil. Three years later, in Communist Poland, he defended the "innate" right of workers to form unions. This Pope, who encouraged his compatriots to engage in "unrelenting resistance to abusive domination," continued to preach "forgiveness" and "reconciliation" to the oppressed classes of Latin America, South Korea, and the Philippines.

Thus, the dominated are interchangeable pawns on the chessboard of power relations. The example of the Jews is well known: sometimes rejected as capitalists and sometimes as Bolsheviks, they have also been accused of being both at once (Teboul, 1977, 173-4). Similarly, homosexuals embodied capitalist decadence from the perspective of Soviet leaders, at the same time that they were a Communist fifth column to hardline right-wingers. No doubt because they are militants by definition, feminists are even more versatile: denounced as "agents of Communism" in the West and "agents of imperialism" in the East, they were labelled "a neocolonialist plot" in the Third World (Morgan, 1984, 4).

However, sometimes this game can be played on another level, with the same dominant group adopting opposite areas of reference to defend its privileges in a specific place. Thus, Québec anglophones attempted to resist measures to assert French as the predominant language in the 1970s by presenting themselves *alternately* as the linguistic majority in North America and as a Canadian minority equivalent to distressed francophones in other provinces. In the first case, they invoked the principles of democracy (majority rule) to impose their language; in the latter case, they claimed their right to be different in seeking to contain the expansion of French.

Blacks have long seen the double standard applied to their detriment. Experts very soon focused on their "case." Their degree of intelligence and level of mental health were particular objects of "observation." Thus, medical studies under the slaveholding regime saw the effect of an *innate* insensibility to civilization in the lower rate of mental illness that they claimed to find among Blacks, and then interpreted the supposed rise in this rate after the Civil War as the sign of a *constitutional* inability to adapt to freedom (Willie *et al.*, 1973, 30-9). This same type of judgment was applied to other racial groups.

Thus, for a time, Native North Americans were deemed to be too simple-minded to be crazy (ibid., 36). Westerners hardly believed otherwise when they treated the colonized as "children" who, according to the double standard, were brutes to be tamed or creatures *both* content with little and inclined to seek uncontrolled satisfaction of their needs (Astier Loutfi, 1971, 65; Memmi, 1972, 85).

In no case are the oppressed presented in a favourable light, and never are they really allowed any margin of control over their fate. What they are granted with one hand is taken away with the other. Victims are locked into an insoluble dilemma, which often leaves them no choice but the lesser of two evils. By operating on several fronts, the dominator ensures that he preserves his control of the dominated. Although sometimes spectacular, even his concessions will only be superficial.

When the United States reduced the age of majority from twenty-one to eighteen in 1971, thus giving the right to vote to part of the country's youth, it was a much with the intent of expanding the pool of recruits for the Vietnam War as of recognizing the maturity of its younger citizens. Not only were similar constitutional amendments proposed during the Second World War and the Korean War, but the amendment finally accepted in 1971 gave members of this age group only civil rights: they were still denied the right to control their own bodies (through the capacity to consent to treatment, for example) or their property (through the right to enter into contacts, among others) (Wilson, 1978, 22).

Whether it modulates the dictates of conventional wisdom or moulds the verdicts of experts, the tactical versatility of the discourse allows the dominator to retain control of power by controlling the discourse. Holding the majority or even, in some cases, a monopoly on the rights to decide the production of meaning, he can change the fundamental rules of his relations with the dominated as he wishes. The defence of his interests requires that the result always be the same: either he will win, or the dominated will lose.

To have any hope of emerging from their alienation, the victims have no choice but to dismantle the logic that systematically traps them. Changes in coherence must be pinpointed, and regular care must be taken to ensure that no double standard is applied. Such prudence should apply particularly to the views of authority: the subjectivity of the specialist is no less present just because it is unacknowledged.

Of all experts, scientists seem to have the firmest foundation in their protestations of objectivity and claims to respect the facts. Thus, the oppressed must give their closest scrutiny to the scientific discourse as they move toward emancipation. From this study, they will often realize that, in addition to sometimes flagrant contradictions, which again stem from tactical versatility, the dominant discourse poses more general problems of *method*, betraying the implicit biases of researchers. These biases may pertain to the criteria adopted in their approach and sometimes to the chosen object of study as well.

In other cases, *errors* are involved. These errors may be subtle or gross, involuntary or deliberate. The history of science is full of monumental blunders committed by influential people who were sure of their facts. Such errors have occurred in every era, with some of these luminaries believing, for example, that everything that existed to be discovered had already been discovered. This was the opinion of one of Emperor Vespasian's great military engineers, Julius Fontinus, in the first century of the Christian era. It would be raised anew by the director of the United States Patent Office in 1899 when he asked President McKinley to close that agency, arguing that everything that could be invented had already been invented (Morgan and Langford, 1981, 145; 64). At the end of the nineteenth century, in the midst of the great scientific boom generated by the Industrial Revolution, England's very prestigious Royal Society claimed to have sufficient evidence to declare that there was no future in radio, X-rays, or heavier-than-air flying machines (Morgan and Langford, 1981, 19, 116, 28). Even in the twentieth century, a winner of the Nobel Prize for physics (Robert Millikan) and a winner of the Nobel Prize for chemistry (Lord Rutherford) expressed disbelief in atomic energy. American Admiral William Leahy, an "explosives expert," denied the possibility of military use of the atom in 1945, telling President Truman, just before the Alamogordo test, that the bomb would not explode (ibid., 46, 145).

While it easy, with the benefit of hindsight, to have a good laugh at such blunders, the history of their repeated appearance is laden with warnings for non-experts who are tempted to lend unconditional credence to current scientific authorities. Tough scientific judgments should not be refused systematically, they should be examined with a critical eye. Recommended in the case of "exact" sciences, which do not always have immediate implications in people's lives, this reservation is all the more pertinent when there is a risk that research will have a direct influence on human relations.

It was relatively unimportant that physicists temporarily took the wrong path when they believed that they had finally established the structure of the atom in the late 1920s. But it was very serious indeed that, in the same period, under the influence of psychometricians who later admitted that they were wrong, laws were adopted barring allegedly inferior ethnic and racial groups from immigrating to America. Often entire generations have to pay the price for the mistaken ideas of a handful of scientists. The anthropologist Manouvrier criticized the conclusions of his former teacher, Paul Broca, deploring their disastrous effect on women, and his observation are valid for all categories of oppressed people:

> Women displayed their talents and their diplomas. They also invoked philosophical authorities. But they were opposed by *numbers* unknown to Condorcet or to John Stuart Mill. These [Broca's] numbers fell upon poor women like a sledgehammer and they were accompanied by commentaries and sarcasm more ferocious than the most misogynist imprecations of certain church fathers. The theologians had asked if women had a soul. Seven centuries later, some scientists were ready to refuse them a human intelligence. (In Gould, 1981, 26).

Broca's craniometry certainly fell into disrepute, but women of his period had plenty of time to pay the price. Their daughters and granddaughters had to reckon with the possibility that another "scientific" theory would come along to defend the same thesis of intrinsic female inferiority in some other way. At the turn of the twentieth century, anthropometry also attempted to demonstrate, with Cesare Lombroso, that like "savages" and children, women were akin to criminals. More inclined to vengeance, jealousy, and vanity, they supposedly did not have the same level of compensating tendencies as men, tendencies that would allow them, as much as men, to claim achievement of a balance between duties and rights, or between egoism and altruism (in Callu, 1978, 377). This "truth," obvious to Lombroso, would be called into question just as Broca's was (ibid., 383).

Other "facts" considered indubitable since the beginning of the century are strongly contested today. Research like that of Masters and Johnson or the Hite Report on women, for example, upset the Freudian certainties about the necessity for "real" women to achieve vaginal orgasm. Apart from the painful constraints that this dictate imposed on women for decades, it is astounding that people could believe that there was only one way to reach orgasm and that experts had the right to determine the degree of orthodoxy of the pleasures of an entire gender.

Psychoanalysis did not spare children any more than women in matters of sexuality. Freud's 1905 decision (taken up by most of his disciples) to ignore the reality of incest committed by parents, seeing it instead as the result of a child's *fantasy* (Miller, 1984), contributed to the denial of the sexual abuse to which children were victims, just as the silence of pediatricians made it possible to cover up physical violence against them.

By finally dealing with this question (in the past few years), psychologists and sociologists also cast doubt on certain "obvious facts" regarding homosexuality. Contrary to the common opinion that homosexuals are automatically inclined to pedophilia, it is now recognized that adults who molest children are most often heterosexuals who victimize *little girls*. Those who choose boys are not necessarily homosexuals themselves and the cases of lesbians who can be accused of this kind of behaviour are very rare (Scacco, 1982, 147). In addition to the fact that they have no contact with homosexuals, pedophiles will often be married men, even religious ones (Schofield, 1965, 149–50). Even sexual assault on an adult male by another man is committed more by heterosexuals than by homosexuals (Kempe, 1984, 39).

Other stereotypes concerning gays have proved to be unfounded when subjected to analysis. For example, there is the depiction of the homosexual as someone who almost inevitably is unhappy at age thirty of forty: left alone and depressed because he is perceived to be aging by his peers, he then preys on children. Yet a survey of elderly American homophiles not only challenged this thesis but discovered the existence of strong solidarity networks within this group and a lesser apprehension of social repression than among young people of the same tendency (Berger, 1982, 185–6). Similarly, a wider sociological study of American couples showed that, far from having a monopoly on non-egalitarian relationships (based on age or degree of wealth), as claimed by a certain literary and film tradition, lesbians are less involved in power relationships than other types of partners (female-male, male-male): whether in terms of work, money, sharing of duties, or sexuality, lesbian couples are less conditioned by the quest for power.[16]

Thus, a number of errors have been committed concerning the identity of dominated groups by experts who sometimes were the leading lights of their eras, and who were followed by generations of disciples who then invoked their authority to mould other victims to untrue theories. Automatically inclined to think of social relations in hierarchical terms, these researchers unconsciously proved their own bias rather than the real inferiority of the oppressed. But it sometimes took decades until such errors became obvious, to the detriment of the groups subjected to them.

But there is an even more serious problem. More than merely committing errors out of prejudice, some researchers used *fraudulent procedures*, which were only discovered long after the fact. There have been several such cases in the history of science. There is no need to go very far back in time: the 1980s were marked by a series of frauds (particularly in medical biology) committed by certain researchers at the most prestigious universities (Geneva, Harvard, Yale).

Whatever the motives that might impel certain individuals to falsify the results of their experiments (desire for career advancement, the pressures of frenzied competition), these cases show the inevitable role played by subjectivity in the development of even the "purest" sciences. It is likely that such subjectivity is manifested in even more sensitive areas of research with an impact on human societies. In these situations, the incentive for fraud would stem less from competition than from an unacknowledged desire to justify the established order and the privileges of a dominant group.

Many such cases have occurred in the past century and a half, sometimes discovered too late to prevent harm, or discovered without automatic correction of the consequences. Thus, the 1924 American law that established immigration quotas for Jews, Slavs, and Latins was not repealed when the same psychometricians responsible for its creation admitted, only a few years later, that their hypotheses and statistical measurements had been invalid. While one of them admitted having completely changed his opinion regarding the definition of the intelligence quotient, and another stated that he now favoured explanations based on the influence of environment rather than heredity, a third acknowledged that the theoretical structure on which his research was based had "collapsed completely" (Gould, 1981, 174–233).

Falsifications were even committed, some of them undoubtedly unconscious (like those of craniometrician Samuel G. Morton on the races, in the nineteenth century) and others clearly deliberate. American psychometrician H.H. Goddard, for example, altered photographs of immigrants to suggest mental retardation (Gould, 1981, 68–9, 27). This was also the case for Cyril Burt, whose data, largely false, were used to determine the educational orientation of students from different English social classes for several decades. Before the hoax was exposed finally in 1972, American psychometrician Arthur Jensen had used Burt's "results" as the foundation of his own analysis of Blacks in the United States (Stepan, 1982, 186).

Burt's prestige in England was so great that he was knighted. Truth and status do not necessarily go hand in hand. A researcher's influence, initially acquired through the quality (real or supposed) of his works, often lends weight to his judgments. There are no few examples of scientists who step outside their own fields to express opinions on fields that are foreign to them.

The opinions of a leading authority are always likely to carry more weight with the public, even when he talks about a question outside his field of expertise. Thus, the Nobel-Prize-winning physicist William Schockley added to the influence of a certain part of the American Right in recent years by endorsing the conclusions of psychometrician Arthur Jensen about racial inequality. It mattered little to those who profited from his prestige that Shockley, a specialist in semiconductors and transistors, was expressing his views on the relationship of intelligence ... with genetics.

The numerous cases of scientific error and fraud, laden with consequences (especially when endorsed by some famous authority), should serve as a warning. The argument of those who invoke "the existence of an abundant literature on the subject" to justify some inequality has been subject to enough wrongful use. But while spectacular, error and falsification are only two reasons *among others* to give a very critical reception to the verdict of specialists on social relations. The frequent fluctuations in the scientists' respect for the facts are reflected far more often in implicit biases than in flagrant twisting of the truth.

If "facts are facts," and if all specialists have been trained in the same discipline of scientific rigorousness, how can their opinions diverge to such a degree? How can this be explained without bringing in a third factor, a parameter not identified in the minds of the researchers themselves, a fundamental difference in *convictions* or *interests*?

One need only consider the way homosexuality was declared normal, almost overnight, after being treated as a disease for a century, to question the value of "facts." Indeed, the American Psychiatric Association decided in 1973 to strike homosexual orientation from its code of mental disorders. After discussions between the decision-making bodies qualified to rule on such matters, and a *majority* vote by the Association's members (Marmor, 1980, 393), the experts agreed to reverse a century-old practice. Thus, all alienating therapies (psychoanalysis) and assaulting therapies (electric shock, emetic absorption) to which lesbians and gays had been subjected before that fateful day had been wrongly imposed! Lives and careers had been shattered because the specialists had decreed a certain way of loving to be abnormal. Now these same specialists were changing their minds ...

If the varying conclusions reached by scientists are likely to raise questions about the role played by subjectivity in their work, no doubt the starting point of this research is also tinged with implicit biases. Though no field of knowledge should be barred to investigation, there is reason to wonder about the selective nature of researchers' interest in choosing certain objects to study rather than others.

The tendency of experts to look for differences between various categories of human beings is curious enough, but the type of groups chosen to make comparisons often betrays non-scientific concerns, frequently deriving from the desire to preserve privileges that the dominant group fears to lose or wishes to justify. For example, it is no accident that American psychometricians at the beginning of the century chose to study races, while their British colleague Cyril Burt preferred social classes. In the former case, it was an ethnic group (Anglo-Saxons) who felt threatened, while in the latter, it was the property-owning elite. The cavalier manner in which men of science establish their scales of priorities is very instructive. Thus, Burt dismissed variations in innate intelligence between races and genders as insignificant, but judged those existing between classes to be fundamental (Gould, 1981, 284).

A group of psychobiologists, with greater subtlety adopted a similarly discriminatory approach in a book entitled *Human Variation: the Biopsychology of Age, Race and Sex* (Osborne et al., 1978). After the inevitable statement of principles describing their indestructible attachment to scientific objectivity (ibid., 1–3), the authors of this work (dedicated to the father of eugenics, Francis Galton!) tried to rank the three categories of identity according to their importance for research. Thus, while age-based comparisons were declared to be difficult and the establishment of psychophysiological differences between the genders was dismissed as "not a high-priority topic" (ibid., 24–5), the largest number of articles were devoted to the theme of race. Though much less numerous than those dealing with Blacks (the target race), some of the commentaries nevertheless provide a highly instructive analysis about the intelligence of women (ibid., 171–93). Thus, while there is no difference in intelligence quotient between the genders, according to the researchers, there would be a difference in the *variability* of IQ test measurements, with male variability being "greater" (more males than females being either retarded or *very brilliant*). In support of their thesis, the authors cited the psychologist Havelock Ellis, who had already noted this phenomenon in 1904: "In males generally there is an organic variational tendency to diverge from the averages, in women, as in females generally, an organic tendency ... to stability and conservatism, involving a diminished individualism and variability" (ibid., 172).

Apart from the very unscientific semantic slippage, allowed by Ellis and the psychobiologists who endorsed him, between the group and the individual, it can be noted that males, once again, represent the norm. Far from being "less balanced" (which would be possible if the criteria adopted were the "happy medium," for example), men are declared to have "greater" variability. Since individualism, like variability, is posited as automatically superior (?), these two traits, of course, will appear to be "diminished" in women.

The authors' subjectivity, already flagrant in the text on women, appears even more evident in the treatment they reserve for race. On the pretense of providing a general assessment of all the articles in the book (whose title gave the illusion that it also dealt with gender and age), the conclusion, to all intents and purposes, focuses only on the racial question and finds Blacks to be irremediably inferior (ibid., 381–4). Because of this inferiority, according to the author, only their subordination to Whites could improve their lot. Thus, in addition to "rescuing" Africans from disease, plantation slavery supposedly assured them of a life without joblessness, famine, and war. Deprived of "discipline and protection" by emancipation, Blacks could only fall into drugs, prostitution, and gambling. The current state of Africa would confirm this view of things, the author concluded, because this continent, since decolonization, had been delivered to the dictatorship of a few local families devoid of any scruples.

Once it is considered that there is irrefutable proof of the relative superiority and inferiority of different groups, psychobiology inevitably leads to eugenics, according to which only the most intelligent would be encouraged to reproduce (ibid., 24).

But arguing in favour of intellectual competition between the races is like playing with fire, and those who get involved in this game can burn themselves. The author of the conclusion considered it appropriate to downplay an observation reported in another article in the book according to which Japanese and Chinese have intelligence quotients superior to those of Whites. But this superiority, considered to be "significantly above" average by this particular author (ibid., 283), is cited in the other writer's conclusion as evidence of a "comparable" level of intelligence between Whites and Asians (ibid., 381).

In addition to the obvious liberties taken by some scientists with certain "facts," there is nothing innocent about the preference they display for this object of study over another. To ensure a minimum degree of rigorous analysis, the implicit parameters of scientific work, namely the identity of the observer "subject" and of the observed "object," must be taken into account.

For example, the definition of a "problem" cannot be completely neutral. It is no mere accident that most psychological theorists have written mainly about women (Chesler, 1983, 75), or that they have devoted four times as many studies to homosexuals as to lesbians (in

Marmor, 1980, 300). Psychoanalysts have sought the cause of rape, incest, pedophilia, and even homosexuality mainly in the mother or wife of the aggressor. But it is male homophilia that is of primary concern to the experts, because when a member of the dominant group renounces his role as universal model, it is regarded much more seriously than the deviances of someone who already belongs to an inferior group.

If the identity of the dominated conditions the orientation of the research, then it is also relevant that the researchers themselves come from one community rather than another. One of the authors of the previously mentioned book on psychobiology noted that opinions on the variability of IQ measurements are often split along gender lines (Osborne et al., 1978, 172). Likewise, the fact that 90 percent of psychiatrists are men is likely to have definite consequences for women (Guyon-Bourbonnais, 1981, 49), and their middle-class value system automatically places them in an ambiguous position in relation to clients from less privileged social backgrounds (Hollingshead, 1958, 253–303).

Thus, research cannot claim to escape the dynamics of power relations any more than action. For a long time, the dominant subject has taken the dominated as the object of study, trying to measure them against the universal yardstick that he believed he represented. While often biased, he undoubtedly has acted in good faith just as often. On some occasions, however, the tone of these researchers has betrayed their true intentions (one need only consider Léonce Manouvrier's reflection on the sarcastic attacks of craniometricians on the women of their era, or the virulent comments of certain American psychobiologists regarding Blacks). Sometimes silence is even more eloquent. For example, it is amazing that specialists in the relations between women and men, such as Krafft-Ebing, Freud, Adler, and Jung, have ignored the essential reality of rape (Brownmiller, 1975, 1).

But most often, the phenomenon of selective omission shows itself through the questions asked and the criteria chosen to answer them. Thus, what is required in one case will not necessarily be required in another, or a specific standard will be applied differently, depending on the case. For example, there is reason to wonder if psychoanalysts are as consistent in looking for the cause of certain men's genius in their wives or mothers as in holding women responsible for the acts of rape or incest committed by other men. There is still cause to question the reason why contemporary neurologists are much more concerned about the degree of cerebral hemispheric bilateralism, which would distinguish men from women, than the comparable phenomenon that separates left-handers from right-handers. Finally, why are psychologists and sociologists so interested in the potential effects on children of the fact that their mother works outside the home, and so little in the potential effects on women of staying home (Janssen-Jurreit, 1982, 220)?

Similarly, it seems curious that not only are the causes of heterosexuality not questioned, but that homophiles, almost exclusively, are attributed personal characteristics (narcissism, among others) or family characteristics (such as a dominating mother and a weak father) that are also widespread in the majority. How can it be explained that the same family structure produces different effects on the sexual orientation of various children, or that parents, exemplary by the psychoanalysts' definition, have gay daughters or sons, while others, whose behaviour is more pathogenic, have "normal" children?

Despite its wide variety of manifestations, the type of family structure has been blamed for the poor socio-economic position of American Blacks, in particular. Published in the 1960s, the report of sociologist Daniel Moynihan, who was commissioned to establish the causes of the phenomenon, betrayed the same implicit biases through the type of questions asked and criteria adopted. While it found that the unemployment rate was higher among the Black population of the United States, the report, though ordered by the Department of *Labor*, disregarded the problems of discrimination in employment and in the unions, focusing its attention on a matriarchy deemed to be primarily responsible for the problem (unemployment, but also crime and drugs) (in Ladner, 1973, 103–4). Black men were supposed to have both exaggerated "virility" (as the absent fathers of numerous children) and to be in danger of emasculation (as sons who were the victims of overpresent mothers). Family instability thus ended up being categorized as an inherent feature of the African-American family, rather than being linked to a more general situation of poverty (underprivileged White families exhibit comparable traits) (Ryan, 1976, 68).

There is a great risk that the researcher will portray the effect as the cause and attribute characteristics that are also distributed throughout the general population to a limited group. Not only must the questions be relevant and free of traps, but the criteria chosen to evaluate the phenomena should also be subject to critical analysis. In making comparisons between the races, for example, will the scientist focus on the *quality* of the characteristics or on their *variety* (Jacquard, 1978)? The entire direction of the research will depend on the answer to this question. In the former case, the researcher will be following in a Social Darwinist tradition, which justifies the "natural" dominance of the fittest; in the latter case, the approach will be closer to population genetics, which establishes the random character of physical differences among human beings, as well as the diversity of their strategies for adapting to their environment.

How can an expert establish a hierarchical scale of values by which "quality" can be measured objectively? Nineteenth-century craniometricians tried to achieve this by taking the degree of resemblance to the ape as the standard of inferiority. But once again, what criteria are the basis for this resemblance: hair texture, a prognathous jaw, or distribution of body hair? To judge by these characteristics alone (since others exist), the human types closest to the apes would be Asians, Africans, and Whites respectively (Berry and Tischler, 1978, 50).

The more general comparison with the animal kingdom currently made by sociobiologists also requires caution. On what epistemological foundations can they base the fundamental likening of animal societies to that of *Homo sapiens*? Is there any such thing as universal animal behaviour? If not, which particular species will be taken as the point of reference? With no really satisfactory answers to these questions, profound inequalities have nevertheless been postulated between human groups.

To measure the more specific differences of intelligence between various classes, psychometricians instead chose to base their evaluations on social success, thus establishing an equation between intelligence and the capacity to acquire wealth and power. Apart from the questionable assumption that everybody is interested in dedicating their lives to this sole objective, there is reason to wonder, as does Noam Chomsky, whether unscrupulousness and willingness to submit to the whims of authority also play a major role in social mobility (in Block and Dworkin, 1976, 285–98).

The use of IQ, already perilous in the sphere of social relations, is no less dangerous when it evaluates competence in terms of age. Precautions must be taken so that older people are not penalized unduly, since their low percentage of the total population already handicaps them statistically. Cultural variations between the tested generations must be taken into account, as well as errors induced by the incidence of diseases not related to aging as such (heart ailments, for example), or by factors unrelated to intelligence, such as motivation or speed (Levin and Levin, 1980, 13–14).

In addition to simple honesty, scientific discipline requires not only that all the parameters relevant to a field of research be taken into account, but that the relationship between these parameters be interpreted as rigorously as possible. It is hard enough to adhere to this imperative in any type of intellectual endeavour, but the difficulty increases when the expert's interests are challenged indirectly by the results of his work. Since the standards he adopts as the reference points of his research most often are those that the dominant group has imposed on society as universal, the implicit biases of his thinking are not always immediately obvious to the oppressed.

What such examples of bias have in common is that they all show distortions of meaning. A characteristic normally considered positive will be reinterpreted by the scientist to the detriment of the dominated group in which its presence is detected. Thus, after noting faster sensory perception in Native North Americans, a late-nineteenth-century psychologist concluded that Whites were superior: instead of being *slower*, the "researcher" benevolently transformed them into *more* delicate creatures, *more* inclined to reflection than the first group (Berry and Tischler, 1978, 63). Women were subjected to the same type of judgment in the early 1920s. Noting the speed with which women learned foreign languages, one linguist saw this phenomenon as another proof that they were unsuited for deep thinking (in Yaguello, 1978, 58). In the 1950s, a geneticist, noticing the smaller size of the Y chromosome (carrying the male determinant) compared to the X chromosome (responsible for female factors), concluded from the male chromosome's "incomplete" appearance that "man is the creative one" (Janssen-Jurreit, 1982, 188).

Thus, the oppressed will never appear to be superior. To prevent this, the oppressor is not afraid to resort to the most unconvincing explanations. But more often than not, he is satisfied to say nothing about characteristics that, if they were specific to the dominant group, would have been interpreted by him as a sign of intrinsic excellence. Thus, even though the X chromosome is not only larger but, it seems, less inclined to carry hereditary diseases and more capable of regeneration than the Y chromosome, even though the ovum is larger than the sperm, and even though women, on the average, live longer than men (Janssen-Jurreit, 1982, 1988–90), the thesis of the female gender as the "weaker sex" has always predominated.

Though contestable, if not ridiculous, this type of competitive approach in the interpretation of facts has modulated the comparative study of dominated and dominant groups for decades. The silences or distortions of meaning to which scientists have resorted are just as revealing of their biases as the direct assertions they may have made about the oppressor's innate superiority. Rather than being drawn into vain competition, the dominated, when seeking emancipation, must endeavour to drive these silences and distortions from their hiding places.

Silences and distortions make it possible to maintain the fiction of the victims' irremediable inferiority. The deck is stacked against them from every angle. For example, while some researchers fail to draw positive conclusions for women from the comparative morphology of female and male chromosomes, others apply their selective logic to the observation of the brain. Thus, while thinkers like Aristotle, Thomas Aquinas, and Freud saw a woman as a sort of failed man, no scientist today seems ready to develop opposing theses from the fact that the primordial gender of the human embryo is female.

Contemporary experts seem to find it more pressing to establish the relative degrees of "lateralization" of the brain, the better to give women a *lower* rating. If this characteristic paradoxically seems to play in women's favour, an expert will always be on hand to correct this impression. Observing, for example, that girls seem to be more successful in school than boys, one Alberta psychiatrist had a ready-made neurological explanation. He argued that the school system, by focusing on verbal activity and the analysis of detail, favours female brain function. Therefore, he wrote, it should be no surprise that boys account for 90 percent of severe learning disabilities and thus for the vast majority of school drop-outs.[17] Since the school system was designed, almost in its entirety, under the direction of *male* civil servants, there is reason to wonder why they sought to stimulate the brain function of the opposite sex to such an extent.

Even when confronted with the most troubling facts, some specialists, faithful to their deep-seated belief in the inferiority of the dominated, prefer to reinterpret data contrary to their point of view, rather than admitting its validity. They reinterpret this data to serve the dominator's advantage and, if necessary, by altering the questions asked and the criteria previously chosen to obtain the information. Convinced, despite the results of the Masters and Johnson experiments (1979, 209), that homosexual orgasms cannot be complete, one psychoanalyst, Kronemeyer, proposed to redefine orgasm. After professing faith in the virtues of "objectivity" (1980, 4), he discarded as the product of "pure speculation" the laboratory observations made by the two American sexologists. "We have yet to be able scientifically to evaluate degrees of orgasmic health," he declared, explaining his opposition (ibid., 160). Even climax is not neutral, and some difference will be found somewhere that can be elevated to a criterion of "orgasmic health." It would seem to be the turn of homophiles, after women, to learn the catechism of orthodox pleasure.

The expert's knowledge sometimes seems to have been acquired by osmosis, since its origin has little to do with how much progress research has made in a given period. The specialist will appear indifferent both to the fact that our knowledge is not far enough advanced and to the possibility that other, unrecognized information exists. For example, many studies on homosexuality at the beginning of the twentieth century revealed an equivalent degree of mental health in *comparable* samples of the homophile and heterosexual populations. Clinical and sociological studies conducted in the United States in the 1920s and 1930s showed this in the case of lesbians (Faderman, 1981, 325–6). Other surveys in the 1950s and 1960s also made it possible to point out that the difference between gays and heterosexuals in the same environment (in prison, in therapy, in everyday life) is less than the difference between individuals of the same sexual orientation in different environments (Schofield, 1965; Hooker, 1969; Marmor, 1980, 299).

But, like Kronemeyer, several experts prefer to ignore these findings. They even ignore the warnings of colleagues who point to our current lack of knowledge of the origins of both heterosexuality and homosexuality (Masters and Johnson, 1979, 411). Thus, factors other than the facts dictate the insistence of certain scientists in considering homosexuality to be pathological. Since most of the publications that regard this sexual preference as a medical problem have been published in countries (the United States and Great Britain) where judicial repression of homosexuality has been most severe (Schofield, 1965, 161), this is a clear indication of the role of cultural influences in the definition of disease by experts.

Thus, oppressive theses are sometimes defended on the basis of a society's values, rather than "objective" considerations: the intensity of belief compensates for the lack of knowledge. Although there has been much progress in recent decades, sexuality is one of the fields still insufficiently explored, or insufficiently enough that it is necessary to ensure that standards of behaviour, and even of sensibility, are not imposed arbitrarily on all individuals. Besides, what foundation can there be for scientific research that would have the open or implicit purpose of establishing criteria for the morality or orthodoxy of specific practices?

If little is known about sexuality, even less is known about intelligence. Once again, the inferior status of entire groups is "objectively" maintained. Not only is the very concept of intelligence difficult to define, but its relationship to both heredity and environment is impossible to clarify. Too many variables come into play, and their networks of interaction are too complex for unequivocal links of cause and effect to be isolated systematically. Ultimately, to reduce the number of these variables, it would be necessary to ensure that the environment is absolutely identical for everyone. In this case, perhaps, the role played by genetic determinants could emerge clearly.

But even if such an operation were possible, the relationship would still be obscure between the various combinations of genes and the many forms of behaviour or intellectual activity that would have to be explained. The concatenation of mechanisms presiding over both genetics and behaviour is still unknown in most cases. In any event, even granting the hypothesis that a type of behaviour or faculty is genetically based does not mean that it is genetically *determined*: the environment often dictates whether or not such behaviour develops, and whether such a faculty is used in one particular way rather than another. For example, the fact that the language function is genetically based in humans does not dictate the type of language they will speak (in Montagu, 1980, 97). Similarly, if it is posited that the *potential* for aggression is innate, peaceful periods in history would also tend to show that the environment determines whether this propensity is exercised (Gould, 1981, 330–1). But when innateness is defined as potential, it no longer has any precise meaning, and the characteristic specific to human beings then becomes their high degree of flexibility.

Like those who believe in the determining influence of heredity on behaviour or on levels of ability, psychometricians, sociobiologists, and neuropsychologists often tend to give a general meaning to partial observations and seek to translate theories, often very recent and developed from these observations, into concrete applications. While sociobiology was born only in the mid–1970s, the strong comeback of psychometry and the emergence, in neuropsychology, of a marked interest in the hemispheric asymmetry of the brain only date from the beginning of the same decade. The relatively recent conclusions of these three disciplines remain controversial. The hopelessly entangled circuits formed by billions of brain cells are no better known than the complex relationships between heredity and environment.

However, an old fascination with the precise topographical location of functions or behaviour patterns still persists among scholars.[18] Although it has not been possible to reproduce scientific experiments conclusively, and although their results remain uncertain or contradictory, researchers continue to seek to base the status of women in society on the postulate that rigid gender differences exist in the asymmetry of the left and right hemispheres of the brain. Despite the fact that variances among individuals in a group are greater than those between the different groups themselves, trends and averages pertaining to differences in *proportion* and *degree* come to be presented as *natural* oppositions, applicable to all members of a group.

These slight differences count for little in the cases where they appear at all. The media prefer to play up the few more sensational experiments that seem to prove the existence of such dissimilarities rather than publish the much more frequent conclusions showing no cognitive differences between women and men. The propensity to present scientific "data" as absolute, thus escaping the general context of the research from which it is obtained at a given time, results in an inordinate interest in the thesis of cognitive differences between the genders.

The fascination exercised by the hypothesis of a cerebral location of functions or behaviour patterns is only one example, among others, of researchers' more general obsession with looking for a *cause* and, what is more, for a unique cause. This quest, while eminently satisfying to the mind, also responds to a need for control. Once the precise origin of a phenomenon seems to be established, it becomes necessary to accept it as inescapable. In the dynamics of power relations, this implicit postulate will serve to interpret an existing domination as the result of a natural imperative.

For this operation to be effective, it must be simple. Thus, theorists are often satisfied with isolating one variable and presenting it as the determining factor, so that the other factors considered inevitably must be articulated around it. But most often, this variable will ultimately be revealed as false, either because it is untrue or because it is necessarily partial. The quest will have to be renewed constantly, but almost always, only a single cause will be sought. Researchers will believe they have found it in a specific group of genes, in a particular brain structure, or in some animal species. Imprinted with the symbolic value devolved upon origins, the chosen cause is sometimes elevated to a universal principle: sociobiology, which claims to replace the social sciences and serve as the sole foundation for moral laws, is perhaps the most complete example of this phenomenon.

The chosen cause will carry all the more conviction if it is already deemed obvious. Thus, it will have to be part of a system of thought with a self-sufficient logic that instantly appears to be flawless. This is why the causality principle is so often part of the dialectic of the *circular argument*: the initial proposition and the conclusion become confused, and the proof, yet to be established, is already present in the question. The demonstration of this proof constantly revolves around its own axis, inevitably making it possible to find the answer being sought.

Circular argument is central to anthropomorphic reasoning. By taking himself as the reference point, man ensures that when he compares himself to certain beings he will see his own reflection in the mirror. For example, man has attributed human traits to God while claiming to have been created in his image. When animals are regarded as a paradigm of Nature, those who argue the principle of man's animality will believe they have found signs of human behaviour in these creatures. Well before the sociobiologists, one late-nineteenth-century anthropologist claimed to have observed cases of "criminality" and "sexual perversion" among the beasts (in Katz, 1976, 41).

Reliance on circular argument goes beyond mere anthropomorphism. Paul Broca resorted to it when, incapable of proving his hypothesis of an increase in human cranial capacity over the centuries, he *postulated* that the Parisian cemetery skulls he measured must have belonged to individuals of different classes (the aristocrats having larger skulls and the members of the popular classes having smaller ones) for their average capacity to vary so little from one period to another. In short, when the data was too resistant, he used his unproven hypothesis to alter its interpretation (Gould, 1981, 96).

The method scarcely differs in the various means employed to discredit homosexuality. Thus, the historical approach claims that an increase (?) in homophilia means that a society is sliding into decadence, and that decadence itself is augured by an upsurge of homosexuality. One psychoanalytical theory draws upon the same logic, as illustrated by the following dialogue:

- A man is homosexual because he did not have a strong father with whom he could identify.
- But not all men who grow up in this context necessarily turn out to be homosexuals.
- No doubt these men had an uncle or a neighbour who served as a father figure.
- But how can one be sure that this homosexual did not identify with an uncle or a neighbour?
- The very fact that he is a homosexual proves that this was not the case. (Schofield, 1965, 165–6)

Circular argument, distortion of the meaning of a proposition, reinterpretation of data – every effort is made to maintain the fiction of the oppressed's inferiority and the resulting necessity for their subordination to the dominator.

This is why the first aspiration of the dominated, when they embark on the road to emancipation, is to participate in the development of society and knowledge as they are. Far from contesting the proposed ideal human type or the basic rules of objectivity that they have learned, they will claim to be just as fit as the dominator to conform to the ideal or live by the rules. At this initial stage of their liberation, the oppressed are not yet aware that the standards by which they agree to be measured do not have an existence independent of hierarchical relations.

Only gradually will the oppressed understand that they cannot win at a game with rigged rules that are likely to be changed as soon as they seem to work to their advantage. Forced to look inward for a secure anchorage, they will learn to know their own identity.

There are several stages in the process of emancipation, and the oppressed who pass through them must meet new challenges at every turn, as well as new ambiguities. These different phases involve dilemmas or pitfalls that rarely can be resolved definitively. Yet the dominated do not have models to help them take their bearings in this unexplored territory. In the first stage, not only must they renounce the model supplied by the dominator, but they sometimes must refrain from following in the footsteps of predecessors who took the wrong path.

Nonetheless, it is in the very essence of emancipation for those who undertake it to question themselves as it unfolds. The most likely guarantee that the vigour of this process will be maintained is the constant obligation to reconsider the models one adopts. Liberation is a process, not a culmination. The oppressed, by applying a critical approach to their own discourse, will gain more in subtlety than they would seem to lose in coherence.

STAGES OF EMANCIPATION

For the oppressed, liberation means not only being able to participate in the shaping of their own lives and environment but gaining access to the resources that make this participation possible (Boulding, 1979, 7). There are three fundamental realms that must be conquered by anyone aspiring to emancipation, often after centuries of subjugation: identity, autonomy, and power. Since it precedes the others, the rediscovery of identity necessarily sets the conditions for the acquisition of autonomy and power.

So long as the dominated do not know who they are, they remain defined by the oppressor, trapped in a discourse that denies them. Under these conditions, no liberation is possible, since before the oppressed become conscious of the unjustified nature of their subordination, it is essential that they reject a supposedly basic inferiority. This rejection may be obscure or fleeting at first, but it will be reinforced by the impetus of the broader opposition it engenders.

Once the victims have reappropriated their true identity, they will be able to determine which rules they choose to obey. Having already challenged the reductive definition that the dominator has imposed on them, they will be able to reject the resulting subjugation. Liberated from his discourse, the dominated will also seek emancipation from his tutelage.

But for the autonomy they have captured to be maintained, the oppressed must demand a share of power. Having managed to escape from the grips of an alienating control and belief system once is not enough to lay the foundations of equal status. Only a profound upheaval in power relations and modes of production of meaning will prevent the dominated from being "put back in their place" some day. This lengthy task goes far beyond obtaining a few formal guarantees on which the oppressed might be tempted to rest their case. In social relations, the gains are rarely final, and there is often a risk that the degree of control "conceded" by the oppressor will be taken back.

Triggered by an increasingly precise impression of the innate injustice of the established order and the systematically erroneous nature of its underlying discourse, the unease that victimized individuals first feel in isolation leads to the awareness that the inferior status imposed on them pertains to their community as a whole. The dominated group's participation in power has consequences for other individual members, whose lot it thus helps to improve. In this manner is the cycle completed, and the liberation process that commenced with a personal revolt ultimately has the effect of changing a multitude of lives.

But for this initial revolt to bring about such an upheaval, there is a need for interdependent research and action. Even though emancipation begins and ends with the individual, he or she has only collective means of ensuring its progress, means that include the reappropriation of identity through an investigative effort so vast that it must be shared with others, and the acquisition of autonomy, and then of power, access to which would remain permanently closed to anyone relying solely on individual strength to shake the established order.

The oppressor makes no small contribution to modulating the course of the liberation of the dominated. Not only does he actively resist the sharing of power, but he implicitly imposes himself as the reference point against which the oppressed, for some time, will continue to measure themselves. Still endorsing a world-view that affirms their inferiority, the victims will initially remain ignorant of the deep kinship that binds them to their peers and will only be able to conceive of liberation as individuals. In their first attempts at emancipation, they will claim abilities equivalent to those of the dominator and seek to live up to the same ideal model of humanity.

The Quest for Identity

Because the established discourse claims to be universal and objective, the initial tendency of dominated individuals seeking emancipation is to measure themselves against the dominator on his own ground. Believing that they are obeying external laws, they will affirm that they can perform "as well" as the oppressor. At this initial stage of their liberation, the only thing they will dare to challenge is the thesis of their own innate inferiority.

What the oppressed demand, in fact, is an opportunity to "show what they can do." Readily conceding that the dominator has been more successful at meeting the high requirements of universality and objectivity, they will even adopt the oppressor as their mentor. Because of what he is, the dominator has "nothing to prove." Even if they sometimes observe some defects in him, the oppressed will believe that these are the exceptions that prove the rule.

In exchange for recognition of the right to equal opportunity for all, the victims will readily submit to the criteria of excellence so fortunately embodied by the representatives of the established order. Everything that relates to these authority figures in any way will be valued by the oppressed as a symbol of this excellence. In adopting the manners, style of expression, and even the apprearance of the dominator, the victims believe they are coming closer to an ideal human type. It is one of the major paradoxes of the quest for identity that self-affirmation first requires *imitation of a supposedly original model*.

Women who believe they are more "effective" in suppressing their reactions in the workplace, or Jews who "discreetly" hold back from speaking too exuberantly in front of Anglo-Saxon Protestants, subject themselves to this logic, which requires the oppressed to deny part of themselves to ensure that they are well received. "Good adjustment," for stigmatized individuals, means trying to be considered essentially the same as others, while making sure to avoid putting themselves in situations or behaving in ways that would make it difficult for people to do more than pay lip service to accepting them (Goffman, 1963, 121).

"You have to show the world that you're like everybody else," a female patient at the Louis-Hippolyte-Lafontaine psychiatric hospital told an interviewer (Provencher, 1982, 11). Like everybody else, because mental patients are human beings, and like everybody else, because there are many human beings who could become mental patients. But once they leave the hospital, the mentally ill will try to conform to the implicit model represented by the "normal" individual, rather than the other way around. Just as women or Jews show self-censorship in the way they speak, the same mental patients who demanded equal status when they resided in an institution will now conceal their past, banishing the expressions they used there from their vocabulary and deliberately employing "big words" as a sign that they have changed (Edgerton, 1967, 163).

African-Americans provide perhaps the most spectacular example of the initial propensity of the dominated to copy the dominator in the belief that this is the way to achieve universality. In the early 1960s, a number of Blacks even felt it necessary to have their hair straightened and use whitening creams. It was a long way (if not chronologically, at least mentally) to the Afro hairstyles and brightly coloured clothing that Whites themselves would later adopt.

While necessarily collective in their composition, even the organizations defending the rights of the dominated are conservative at the start of the emancipation process. Created in 1909, the National Association for the Advancement of Coloured People (NAACP) had been fighting for decades for the legal and political equality of Blacks when the civil rights movement of the Reverend Martin Luther King embarked, in the 1950s, on a peaceful struggle for the *integration* of African-Americans into the majority institutions. Although the methods used (freedom marches, sit-ins, occupation of segregated facilities) contrasted sharply with those of the NAACP, the new movement still aspired to the model of a humanistic White society.

The evolution of the feminist movement was not very different. Its first initiatives, at the turn of the twentieth century, also focused on political and legal objectives. In addition to the long struggles waged discreetly in the courts to force a more open interpretation of the existing laws, the efforts of that era's activists crystallized when they won the right to vote, so that they could change the laws themselves. Although it placed more emphasis on access to social equality, the National Organization for Women, founded in 1966 by Betty Friedan, still relied on the virtues of liberalism to bring about change. Indeed, the movement initially identified automatically with the values of the White middle-class population.

Beginning very early in the nineteenth century, the struggle by society's lower classes to improve their lot would take a slightly different path. Although the right to vote was extended gradually to all social classes[19] during the following decades, the labour movement's demands quickly became more radical. Especially in the wake of Marxism, union organizations and then political parties were established with the aim of overthrowing the established order. The hazards of the struggle and the pressure of different traditions would produce opposite results, depending on the country.

Thus, while labour militancy evolved in France and Germany (until the Social Democratic congress of 1959) into competition between a reformist and a revolutionary wing, labour in Great Britain, Canada, and the United States hewed to a more or less marginal socialism (the British Labour Party and the Canadian New Democrats being less to the left) and to a business unionism geared primarily to the improvement of wages and working conditions for its members.[20] In predominantly Anglo-Saxon cultures, the tendency thus remained one of integration rather than of confrontation, with the less affluent accepting the foundations of the economic system and seeking, as their main objective, to benefit from it in turn. In the United States, in particular, the "American dream" still continues to sustain faith in the possibility that any sufficiently determined individual can climb the social ladder.

Thus, movements emerge in the emancipation process that inevitably stake everything on integration. Regardless of whether it is maintained subsequently, this gamble comes relatively early in a movement's history. This phenomenon, particularly easy to define in the case of African-Americans and women, is fairly evident in the more recent struggle of homosexuals.

Although such British pioneers as Havelock Ellis and Edward Carpenter, influenced by the reform movement launched by Magnus Hirschfeld in Germany, tried early in the century to contain the rising oppression against homophiles, it was only in the 1950s that more broadly based attempts began in the West to have lesbians and gays accepted by society as a whole. But in every country in which it arose, the liberation movement very soon took on conservative features. Whether in the case of the Mattachine Society and the Daughters of Bilitis in the United States, the Arcadie Group in France, or the Homosexual Law Reform Society and the Kenric Collective in England, the marching orders were to adopt the trappings of middle-class respectability and encourage dialogue with the "experts" (d'Emilio, 1983, 106–13; Girard, 1981, 44–67; Weeks, 1983, 171–9). This concern with reassuring the majority would be reflected in the recommendation that women avoid wearing trousers or cutting their hair too short.

The decision to be "reasonable" was not risk-free, however. Black, feminist, or homosexual activists of the 1950s and 1960s would learn this quickly. One of the major challenges encountered by dominated individuals seeking integration is the constant and superior effort they must invest to achieve this goal. Whatever the place made for them by the dominator, it is always conceded as a favour. If they make the least error, everything they have gained may be called into question. To obtain equal rights, they must show that they are twice as competent. Only the oppressor has the privilege of failure or of being simply average in ability, without suffering the suspicion of intrinsic inferiority.

Since the members of the dominated group are compelled to pay a heavier price to "rise" in the hierarchical order, such heights are reserved for a select few. Too busily engaged in persuasion, they rely more on the good faith of the oppressor than on their own strength. Inclined to respect a system that evolves only at the slowest pace, they continue to play with a deck stacked by the courts and by the legal system.

The very successes gained by a minority of the oppressed risk confirming the dominator's conviction of his more general superiority. Co-opted by the oppressor, the efforts made by "token" dominated individuals may soothe his troubled conscience and help prop up an established order henceforth less vulnerable to charges of exclusivism.

It is by becoming increasingly aware of the ambiguity of their position in relation to the oppressor that the victims will alter the course of their emancipation, and even rethink the very objectives they had proposed to achieve. Having tried in vain to live a form of equality that required the denial of their identity, they will now find it necessary to turn toward their own people, so that they can have both.

Thus begins the transition between the first and second stages of emancipation, as the discourse of the dominated takes on a more radical content and a more demanding tone. Abandoning reformist and often purely legalistic ventures, this discourse will translate into the will to transform existing structures. In short, the liberation movement will gradually cease to revolve around integration into the dominant model and will become the means of discovery of a difference.

Now aware that they have been tricked, the oppressed will begin by reconsidering their entire relationship with the oppressor. They will discover that not only has the dominator remained the centuries-old possessor of wealth, status, and power, but that his discourse has legitimized this unequal distribution. Trapped by the tactical flexibility of this discourse, the oppressed could only figure as the eternal loser. Their new quest for identity henceforth will require them to *demand recognition of their status as victim.*

This demand strikes at the very heart of the dominant pedagogy. Not content merely to denounce the very real injustice to which they have been subjected, the dominated can now dismantle the entire myth of their own supposed role in this matter.

Once again, it is essential that the right victims be identified and that recognition of the wrong they have suffered not benefit anyone else. Such situations have often arisen in history. Thus, though women were blamed for it in many instances, rape has been considered a crime for centuries. However, this crime was perceived as being directed against the father (if the victim was a virgin) or against the husband (if she was married). Even today, raping the wife of one's adversary is considered to be a way of injuring him in a conflict (Brownmiller, 1975, 8–119).

A similar slippage in the definition of victim status has occurred in the case of pornography, particularly as it relates to children. Choosing to ignore the opinion of those of its members who pointed to the harmful consequences of pornography for the young (by encouraging sexual abuse, for example), an American commission of inquiry recommended, in 1970, that legislation on pornography be liberalized, after citing the supposedly few negative effects of pornographic materials ... on its consumers (in Lederer, 1982, 68–9). Since adult males did not seem to run any risks, there was no cause for concern.

More recently and on an even vaster scale, those who suffered most from an economic catastrophe were denied victim status by the dominator. Either they were downgraded to the status of some victims among others, or they were held to be mainly responsible for their misfortune. While the 1982 recession caused hundreds of thousands of layoffs, bankers and industrialists denounced salary scales and blamed the unions. Choosing to forget the earlier example of 1929, when wages clearly rising more slowly than profits and a 40 percent drop in union membership in one decade had played no role in triggering the Depression, a number of companies, *which had remained in a good financial position*, invoked the same reasons to demand wage concessions from their employees in 1982. While the recession was portrayed as a disaster hitting the entire world without distinction, unions were compelled to lend their money to companies (like Maislin) whose management errors, more than the general economic climate, had brought them to the verge of bankruptcy. Barely two years later, senior executives of major American corporations (especially in the automobile industry), who had held the growth in their employees' wages to 2.6 percent, granted themselves 13 percent "catch-up" raises. According to the results of studies presented to the United States Congress, incomes of American CEOs generally increased by more than 210 percent between 1980 and 1990, while those of workers grew by only about 50 percent and the profits of the companies for which they worked rose by slightly less than 80 percent. If responsibility for apportioning blame is left to the oppressor, the dominated, more often than not, will be found guilty for the disaster afflicting them, or their plight will be attributed to imponderable factors caused by impersonal calamities.

However, there is no need for the oppressed to be the target of an immediate or flagrant injustice in order for them to be entitled to claim victim status. A situation of structural inequality may justify this demand. The comparative position of French Canadians and Anglo-Quebecers in North America is a good illustration of this reality. A specious argument would have it that the two minorities share an equivalent plight: both are threatened by dominant majorities unconcerned about preserving their identity (Anglo-Canadians for the first group, and French-Quebecers for the latter), with both being reduced to struggling for their survival. Yet such a parallel only masks the precarious position of *all* francophones on this continent. While English-speaking North Americans account for 240 million people in a total of 58 states and provinces within two federations (the United States and Canada), the population of French origin amounts to scarcely 20 million, of which 5 out of the 6 million not yet assimilated are concentrated in Québec, the only state with a francophone majority.

Thus, it is a matter of some importance that the status of victim be claimed by the group that has suffered from inequality. Far from reflecting a propensity to complacency and self-indulgent misery, such a demand prevents the dominated from having to beg for a problematical improvement in their condition, and instead allows them to demand that justice be done.

It is often at this stage that the oppressed will decide to give themselves a name, as a conclusive sign of their dealienation. Naming is one way of appropriating a living being or an object. By changing or taking over the name they have been given, the victims display their will to retake possession of themselves. By deciding to call themselves by a name of their own choosing, they take away the dominator's power to define them.

There is no need to reinvent language for this purpose. The dominated sometimes will be satisfied to take pride in claiming a title of which they had previously been ashamed. Thus, some will more readily say they are "Jews" in a society in which they had long preferred to keep quiet about their origin. Women who used to be uncomfortable with the word "lesbian" will no longer hesitate to identify themselves as such. To mark their determination to recapture a tradition intended to humiliate them, some will even proclaim themselves "dykes" (or *"gouines"* in French) and gays will call themselves "queens." People with a handicap even use the words "cripples" or "crips." Some African-Americans have pushed the demand for victim status to its limits. Taking on an entire past that had sought to entrench their anonymity, but this time to their advantage, the "Black Muslims" of the 1960s, like Malcolm X, followed their first names with the X of namelessness and personal negation (Guillaumin, 1972, 74).

But more often than not, the break with an ancient code is reflected in the *transformation* of the conventions of *language*. Periods of social upheaval have provided striking examples of this phenomenon. Thus, the French and Russian Revolutions gave rise to general use of the familiar pronoun, in addition to the replacement of the words *"Madame"* and *"Monsieur"* and their Russian equivalents with "Citizen" or "Comrade" (Yaguello, 1978, 182–3). Reflecting the rise of many emancipation movements, the 1970s and 1980s have been the most fertile period for linguistic evolution. By changing the way they are designated, various types of oppressed both provoke and reflect the development of a new discourse on their identity. Expressions that were automatically degrading (like "unwed mother," or *"fille-mère"* in French), or which had acquired degrading implications (like "homo" for homosexual), have now been replaced with other designations, more neutral ("single mother" or *"mère célibataire"* in French) or more positive ("gay").

The status of the elderly has evolved as well, with older individuals ceasing to be "old people" and becoming "senior citizens" or even "golden agers." Even references to variations in health or physical and mental wellness have changed. Gradually, the concept of being "differently abled" or "physically challenged" is replacing the older terms "infirm" or "disabled," no doubt too stained with negative connotations. Similarly, the "blind" are now designated as "visually handicapped" or, more progressively, "visually challenged," and the "deaf" as "hearing handicapped" or "hearing challenged." The English-speaking handicapped totally reverse the perspective when they label healthy people as "temporarily able-bodied."

The even more decried notions of "psychiatric illness" and "madness" have given way to the more positive concept of "mental health." Persons who successively were labelled "inmates" of the asylum or "patients" of the psychiatric hospital now figure as "clients" or "consumers" of services (Boudreau, 1984, 155).

The recent evolution of language is not limited to a few groups of stigmatized individuals. Peoples, if not entire continents, have embarked on the renaming process. Anti-colonialist uprisings, often denounced as "outbursts of fanaticism," have become "national movements" (Astier Loutfi, 1971, 91). Third World countries, created as a result of these uprisings, have been re-labelled "developing countries" instead of "underdeveloped."

A similar phenomenon has occurred in the West, with the resurgent militancy of ethnic groups long relegated to inferior status. These groups have refused the reductive label of "regionalist" to refer to movements promoting the demands of their territorially concentrated members. Aware that it was in the interests of centralizing forces in Europe to label the areas that had fallen under their control as "regions," they now demand the status of "nations" (with or without a state) or "national minorities" (Petrella, 1978, 30–5). With the addition of ideological issues to inter-ethnic conflicts, victims of Russian or Soviet imperialism[21] restored their countries to the cultural influence of the West by choosing to refer to "Central" rather than "Eastern" Europe.

North America is not exempt from this lexical questioning through which both racial and ethnic groups are seeking redress. While "Negroes" gradually became "Blacks" and then "African-Americans," "Eskimos" transformed themselves into "Inuit," and the undifferentiated status of "Indians" evolved into that of "aboriginal peoples" (the first inhabitants of the continent). "Ethnics" rediscovered their heritage in the United States, while "New Canadians" or *"Néo-Québécois"* expressed their desire to be known under the less time-bound heading of "cultural communities." Québec's French Canadians had already discovered a "national" identity, seeing their "province" of residence as a "State" and themselves as *"Franco-Québécois"* (French Quebecers) rather than as "French Canadians."

Since their emancipation movement is one of the most important of the past three decades, women have not rested on the fringes of the general trend toward self-affirmation. American women, in particular, sought ways to end the systematic distinction in the English language between the status of married and single women: thus Mrs. and Miss were merged into a more neutral Ms. The operation was more difficult in French, where *"Madame,"* in many cases, emerged as the sole form of address, except where using a person's first name and surname alone was considered sufficient. In both languages, however, use of the word girl (*fille*) instead of woman (*femme*) was criticized, especially when it was used parallel to man (*homme*) instead of boy (*garçon*).

More comprehensively, feminists called for a profound transformation of language by seeking a more balanced use of feminine and masculine pronouns and word endings, and by challenging the pretensions of "man" to represent all of humanity. Thus, in the

French language, words for which only a masculine form existed were feminized (*individue, professeure*), the determining weight of order was reversed (by referring to an *ethnologue-femme* rather than a *femme-ethnologue*, for example), or alternative precedence was applied in common phrases ("*celles et ceux*" or "*ceux et celles*") (Michard-Marchal, 1982, 192–3). In English, "chairman" was replaced with "chair" or "chairperson," and attempts were made to refer to "women and men" instead of "men and women."

With consciousness of identity came an accentuated awareness of a general condition of oppression, which itself required a redefinition of language. In this context, rape ceased to be categorized as a crime of passion to become an act of violence, and the struggle against pornography was identified with resistance to a multi-billion-dollar hate literature industry rather than an attempt at censorship. Equality has also come to mean equal opportunity, as shown in the evolution from "equal pay for equal work" to "equal pay for work of *equal value*."

The quest for identity thus involves both a challenge to the oppressor's discourse and behaviour and the victim's rediscovery of self. After attempting to model themselves on the oppressor, victims will come to count more on themselves and their peers, and even to embark on a systematic critique of a dominator reduced to his solely negative dimensions. Thus, the language of the oppressed will be articulated around the notion of difference. Far from claiming to support comparison with the oppressor, the oppressed will seek to distinguish themselves from the dominant group.

Having noted the faults of the established order, the victims will be inclined to propose their own difference as conforming more to an ideal type of humanity. While exalting the discovery of their new identity, they will find virtues in themselves that often will be the opposite of what the oppressor represents. They will even glory in possessing some feature previously considered a mark of inferiority.

Once pride has been affirmed, the exaltation of the difference translates into a discourse that both attests to a discovered identity and contests an alleged superiority. In this sense, the oppressor, in part, continues to be the reference point in terms of which the dominated continue to define themselves. But this time, the dominated set the agenda and the oppressor is called to account. In the same way that the dominant discourse portrayed the oppressed as an eternal loser, now the victim will seem incapable of finding anything good to say about the oppressor.

The second stage of liberation thus obeys a certain Manichaean logic, attesting to the scope of the domination that has been suffered as it prepares the way for new social relations. By swinging the dialectical pendulum in a direction opposite to its centuries-old course, the discourse of the oppressed creates the impression of two extremes that the groups involved will be inclined to flee, seeking a "moderate" path which will result in a redressing of the victims' grievances.

Toward Autonomy

In the same way that it makes the dominated conscious of their own worth, the second stage of the emancipation process calls upon them to challenge the oppressor's superiority. Not only do they realize that there is nothing universal about the model of humanity imposed upon them, but they perceive that even the dominator does not live up to the requirements to which he claims to subject them.

The dominated ultimately hold the oppressor responsible for the general state of the world. Thus, as his admiration faded when he was faced with Whites capable of producing Nazism, Black writer James Baldwin also observed the more general flaws of western civilization, which had to replace the wizard with the psychiatrist in order to heal its permanent anxieties (1963, 73; 140). In an article evocatively entitled "A Last Word from the First Americans,"[22] Sioux lawyer Vine Deloria explained the aboriginal peoples' reluctance to celebrate the bicentenary of United States independence. Not only were Natives amazed at the damage caused in only two centuries by the unreasoning exploitation of the environment by the European conquerors, but a two-hundred-year anniversary was scarcely impressive to the original inhabitants of a continent who had much more ancient events to commemorate.

The critique of the outside world by a resident of a Québec psychiatric hospital is perhaps the most devastating radical analysis at which a victim can arrive. This "mental patient" is surprisingly lucid:

Accidents, fires, wars, hassles: it never stops. Crime too. ... Everybody's in a hurry, everybody looks unhappy, everybody looks more miserable than we are inside. No! I'm telling you, I'm not tempted to leave here. (In Provencher, 1982, 51)

It is only one step from the challenging of the universe created by the dominator to the development of a sense of relativity in the oppressed. While the victims may not envisage a specific alternative model right away, at least they will begin to have the impression that it is possible to see things in a different way. In the words of another "inmate" of the same hospital:

[My husband and children] often have told me to put both feet on the ground and look reality in the face. Reality, reality! What's reality? Theirs? Mine? I'm beginning to think there ought to be several. (In Provencher, 1982, 68)

Soon, however, the dominated will think they have found an alternative path in the implicit values they believe are specific to their own group. Marked by the aspiration for autonomy, the second stage of emancipation is one of *discovering the difference*, a discovery that is reached through the process of proclaiming pride. "Black is beautiful," African-Americans affirmed in the late 1960s to contest the dominant aesthetic criteria, which negated them. "Small is beautiful," said the adherents of regionalist and nationalist movements reproached by established nationalisms for their status as "small peoples" threatening the unity of "great nations." As a clear indication of its will to take control of its own destiny, the francophone nucleus of one of these small peoples would soon repeat *"Québec sait faire!"* reaffirming its competence both to itself and to others.

The slogan "Gay is good" was taken up by homophiles in the United States seeking to put their preference forward as both an agreeable and morally justifiable lifestyle. In France, *"J'en suis et j'en suis fier"* became the equivalent of the American theme of "Gay Pride." In another example of exaltation of the very thing previously used to diminish them, ex-psychiatric patients did not hesitate to demand a "right to be crazy." While some demanded new respect for the "feeble" minds formerly attributed to them, others, such as the feminists, insisted on the same respect for the bodies that women are now seeking to reappropriate by celebrating their sexual (even genital) and reproductive specificity.

In so doing, these emancipation movements necessarily became more radical, especially since some of them then drew their inspiration from the philosophy of decolonization, both the paradigm and the harbinger of a better *world*.

In this context, during the latter half of the 1960s, a hitherto latent tension within the American civil rights movement resulted in the formation of a wing that rejected the integration of African-Americans into the White majority as a dead-end street and instead sought to have them win control of their own institutions. Likewise, feminists, rightly labelled radical, challenged the very foundations of a society that they described as patriarchal and, like Blacks who adopted Afro hairstyles and wore colourful clothing, denounced the trap represented for women by the pedestal of beauty by choosing to do without fashionable clothes and cosmetics.

A student movement had already been created that immediately posed a radical challenge to the social and economic system it deemed both bourgeois and paternalistic (*"Don't trust anybody over thirty*"). Again symbolic of a fundamental critique, conventional clothing gave way on university campuses to jeans and T-shirts, or simply to odds and ends bought at army surplus stores. The Bolsheviks in Russia, and later in the USSR, had long ago demonstrated that revolutionaries set the tone for the radicals who followed them, who could be recognized by their uniform cut of clothing and proletarian caps.

Gay activists did not lag behind. In the early 1970s, they hardened their resistance to oppression by opting increasingly for direct action. Some even decided to openly shock heterosexist culture by pushing its representation of them as "effeminate" men to the most outrageous caricature (the "drag queen").

The successive rejection of White, bourgeois, heterosexist, patriarchal, and paternalistic society would be followed by the questioning of a psychiatric world-view that defended the established order. Launched by practitioners (T. Szasz of the United States, M. Mannoni of France, and R.D. Laing and D.G. Cooper of Britain), the antipsychiatric movement, by the early 1980s, converged with expsychiatric patients, who challenged not only the competence but the right of medical "experts" to decide the degree of "deviance" or "mental illness" of others.

The oppressed's critique of the oppressor, radical in the scope of its challenge to the established order, is just as radical in the depth of the structures it challenges. But at this stage of the liberation process, radicalism also becomes Manichaeism, with the negative picture of the dominator reflecting the mirror image of dominated individuals exalted in their difference. The second phase of emancipation is one of essentialist fascination, induced by the oppressed's (re)discovery of themselves and their peers. During this stage, minority identity is presented as an alternative model.

The dominated, at this point, seem to be proud of what they *are*. This attitude never fails to provoke a certain malaise in liberals of the dominant group who had sympathized with the oppressed up to then. For if people can be proud of what they *do* or, possibly, of what they *have* (or at least of what they had to do to have it), it will seem strangely biased for people to be proud of what they are: members of a particular nation, gender, social class, or age group.

Yet in the case of dominated groups, pride is a precondition for *dignity*, for assuming one's identity. The exaltation of the difference coincides not only with the oppressed's repudiation of the self-contempt previously engendered by the *shame of being* victims and their false portrayal by the oppressor, but also with the updating of their history by the group to which they belong, and thus with an awareness of what they have *done* but has been hidden. What might have passed for immodest self-aggrandizement is really only a cathartic stage in the process of ending alienation.

As essential as it is, this stage poses many dangers in how the dominated seeking emancipation relate to the dominator. One of the major risks is to accentuate the oppressor's propensity to reductionism. Thus, since the early 1980s, journalists frequently have defined the action of minority communities as coming from "pressure groups" (derisively referred to as "politically correct" in the 1990s), thus downgrading the oppressed to the same status as any lobby (the National Rifle Association, for example). This leads people to believe that the emancipation movements are defending *special interests* rather than the principle of the equality of individuals.

In 1984, critics (including those of the liberal *Washington Post*) claimed that the selection process of Geraldine Ferraro as the Democratic candidate for vice-president of the United States had been overly influenced by feminist lobbying. This reasoning is laden with unconscious prejudices, in that it prefers to attribute to the influence of a "pressure group," rather than to the most elementary requirements of democracy, the decision to send a member of the 52 percent majority constituted by the female population of the United States to the White House. Even more insidious, because of their pretensions to completely factual impartiality, wire service articles continued to harp on this theme. Drawing up the list of the main contenders, in July 1984, to be Walter Mondale's running mate on the Democratic ticket, Associated Press described them as follows:

- Gary Hart, the candidate most likely to attract independent voters;
- Geraldine Ferraro, a Catholic woman from the Italian-American community;
- Dianne Feinstein, mayor of a city (San Francisco) controversial for its tolerance of homosexuals;
- Martha Layne Collins, the only female governor in the country;
- Tom Bradley and Wilson Goode, Black mayors of Los Angeles and Philadelphia;
- Mayor Henry Cisneros of San Antonio, popular with the Hispanic community;
- Senator Lloyd Bentsen, the only personality interviewed by Mr. Mondale who does not represent a pressure group.

Out of the list of candidates, all holding important public offices, the wire service failed to mention gender, race, religion, ethnic origin, or sexual orientation in only two cases. WASP, male, and presumably heterosexual, Gary Hart and Lloyd Bentsen were proposed implicitly as the only complete politicians, their identity being deemed to include all categories. Seen automatically as the embodiments of a universal humanity, in relation to which "the others" would be defined as "different," Bentsen and Hart could be considered by the anonymous author of the dispatch as respectively standing above "pressure groups" or as solely capable of attracting "independent" voters.

Thus, without appearing to be aware of the real premises of its judgment, the dominant group considers that respect for equality only means ensuring that women or Blacks, for example, have enough representatives to defend *their* interests in high public office. In no way does it consider it a valid possibility that women or African-Americans could claim to speak, like White male politicians, in the name of *all* citizens.

The dominator's tendency to relegate the oppressed to minority status, while criticizing their supposed lack of concern for the general good, has modulated the discourse of the established order, from the shortcuts in reasoning taken by the "man in the street" to the allegedly impartial comments of "well-informed sources." Though the claims of these circles to universality remain nothing more than pretensions, there is an implicit postulate in this type of approach that a fundamental kinship exists among human beings.

But one recent discourse (although itself part of a tradition) has been developing that, in practice, denies the very principle of equality to which it claims to adhere, taking over the concept of respect for differences hitherto primarily defended by the dominated groups. This reactionary discourse does not so much respect differences as it *imposes* them (Brouillon, 1981, 7). Postulating the profound incompatibility of distinct groups, or a complementarity between these groups requiring the radicalization of their opposing traits, this discourse concludes that it is necessary either to separate them or to subordinate one group to the other. In the first case, a justification was found for apartheid in South Africa, just as racial segregation in the United States was endorsed by the Supreme Court's "separate but equal" doctrine in the last century. This explains the curious phenomenon of the great sympathy manifested by White South African segregationists for the culture of the Black populations (in Kuper, 1985, 325).

The proposed relationship between men and women is perhaps the best example of one group's subordination to another. Despite official recognition of the principle of equality of the sexes "before God," both Orthodox Judaism and Catholicism invoke their "different roles" in reserving the higher religious functions of Torah study and the priesthood for men only. There is no doubt here that difference means inequality. A similar equation can be found in the discourse of American fundamentalists (as in the statements of Phyllis Schlafly) who oppose the Equal Rights Amendment, which would entrench the principle of equality for women in the Constitution, in the name of "respect for the difference" between the sexes.

Thus, the relegation of dominated groups to minority status is crystallized, and the concept of respect for "difference," which these groups had intended to be liberating, results in their own confinement. Academic specialization is a case in point of how this process works. For example, there is a sociology of "deviance," and psychology itself has been subdivided into specific fields for different age groups (child psychology, adolescent psychology, gerontology). The very existence of anthropology assumes a distinction between "civilized" populations and "primitive" peoples (Kinloch, 1979, 21).

It should be no surprise that the culture (understood as meaning all forms of behaviour) of each of the various minorities is labelled a "subculture" in the vocabulary of the social sciences. Although initially useful, the concept of subculture is a trap for the dominated, because it judges their values and behaviour by the implicit yardstick of an ideal *culture* which, in fact, is that of the dominator. In such a context, the subculture most often exhibits negative characteristics, which have the effect of isolating those who participate in it and which, though cultural by definition, sometimes come to be considered *constitutional*. Thus, transmitted from generation to generation in the case of the poor and people of colour, or springing up as a sort of fatality in individuals of advanced age or the mentally handicapped, and even among youth or gays, tendencies would emerge which, while not identical from one group to the next, would reflect a major "difference" in relation to the dominant model of values and behaviour. These tendencies could take the form either of excessive attention to the present and a need for immediate gratification, or of a lack of motivation or sustained effort, or of a ghetto mentality that would incline individuals to seek only the company of their peers (Waxman, 1977, 14–18; Levin and Levin, 1980, 64).

Though necessary to ensure a happy end to alienation, the dominated's exaltation of their "difference" therefore has major pitfalls. Not only do they risk confining themselves to an identity that will serve to "explain" them entirely, but the dominator will find it easy to accuse them of a lack of concern for the universal and reduce them to their difference, the better to exclude them.

The notion of inequality is implicit in the notion of difference. According to one popular saying, "If our Lord had wanted all men to be equal, He would have made them all alike." The underlying assumption is that equality results in similarity (Dumont, 1966, 30).

Yet if differences dictate inequality, this is because an ideal type of humanity is implicitly set up as the standard of measurement of those whose nature it is to be "other." Thus, as understood in the dominant discourse, difference does not evoke the diverse features of fundamentally equal individuals or groups, but rather a primary model which reflects, to those who do not essentially coincide with it, an image that is "lacking." As the centre or the summit, but primarily as a fixed point of reference, this model is intended as both the source of evaluation and the origin of definition. Thus, difference is neither neutral nor free; it is the product of dependence and domination (Guillaumin, 1979, 14–15).

The dominator is thus the only person who is not different from anyone: he simply *is*. This is why it is the role of the oppressed to be "other." Colette Guillaumin's observation regarding women is valid for all dominated groups:

We have accomplished the grammatical and logical *tour de force* of being different all by ourselves. It is our nature to be different. We are always something "more" or "less." We are never the term of reference. (Guillaumin, 1978, 16)

Thus, women *by themselves* can figure, in the French language, as "*personnes du sexe*" ("persons of gender"), or groups deemed to be more or less foreign can be considered "ethnic" *in and of themselves*. It will be noted that in the dominator's case, occupying the entire field of an identity is less a mark of reductive intent than of the strengthening of individuality (to be "aristocratic," to have "class").

Activists of emancipation movements thus must be aware that the road followed for a time by the oppressed of the exaltation of difference is a minefield. Coinciding with the (re)discovery of their history, the phase of self-pride should be only a phase, a state in the process of finally assuming their identity. Once they have overcome the shame of being inferior, it is time to refuse subordination and aspire to control their own destiny, which necessarily requires recognition of the principle of equality.

This equality is not demanded as a consequence of similarity, but rather as the *first foundation* of tolerance. This equality is a postulate and not a measure of resemblance. For what kind of resemblance could it be? A resemblance to an ideal human type, now known to borrow the traits of a dominator who imposes them as universal? And if not, then a resemblance to whom? If there is no longer any group that can claim to serve as a model for others, neither is there one that can claim to represent them all. Each group is *different from* the others, starting with the various dominant groups, who themselves differ from the dominated.

If there is no possible standard of similarity, neither can there be much of a criterion of equality. The equality at issue is the one established "in law" (Jacquard, 1978, 187–8). This does not deny the differences but treats them as secondary accidents rather than as the source of equality. As Tzvetan Todorov wrote: "Men must be recognized as equal to admit that they remain different... Tolerance based on equality has no limits: reciprocally, any non-egalitarian discrimination is condemnable" (Todorov, 1986, 12).

Like the principle of equality on which it depends, tolerance is a postulate. It must be accepted as such, for its own sake. Though undemonstrable, the principle of tolerance is no less legitimate. It is certainly more legitimate than the principle of similarity, which, when analyzed, is revealed to be indefensible. Its practical consequences are clearly more positive for dominated groups, since it does not have the automatic effect of denying their right to equality. On the other hand, the postulate of tolerance does not so much deny differences as it strips them of the essentialist character given to them by the dominant discourse, the better to show the relativity that they entail.

Although they have their own traits, specific by definition, the various identities are indeed relative. They take on reality only through contrast. This is why the notion of diversity is more likely to have a fortunate outcome than the notion of difference, which is still too heavily burdened with non-egalitarian presuppositions (d'Eaubonne, 1977, 162). In both cases, however, the dominant group must be identified systematically. It must be detected and named wherever it continues to hide behind the appearance of a "universal" discourse. It is important to recall, for example, that a masculinist lobby has existed for two hundred years to settle successive elections to the United States presidency, yet, precisely because it was unique, this monopoly went unchallenged. Moreover, when mayors of American cities are considered as possible candidates for vice-president, it will have to be pointed out that these individuals are white-skinned and, if applicable, that they run cities intolerant of homosexuals.

In short, the hidden presence of the dominant groups must be exposed until it becomes glaringly obvious that none of them can claim to be the perfect human type. Eventually, it will sink in that the notion of an ideal culture, as a yardstick against which "different" individuals and groups have been measured, is only one *subculture* among others, a subculture of adult White males with solid incomes, men presumed to be heterosexual and mentally and physically balanced. Since this *pressure group* has succeeded in imposing the belief that its own specificity coincides totally with universal Man, its values and behaviour have been elevated to the status of the only *politically correct* culture for centuries.

Aware that they benefit, due to certain aspects of their personality, from privileges devolved upon the dominant groups, otherwise dominated individuals understand the importance of literally spelling out their identity when they sign a work that the public might be tempted to consider "universal." In the tradition of theorists or researchers who insist on their *subjectivity* in the prefaces to their works, writers immediately will introduce themselves as having a *relative identity*. "I was born in 1960. I am white, gentile, middle class, ablebodied,"[23] one of the authors of a collection of feminist and lesbian articles published in England wrote. As laboured as it may seem, this enumeration has the merit of emphasizing the diversity of ways of being, thereby drawing attention to the true identity of artists and intellectuals, and even of experts, who have the illusion, if not the pretension, of maintaining a universal discourse.

By endeavouring to put the dominant group "in its place" (as one group among others), the oppressed display not only their desire for autonomy but their new awareness of needing some margin for control in society as a whole. After having assured themselves that equality is a principle of law, they must see that it is transformed into fact. In short, it becomes necessary to seek power. While in theory tolerance should be a postulate, in practice it is the result of a power relationship (Casamayor, 1975, 169). Indeed, recognition of a group's equal status can already be considered a measure of its existing influence. Exposure of the oppressor's claims to a universal and objective discourse is no guarantee that he is ready to renounce his privileges. Systematic reliance on tactical flexibility in his discourse, as well as the many methodological shortcuts taken by the experts who speak on his behalf, are constant evidence of his manifest determination to defend his interests.

Once the oppressor's good *conscience* has been found lacking, there is a risk that his good *will* in initiating the redistribution of status, wealth, and power will follow the path of greatest resistance. A frequent observation made by those who have attempted to "obtain" recognition of their rights from the oppressor is that autonomy is taken, not requested. The power demanded, which is total (at least in a legal sense) when it signifies control of the State by one people or by a social class, will often take the form of mere participation in decision-making for a dominated group previously denied the means to act or influence the discourse.

While some dominated individuals, despairing of being able to change the course of the dominant society at a particular point in its history, choose to live apart (as in the case of the lesbian feminists known as "separatists," the "Black Muslims," or popular anarchist groups), most prefer to endeavour to change it, either by working from within or by challenging its very foundations. Whether these activists define themselves or are considered reformists (some would say "moderates") or radicals, even revolutionaries, all seek some degree of power to balance or totally reverse a relationship that put their specific oppressed group at a disadvantage.

The Pursuit of Power

Victims very soon have to give up the grand illusion that there is some higher ideal in which the reconciled aspirations of both the dominated and the dominators will ultimately converge. Experience has taught the oppressed that there is no final destination, and that the struggle against oppression is never really over. As worthy of respect as they may be, the institutions that settle disputes are also parties to the conflict.

Because the oppressor possesses power, he also has the power to preserve it (Spender, 1983, 9). Yet since power will provide them with the means to be autonomous, the oppressed have no other choice than to struggle to take power for themselves. Thus, the second and third phases of oppression are linked to each other. By *acting*, the dominated oblige the dominator to *react* (ibid., 738). Though fundamentally necessary, this reversal of the power relationship should be directed at capturing the power *to* rather than the power *over* (Morgan, 1984, 30), and at gaining the power to do *something* rather than the power over *someone*. One thing is sure, however: this process is possible only through a collective struggle.

History shows that this struggle, when it involves an identity based on affiliation to a group, sometimes takes a violent form. Whether through a general strike or through a revolutionary uprising, unions and political parties, beginning in the nineteenth century, sought to ensure control of the State by the working class. Even when they aspired only to improve wages and working conditions, the conflicts they unleashed translated, at the very least, into a power struggle, if only to limit the scope of management rights, which had started out as absolute.

There is little difference in the struggles that sometimes pit regions and entire "races" against each other. In 1861, the northern and southern states of the United States found themselves caught up in a war that would last four years. Although the primary cause of this war was the conflicting attempts of Northern industrialists and Southern planters to secure control of the West, the plight of the slaves ultimately played a role as well.

While the dominated peoples of Europe did not open hostilities on their own behalf in 1914, they nevertheless profited from the consequences of the war when the Versailles Conference, in 1919, recognized their right to self-determination, a right refused by the continental empires of the previous century.

This same right would soon be demanded, especially after the Second World War, by the African and Asian colonies of the western powers. Whether or not they achieved independence peacefully depended on the degree of repression applied against them by the various colonial regimes. In the late eighteenth and early nineteenth centuries, American colonies of European powers (the future United States as well as certain Latin American colonies) had to rebel to obtain control over their own destinies. A commitment to social change would more often accompany the nationalist movements of the twentieth century. Though this twofold commitment to progress often took on the character of an uprising, this was not an absolute rule.

Québec's evolution is special because it has been influenced by the general context while partially following its own logic. Although activists referred both to the principle of national self-determination and the historical example of decolonization, the Québec situation was more similar to that of the American colonies seeking liberation in the eighteenth and nineteenth centuries than to that of the Asian and African countries making a political break with a totally alien western culture. Not only did Québec's dominated francophones and dominant anglophones occupy the same territory and share a common European heritage, but the former enjoyed a high standard of living, even if they did not control their economy. Thus, the social reforms achieved in the 1960s could be called a "Quiet Revolution," and the pro-sovereignty impulses manifested during that period led to simple autonomist arrangements (with Québec deciding to remain in Canada) two decades later. But in the early 1990s, the constitutional debate resumed in full force, in a climate of insidious tension that never completely faded away.

The unique fate of the Jews also took a dramatic turn both after and *because of* the Second World War. The Jews of Europe having been the victims of an attempt at genocide by Nazi Germany, the survivors decided to establish their own state. Receiving support from a West suffering from a bad conscience (based on an 800-year tradition of anti-Semitism, the Allies had been guilty of indifference to their fate), Ashkenazi Jews settled in a land already occupied by the Palestinians. As one diaspora replaced another, wars between Israelis and Arabs regularly inflamed the region. In recent years, this tragedy, which, in the words of one Israeli writer, pits "two peoples who are both right" against each other, spread, through terrorism, to the West, which up to then had been spared the violence of which it was the remote instigator.

But the use of force as a means of obtaining justice is not solely the product of ethnic conflicts with international implications. The use of violence also came to mark the liberation movement of African-Americans. Exasperated by the high psychological, and often physical, cost incurred in the use of non-violent tactics to obtain racial equality in the United States, some ended up resorting to force. In addition to the urban riots of the "long hot summers" of the latter half of the 1960s, the Black Panthers soon became known for their Maoist rhetoric and terrorist methods. Created in the 1930s, the "Black Muslims" sect now spoke the language of power, and, in an exhilarating phenomenon for African-Americans little accustomed to inspiring it, gained police respect (Baldwin, 1963, 67–8).

The key word in this period was power, sometimes linked to the use of violence but mainly conceived as a means of assuming one's identity and establishing autonomy. Activists in the 1960s did more than follow the specific example of the Black Panthers or the Black Muslims: they were engaged primarily in a general quest for "Black Power." Having gradually migrated from the southern United States to the cities of the north and west, the population of African origin began to use their purchasing power as a political tool. Accounting for 12 percent of the American population, they could bank on the fact that they had now spread through almost all of the United States, while remaining concentrated in one region (the South), where the real exercise of their voting rights could finally bring about change.

Other dominated groups profited from the lessons of the Black movement. While Chicanos abandoned the legal approach of the League of United Latin American citizens to adopt more radical methods of political and social action in states like California, Texas, and Arizona (Olson, 1979, 389), the aboriginal peoples of North America learned the virtues of "Red Power," evoking their historic rights, if not their demographic clout. Even in Europe, ethnic groups who had been ignored, when they were not oppressed outright, now dared to demand "regional power" (in Gras and Linet, 1977, 428).

In the past, when young people were associated with the use of force, they most often were involved in nationalist or class struggles.

But in the latter half of the 1960s, a phenomenon unique in history occurred: the eruption of a movement of youth *as youth*. A radical mixture of politics and counter-cultural idealism, this youth revolution soon took on an international character (Essler, 1971, 40). Challenging the established order (including the traditional Left) at the same time that it sought everywhere to be joyful and free (as in France's 1968 "May Revolution"), this revolt also took the form of active, sometimes vehement protest against the Vietnam War. In the United States, it not only linked up with a civil rights movement itself becoming less sensitive to the effectiveness of non-violence, it also gave rise to the birth of a New Left, critical both of the situation of the poor and of all values (including that of "objective" knowledge in education) conveyed by the White western bourgeoisie. A quest for power emerged in this case as well, and the concept of "Student Power" surfaced in turn.

Linked ideologically to the Black movement (at least in the United States) and to the more general struggle against imperialism and against all kinds of "establishments," "Student Power" nevertheless had scarcely anything to say about the emancipation of women. While the young men who aspired to this power wanted to claim kinship with a sexual revolution that cast down a number of ancient taboos, they nevertheless did not challenge the foundations of sexism. Women decided to split away and defend their own cause. This position would coincide with a radicalization of the feminist movement, a radicalization that, apart from its critique of patriarchal structures, was based on the belief that "the personal is political." Thus, the very foundations of the old dichotomy between public and private life were undermined.

It was during the same period, in the early 1970s, that "Gay Power" emerged. Triggered by the examplary act of resistance (by "effeminate" men, no less!) in the Stonewall riot against an umpteenth police raid on the homosexual bars of New York, the "Gay Power" movement did not hesitate to occupy the offices of homophobic publications, to interrupt meetings of "experts" advocating aversion therapies, or, like the feminists, to warn politicians that they had better take a stand on the condition reserved for homosexuals by society. (Twenty years later, they would be joined by bisexuals, as evidenced by the march on Washington in the spring of 1993.) Inspired in part by the American example, European emancipation movements formed common fronts (such as the Gay Liberation Front in England and the *Front homosexuel d'action révolutionnaire* in France). Torn between a gay militancy cross-bred with male chauvinism and a feminist movement often hostile to them, politically committed lesbians also formed a radical movement.

As the 1970s progressed, other dominated groups organized, inspired by the example of the activists of earlier years, including some (from the New Left and the civil rights movement) who seemed to have lost steam by then. Thus, "Gray Power" or a "Gray Panther" movement developed, demanding economic equality for the elderly and challenging the validity of compulsory retirement.

By the beginning of the 1980s, the dominated groups in whose name the established order still claimed to speak indirectly obtained a voice, as in the case of children, for example. Since women continued to be the main caregivers and since the abuses committed against them by adults mainly affected girls, the feminist movement made the defence of children one of its objectives.

Also vulnerable, the mentally handicapped began to find champions, and also tried to speak for themselves. The more demanding nature of their requests fit in not only with the hard line adopted by the theorists of the anti-psychiatric movement but with other liberation movements as well. From the simple plea expressed in J.C. Pagé's 1961 work, *Les fous crient au secours*, they moved on to critical denunciation in the 1980s. The first step in the liberation process was taken with *Erreur sur la personne*, which proposed to demonstrate the "similarity between the mental patient and his fellow citizens" (Provencher, 1982, 26), while the second and third phases of emancipation would be illustrated, in 1984, by *La folie comme de raison*, a publication of the *Solidarité-Psychiatrie* collective that called for "the right to be crazy."

The physically handicapped had already established associations to defend their rights in the 1970s. These associations demanded better integration into society by proposing that jobs be opened to them and that homes, public places, and means of transportation (private or public) be adapted to their needs. History will no doubt remember the strike in March 1988 by the deaf students of Gallaudet College in Washington as the turning point in the social evolution of the handicapped. Supported by comrades from every corner of the world, these students drew upon the precedents created by the Black and feminist movements to demand that the administrators of their institutions henceforth be chosen by their own community. This worldwide solidarity movement appeared again, four years later, at "Independence 92," an international conference on handicaps, held in Vancouver, a conference that brought together representatives from more than a hundred countries.

It has thus become increasingly obvious that emancipation for different oppressed groups not only speaks a similar language but follows approximately the same historical stages. The post-war decades have shown that liberation movements are linked to each other chronologically, with the newest borrowing their emancipatory rhetoric from the older ones.

What is more, if one judges by the *numbers* represented by all of the oppressed, their sheer weight alone should enhance the logical ties that already join them together in solidarity. Although there are many overlaps between groups, it should be remembered that the Third World accounts for three-quarters of the world population (from a demographic standpoint, it would be even more appropriate to refer to the "First" World), or that children (Boulding, 1979, 7) and women represent more than 50 percent. The scope of poverty is also dumbfounding. While one-third of the inhabitants of the southern hemisphere are hungry and undernourished, one out of every four people in the world is homeless. The West itself is faced with an unemployment rate that averaged nearly 10 percent of all workers in 1992 for OECD countries, or 30 million individuals.

There seems to be something fateful about the 10 percent figure, since it emerges as the most frequent proportion represented by several dominated groups. Ten percent is the approximate share of the population represented by handicapped individuals (Veil, 1982, 267–8) and (though it is debatable) homosexuals throughout the world, by Blacks in the United States (11 percent, in fact), and by the elderly in the western world. However, with extended life expectancy and a falling birth rate, the demographic clout of the elderly in the industrialized countries is bound to increase. On the other hand, while 3 percent of the population live with an intellectual handicap (*Les personnes handicapées au Québec* I, 1984, 36), it would appear that about one-third of the individuals residing in these countries visit a psychologist or a psychiatrist during their lifetimes.

In societies where pluralism is taking on an increasingly cultural (rather than religious) character, the question of demographic ratios between groups of different ethnic origins is finally arising. Out of all the independent states on the globe in 1971, only 9 percent were ethnically homogeneous, while 30 percent had single major ethnic groups representing less than 50 percent of their population and 40 percent had at least five important ethnic groups.[24] North America historically has been a land of immigration. With the exception of 2 million Natives descended from aboriginal peoples brutally conquered in the past, Canada and the United States are the products of the influx of 12 million and 47 million immigrants respectively since the beginning of the seventeenth century.[25] Even western Europe now has to reckon with ethnic minorities representing from 7 percent to 14 percent of the population, depending on the country.[26] The even older question of regions still remains relevant, with 50 million

Europeans living in conditions that have provoked their discontent in this regard (Gras and Gras, 1982, 19). A more global challenge, though the number of individuals immediately concerned seems more limited, is the precarious existence of 17 million refugees around the world at the beginning of the 1990s.

In absolute figures, all dominated groups, taken together, thus form a strong majority of the world's population. If one considers the fact that most persons making up these groups have one or more close relations among the members of the dominant group, this majority should rise to sufficiently respectable proportions for relationships of domination to be extinguished. The deep kinship between the discourses of the various oppressed groups seeking emancipation, as well as the chain reaction linking their liberation movements, should fuel the solidarity between different victims of intolerance. Yet it must be observed that these victims all too often do not find it relevant to co-operate, and treat each other as adversaries.

According to Christiane Rochefort, "oppressed groups are objectively allies. All they have to do is realize it" (1976, 41). However, it appears that for such a higher state of consciousness to bear fruit, the real obstacles to a truly common struggle must be taken into account. There are many *centrifugal* factors to contend with, the most important being that those who are dominated in one way often prove to be dominant elsewhere.

Prudence is even more essential in relations with a dominator who is quite capable, when necessary, of mounting a specific discourse against emancipation movements. The very identity of activists may cause them problems from the outset and help to discredit their discourse and action before they have even begun.

Two situations may arise: either the activists (or thinkers) belong to the dominated group (most often) or they come from the dominant group. In either case, however, they risk attracting the wrath of both groups at once. If they come from the dominated group, the oppressor will feel entitled to accuse them of "subjectivism" and will call the validity of their discourse into question. But these members of the dominated group will not find favour in the eyes of their peers, either. For example, they will be accused of being "not competent enough" (a complex of alienation) or of having "betrayed" their own people by "making it" in their struggle (Marsalla and White, 1982, 344; Berry and Tischler, 1978, 230).

Activists (or theorists) who come from the dominant ranks will also be called "traitors" or "turncoats" by their own group: a traitor to his sex when a man is a feminist (Strauss, 1982), or traitors to their race when a White or an "Aryan" sides with Blacks or Jews ("nigger-lovers" or "Jew-lovers"), or traitors to their class when members of the bourgeoisie become revolutionaries. The dominated whom they seek to defend will often react with suspicion, initially regarding their motives as questionable.

In general, activists (or researchers) will be charged with the major offences of opportunism and extremism. Opportunism, because they will be accused of "making a career on the backs of the oppressed" and "profiting" from an emancipation movement to "succeed" or "enrich themselves" (Friedan 1981; Memmi, 1972, 111; *L'écran handicapé*, 1983, 115); extremism, because the new point of view that they defend will be deemed to depart from the "happy medium" and will thus be a virtual threat to both the victim and the oppressor. The oppressors will have a fine time playing the moderates against the extremists "on both sides" (treating White racists and African-Americans who have run out of patience as two sides of the same coin), or projecting the abuses for which they are themselves responsible onto the activists (Pinochet accusing the Chilean Communists of "profiting" from the economic recession), or claiming to protect the dominated against the ill will of false representatives (the Anglo-Québec establishment championing the right of francophone workers to speak English against the wishes of "bourgeois" nationalists).

The oppressor's self-righteousness in relation to the victims thus extends into the belief that he is striking at personal ambition and fanaticism expressed through militant discourse. He will play up criticism of dissident intellectuals "cut off from ordinary people," ordinary people of whom he claims, despite his privileged status, to be the sole true interpreter. People of action will not be treated any more mildly: he will see them as "new pretenders to power," ready to abuse the "guileless masses" that he himself aspires to shield with his "disinterested" protection (in Grimal, 1965, 29–30).

Having already declared himself to be the prey of the dominated, the oppressor, with even stronger purpose, will pose as the victim of the militants who call for their emancipation. Calling the redress of the inequalities he has maintained a form of "reverse discrimination," the dominator will use the specious argument that the oppressed are tyrannizing those who had initially deprived them of their rights. Sometimes forced to recognize the wrongs he has caused, he will hasten to claim that "two wrongs don't make a right." A White American who is not offended at the fact that a disproportionate number of Blacks were sent to Vietnam or that African-Americans sometimes account for up to 40 percent of "Death Row" prisoners in the nation's penitentiaries will nevertheless find it unacceptable that affirmative action is intended to increase their presence in institutions of higher learning. The dominator will even consider it a form of oppression that it is no longer possible for him to oppress. A Canadian organization, Real Women, cried injustice because the federal minister responsible for the Status of Women refused to give it funding to promote its non-egalitarian views on what a "real" woman is and to fight against the extension of rights to the gay minority.

The offended reactions, even the apocalyptic prophecies, that often greet proposals favourable to the dominated groups are nothing new. Those who opposed the Napoleonic Code's secularization of marriage, legalization of divorce, and decriminalization of homosexual practices predicted the end of the family and the proliferation of homophilic orgies in the streets (in Marmor, 1980, 93). Conservatives of the 1920s feared the death of the planet, after that of the family, because women were given the right to vote (Faderman, 1981, 334). Even today, feminists are regularly tarred with epithets like "wild-eyed" and "aggressive" (or *déchaînées*, *agressives*, and *enragées* in French). On another front, while anglophone Canadians accused Franco-Manitobans of "blackmail" for seeking to enforce their constitutional rights, which had been flouted for ninety-four years, French Quebecers concerned with defending their language, by adopting Bill 101, were compared to the supporters of Idi Amin Dada and the gauleiters of Adolf Hitler.[27]

The oppressor's discourse does not always adopt such a vehement tone. More adroitly, he will present himself as even-handed and open-minded. In the name of equality, for example, he will refuse to grant "special rights" to "particular" groups. "It would be unfair to heterosexuals, who are required to be abstinent, to admit gays into the armed forces," said one high-ranking military officer.

Apparently converted to the virtues of egalitarianism, the dominator also shows he is sensitive to factors of disunion. His discourse presents the established order as a harmonious whole in which any opposition challenge would seem gratuitous. From this perspective, defending a cause, and even defending oneself, will automatically be classified as an aggressive act. Federalists have long accused proponents of Québec sovereignty of "dividing families." Feminists have been charged with "driving" men "traumatized" by new and *equal* relationships to homosexuality.

The oppressor, who has already tried to put the burden of proof on the shoulders of the victim, will now endeavour to have activists bear the blame for conflict. Often he will express nostalgia for an era when "everyone got along so well," an era when women and children willingly submitted to the authority of the "head of the family," or when homosexuals did not "attack" the majority by "flaunting themselves."

It was the defenders of Dreyfus who triggered the development of anti-Semitism in France, claimed Pierre Boutang on the French program *"Apostrophes."*[28] Eleanor Roosevelt swayed "class against class and race against race" when she insisted on inviting Black singer Marian Anderson to sing at the White House, one of the Daughters of the American Revolution indignantly charged (Warwick, 1980, 105). Western liberals have adopted a paternalistic attitude to South Africa and are using it as a laboratory for their grand social theories, lamented the South African ambassador to Canada, Glenn Babb, before returning home.

Declared to be troublemakers, activists will sometimes be tempted to make concessions to the dominator. Some will resort to the proven tactic of creating a foil, offering the least unorthodox dominated group the advantage of proposing an adversary to the oppressor which they can both reject, thus making their own demands seem moderate. This is why feminists have considered it opportune to ignore and even justify the marginalization of their lesbian sisters, or why gays themselves have ridiculed those of their peers whom they consider "effeminate." Even the physically handicapped sometimes play upon the negative perception that society has of some of them (*L'écran handicapé*, 1983, 129), with the blind being better accepted than the deaf, and the mutilated better regarded than the paralysed (Veil, 1982, 216).

In a curious irony, activists of an oppressed group risk finding themselves shoulder to shoulder with dubious allies. Corporations or pressure groups, sometimes for completely opposite reasons, have an interest in defending the same demands. The dominated then face the dilemma of involving themselves in a tactical association that, in the long run, may provide ammunition to adversaries who today are allies of circumstance.

Feminists have scarcely been exempt from such dilemmas. For example, on the question of abortion, they were on the same side as the owners of magazines like *Playboy*, while those feminists who favour censorship against pornography find themselves equivocal partners in the ranks of various fundamentalist religions. There is nothing new about this type of conflict. When British feminists and socialists at the turn of the century fought for motherhood to be a free choice, exercised under the best possible conditions, they were guaranteed the support of racists and imperialists (Rowbotham, 1974, 106). Even today, the demands of middle-class White women for the right to choose abortion are in apparent contradiction with the fears of women from ethnic and "racial" minorities who have a long history of forced sterilizations, or with those Third World feminists who are well aware that the means of contraception received in their countries are supplied by the United States and the World Bank (Morgan, 1984, 26). Finally, feminist and nationalist Irishwomen who can freely determine the use of their bodies in England are denied freedom of choice in an independent Catholic Ireland.

It is therefore not rare that, in endeavouring to solve a problem in one area, activists from dominated groups are placed in the position of creating a new one elsewhere. Aware that they sometimes have to choose between a course of action riddled with pitfalls and a complicit passivity to the established order, activists risk jumping from the frying pan into the fire and paying for their aspirations toward progress with even greater confusion. The questionable aid they receive from allies who are more circumstantial than real makes no small contribution to this obfuscation of the issues. While they sometimes adopt a discourse similar to that of the oppressed, these allies most often hark to opposing values (including the hierarchical ranking of human beings) and always have different objectives in mind (the confirmation or hardening of the status quo, for example). If alliances are intended to be permanent, they will have to be made with more natural partners.

To be "natural," the eventual partners of dominated groups seeking emancipation must necessarily share their resolve to transform non-egalitarian relations between identity groups, and thus to be part of the progressive forces of society. This primarily applies to so-called left-wing organizations, which claim to be driven by a commitment to change rather than by the desire to conserve the status quo (a motivation attributed to the Right). An essentially relative notion, "the Left" has evolved on the social and political chessboard along with historical shifts in issues, with former progressive movements serving as the right-wing point of reference for other, more recent initiatives. Thus, initially identified with liberalism, the western Left became linked to socialism, and then to Communism, which itself ultimately became confused with the defence of a new established order. The historical trajectory of the Left followed the path of the American War of Independence and the French Revolution, before moving in the direction of the Soviet Revolution, the results of which eventually would be contested by the Trotskyists, the Maoists, and the radicals of the New Left.

It is therefore no surprise that, while all kinds of oppressed groups have been able to find natural allies in left-wing movements, the positions taken by the latter over the past two centuries have sometimes varied and thus have disappointed the hopes placed in them. Although, by definition, they are more inclined than the Right to struggle on behalf of the victim, this does not necessarily mean that they *always* espouse the victim's cause. Not only are the forces of the Left divided, but they may choose to dedicate themselves to the liberation of one dominated group without being concerned about that of another, and may even work to the detriment of an oppressed group.

Founded on respect for individual rights and freedoms, which aristocratic privileges had hitherto stifled, liberalism did not consider it appropriate, for example (except for a fairly brief time in France), to extend to all men of the lower classes the voting rights that the American War of Independence and the French Revolution had won for members of the bourgeoisie. The property qualification for voters, which favoured the property-owning classes, continued to prevail for varying periods of time, depending on the country. Women had to wait nearly a century and a half to be granted the same voting rights. In 1793, the French Revolution explicitly denied them the status of citizens (on the same basis as children, the insane, and criminals), until the Napoleonic Code made them into legal and intellectual minors (Callu, 1978, 18–19). The revolutionaries justified this exclusion in the name of the same "Nature" that they had invoked against privileges.

Nevertheless, it was the French Revolution that allowed Jews to obtain citizenship and "emancipated" them from the centuries-old social barriers erected against them. With a tardiness paralleling their delay in granting universal male suffrage, the United States and England followed a similar course a few years later. It should be remembered that Native Americans were recognized as citizens only in 1934, and that, in the western world, Blacks continued to be denied the very status of "persons" and not only that of citizens. After a first attempt at abolition during the French Revolution, the slave trade, and then the institution of slavery itself, were suppressed only in the nineteenth century by England and France. A civil war was even necessary to end slavery in the United States.

For European liberalism, the question of slavery gave way to the colonial question. Generous in its intentions toward its colonies, Revolutionary France nonetheless resolved never to break the ties of dependence that formed the legal basis of its universal aims. Republicans justified the conquest of Algeria in 1830, for example, in the name of France's pretensions to a "civilizing mission" (Merle, 1969, 23–32). Indeed, the nineteenth century was the age of the grand imperialist thrust of the western powers into Africa and Asia. The universalist French revolutionaries also engaged in imperialism within their own territory, as the Jacobin tradition fostered centralization and even the destruction of regional dialects. For the Left of that period, the "provinces" represented the reactionary forces, which is what they would long continue to embody for socialists and Communists.

The status of full citizenship, the primary condition for the exercise of civil rights, thus was not extended to everyone. While the male members of the lower classes, for fiscal reasons, were treated as second-class citizens, entire categories of people were deemed unfit for citizenship. Unfit, because their "race" had reduced them to the status of slaves; unfit, because they were stricken with a disability due to their age, gender, or state of mental health; or unfit because, as the study of the plight of homosexuals in Anglo-Saxon countries has shown, their sexual orientation rendered them unworthy of the title of citizen.

Arising from the Industrial Revolution, which cruelly exposed the deficiencies of exclusively individual rights, socialism would subordinate the emancipation of various oppressed groups to that of the workers. This does not mean that the socialists were less sympathetic to these groups than the liberals. But while women and homosexuals, for example, frequently had to defend themselves to the socialists for promoting a cause judged to be too individualistic, national and regional movements were perceived as unorthodox competitors in the sphere of collective rights. What is more, these different groups were sometimes portrayed as reactionary forces to be neutralized, if not destroyed.

Women, who had found a few liberal champions in Tom Paine, Condorcet, and John Stuart Mill, certainly received support from several socialist theoreticians, both "utopian" (Charles Fourier, Saint-Simon, Robert Owen) and Marxist (Friedrich Engels, August Bebel). But like the liberals, Proudhon would deny them the right to equality in the name of "nature" (in Gallant, 1984, 65). In practice, the trade union movement in the nineteenth century also called for the return of women to the home rather than pay equity between the genders, and some of its members excluded women automatically from their ranks. After the First World War, socialists and Communists carried on the reluctance displayed by earlier left-wing organizations to recruit women, publicly questioning their allegedly innate conservatism (Rowbotham, 1974, 163) and accusing working women of being "inert masses" (Dufrancatel, 1979, 181). While American trade unionists and socialists in the 1920s claimed that the Equal Rights Amendment, the first constitutional amendment proposed to ensure equality for women, was a symbolic measure aimed at bourgeois women in the Republican Party, French radicals and socialists of the Popular Front opposed women's suffrage in 1936, alleging that the Catholic Church influenced them conservatively.

The reaction of socialists to homosexuals was equivocal as well, marked at first by the open-minded attitude of certain leaders and then by rejection on the part of the movement as a whole. Decriminalized by liberalism in Napoleonic France, homosexuality continued to be the object of legal condemnation in countries of Germanic and Anglo-Saxon traditions. Through their (fruitless) opposition to a particularly repressive piece of German legislation (paragraph 175 of the Penal Code), men like Lassalle, Bernstein, Bebel, and Kautsky, at the turn of the twentieth century, expressed the first socialist viewpoint on the question. In the same period in England, it was socialists once again (if not all socialists) who supported the cause of gays through the efforts of Edward Carpenter. Finally, in 1917, the Bolsheviks themselves abolished the homophobic laws enacted under the Czarist regime.

Starting in the 1930s, however, Stalinist laws again made homosexual practices a crime. The Left then began to denounce homosexuality as a form of "fascist perversion" and bourgeois decadence. This about-face had dramatic consequences for certain individuals caught up in the toils of the Second World War. Prisoners in Nazi concentration camps who wore the pink triangle (the colour derisively imposed by Hitler's regime) had to suffer from the actions of political deportees who did not hesitate to draw up extermination lists for the SS, putting homosexuals first among those who would be worked to death (Heger, 1981, 23–4). In more recent years, the Dachau International Committee rejected a proposal for a commemorative plaque honouring the gays who had lost their lives there, and it is now known that homophiles are persecuted in Castro's Cuba and shot in Communist China.

Ambiguous regarding women and curiously favourable to homosexuals, the initial attitude of the Marxist Left to ethnic groups (dominated or not) was automatically hostile. Regions had already been perceived as reactionary entities by liberals; socialism also saw the rise of nationalism as the doing of bourgeois forces. Socialists thus advocated the development of an international working-class consciousness beyond, and even at the expense of, feelings of national affiliation ("Workers of the world, unite!"). However, this theoretical position was countered by the outbreak of the First World War. After declaring their aversion to participation in the conflict, European socialist parties opted, to the detriment of international proletarian solidarity, for a "sacred union" with the more conservative parties of their countries. The unity of the Left was fatally compromised by this split, as shown by the creation, at the end of the war, of henceforth competitive socialist and Communist parties.

Ironically enough, Stalin himself would not hesitate to appeal to Russian nationalism during the Second World War, which the Soviets would then name the "Great Patriotic War." The social revolutions that occurred around the globe in the post-war years had all the greater chance of success if they were accompanied by a nationalist impetus. This was shown by the evolution of certain countries toward decolonization, the best examples being China and Cuba. This reality troubled the European Left, which believed it had "surpassed" the nationalist reflex. Indeed, with the exception of Proudhon, the "utopian" socialists of the nineteenth century had tried to justify colonialism in the name of universalism (Merle, 1969, 37). It was only one small step from this position to a revisionist approach to the issue of colonialism. Today, one segment of the Left proclaims itself disillusioned with Third-Worldism and disappointed with the despotic regimes of Africa and Asia, thus denying them the right to make mistakes, a right that the West itself has largely exercised (Amin et al., 1979).

Not always free of nationalist reactions, the Left did not necessarily succeed in solving the challenge posed by racism to its members. In the nineteenth century, Fourier and Proudhon were hard on the Jews (Poliakov, III, 1968, 471), and even today, anti-Semitism persists in the former USSR. In the post-slavery United States, at the turn of the twentieth century, the Socialist Party of Eugene Debs was indifferent to the condition of Blacks, an indifference that it attempted to justify by the ideological precedence of the labour question (Davis, 1983, 151). As for North American trade unions (which, it is true, practised business unionism), they had a long tradition of excluding Blacks or practising segregation against them (Marwick, 1980, 123) and of denouncing the Japanese and Chinese "yellow peril" (Olson, 1979, 395; Labelle et al., 1980, 16). Although they are more to the left on the political spectrum, French unions like the CGT (Communist) or the CFDT (Socialist) have not always ensured that foreign workers (except, more recently, Italians and Spaniards) feel accepted in their ranks (Granotier, 1979, 271).

In addition to the challenge of racism, there are the dominating relationships between unequal ethnic groups, relations in which the Left has perceived the need for a struggle against the demon of ethnocentrism. Thus, in the name of Soviet principle, Russian nationalism was imposed on the other peoples of the USSR, and genuine local Communists who appeared to threaten the establishment of Soviet hegemony in the various countries of Central Europe were eliminated. Though in a less immediately dramatic way, the Canadian New Democratic Party, alongside the big corporations that it otherwise denounced, endeavoured to contain the aspirations of a secular and social democratic Québec to self-determination in the 1980 referendum and then, one year later, to support a constitutional package from which the only francophone province in Canada was excluded.

Finally, the Left has sometimes forgotten the interests of the very groups of which it claims to be the leading representative. Periods of economic crisis (including those of 1929 and 1982) exposed the propensity of unions not only to call for the return of women to the home, the more or less forced early retirement of older workers, and the repatriation of foreign workers to their countries, but to choose to defend those who already had jobs rather than non-union workers or the unemployed (Marwick, 1980, 190–2). But there are even more troubling examples. Established in the name of the principles of proletarian revolution and remaining the only model of their achievement for thirty years, the Soviet regime in the Stalin era nevertheless exhibited the traits of a once again non-egalitarian society. The dominant class that emerged, if it did not actually own the means of production, nonetheless monopolized power and maintained its control over a State that, according to Marxist theory, was supposed to wither away. With time, the presence of practically unremovable leaders stamped the system with a periodic tendency to gerontocracy.

It was in part in reaction to the Soviet model and, in general, to a Left that it perceived as having become bourgeois that the New Left appeared in the late 1960s. Critical of all structures and values that might seem traditional, the adherents of the Youth International Party (the "yippies") nevertheless continued to convey very conservative, even oppressive notions regarding groups that had been marginalized for centuries. Though libertarian for themselves, students did not mean to include the practice of homosexuality in the sexual revolution and only conceived of women's participation in the form of constant availability to their male partners.

Women (just as young as they) who aspired to promote the emancipation of their gender were treated as though they were sexually frustrated and were advised to shut up, or even expelled from meetings (Hymovitz and Weissman, 1978, 348; Fitzgerald et al., 1982, 16; Collectif Clio, 1982, 482–3; Touraine, 1978, 145–6). In the view of these radicals, raising the problem of the status of women was a form of cultural reduction of the fundamental stakes of the struggle, which were primarily economic. To this traditional criticism, they added the accusation that only the interests of middle-class women were being promoted. Yet nobody seemed to be offended that the students themselves, like the great professional revolutionaries (Marx, Engels, Lenin, Trotsky, Mao, Castro, and even the hero of the 1960s, Che Guevara) were members of the bourgeoisie!

The New Left did not support homosexual activists any more than it had accepted the demands of the feminists as legitimate. On the contrary, its opponents were frequently labelled "faggots" or, in French, "*pédés*" or "*tapettes*" (as in the reference to Pierre Trudeau in the FLQ Manifesto), betraying the implicit (and traditional) association between the revolutionary will and a certain concept of virility (Altman, 1976, 182–95; Ménard, 1982, 244). As it long had done, the Left criticized homosexuals for their supposed accommodation with bourgeois sentimentalism and their indifference to the oppression of others. The charge brought against them by activists including, in the Third World, an organization as respectful of human rights as Amnesty International was not so different. According to these critics, there were more important causes than the defence of people whose lifestyle was the result of "western ennui." Thus, Amnesty International remained silent on the persecution of gays until 1991.

In the past two centuries, the progressive forces seeking to rectify social inequalities in the West thus have not always extended their commitment to change to all dominated groups. There have even been cases in which these forces have sanctioned the oppression of such groups. This attitude was sometimes inspired by the internal logic of their own theories, and sometimes by an oppressive tradition that they carried on unknowingly. As shown more specifically by the plight of women, homosexuals, and ethnic or "racial" communities, even though the victims received support from the Left more often than from the Right, this support was never constant or automatic. There were even cases in which activists of other dominated groups had to count liberals, socialists, Communists, and even members of the New Left among their adversaries. It thus became necessary to seek emancipation distinct from if not in competition with, that of the lower social orders.

However, just as the champions of the Left and of the oppressed do not necessarily have the will to join in common fronts, there is no spontaneous solidarity uniting these groups with each other. For example, conflicts of interest pit groups against each other, in the same way that such conflicts oppose all of them to the dominator. But the ultimate paradox of power relationships is that the dominated, precisely *because* they are victims, will sometimes be inclined to act as oppressors in turn. Far from identifying with other people in distress, they will prefer to alleviate the shame of being victims by crushing those who are weaker than they. This is a particularly pernicious process, based more on an indefinitely renewed contempt (for oneself and for other victims) than on the simple competition that motivates groups placed in a conflict of interests.

Such conflicting interests are frequent. The case of the tumultuous relations between Irish and French Canadians, for example, is well known. Both Catholic and both subject to English domination, they contended for control of the Church hierarchy and to obtain industrial jobs in Canada and New England. Unemployment also generally induces conflicting interests: since the two energy crises, young people have found themselves competing with migrants, retirees, and the handicapped on the secondary job market (*Le chômage des jeunes*, 1980, 10).

Competition for income is sometimes combined with a struggle for power. Thus, under the seniority principle often prevailing in the field of employment, the last hired under affirmative action programs will be the first to be laid off in the event of recession. It may even happen that these programs are only incentive-based or stipulate neither deadlines nor quotas for certain groups (the handicapped, for example), while more energetic measures have been taken to favour others (especially members of racial minorities and women) (Bowe, 1978, 15, 31).

Finally, the oppressed can be divided according to status. One need only recall the insidious tension between African-Americans and Jews, each group laying claim, through their respective experience of two and a half centuries of slavery or genocide, to the title of greatest victim. In other cases, competition for status passes through a stage of competition for specificity. In the area of institutionalization, for example, the poor, the handicapped, and the elderly have to fight to gain respect for their differences and resist being lumped into the same category.

However, solidarity is even more problematic when the very identities of different dominated groups come into opposition with each other. The dynamics of oppression then demand that self-assertion be achieved by negating the dignity of another. Subjected to the dominator, the oppressed carve out a territory in which they are the masters. The hierarchical nature of the relations that men seek to maintain with women within dominated ethnic or social groups is a good illustration of this process. Since women are perceived as the only "property" remaining to them, men will label women's egalitarian urges "emasculation." This was the discourse of many working-class males in the nineteenth century (Dufrancatel *et al.*, 1979, 167–8). As statements by Eldridge Cleaver and Stokeley Carmichael show, it was also taken up by Black Power militants in the 1960s.[29] Aboriginal feminists who called for independent participation in the Canadian constitutional talks in 1992 had not forgotten either that male band chiefs, for eleven years, had opposed the demands of Indian women to regain their Native status. In the Third World, some even see excision as a right to be upheld against the "colonialist" influence of western feminism (in *Enjeux ethniques*, 1983, 61).

A similar phenomenon occurred in the West in the last century, when an anti-slavery congress, held in London in 1840, decided to exclude women from its deliberations. Although the first feminists were also militant abolitionists, suffragists did not hesitate either, at the turn of the twentieth century, to invoke eugenic arguments to obtain voting rights for White women that had been granted only the Black males (Hymovitz and Weissman, 1978, 86; Davis, 1983, 70–115).

But most often, certain dominated groups seek to set themselves apart from other dominated individuals who might add to the burden of their already despised condition. Thus, the "poor Whites" of the South rejected ties with Blacks. Similarly, people of an inferior social or "racial" group might more readily reject the mentally ill (Dear and Taylor, 1982, 55–8).

Likewise, the men of an ostracized community will be particularly hostile to gays, perceiving homosexuality as the effect of the dominant group's desire to emasculate members of their gender (Cleaver, 1968, 102–3), unless the dominant group itself is accused of decadent homophilic tendencies (Fanon, 1952, 147). Gays are charged with having the same aims as feminists, namely a desire to destroy male virility.

Yet despite all kinds of divisions that have pitted the oppressed against each other for centuries, real *solidarity* is emerging, particularly in the past decade, and has survived the apparent splintering of militancy. Alliances are developing between local or national groups, which often work on specific issues in a sort of parallel "front" of everyday struggles. Sometimes the sole connecting factor for these alliances is the will to create a rallying point for those abandoned by the established order. This was one of the meanings of the Rainbow Coalition of U.S. Democratic presidential candidate Jesse Jackson. The ecology and anti-nuclear movement also became a crystallizing point for categories of activists as apparently different as regionalists, eco-feminists, and certain grassroots groups.

Anxious to tilt the balance of power in their favour, other dominated groups, like women, Amerindians, and francophones in Canada in November 1981, will seek a tactical rapprochement capable of triggering a better response to their demands (constitutional, in all three cases). More articulately, and more vilified, the "Loony Left" in England is waging a struggle to correct the threefold inequality caused by the present relations between classes, races, and genders. In general, there is a more lively awareness that attacks on the rights of a specific group (by skinheads and neo-Nazis, for example) are a virtual threat to others. This seems to have been understood by the ethnic and racial minorities who voted against a proposition to exclude homosexuals from teaching positions in California, as well as by the women's groups who expressed concern about manifestations of racism against Blacks and Jews in Alberta.

In addition to the effective solidarity emerging among activists of various oppressed groups, there are the increasingly frequent convergences of issues in the reports of public organizations concerned with social progress, as well as the theoretical studies proposing a synthesis of dominating relationships. While organizations seek more immediately practical solutions, theorists are endeavouring to find a parameter of identity which would logically include all others. Yet the two approaches can complement each other, since the very evolution of this analysis tends to show that the quest for a universal category of identity depends on a pragmatic approach.

It is easier to theorize about the fundamental nature of a specific type of domination than to prove it. Establishing a hierarchy of horrors among various forms of oppression also presumes the existence of an impossible consensus on the method of evaluation selected. To claim to include all forms of intolerance, the chosen parameter of identity therefore must obey criteria that are primarily practical. The more frequently a parameter overlaps with others, the more valid its pretensions of universality will seem. It then will become more auspicious to seek common solutions to dominating relationships now intersected by a single, coherent line.

The different courses followed in looking for a common thread in the dynamics of intolerance have one thing in common: they use categories of identity as reference points. Thus, the notion of *social handicap* is sometimes evoked as a metaphor for deficiency in the victimization process. By extending to the collective realm a disadvantaged condition more often associated with an individual's physical or mental state, this analogy highlights the inadequacies of the principle of equality before the law when not combined with real equal opportunity.

But symbolic convergences have crystallized most often around the automatically collective concepts of *colonization* and *class*. These symbolic convergences have historical consanguinity as well, if one recalls that the movement for emancipation of African and Asian countries from western control was the first to arise after the Second World War.

Understood as a synonym for alienation, the term "colonization" was then applied to all situations of dependency, including that of children, as evidenced by the evocative title of Gérard Mendel's book *Pour décoloniser l'enfant* (Decolonizing the Child), published in the early 1970s.

However, it is mainly "racial" minorities that have claimed the parallel with colonized peoples, starting with the Black Power movement in the United States. The awareness of a privileged link with African, Asian, and Latin American countries even developed, in recent years, into one of effective kinship with the Third World among immigrants of colour in Canada, the United States, and Great Britain.

Aboriginal peoples, as the first inhabitants of the North American continent, also identify with the populations of the southern hemisphere. But in this case, as in that of the regionalist and nationalist movements of the northern hemisphere, they have preferred to talk about "internal colonialism." While Robert Lafont proposed an entire program for regional decolonization in *Décoloniser en France: les régions face à l'Europe* (1971), Michael Hechter entitled his book *Internal Colonialism: the Celtic Fringe in British National Development* (1977).

In a variation on the same theme, Michel Foucault noted the existence of exclusion zones where "regional sexualities" were bottled up (1976, 66), and the American writer Jill Johnston proposed the formation of a "lesbian nation" as a solution to the condition of women (1973), an appellation that anticipated the "Queer Nation" movement of the 1990s.

As indicated in the references previously mentioned, comparisons with the plight of the colonized to designate the various manifestations of alienation were particularly frequent in the 1970s. But it was also during that period that the relationship with social class began to be confirmed, a relationship that continues to fuel reflection.

Used to account for economic exploitation, this relationship also gave rise to the concept of "proletarian nation" or "people-class" (*"peuple-classe"*). Already applied to regions and ethnic groups in Great Britain and France sometimes said to be on the fringe, which had been sacrificed on the altar of the nation state, this concept also served to describe the situation of the French population in Canada, a situation that the Royal Commission on Bilingualism and Biculturalism would show to be all the more economically inferior to that of anglophones residing in Québec.

In the wake of the student movement of the late 1960s, the term "chronological underclass" was also invoked to designate the youth generation (Rochefort, 1976, 52; Silverstein, 1973, 1). Originally used to describe an overall condition of dependence, it has now taken on precise economic traits. Following a demographic imbalance, which paradoxically worked to the advantage of the radical generation of 1968, and a series of economic recessions, the complete solution of which is always put off to a later date, many young people in the 1980s and 1990s would provide a reserve of cheap labour and become the prime target of unemployment, even creating a subproletariat employed on a part-time, minimum-wage, and freelance basis.

Things have been no different for women, whose living conditions have deteriorated in many cases. Today, even the most liberal feminists have to take note of the feminization of poverty and the double workload of more privileged women.

In the late 1970s, radical feminists like Colette Guillaumin (1978) and Shulamith Firestone (1979) were already proposing an analysis based on the existence of a "gender class" to account not only for invisible and unpaid housework but for the task of reproducing the producers. In relationships dictated by gender, in which women are defined as economic objects, the work and bodies of women thus would be completely appropriated, an ultimate manifestation of this exploitation being the sexual harassment to which women are subjected on the job.

But the concept of class, though a fertile aid to understanding the dynamics of certain identity-based relationships of domination, does not describe all of these relationships or every one of their aspects, any more than the concepts of colonization or social handicap did.

The identification of one type of oppression as more fundamental than all others thus remains elusive, at least if one continues to define "fundamental" as the deepest and most irreducible foundation of identity. In concrete terms, this quest is based on the principle that it is possible to measure the respective weight of each disadvantage affecting an old, poor, handicapped, Black lesbian, for example.

Although most often enunciated implicitly, this challenge has been raised repeatedly as each of the various emancipation movements has emerged. Thus, for Albert Memmi, racism was not only "the symbol" but also "the epitome" of all oppression (1973, 8). On the other hand, radical feminists saw the domination of women by the male gender as the primary source of the evils of a comprehensively patriarchal society.

Finally, in the Marxist view, generational conflict, the war between the genders, and inter-ethnic confrontations could only be resolved through the class struggle. Even homosexuality, like mental illness, was perceived as "the result of social contradictions" (in Jacerme, 1974, 210).

More often than not, however, these assertions are presented as postulates and primarily reflect the special attention paid by certain thinkers and activists to the condition of a particular dominated group.

While maintaining a bias of this nature, some of them have endeavoured to get around the difficulty by choosing to consider as fundamental something that is in fact universal. By breaking down the dynamics of different relationships with the other, within the different parameters of identity, it becomes possible to pinpoint the dimensions of domination that affect the greatest number.

Thus, since most individuals have to pass through different life cycles, it was possible to propose age as a universal criterion. If one is to believe Christiane Rochefort, childhood, in particular, would be the "mould of all oppressions," since each individual is conditioned, during this initial stage of existence, to internalize submission to authority (1976, 41–51).

Specialists in physical or mental health invoke a similar logic when they recall that we are all only "temporarily able-bodied," and that, since disease knows no barriers of age, class, gender, or ethnic origin, the ostracism imposed on the handicapped is, according to Jean Schmidt, "the first [oppression] of all" (in *L'écran handicapé*, 1983, 107).

Like Dennis Altman, theorists of sexual orientation also maintain that "everybody is 'normal' and everybody is homosexual," since human beings, to various degrees, as Kinsey showed, have versatile sexual tendencies (1976, 210–13). In this sense, homophobia would in fact reflect an attempt at repression within oneself, and the very concept of "sexual minorities" would no longer mean anything.

Thus, in the case of age, sexual preference, and physical or mental health, the "other," to some extent, would be within us, providing the foundation for the universal nature of our relationship with it. Even when the "other" acquires reality external to us, the relationship cultivated with him or her in certain cases would at least be charged with the potential for affection or intimacy.

While it is possible to talk of the "hatred" that the class or race "enemy" is capable of inspiring (a hatred embodied in totalitarian political regimes, for example), it is automatically postulated that love is the universal basis of the bond that can be established between the generations or between the genders.

But if, with the exception of the "hard" categories of identity based on affiliation to a group (class or ethnic), the solution to the problem of oppression requires more harmonious relations with others, *most of which can be considered universal*, then the impasse remains intact and we will not have found one convergent parameter.

While a vertical approach proved to be ineffective, it should be possible to find a way out by proceeding across group lines. In other words, by resorting to a *comparative* analysis of different relationships of domination, and by taking systematic cross-sections of their *practical* implications, it is inevitable that constants will emerge, pointing in the direction of a single convergent parameter.

Indeed, when the network of parallels between the various categories of identity is established, one thing becomes obvious: the gender of the individual concerned runs through all of them like a common thread. In each type of relationship of domination, the woman's burden is almost always heavier to bear than that of the man because, in addition to the oppression suffered by both, she also carries the weight of her own condition, which increases this oppression.

First of all, her sexuality places her at a disadvantage both as the dominator and as the dominated. As the dominator, sexual transgression is especially prohibited to her. As the dominated, she is deemed to be available to the dominator and perceived by oppressed males as the prime outlet of their own alienation. The requirements of beauty imposed on the "fair sex" also weigh heavily upon elderly or handicapped women (Topliss, 1982, 183), who are already disadvantaged by pension plans based on the interests of the husband and by rehabilitation programs geared to accidents on the road and in the workplace, in which men are more often the victims.[30]

From the outset, women are also considered to have the principal responsibility for nurturing children, the aged, the sick and the handicapped, and even men, and their time is deemed to be indefinitely available (Guillaumin, 1978, 2, 10). Governments, claiming to humanize care by entrusting it "to the family," implicitly place the burden of deinstitutionalization on the shoulders of women.

Although they account for one-third of the work force and two-thirds of the hours worked around the world, women have only 10 percent of the income and 1 percent of the property (Morgan, 1984, 1). Regardless of social class, ethnic origin, or economic region, they are becoming even more impoverished, both in the industrialized countries and in the Third World (Scott, 1984, ix). In the case of widows, handicapped women, and mothers heading one-parent families, among others, the feminization of poverty, in turn, is increasing the number of poor children.[31]

Elderly women living alone are also vulnerable, and the problem is accentuated when membership in a visible minority compounds the factor of old age. Even before the recession of the 1980s, older Black women ran a five-times-greater risk of living under the poverty line than White men of the same generation (Macdonald and Rich, 1984, 10; 61).

In the same period, the OECD noted the particularly dramatic situation of girls in youth unemployment. Ten years later, young and sometimes responsible for a family, they would account for the highest percentage of the marginally employed.

When they are immigrants, if they are not employed as housemaids or cheap labour, they will have to remain isolated at home and ignorant of the language of their adopted country (Labelle *et al.*, 1980, 51). Their daughters will risk being caught between the hostility of the people of the host country and the oppression of family structures that brothers, as well as parents, often wish to maintain.[32]

More often than men in the same condition, handicapped women will be advised not to have children, with the postulate implicit that a disabled husband can count on his female partner to earn a livelihood *and* take care of a family, but not the reverse.[33] This also explains why handicapped women (or women declared to be mentally handicapped) were sterilized more often without their knowledge than men.

Already heavily underprivileged in economic terms, women also have to face endemic physical violence. In addition to harassment, rape and outright murder hang over the entire female gender as a threat and strike directly at its members. Conjugal violence is the most widespread form of violence in the world.

Force may be used against women not only by a spouse but by a former lover, an ex-husband, or even a male family member. If this spouse belongs to a dominated social class or ethnic group, this will often be considered a mitigating circumstance for a man, who will be excused for wanting to at least exercise power "in his own home."

Not necessarily sheltered from violence in their own (?) homes, women are in even greater danger during collective upheavals. If they account for 80 percent of the world's refugees, this is because, in the best of cases, they rarely enjoy freedom of movement equal to that of men, or because, as victims of a victor who had exercised "his rights" over them, they rot in refugee camps after being rejected by their communities (Jacques, 1985, 146–7).

In many Third World countries (South Asia and West Asia, China, North Africa), the more deplorable state of nutrition and health care for the female population gives men the demographic advantage compared to women. Thus, more than 100 million women can be said to be "missing."[34]

Female children are targets of violence just like their elders. Not only are they the prime targets of incest and sexual abuse, at least in the West, but they have been and continue to be more subject to infanticide in cultures that practise it. One million children die each year because they are girls.[35]

The only case in which women are less oppressed than men is that of sexual orientation. As the history of judicial repression shows, society tolerates homosexuality in men much more poorly than in women. But this difference in treatment actually strengthens the thesis that the domination of women by men is the most universal form. Indeed, the orientation of gay males is perceived, though wrongly, as a degrading desire to become a woman, that is to say, a member of the "weaker" sex.

Whatever parameter of identity is considered, the gender of the person concerned thus always modulates the dynamics of relationships of domination. Gender inevitably accentuates the negative consequences for status and power that are the price of membership in a dominated group, and also tremendously increases both the economic disadvantages and the negative impacts on health and safety.

This results in a chain reaction beyond the fundamental field of identity, shaping the way people think and behave. Omnipresent, though unequal depending on the culture, the threat of violence weighing down upon women restricts their freedom of action all by itself. These restrictions can be categorized as a form of apartheid both in time (after dark, for example) and in space (in isolated areas, among others).

Women's freedom of thought is no less exempt from restrictions. What is most universal in the allegedly universal religions is a common devaluation of their spiritual status and an obligation to submit to the standards established by male authority.

The right of women to speak is most often limited, if not denied. As occasions for men to sin, or subject, by the very nature of their identity, to ritual impurity, they are most often barred from access to divine ministry, and even to the main liturgical activities.

Not only are women the most frequent victims of multiple forms of oppression, but they are universally considered to be a problem. Religion, science, law, and even folklore, in the spirit of *"cherchez la femme,"* have all sought out the woman, or the mother, or the "daughter of Eve," holding her responsible for natural and historical catastrophes. According to this logic, the lives, sexual orientation, and health (even the physical health) of individuals primarily depend on women. Through sexuality, they are also responsible for incest (against children), rape (against other women), and the unbalanced psychological state of men with whom they have (or do not have) physical relations. Whole societies can suffer from their harmful influence, since, according to some, "matriarchy" causes delinquency and unemployment in underprivileged classes and ethnic groups.

Universally victimized and seen as the problem, women therefore hold the key to solving the challenge of identity-based intolerance.

Not only do women account for half the population, but they bring *everyone* into the world (in Callu, 1978, 147). Thus, all demographic problems primarily concern them. Breaking with the traditions of the colonizing countries that imposed a patriarchal structure where the family or the tribe might have been egalitarian, and with the bias of international administrations that put credit and agricultural technology in the hands of men alone (Etienne and Leacock, 1980, 18–19; Giddens and Held, 1982, 452), major international organizations like UNICEF (since its 1980 report on the state of children in the world) and the United Nations Fund for Population Activities (1992) even affirmed that, of all the measures taken to improve health and nutritional conditions in the Third World, it is those that develop education for girls and give women the right to property that offer the most promise.

All by itself, a general improvement in the status of women would set off shock waves, which would not only make a radical change in the lot of every group of individuals who are oppressed because of what they are, but would also overturn the foundations of the world's "great" religions, as well as the spatial and temporal reference points of society.

This does not mean that the inequalities existing among women themselves would vanish and that all dominating relationships would be resolved at one blow. But at least these relations, from then on, could be understood in terms of their own characteristics, and cases of multiple oppression could be unburdened of the factor of sexual affiliation which until then would be one of their inevitable components.

In the dynamics of power, the relations between men and women are not necessarily more fundamental because they are more universal; but they necessarily are more universal because they intersect with *all* forms of oppression.

Conclusion

It has become fashionable in some circles to claim that emancipation movements are "out of style." Activists who continue to defend a cause are supposedly merely "nostalgic" for a past era, and theorists interested in analysing the relationships of domination give the impression of sailing against the current in an era completely focused on practical concerns. It is even the "in" thing among those who have benefitted from the struggles waged by the previous generation to mock its "extremist" character so that they can pass for "moderates."

The very notion of the victim has become synonymous with self-indulgent misery now that individuals are considered to be primarily responsible for their fate and encouraged to fulfil duties rather than assert their rights. To be labelled a victim is perceived increasingly by the oppressed as an insult rather than as a status on which to base their demands. Yet if the dominated no longer exist, this means, by definition, that there is no more dominator: the dominator has gone out of fashion as well. This is what is implied by the numerous appeals for concerted action and consensus.

Because the affirmation of establishment values, for the time being, seems to be prevailing over radical challenges, some have hastened to declare the end of ideology. But isn't this a time of rampant economic neo-liberalism and social neo-conservatism? Aren't integrist and fundamentalist religions on the rise? Activism may appear outmoded, but the problems have not gone away. It is somewhat suspicious how hastily the media (among others) have insisted on portraying only important phenomena as mere fads. The death knell has been sounded far more often for feminism, for example, than for dieting, or for the preoccupation with fashion.

Tolerance, more than any other value, should remain a constant goal. The personal sufferings and collective waste caused by oppression are incalculable. Antoine de Saint-Exupéry could see "murdered Mozarts" among underprivileged children. The commemoration of the hundredth anniversary of the Metropolitan Opera, in the fall of 1983, gave an even more physical impression of the radical absence of talents that have never been developed: while seven young Black female singers, along with the greatest voices of our age, celebrated the centenary of the famous opera house, not one African-American woman or man was "visible" in the imposing gathering of older singers assembled by the "Met" management at the end of the show.

For African-American artists, the tradition dated back barely two generations, and none of them was entitled to a place among the elders. It will never be possible to write the history of what could have been. It is all the more difficult to render justice to those whose talents were so irredeemably stifled that the loss cannot fully be imagined. One need only consider what America would be like today if it were as totally segregationist as it was forty years ago, if singers like Kathleen Battle, Myra Merritt, and Leona Mitchell possessed the same voices and the same gifts but could not acquire the musical training allowing them to make a career in opera. Yet there were indeed women in the past whose voices were just as beautiful but were never heard.

Transposed into every field of endeavour, this absence represents an immeasurable loss for humanity. But if society loses, it must never be forgotten that it is individuals who pay the psychological and material price for this denial of existence. Even beyond the violence sometimes exercised against them, the humiliation, frustration, and wasted potential that are their daily lot affect the victims *personally*, even when they number in the millions. Except in our perception, there is nothing collective about the tragedies of intolerance. Every nightmare is unique. The mind can sometimes grasp the tragedy of an individual, and sometimes statistically comprehend that of a community, but the drama of each and every individual hidden behind these statistics surpasses understanding.

Because it is impossible for us to be fully aware of the scope of such waste and suffering, the struggle for tolerance can never really end.

Notes

CHAPTER ONE
A UNIVERSAL DISCOURSE

1 N.F. Cantor, *Medieval History: The Life and Death of a Civilization* (New York: Macmillan, 1963).
2 T. Frank, "Race Mixture in the Roman Empire," *The American Historical Review* 21 (1916): 689–708.
3 John Cowper Powys, *Ducdame* (New York: Doubleday, 1925).
4 A.-M. Jaton, "La femme des Lumières, la nature et la différence," in *Figures féminines et roman*, ed. J. Bessière, (Paris: PUF, 1982), 75–85.
5 Reported in *The New York Review of Books*, 14 June 1984, 35.
6 In C. Degler et al., *The Democratic Experience. A Short American History* (Glenview (Ill.): Scott, Foresman & Co., 1977), chap. 17.
7 D. Juneau, "Les autres 'ethniques,'" in *Enjeux ethniques*, 1983, 4.
8 DSM: *Diagnostic and Statistical Manual*; ICD: *International Classification of Diseases*.
9 Opuscule, Montreal, 1982.
10 Reported in *Ms.*, November 1986, 8.
11 M.F. Toinet, "Les minorités et l'information," in *Le facteur ethnique aux États-Unis et au Canada*, eds M. Lecomte and C. Thomas (Université de Lille: 1983), 81–5.
12 Or at least those of the years 1976–77.
13 O. Sacks, "The Revolution of the Deaf," *New York Review of Books*, 2 June 1988, XXXV, 9, 23–8.

CHAPTER TWO
THE LANGUAGE OF OBJECTIVITY

1 Even today, this postulate prevails implicitly in the most innocuous forms.

In restaurants, for example, wine is automatically offered to the man for tasting.
2 Cited in R. Morgan, *Sisterhood is Powerful* (New York: Random House, 1970), 34.
3 Gustave Welter, *Histoire de Russie*, 4th edition, 1963, 232.
4 In laughing at his drunkenness and nakedness.
5 At the present time in Québec, psychotropic, sedative, and hypnotic drugs are administered mainly to persons dependent on social assistance (Lamontagne, 1985, 35).
6 Height itself is affected by the quality of nutrition.
7 Konrad Lorenz, *Studies in Animal and Human Behavior* (London: Methuen, 1971), II, 172. Emphasis added.
8 P. Thuillier, "La sociobiologie à l'assaut de la culture," in *L'état des sciences* (Paris and Montreal: Découverte-Maspero/Boréal, 1984), 122.
9 Cited in E. Jones, *La vie et l'oeuvre de Sigmund Freud*, 2, (Paris: PUF, 1961), 445.
10 C. Degler, *op. cit.*, chap. 10.
11 F. Bergeron, "Ernst Zündel: un nouveau procès de Nuremberg à Toronto?" *La Presse*, 14 January 1984.
12 J.P. Deriennic, "Faut-il reconnaître le génocide arménien?" *Le Devoir*, 4 June 1984.

CHAPTER THREE
ALIENATION

1 A.-M. Alonzo, "Cuir-et-chrome," *La vie en rose*, 23 February 1985, 26.
2 *Nana* (Zola), *Sappho* (Daudet), *La maîtresse de Paul* (Maupassant).
3 See, among others, *La fille aux yeux d'or* by Balzac, *La Pharisienne* by Mauriac. In film, *Les Biches* by Claude Chabrol is a good example.
4 See *Marjorie Morningstar* (Herman Wouk), and certain types of intellectual women, always dissatisfied, in the novels of Philip Roth and Saul Bellow.
5 On this subject see C. Doudna, "American Couples: Supporting New Findings," *Ms.*, November 1983, 116–9, which reports on a study by sociologists Philip Blumstein and Pepper Schwartz.
6 C. Brisset, "Trente millions de mutilées," *Le Monde*, 1 March 1979, 22. The World Health Organization ventures the figure of 80 million in 1993.
7 Prudent estimates set the number of victims at 100,000 or 300,000 (eds, A.C. Kors and E. Peters, *Witchcraft in Europe*, [Philadelphia: University of Pennsylvania Press, 1972], 13). The vast majority of them were women.
8 Kors and Peters, *op. cit*; E. Clark and H. Richardson, eds., *Women and Religion* (New York: E. Mellen Press, 1977), 116. More than half of

the "witches" were single women, especially spinsters and widows. This means they were often old (in Bridenthal and Koonz, 1977, 133).
9 R. Bridenthal et al., *When Biology Became Destiny: Women in Weimar and Nazi Germany* (New York: Monthly Review Press, 1984), 27.
10 B. Bouthoul, *Le phénomène-guerre* (Paris: Petite Bibliothèque Payot, 1962), 146–51.
11 *La Presse Plus*, 16 June 1984, 6.
12 Account of an American report cited by *The Gazette*, 30 June 1984.
13 Study by the Ligue des droits et libertés cited in *Le Devoir*, 25 October 1984.
14 Interview given on the program "Visage" of the Radio-Québec television network, 13 December 1984.
15 E.D. Genovese, *The World the Slaveholders Made* (New York: Vintage Books, 1971), 195–201.
16 Judgment of 17 September 1984.
17 J.P. Proulx, "La bataille du français au Manitoba", *Le Devoir*, 3 February 1984.
18 J. Richer, "Les femmes des presbytères," *L'Actualité*, September 1984, 57.
19 In M. Niveau, *Histoire des faits économiques contemporains*, 3rd ed. (Paris: PUF, 1970), 126.
20 A.-M. Malavoy, "La guerre au jour le jour," *Critère*, 83, (Autumn 1984): 23.
21 J.J. Gayford, "Battered Wives," in *International Perspectives on Family Violence*, eds R.J. Gelles and C.P. Cornell (Toronto: Lexington Books, 1983), 129–35.
22 In this regard, see films or books like *Z*, *The Conformist* or *Rome, Open City*.
23 Thesis denied by a survivor of the camps (Heger, 1981, 20).
24 See "Les Arabes et nous," *Le Nouvel Observateur*, 30 November 1984, 55.
25 Cited in a review of the book by Julian Sher, *White Hoods: Canada's Ku Klux Klan*, in *The Gazette*, 24 September 1983, I-2.
26 Cited in *The Gazette*, 4 September 1982, B-5.
27 More than 90 percent of proverbs concerning women cited by *The Penguin Dictionary of Proverbs* (Harmondsworth, 1983) are negative.
28 J. Bayley, "Only disconnect," *The New York Review of Books*, XXXII, 13, 15 August 1985, 19.
29 A. Francos, *Il était des femmes dans la Résistance* (Paris: Stock, 1978), 101–2.

CHAPTER FOUR
EMANCIPATION

1 C.S. Ford and A.C. Beach, *Patterns of Sexual Behavior* (New York: Harper, 1951).
2 Particularly in his *Three Contributions to the Theory of Sex* (1905). Freud's

position should not be confused with that of his disciples on this question.
3 Leo XIII's encyclical *De Rerum Novarum* only dates from 1891.
4 I Tim. 1:10 and I Cor. 6:9–10.
5 As examples, see P. Duroc, *Homosexuels et lesbiennes illustres, 1983*, (Brussels: Les auteurs réunis, 1983) and the humorous calendar by M. Greif, *The Gay Book of Days*, (Secaucus: A Main Street Press Book, 1982).
6 *The Democratic Experience* by Carl Degler et al. is a good example of this type of reductionism.
7 D. Morris, *The Naked Ape* (New York: McGraw Hill, 1967).
8 D. Symon, *The Evolution of Human Sexuality* (Oxford: Oxford V.P., 1979); D. Barash, *Sociobiology and Behavior*, 2nd ed. (New York: Elsevier, 1982).
9 In *Totem and Taboo* (1913).
10 Elisabeth Badinter reported the results of surveys conducted in France on the attitude of fathers, which revealed that some of them would like to experience pregnancy (*Le Devoir*, 18 October 1980).
11 One example: "Since *women* everywhere bear the 'double job' burden of housework in addition to outside work, *we* are most gravely affected by the acknowledged world crisis in housing" (Morgan, 1984, 3, emphasis added).
12 In the USSR, the "crime" of political dissidence could be treated as a psychiatric illness, with the use of personality-destroying drugs (Boukovski, 1971).
13 For example, eating pork, or fish and seafood without fins and scales.
14 In his "Apostolic Exhortation on the Cult of the Virgin Mary" (March 1974), Paul VI proposed Mary as the "outstanding model of the feminine condition".
15 It is the father who has the *mitzvah*.
16 See C. Doudna, "American Couples: Surprising New Findings," *Ms.*, November 1983, 116–9, on the study by sociologists Philip Blumstein and Pepper Schwartz.
17 P. Sormany, "Le cerveau a-t-il un sexe?" *L'Actualité*, November 1980, 36.
18 In the seventeenth century, Descartes saw the pineal gland as the centre for transmission of outside impressions to the soul. In the nineteenth century, a special science (phrenology) emerged to map the activities of the brain.
19 To their male members.
20 Except during the 1970s in Québec, when it became more radical.
21 The Czech writer Milan Kundera, among others.
22 "A Last Word from the Frist Americans," *The New York Times Magazine*, 4 July 1976, 80.
23 Caroline Claxton, in *Girls Next Door*, eds J. Bradshaw and M. Hemming, (London: The Women's Press, 1985), 177.

24 Assessment provided in *Le Devoir* of 5 March 1985, special section on minority rights, *Les droits des minorités*.
25 Figures supplied by the historian Michel Brunet (in *Migrations et communautés culturelles*, 1982, 17).
26 *L'état du monde 1984* (Paris and Montreal: La Découverte / Boréal Express, 1984), 548.
27 See the letters to the editor in the *Montreal Star* in 1977, among others.
28 19 August 1984 (rebroadcast by Radio-Québec).
29 In R. Morgan, *Sisterhood is Powerful* (New York: Random House, 1970), 35–6.
30 G. Escomel, "Handicapés au carré," *La vie en rose*, (February 1985) 23: 27–8.
31 L. Leboeuf, "Les femmes et la pauvreté," *Service social*, XL, 3, (1991): 24–41.
32 In "Les Arabes et nous," *Le Nouvel Observateur*, 30 November 1984, 48.
33 Escomel, *op. cit.*, 27–8.
34 Sen Amartya, "More than 100 Million Women Missing," *New York Review of Books*, 20 December 1990, 61–6.
35 C. Trudel, "Priorité aux enfants dans le nouvel ordre mondial," *Le Devoir*, 19 December 1991, p. B-1.

Thematic Bibliography

GENERAL STUDIES

Achard, P. et al. 1977. *Discours biologique et ordre social.* Paris: Le Seuil. 288 pp.
Adam, B.D. 1978. *The Survival of Domination: Inferiorization and Everyday Life.* New York: Elsevier. 179 pp.
Adorno, T.W. et al. 1964. *The Authoritarian Personality.* New York: Wiley. 2 vol.
Allport, G.W. 1955. *The Nature of Prejudice.* 3rd edition. Cambridge (Mass.): Addison-Wesley. 537 pp.
Ariès, P. and G. Duby, eds. 1985–1987. *Histoire de la vie privée.* Paris: Le Seuil. 5 vol.
Becker, H. 1963. *Outsiders.* Glencoe (Ill.): Free Press, 179 pp.
Berger, T.R. 1981. *Fragile Freedoms: Human Rights and Dissent in Canada.* Toronto: Clarke-Irwin. 298 pp.
Bettelheim, B. and M. Janowitz. 1964. *Social Change & Prejudice, Including Dynamics of Prejudice.* New York: Free Press of Glencoe. 337 pp.
Block, N.J. and G. Dworkin, eds. 1976. *The I.Q. Controversy. Critical Readings.* New York: Pantheon Books. 557 pp.
Bresson, Y. 1977. *Le capital-temps: pouvoir, répartition et inégalités.* Paris: Calmann-Lévy. 218 pp.
Caplan, A.L., ed. 1978. *The Sociobiology Debate: Reading on Ethical and Scientific Issues.* New York: Harper & Row. 514 pp.
Carbonel, C.-O., ed. 1975. *Le message politique et social de la bande dessinée.* Toulouse: Privat. 181 pp.
Casamayor, L. 1975. *La tolérance.* Paris: Gallimard.
Chesnais, J. 1981. *Histoire de la violence en Occident de 1800 à nos jours.* Paris: R. Laffont. 497 pp.
Claval, P. 1978. *Espace et pouvoir.* Paris: PUF. 257 pp.
Collins, M.W., I.W. Wainer, and T.A. Bremner, eds. 1981. *Science and the Question of Human Equality.* Boulder (Colo.): Westview Press. 158 pp.

Davis, F.J., ed. 1979. *Understanding Minority-Dominant Relations: Sociological Contributions*. Arlington Heights (Ill.): AHM Pub. Corp. 496 pp.
Deconchy, J.P. 1971. *L'orthodoxie religieuse. Essai de logique psychosociale*. Paris: Éd. ouvrières. 373 pp.
Delacampagne, C. 1977. *Figures de l'oppression*. Paris: PUF. 192 pp.
Delumeau, J. 1983. *Le péché et la peur. La culpabilisation en Occident, 13e–18e siècles*. Paris: Fayard. 741 pp.
Dobzhansky, T. 1973. *Genetic Diversity and Human Equality*. New York: Basic Books. 128 pp.
Dumont, L. 1966. *Homo Hierarchicus*. Paris: Gallimard. 445 pp.
Ehrlich, H.J. 1973. *The Social Psychology of Prejudice*. New York: John Wiley and Sons. 208 pp.
Eysenck, H.J. 1973. *The Inequality of Man*. London: Maurice Temple Smith. 288 pp.
Franklin, J. 1975. *Le Discours du pouvoir*. Paris: Union générale d'éditions. 429 pp.
Freire, P. 1974. *Pédagogie des opprimés*. Paris: Maspero. 202 pp.
Gabel, J. 1970. *Sociologie de l'aliénation*. Paris: PUF. 216 pp.
Goffman, E. 1963. *Stigma. Notes on the Management of Spoiled Identity*. Englewood Cliffs (N.J.): Prentice-Hall, 147 pp.
Gould, S.J. 1981. *The Mismeasure of Man*. New York, London: W.W. Norton & Co. 352 pp.
Gourgues, M. and G.D. Mailhot, eds. 1986. *L'altérité. Vivre ensemble différents*. Paris, Montreal: Cerf/Bellarmin. 455 pp.
Gross, B.R., ed. 1977. *Reverse Discrimination*. Buffalo (N.Y.): Prometheus Books. 401 pp.
Guillaumin, C. 1979. "Questions de différence," *Questions féministes*, 6: 3–23.
Haskell, T.L., ed. 1984. *The Authority of Experts. Studies in History and Theory*. Bloomington: Indiana University Press. 278 pp.
Jacquard, A. 1978. *Éloge de la différence: la génétique et les hommes*. Paris: Le Seuil. 224 pp.
Kinloch, G.C. 1979. *The Sociology of Minority Groups Relations*. Englewood Cliffs (N.J.): Prentice-Hall. 243 pp.
Lerner, M.J. 1980. *The Belief in a Just World. A Fundamental Delusion*. New York: Plenum Press. 209 pp.
Levin, J. 1975. *The Functions of Prejudice*. New York: Harper & Row. 150 pp.
Lewontin, R.C., S. Rose, and L.C. Kawin. 1984. *Not in Our Genes: Biology, Ideology and Human Nature*. New York: Pantheon. 322 pp.
Marcil-Lacoste, L. 1984. *La thématique contemporaine de l'égalité*. Montreal: PUM. 243 pp.
Memmi, A. 1973. *L'homme dominé*. 2nd edition. Paris: Payot. 232 pp.
Miller, A.G. ed. 1982. *In the Eye of the Beholder: Contemporary Issues in Stereotyping*. New York: Praeger. 531 pp.

Miquel, P. 1978. *Les oubliés de l'histoire.* Paris: Fernand Nathan. 2 vol.
Montagu, A., ed. 1980. *Sociobiology Examined.* New York, Oxford: Oxford University Press. 355 pp.
Moreau de Bellaing, L. 1990. *Sociologie de l'autorité.* Paris: L'Harmattan. 171 pp.
Morgan, C. and D. Langford. 1981. *Facts and Fallacies.* London: Webb and Bower. 176 pp.
Pellerin, R. 1983. *Théories et pratiques de la désaliénation.* Montreal: L'Hexagone. 200 pp.
Rokeach, M. 1960. *The Open and Closed Mind: Investigations into the Nature of Belief Systems and Personality Systems.* New York: Basic Books. 447 pp.
Rose, H., S. Rose, et al. 1977. *L'idéologie de/dans la science.* Paris: Le Seuil. 257 pp.
Ryan, W. 1976. *Blaming the Victim.* 2nd edition. New York: Vintage Books. 351 pp.
Sagarin, E. 1971. *The Other Minorities: Nonethnic Collectivities Conceptualized as Minority Groups.* Waltham (Mass.), Toronto: Xerox College. 352 pp.
Scherer, J. and G. Shepherd, eds. 1982. *Victimization of the Weak: Contemporary Social Reactions.* Springfield (Ill.): Charles C. Thomas. 288 pp.
Schur, E.M. 1980. *The Politics of Deviance: Stigma Contests and the Uses of Power.* Englewood Cliffs (N.J.): Prentice-Hall. 241 pp.
Simon, M. 1985. *Les droits de l'homme. Guide d'information et de réflexion.* Lyon: Chronique sociale. 177 pp.
Todorov, T. 1986. "La tolérance et l'intolérable," *Lettre internationale,* 8: 11–14.
Torrelli, M. and R. Baudoin. 1972. *Les droits de l'homme et les libertés publiques par les textes.* Montreal: PUQ. 387 pp.
Tort, M. 1974. *Le quotient intellectuel.* Paris: Maspero. 184 pp.
Vant, A., ed. 1986. *Marginalité sociale, marginalité spatiale.* Paris: CNRS. 272 pp.

SPECIFIC STUDIES

Age

Les âges de la vie: actes du colloque/VIIe Colloque national de démographie. Strasbourg. 5, 6, 7 May 1982. Paris: PUF. 211 pp.
Attias-Donfut, C. 1988. *Sociologie des générations. L'empreinte du temps.* Paris: PUF. 249 pp.
Chudacoff, H. P. 1989. *How Old Are You? Age Consciousness in American Culture.* Princeton (N.J.): Princeton University Press. 232 pp.
Eisenstadt, S.N. 1964. *From Generation to Generation: Age Groups and Social Structures.* New York: The Free Press. 357 pp.
Mannheim, K. 1952. "The Problem of Generations," in *Essays in the Sociology of Knowledge,* edited by P. Kerskemeti, 276–320. New York.

Mead, M. 1979. *Le fossé des générations: les nouvelles relations entre les générations dans les années 1970.* Paris: Denoël/Gonthier. 185 pp.

Mendel, G. 1974. *La crise des générations.* 3rd edition. Paris: Payot. 272 pp.

Philibert, M. 1968. *L'échelle des âges dans la philosophie, la science et la société. De leur renversement et des conditions de leur redressement.* Paris: Le Seuil. 420 pp.

CHILDREN

Ariès, P. 1973. *L'enfant et la vie familiale sous l'Ancien Régime.* Paris: Le Seuil. 316 pp.

Boulding, E. 1979. *Children's Rights and the Wheel of Life.* New Brunswick (N.J.): Transaction Books. 179 pp.

Bremner, R.H. et al.. 1970–1974. *Children and Youth in America. A Documentary History.* Cambridge (Mass.): Harvard Univ. Press. 3 vol.

Chombart de Lauwe, M.J. 1979. *Un monde autre: l'enfance, de ses représentations à son mythe.* 2nd edition. Paris: Payot. 456 pp.

Chombart de Lauwe, M.J. and C. Bellan. 1979. *Enfants de l'image. Enfants personnages des médias/Enfants réels.* Paris: Payot. 300 pp.

Crubellier, M. 1979. *L'enfance et la jeunesse dans la société française 1800–1950.* Paris: A. Colin. 389 pp.

Davet, J. et al. 1979. *Fous d'enfance. Qui a peur des pédophiles?* Paris: Recherches. 216 pp.

De Mause, L., ed. 1974. *The History of Childhood.* New York: Psychohistory Press. 450 pp.

Erickson, E.H. 1976. *Enfance et société.* 6th edition. Neuchâtel: Delachaux et Niestlé. 285 pp.

Fontana, V.J. 1983. *Somewhere a Child is Crying. Maltreatment Causes and Prevention.* 2nd edition. New York: American Library. 254 pp.

Greer, G. 1984. *Sex and Destiny: The Politics of Human Fertility.* London: Secker & Warburg. 541 pp.

Henning, J.S., ed. 1982. *The Rights of Children: Legal and Psychological Perspectives.* Springfield (Ill.): Thomas. 285 pp.

Huston, N. 1979. *Jouer au papa et à l'amant: de l'amour des petites filles.* Paris: Ramsay. 190 pp.

Ishwaran, K., ed. 1979. *Childhood and Adolescence in Canada.* Toronto. McGraw-Hill Ryerson. 386 pp.

Jenks, C., ed. 1982. *The Sociology of Childhood: Essential Readings.* London: Batsford Academic and Educational. 299 pp.

Kempe, R.S. and C.H. Kempe. 1984. *The Common Secret: Sexual Abuse of Children and Adolescents.* New York: W.H. Freeman and Co. 284 pp.

Kuhn, R.C. 1982. *Corruption in Paradise: the Child in Western Literature.* Hanover (N.H.): University Press of New England. 264 pp.

Lapouge, B. and J.L. Pinard-Legry. 1984. *L'enfant et le pédéraste.* Paris: Le Seuil. 128 pp.

Lemieux, D. 1984. *Une culture de la nostalgie. L'enfance dans le roman québécois, des origines jusqu'à la période contemporaine.* Montreal: Boréal Express. 244 pp.

Masson, J.M. 1984. *Le réel escamoté. Le renoncement de Freud à la théorie de séduction.* Paris: Aubier. 254 pp.

Mead, M. and M. Wolfenstein, eds. 1955. *Childhood in Contemporary Culture.* University of Chicago Press. 471 pp.

Mendel, G. 1971. *Pour décoloniser l'enfant. Sociopsychanalyse de l'autorité.* ("PBP" 188). Paris: Payot. 261 pp.

Miller, A. 1984. *Thou Shalt Not Be Aware: Society's Betrayal of the Child.* New York: Farrar, Strauss, Giroux. 331 pp.

Parr, J., ed. 1983. *Childhood and Family in Canadian History.* Toronto: McClelland & Stewart. 221 pp.

Pelton, L.H., ed. 1981. *The Social Context of Child Abuse and Neglect.* New York, London: Human Sciences Press. 331 pp.

Pinchbeck, I and M. Hewitt. 1969–1973. *Children in English Society.* London: Routledge and Kegan Paul. 2 vol.

Pollock, L.A. 1983. *Forgotten Children. Parent-Child Relations from 1500 to 1900.* New York, Cambridge: Cambridge University Press. 352 pp.

Pollock, L.A. 1987. *A Lasting Relationship. Parents and Children over Three Centuries.* Hanover (N.H.), London: University Press of New England. 319 pp.

Primault, M., H. Lhong, and J. Mabieu. 1961. *Terres de l'enfance. Le mythe de l'enfance dans la littérature contemporaine.* Paris: PUF. 202 pp.

Rémy, F. 1984. *40,000 enfants par jour.* Paris: Laffont.

Rimbaud, C. 1980. *52 millions d'enfants au travail.* Paris: Plon. 199 pp.

Rochefort, C. 1976. *Les enfants d'abord.* Montréal: l'Étincelle. 196 pp.

Rush, F. 1980. *The Best Kept Secret. Sexual Abuse of Children.* New York: McGraw Hill. 226 pp.

Les sévices institutionnels (1re partie). 1982. Fourth international congress on mistreated and neglected children. Paris. 168 pp.

Shorter, E. 1975. *The Making of the Modern Family.* New York: Basic Books. 369 pp.

Straus, P. et al. 1982. *L'enfant maltraité.* Paris: Fleurus. 276 pp.

Sutherland, N. 1976. *Children in English-Canadian Society.* Toronto, Buffalo: University of Toronto Press. 336 pp.

Van Stolk, M. 1979. *The Battered Child in Canada.* 2nd edition. Toronto: McClelland & Stewart. 178 pp.

Walvin, J. 1982. *A Child's World. A Social History of English Childhood, 1800–1914.* Harmondsworth (Middlesex): Penguin Books. 236 pp.

Ward, E. 1984. *Father Daughter Rape.* London: The Women's Press. 247 pp.

YOUTH

Alzon, C. 1974. *La mort de Pygmalion. Essai sur l'immaturité de la jeunesse.* Paris: Maspero. 213 pp.

Benoit, F. and P. Chauveau. 1986. *Acceptation globale. Une histoire de générations*. Montreal: Boréal. 121 pp.

Brohm, J.M. and M. Field. 1975. *Jeunesse et révolution: pour une organisation révolutionnaire de la jeunesse*. Paris: Maspero. 171 pp.

Le chômage des jeunes: causes et conséquences. 1980. Paris: OCDE. 172 pp.

Claes, M. 1992. "L'image de l'adolescence dans la presse écrite," *Revue québécoise de psychologie*. 13, 2: 37–51.

Davidson, F. et al. 1981. *Le suicide de l'adolescent: étude épidémiologique et statistique*. Paris: E.S.F. 135 pp.

Erickson, E., ed. 1963. *Youth: Change and Challenge*. New York, London: Basic Books. 284 pp.

Esler, A. 1971. *Bombs, Beards and Barricades. 150 Years of Youth in Revolt*. New York: Stein & Day. 336 pp.

Falchikov, N. 1986. "Images of Adolescence: an Investigation into the Accuracy of the Image of Adolescence Constructed by British Papers." *Journal of Adolescence*, 9: 167–180.

Feuer, L.S. 1969. *The Conflict of Generations: The Character and Significance of Student Movements*. New York, London: Basic Books. 543 pp.

Gillis, J.R. 1974. *Youth and History: Tradition and Change in European Age Relations, 1770–Present*. New York, London: Academic Press. 232 pp.

Handlin, O. and M.F. Handlin. 1971. *Youth and the Family in American History*. Boston, Toronto: Little Brown. 326 pp.

Jeunesses: des illusions tranquilles. 1986. Montreal: Éditions VLB. Montreal. 234 pp.

Johnson, P. 1983. *Modern Times: the World from the Twenties to the Eighties*. New York: Harper & Row. 817 pp.

Keniston, K. 1968. *Young Radicals: Notes on Committed Youth*. New York: Harcourt Brace & World. 368 pp.

Kett, J.F. 1977. *Rites of Passage: Adolescence in America 1790 to the Present*. New York: Basic Books. 327 pp.

Lapassade, G. 1969. *L'entrée dans la vie. Essais sur l'inachèvement de l'homme*. 3rd edition. Paris: Éditions de Minuit. 256 pp.

Menu, M. 1973. *Le mythe de la jeunesse*. Thesis. Université de Lille III, 524 pp.

Meyer Spacks, A.P. 1981. *The Adolescent Idea: Myths of Youth and the Adult Imagination*. New York: Basic Books. 308 pp.

Musgrove, F. 1974. *Youth and the Social Order*. London: Routledge & Kegan Paul. 168 pp.

La prostitution des jeunes. 1984. Montreal: Convergence. 146 pp.

Sauvy, A. 1970. *La révolte des jeunes*. Paris: Calmann-Lévy. 269 pp.

Schiamberg, L.B. 1973. *Adolescent Alienation*. Columbus (Ohio): C.E. Merrill Pub. Co. 148 pp.

Silverstein, H. 1973. *The Sociology of Youth: Evolution and Revolution*. New York: MacMillan. 472 pp.

Touraine, A. et al. 1978. *Lutte étudiante*. Paris: Le Seuil. 384 pp.
Williams, S. et al. 1981. *Les jeunes sans emploi: trois stratégies*. Paris: OCDE. 258 pp.

OLD AGE

Achenbaum, W.A. 1978. *Old Age in the New Land: The American Experience since 1790*. Baltimore: Johns Hopkins University Press. 237 pp.

Ariès, P. 1976. *Histoire des populations françaises et de leurs attitudes devant la vie depuis le 18e siècle*. Paris: Le Seuil. 412 pp.

Binstock, R.H. and E. Shonas, eds. 1976. *Handbook of Aging and the Social Sciences*. New York: Van Nostrand Reinhold. 684 pp.

Birren, J.E. and B. Woodruff, ed. 1983. *Aging: Scientific Perspectives and Social Issues*. 2nd edition. Monterey (Ca.): Brooks/Cole Pub. Co. 460 pp.

Cole, T. R. 1991. *The Journey of Life. A Cultural History of Aging in America*. New York: Cambridge University Press.

Cowgill, D.O. and L. Holmes. 1972. *Aging and Modernization*. New York: Appleton-Century-Crafts. 331 pp.

La culture et l'âge. 1984. ("Questions de culture," 6). Québec: IQRC. 198 pp.

De Beauvoir, S. 1970. *La vieillesse*. Paris: Gallimard. 2 vol.

Fischer, D.H. 1977. *Growing Old in America*. New York: Oxford University Press, 242 pp.

Freeman, J.T. 1979. *Aging, its History and Literature*. New York, London: Human Sciences. 161 pp.

Guillemard, A.M. 1976. *La politique d'intégration de la vieillesse: genèse et usages sociaux d'un retournement doctrinal*. Paris: Centre d'étude des mouvements sociaux. 344 pp.

Gutton, J.P. 1988. *Naissance d'un vieillard. Essai sur l'histoire des rapports entre les vieillards et la société en France*. Paris: Aubier. 279 pp.

Imhof, A.E., ed. 1982. *Le vieillissement: implications et conséquences de l'allongement de la vie humaine depuis le 18e siècle*. Presses univ. de Lyon. 224 pp.

Lamontagne, F. 1982. *Le stigmate social de la vieillesse et les comportements de maladie*. Thesis (M.Sc.). Université de Montréal. 116 pp.

Levin, J. and W. Levin. 1980. *Ageism, Prejudice and Discrimination against the Elderly*. Belmont (Ca.): Wadsworth Pub. Co. 153 pp.

Marshall, V.W., ed. 1980. *Aging in Canada: Social Perspectives*. Don Mills (Ont.): Fitzhenry and Whiteside. 314 pp.

Minois, G. 1987. *Histoire de la vieillesse de l'Antiquité à la Renaissance*. Paris: Fayard. 442 pp.

Neugarten, B., ed. 1968. *Middle Age and Aging. A Reader in Social Psychology*. University of Chicago Press. 596 pp.

Pacaud, S. and M.O. Lahalle. 1978. *Attitudes, comportements, opinions des personnes âgées dans le cadre de la famille moderne*. Paris: Éditions du CNRS. 148 pp.

Paillat, P. 1982. *Vieillissement et vieillesse*. Paris: PUF. 127 pp.

Ravinel, H. de. 1972. *Vieillir au Québec*. Montreal: La Presse. 168 pp.
Riley, M.M. et al. 1968–1972. *Aging and Society*. New York: Russell Sage Foundation. 3 vol.
Sokolovsky, J. 1983. *Growing Old in Different Societies: Cross-Cultural Perspectives*. Belmont (Ca.): Wadsworth Pub. Co. 259 pp.
Stearns, P.N. 1977. *Old Age in European Society: the Case of France*. London: Croom Helm. 163 pp.

Class

Bernstein, B. 1975. *Langage et classes sociales. Codes socio-linguistiques et contrôle social*. Paris: Éditions de Minuit. 352 pp.
Bertaux, D. 1977. *Destins personnels et structure de classe*. Paris: PUF. 322 pp.
Bourdieu, P. 1982. *La distinction. Critique sociale du jugement*. 2nd edition. Paris: Éditions de Minuit. 672 pp.
Brébant, B. 1984. *La pauvreté, un destin?* Paris: L'Harmattan. 179 pp.
Brizay, B. 1979. *Qu'est-ce qu'un chômeur?* Paris: Livre de Poche. 544 pp.
Broadfoot, B. 1978. *La Grande Dépression: témoignages des années perdues*. Montreal: Québec/Amérique. 395 pp.
Bulmer, M., ed. 1975. *Working-Class Images of Society*. London: Routledge and Kegan Paul. 278 pp.
Chevalier, L. 1978. *Classes laborieuses et classes dangereuses à Paris pendant la première moitié du XIXe siècle*. Paris: Plon. 735 pp.
Coates, K. and R. Silburn. 1970. *Poverty: the Forgotten Englishmen*. Harmondsworth (Middlesex): Penguin Books. 236 pp.
Dolléans, A. 1948–1967. *Histoire du mouvement ouvrier*. Paris: A. Colin. 3 vol.
Durgnat, R. 1970. *A Mirror for England: British Movies from Austerity to Affluence*. London: Faber & Faber. 336 pp.
Eagleton, M. and D. Pierce. 1979. *Attitudes to Class in the English Novel from Walter Scott to David Storey*. London: Thames & Hudson. 159 pp.
Eyraud, F. 1985. *Travail et travailleurs en Grande-Bretagne*. Paris: La Découverte. 121 pp.
Feagin, J.R. 1975. *Subordinating the Poor, Welfare and American Beliefs*. Englewood Cliffs (N.J.): Prentice-Hall. 180 pp.
Forcese, D.P. 1980. *The Canadian Class Structure*. 2nd edition. Toronto: McGraw-Hill Ryerson. 178 pp.
Fourastié, J. and B. Bazil. 1980. *Le jardin du voisin, les inégalités en France*. Paris: Librairie générale française. 352 pp.
Garraty, J.A. 1978. *Unemployment in History: Economic Thought and Public Policy*. New York: Harper & Row. 273 pp.
Geremek, B. 1987. *La potence ou la pitié. L'Europe et les pauvres du Moyen Âge à nos jours*. Paris: Gallimard. 330 pp.
Giddens, A. and D. Held, eds. 1982. *Classes, Power and Conflict: Classical and Contemporary Debates*. Berkeley: University of California Press. 646 pp.

Gilbert, D. and J.A. Kahl. 1982. *The American Class Structure: a New Synthesis.* Homewood (Ill.): Dorsey Press. 386 pp.

Gones, D. 1976. *Silence, on ferme! Les licenciements vus par la base.* Paris: Éditions ouvrières. 156 pp.

Guiral, P. et al. 1969. *La société française, 1815–1914, vue par les romanciers.* Paris: A. Colin. 256 pp.

Hadjinicolaou, N. 1973. *Histoire de l'art et lutte de classes.* 2nd edition. Paris: Maspero. 218 pp.

Harouel, J.L. 1984. *Essai sur l'inégalité.* Paris: PUF. 278 pp.

Harrington. M. 1970. *The Other America: Poverty in the United States.* 11th edition. New York: Macmillan. 191 pp.

Harvey, F. 1980. *Le mouvement ouvrier au Québec.* Montreal: Boréal Express. 330 pp.

Hayes, J. and P. Nutman. 1983. *Comprendre les chômeurs.* Brussels: Pierre Mardaga. 221 pp.

Jaher, F.C., ed. 1973. *The Rich, the Well Born, the Powerful: Elites and Upper Classes in History.* University of Illinois Press. 379 pp.

Jahoda, M. 1983. *Employment and Unemployment: a Social-Psychological Analysis.* Cambridge University Press. 111 pp.

Jones, J. 1992. *The Dispossessed. America's Underclass from the Civil War to the Present.* New York: Basic Books. 399 pp.

Laurin-Frenette, N. 1978. *Classes et pouvoir: les théories fonctionnalistes.* Montreal: PUM. 358 pp.

Lautrey, J. 1980. *Classe sociale, milieu familial, intelligence.* Paris: PUF. 282 pp.

Lawrence, S. 1990. *The Poor in Court: the Legal Services Program and Supreme Court Decision Making.* Princeton (N.J.): Princeton University Press. 207 pp.

Lazarsfeld, P., M. Jahoda, and H. Zeisel. 1981. *Les chômeurs de Marienthal.* Paris: Éditions de Minuit. 144 pp.

Ledrut, R. 1966. *Sociologie du chômage.* Paris: PUF. 547 pp.

Légaré, A. 1977. *Les classes sociales au Québec.* Montreal: PUQ. 197 pp.

Le Masters, E.E. 1975. *Blue Collar Aristocrats: Life Style at a Working Class Tavern.* Madison: University of Wisconsin Press. 218 pp.

Mann, M. 1973. *Consciousness and Action Among the Western Working Class.* London: Macmillan. 80 pp.

Marwick, A. 1980. *Class: Image and Reality in Britain, France and the USA since 1930.* New York: Oxford University Press. 416 pp.

Mathis, A. 1979. *Vivre sans travail: Des chômeurs parlent.* Paris: Le Seuil. 160 pp.

McKibbin, R. 1990. *The Ideologies of Class: Social Relations in Britain, 1880–1950.* Oxford: Clarendon Press. 308 pp.

Monaco, J. 1984. *American Film Now: the People, the Power, the Money, the Movies.* 2nd edition. New York: New American Library. 544 pp.

Mousnier, R. 1969. *Les hiérarchies sociales de 1450 à nos jours.* Paris: PUF. 196 pp.

Noiriel, G. 1986. *Les ouvriers dans la société française, XIXe–XXe siècle.* Paris: Le Seuil, 317 pp.

Palmer, B.D. 1983. *Working-Class Experience: the Rise and Reconstitution of Canadian Labour 1800–1980.* Toronto: Butterworths. 347 pp.

Péju, S. 1985. *Scènes de la grande pauvreté.* Paris: Le Seuil. 295 pp.

Porter, J.A. 1965. *The Vertical Mosaic: An Analysis of Social Class and Power in Canada.* University of Toronto Press. 626 pp.

Prédal, R. 1972. *La société française (1914–1945) à travers le cinéma.* Paris: A. Colin. 347 pp.

La presse et la pauvreté. 1973. Ottawa: Conseil national du bien-être social. 46 pp.

Report of a Survey of Canadians' Perceptions of Social Class. 1978. Montreal: Data Laboratories Research. 32 pp.

Sassier, P. 1990. *Du bon usage des pauvres: histoire d'un thème politique.* Paris: Fayard. 450 pp.

Sennett, R. and J. Cobb. 1973. *The Hidden Injuries of Class.* New York: Vintage Books. 275 pp.

Waxman, C.I. 1977. *The Stigma of Poverty: a Critique of Poverty Theories and Policies.* New York, Toronto: New York Press, Pergamon Press. 148 pp.

Zieger, R.H. 1986. *American Workers, American Unions, 1920–1985.* Baltimore (Md.): Johns Hopkins University Press. 233 pp.

Health

MENTAL HEALTH

Alexander, F.G. and S.T. Selesnick, eds. 1966. *The History of Psychiatry: an Evaluation of Psychiatric Thought and Practice from Prehistoric Times to the Present.* New York: Harper and Row. 417 pp.

Bastide, R. 1977. *Sociologie des maladies mentales.* Paris: Flammarion. 314 pp.

Boudreau, F. 1984. *De l'asile à la santé mentale. Les soins psychiatriques: histoire et institutions.* Montreal: Éditions Saint-Martin. 274 pp.

Boukovski, V. 1971. *Une nouvelle maladie mentale en U.R.S.S.: l'opposition.* Paris: Le Seuil. 237 pp.

Castel, R. 1976. *L'âge d'or de l'aliénisme.* Paris: Éditions de Minuit. 334 pp.

Cellard, A. 1991. *Histoire de la folie au Québec de 1600 à 1850: le désordre.* Montreal: Boréal. 280 pp.

Cooper, D.G. 1970. *Psychiatrie et antipsychiatrie.* Paris: Le Seuil. 187 pp.

Craft, M.J. and A. Craft. 1978. *Sex and the Mentally Handicapped.* London: Routledge and Kegan Paul. 112 pp.

Crocetti, G.M. et al. 1974. *Contemporary Attitudes toward Mental Illness.* University of Pittsburgh Press. 244 pp.

Dear, M.J. and S.M. Taylor. 1982. *Not on our Street: Community Attitudes to Mental Health Care.* London: Plon. 182 pp.

Deleuze, G. and F. Guattari. 1975. *L'Anti-OEdipe.* 2nd edition. Paris: Éditions du Minuit. 494 pp.

Edelson, M. 1971. *The Idea of Mental Illness*. New Haven: Yale University Press. 140 pp.
Edgerton, R.B. 1967. *The Cloak of Competence. Stigma in the Lives of the Mentally Retarded*. Berkeley: University of California Press. 233 pp.
Feder, L. 1980. *Madness in Literature*. Princeton University Press. 331 pp.
Felman, S. 1978. *La folie et la chose littéraire*. Paris: Le Seuil. 354 pp.
Foucault, M. 1961. *Histoire de la folie à l'âge classique*. Paris: Plon. 583 pp.
Fréminville, B. de. 1977. *La raison du plus fort: traiter ou maltraiter les fous?* Paris: Le Seuil. 192 pp.
Gentis, R. 1970. *Les murs de l'asile*. Paris: Maspero. 90 pp.
Gobin, P. 1978. *Le fou et ses doubles: figures de la dramaturgie québécoise*. Montreal: PUM. 263 pp.
Goffman, E. 1961. *Asylums: Essays on the Social Situation of Mental Patients and Other Inmates*. New York: Doubleday. 386 pp.
Grob, G.N. 1973. *Mental Institutions in America: Social Policy to 1875*. New York: Free Press. 458 pp.
Gunn, J. and D.P. Farrington, eds. 1982. *Abnormal Offenders, Delinquency and the Criminal Justice System*. Toronto, New York: Wiley. 384 pp.
Jacerme, P. 1974. *La folie: de Sophocle à l'antipsychiatrie*. Montreal, Paris: Bordas. 223 pp.
Jaeger, M. 1981. *Le désordre psychiatrique. Des politiques de la santé mentale en France*. Paris: Payot. 264 pp.
Kittrie, N.N. 1971. *The Right to be Different – Deviance and Enforced Therapy*. Baltimore, London: Johns Hopkins Press. 443 pp.
Lainé, T. and D. Karlin. 1977. *La raison du plus fou*. Paris: Éditions Sociales. 341 pp.
Laing, R.D. 1965. *The Divided Self*. 2nd edition. Harmondsworth (Middlesex): Penguin Books. 218 pp.
Lamontagne, Y. 1985. *L'ampleur des maladies mentales au Québec*. Québec: Québec Science. 99 pp.
Langlois, L. 1975. *Attitudes envers des malades mentaux qui vivent hors de l'hôpital psychiatrique*. Ministère des Affaires sociales du Québec. 148 pp.
Leighton, A.H. 1982. *Caring for Mentally Ill People. Psychological and Social Barriers in Historical Context*. London, New York: Cambridge University Press. 277 pp.
Mannoni, M. 1970. *Le psychiatrie, son "fou" et le psychanalyste*. Paris: Le Seuil. 267 pp.
Marsella, A.J. and G.M. White. 1982. *Cultural Conceptions of Mental Health and Therapy*. Dordrecht, Boston, London: D. Reidel Pub. Co. 414 pp.
Millett, K. 1990. *The Loony-Bin Trip*. New York: Simon and Schuster. 316 pp.
Pagé, J.C. 1961. *Les fous crient au secours, témoignage d'un ex-patient de Saint-Jean-de-Dieu*. 2nd edition. Montreal: Éditions du Jour. 156 pp.
Pélicer, Y. 1982. *Histoire de la psychiatrie*. 3rd edition. Paris: PUF. 127 pp.

Provencher, S. 1982. *Erreur sur la personne: cinq malades mentaux se racontent.* Montreal: VLB Éditeur. 188 pp.

Rosen, G. 1968. *Madness in Society: Chapters in the Historical Sociology of Mental Illness.* London: Routledge & Kegan Paul. 337 pp.

Ross, R.T. et al. 1985. *Lives of the Mentally Retarded. A Forty-Year Follow-Up Study.* Stanford University Press (Ca.). 203 pp.

Rothman, D.J. 1971. *The Discovery of the Asylum: Social Order and Disorder in the New Republic.* Boston: Little, Brown. 376 pp.

Santé mentale et processus sociaux/Sociologie et sociétés. 1985 (April), XVII, 1. Montreal: PUM.

Santos, E. 1977. *L'itinéraire psychiatrique.* Paris: Éditions des femmes. 132 pp.

Scheff, T.J. 1966. *Being Mentally Ill: a Sociological Theory.* Chicago: Aldine Pub. Co. 209 pp.

Scull, A.T. 1979. *Museums of Madness. The Social Organization of Insanity in 19th Century England.* London: Penguin Books. 275 pp.

Solidarité-psychiatrie. 1984. *La folie comme de raison. Histoires vraies.* Montreal: VLB Éditeur. 246 pp.

Saint-Amand, N. 1986. *Folie et oppression.* Moncton (N.B.): Éditions de l'Acadie. 199 pp.

Szasz, T. 1970. *The Manufacture of Madness. A Comparative Study of the Inquisition and the Mental Health Movement.* New York: Harper & Row. 383 pp.

Townsend, J.M. 1978. *Cultural Conceptions and Mental Illness: a Comparison of Germany and America.* University of Chicago Press. 150 pp.

Vanier, J. 1971. *Ton silence m'appelle.* Paris: Fleurus. 126 pp.

Weinberg, S.K., ed. 1967. *The Sociology of Mental Disorders.* Chicago: Aldine Publishing Co. 367 pp.

PHYSICAL HEALTH

Bowe, F. 1978. *Handicapping America. Barriers to Disabled People.* New York: Harper and Row. 254 pp.

Chicaud, M.B. 1979. *Les enfants de petite taille.* Paris: Fleurus. 273 pp.

L'écran handicapé/Cinémaction. 1983. Dossier compiled by Olga Beher. Paris. Cerf.

Enby, G. 1975. *Let There Be Love: Sex and the Handicapped.* New York: Taplinger Pub. Co. 65 pp.

Finkelstein, V. 1980. *Attitudes and Disabled People.* New York. World Rehabilitation Fund. 104 pp.

Gerhardt, U. 1989. *Ideas about Illness. An Intellectual and Political History of Medical Sociology.* London: Macmillan. 425 pp.

Herzlich, C. and J. Pierret. 1984. *Maladies d'hier, maladies d'aujourd'hui.* Paris: Payot. 295 pp.

Hunt, P., ed. 1966. *Stigma: the Experience of Disability.* London: Geoffrey Chapman. 176 pp.

Krause, E.A. 1977. *Power and Illness, the Political Sociology of Health and Medical Care*. New York: Elsevier. 383 pp.
Laplantine, F. 1986. *Anthropologie de la maladie*. Paris: Payot. 411 pp.
Lenoir, R. 1974. *Les exclus: un Français sur dix*. 3rd edition. Paris: Le Seuil. 180 pp.
Loux, F. and P. Richard. 1978. *Sagesse du corps. La santé et la maladie dans les proverbes français*. Paris: Maisonneuve et Larose.
Maladies et sociétés. XIIe–XVIIIe siècles. 1989. Paris: CNRS. 420 pp.
Mittler, P. 1978. *People and Patients*. London: Methuen.
Munday, D. 1976. *Dorcas: Opportunity not Pity*. Turnbridge Wells (Kent): Midas Books.
Les personnes handicapées au Québec. Dossiers d'information de l'Office des personnes handicapées du Québec, 1984–. Québec. 12 vol.
Sandblom, P. 1987. *Creativity and Disease*. 4th edition. Philadelphia: G.F. Stickley Co. 143 pp.
Segal, P. 1977. *L'homme qui marchait dans sa tête*. Paris: Flammarion. 250 pp.
Sontag, S. 1978. *Illness as Metaphor*. New York: Farrar, Straus & Giroux. 88 pp.
Stewart, W.F.R. 1979 *The Sexual Side of Handicap*. Cambridge: Woodhead Faulkener. 208 pp.
Thomas, D. 1982. *The Experience of Handicap*. London: Methuen. 209 pp.
Thouez, J.-P. 1988. *L'espace et le temps en géographie des maladies*. Montpellier: Université Paul Valéry. 32 pp.
Topliss, E. 1982. *Social Responses to Handicap*. London, New York: Longman, 190 pp.
Veil, C. 1968. *Handicap et société*. Paris: Flammarion. 215 pp.
Veil, C., ed. 1982. *Vivre dans la différence: handicap et réadaptation dans la société d'aujourd'hui*. Toulouse: Privat. 315 pp.
Vivre ensemble?: les barrières psychologiques s'opposant à l'intégration des personnes handicapées: journées d'études et de recherches sur le handicap et les inadaptations. 1982. Paris: PUF. 282 pp.
Zuchman, E. 1982. *Famille et handicap dans le monde, analyse critique des travaux de la dernière décennie*. Paris: Centre technique national d'études et de recherches sur les handicaps et les inadaptations. 181 pp.

Ethnicity, Race, Peripheral Groups

Apostolides, J.-M. 1984. *Les métamorphoses de Tintin*. Paris: Seghers. 293 pp.
Banton, M. 1971. *Sociologie des relations raciales*. Paris: Payot. 422 pp.
Berry, B.A. and H.L. Tischler. 1978. *Race & Ethnic Relations*. 4th edition. Boston: Houghton Mifflin. 433 pp.
Bienvenue, R.M. and J.E. Goldstein, eds. 1985. *Ethnicity and Ethnic Relations in Canada*. 2nd edition. Toronto: Butterworths. 335 pp.

Billig, M. 1981. *L'internationale raciste. De la psychologie à la "science" des races.* Paris: Maspero. 175 pp.

Butcher, P. ed. 1977. *The Minority Presence in American Literature, 1600–1900.* Washington (D.C.): Howard University Press. 2 vol.

Caldwell, G. 1983. *Les études ethniques au Québec: bilan et perspectives.* Québec: IQRC. 106 pp.

Castles, S. 1984. *Here for Good: Western Europe's New Ethnic Minorities.* London: Pluto Press. 259 pp.

Dinnerstein, L. and D.M. Reimers. 1975. *Ethnic Americans: a History of Immigration and Assimilation.* New York: Dodd, Mead & Co. 184 pp.

Di Pietro, R.J. and E. Ifkovic, eds. 1983. *Ethnic Perspectives in American Literature.* New York: Modern Language Association of America. 333 pp.

"Enjeux ethniques. Production de nouveaux rapports sociaux," *Sociologie et sociétés.* 1983 (October), XV, 2. PUM.

Ethnic and Immigration Groups: the U.S., Canada, and England. 1983. New York: Haworth Press. 126 pp.

Ferro, M. 1981. *Comment on raconte l'histoire aux enfants à travers le monde entier.* Paris: Payot. 316 pp.

Foster, C.R., ed. 1980. *Nations Without a State: Ethnic Minorities in Western Europe.* New York: Praeger. 216 pp.

Gardner, R.C. and R. Kalin, eds. 1981. *A Canadian Social Psychology of Ethnic Relations.* Toronto: Methuen. 244 pp.

Glazer, N. and D.P. Moynihan, eds. 1975. *Ethnicity: Theory and Experience.* Cambridge (Mass.): Harvard University Press. 531 pp.

Gossett, T.F. 1963. *Race: the History of an Idea in America.* Dallas: Southern Methodist University Press. 512 pp.

Guillaumin, C. 1972. *L'idéologie raciste. Genèse et langage actuel.* La Haye, Paris: Mouton. 247 pp.

Hall, R.L. 1979. *Ethnic Autonomy: Comparative Dynamics, the Americas, Europe and The Developing World.* New York, Toronto: Pergamon Press. 458 pp.

Halloran, J.D., ed. 1977. *Ethnicity and the Media. Reporting in the United Kingdom, Canada and Ireland.* Paris: UNESCO. 376 pp.

Helmreich, W.B. 1982. *The Things They Say Behind Your Back. Stereotypes and the Myths Behind Them.* New York: Doubleday. 276 pp.

Hepburn, A.C., ed. 1978. *Minorities in History.* London: E. Arnold. 251 pp.

Hunt, C.L. and L. Walker. 1979. *Ethnic Dynamics: Patterns of Intergroup Relations in Various Societies.* 2nd edition. Holmes Beach (Fla.): Learning Publications. 463 pp.

L'immigration au Québec/Cahiers de recherche sociologique. 1984 (September), 2, 2. UQAM.

Kuper, L., ed. 1975. *Race, Science and Society.* Paris, New York: UNESCO. 370 pp.

Lecomte, M. and C. Thomas, eds. 1983. *Le facteur ethnique aux États-Unis et au Canada*. Université de Lille III. 251 pp.

Lévi-Strauss, C. 1952. *Race et histoire*. Paris: UNESCO. 85 pp.

McNeely, R.L. and C.E. Pope, eds. 1981. *Race, Crime and Criminal Justice*. Beverly Hills: Sage Publications. 176 pp.

Memmi, A. 1982. *Le racisme: description, définition, traitement*. Paris: Gallimard. 220 pp.

Migrations et communautés culturelles. 1982. (Questions de culture, 2). Québec: IQRC.

Miles, R. 1989. *Racism*. London: Routledge. 158 pp.

Miller, R.M., ed. 1980. *The Kaleidoscopic Lens: How Hollywood Views Ethnic Groups*. Englewood (N.J.): J.S. Ozer. 222 pp.

Olson, J.S. 1979. *The Ethnic Dimension in American History*. New York: St. Martin's Press. 440 pp.

Paraf, P. 1981. *Le racisme dans le monde*. 6th edition. Paris: Payot. 243 pp.

Pirotte, J., ed. 1982. *Stéréotypes nationaux et préjugés raciaux aux 19e et 20e siècles: sources et méthodes pour une approche historique*. Louvain-la-Neuve: Éditions Nauwelaerts. 165 pp.

Ramcharan, S. 1982. *Racism: Non-Whites in Canada*. Toronto: Butterworths. 138 pp.

Rex, J. 1970. *Race Relations in Sociological Theory*. New York: Schocken Books. 169 pp.

Ringer, B.B. 1983. *"We the People" and Others. Duality and America's Treatment of its Racial Minorities*. New York, London: Tavistock. 1,100 pp.

Said. A.A. and L.R. Simmons. 1976. *Ethnicity in an International Context*. New Brunswick (N.J.): Transaction Books. 241 pp.

Stepan, N. 1982. *The Idea of Race in Science: Great Britain, 1800–1960*. London: Macmillan. 230 pp.

Taguieff, P.A. 1988. *La force du préjugé. Essai sur le racisme et ses doubles*. Paris: La Découverte. 644 pp.

Thomas, A. and S. Sillen. 1972. *Racism and Psychiatry*. New York: Bruner-Mazel. 176 pp.

Van den Berghe, P. 1981. *The Ethnic Phenomenon*. New York, Oxford: Elsevier. 307 pp.

Van den Berghe, P. 1978. *Race and Racism: a Comparative Perspective*. 2nd edition. New York: Wiley. 171 pp.

Van den Berge, P. 1970. *Race and Ethnicity: Essays in Comparative Sociology*. New York, London: Basic Books. 312 pp.

Wieviorka, M. 1992. *La France raciste*. Paris: Le Seuil.

Windisch, U. 1978. *Xénophobie?: logique de la pensée populaire: analyse sociologique du discours des partisans et des adversaires des mouvements xénophobes*. Lausanne: L'Âge d'homme. 182 pp.

Yetman, N.R. and C.H. Steele, eds. 1975. *Majority and Minority: the Dynamics of Racial and Ethnic Relations*. 2nd edition. Boston, Toronto: Allyn and Bacon. 640 pp.

NATIVE PEOPLES

Adams, H. 1975. *Prison of Grass: Canada from the Native Point of View*. Toronto: New Press. 238 pp.

André, A. 1976. *Je suis une maudite sauvagesse*. Ottawa: Leméac. 238 pp.

Assiniwi, B. 1973–1974. *Histoire des Indiens du Haut et du Bas Canada*. Montreal: Leméac. 3 vol.

Bataille, G.M. and C.L.P. Silet, eds. 1980. *The Pretend Indians: Images of Native Americans in the Movies*. Ames: Iowa State University Press.

Berkhofer, R.F. 1978. *The White Man's Indian: Images of the American Indian from Columbus to the Present*. New York: A.A. Knopf. 261 pp.

Brown, D. 1973. *Enterre mon coeur: la longue marche des Indiens vers la mort*. Paris: Stock. 551 pp.

Chamberlin, J.E. 1975. *The Harrowing of Eden: White Attitudes toward North American Natives*. Toronto, Montreal: Fitzhenry & Whiteside. 248 pp.

Delanoe, N. 1982. *L'entaille rouge, terres indiennes et démocratie américaine 1776–1980*. Paris: Maspero. 418 pp.

Deloria, V. 1971. *Custer Died for Your Sins. An Indian Manifesto*. 7th edition. New York: MacMillan. 279 pp.

Dupuis, R. 1991. *La question indienne au Canada*. Montreal: Boréal (Express). 125 pp.

Graugnard, J.F. et al. 1979. *Voix indiennes: le message des Indiens d'Amérique au monde occidental*. Paris: Les formes du secret. 242 pp.

Haycock, R.G. 1971. *The Image of the Indian: the Canadian Indian as a Subject and a Concept in a Sampling of the Popular National Magazines Read in Canada, 1900–1970*. Waterloo Lutheran University. 98 pp.

Jaulin, R. 1972. *L'ethnocide à travers les Amériques*. Paris: Fayard. 431 pp.

Marcil, C. and D. Thibault. 1985. *Le printemps indien*. Montreal: Québec-Amérique. 339 pp.

Monkman, L. 1981. *A Native Heritage: Images of the Indian in English Canadian Literature*. University of Toronto Press. 193 pp.

Morin, G.H. 1977. *Le cercle brisé: l'image de l'Indien dans le western*. Paris: Payot. 320 pp.

Oswalt, W.H. 1978. *This Land Was Theirs: a Study of North American Indians*. 3rd edition. New York, Toronto: Wiley. 569 pp.

Prucha, F.P. 1985. *The Indians in American society. From the Revolutionary War to the Present*. Berkeley: University of California Press. 127 pp.

Savard, R. 1979. *Destins d'Amérique: les autochtones et nous*. Montreal: L'Hexagone. 189 pp.

Smith, D.B. 1979. *Le "Sauvage" pendant la période héroïque de la Nouvelle-France (1534–1663) d'après les historiens canadiens-français des 19ᵉ et 20ᵉ siècles*. Montreal: Hurtubise HMH. 137 pp.

Todorov, T. 1982. *La conquête de l'Amérique, la question de l'Autre*. Paris: Le Seuil. 258 pp.

Vincent, S. and B. Arcand. 1979. *L'image de l'Amérindien dans les manuels scolaires du Québec*. Montreal: Hurtubise HMH. 234 pp.

BLACKS

Baldwin, J. 1963. *La prochaine fois, le feu*. Paris: Gallimard.

Bogle, D. 1973. *Toms, Coons, Mulattoes, Mammies and Bucks: an Interpretative History of Blacks in American Films*. New York: Viking. 260 pp.

Cleaver, E. 1968. *Soul on Ice*. New York: McGraw-Hill. 210 pp.

Fanon, F. 1952. *Peau noire, masques blancs*. Paris: Le Seuil. 238 pp.

Frederickson, G.M. 1971. *The Black Image in the White Mind: the Debate on Afro-American Character and Destiny, 1817–1914*. New York: Harper & Row. 343 pp.

Gross, S.L. and J.F. Hardy, eds. 1966. *Images of the Negro in American Literature*. University of Chicago Press. 321 pp.

Hoffman, L.F. 1973. *Le nègre romantique: personnage littéraire et obsession collective*. Paris: Payot. 302 pp.

L'image du Noir dans l'art occidental. 1976–1989. Paris: Bibliothèque des arts. 4 vol.

Jordan, W.D. 1969. *White over Black, American Attitudes toward the Negro 1550–1812*. Baltimore: Penguin Books. 651 pp.

Kaké, J.B. 1977. *La traite négrière: l'Afrique brisée* ("Histoire générale de l'Afrique", 6). Paris: Afrique biblio Club. 111 pp.

Kimoni, J. 1980. *Une image du Noir et de sa culture: esquisse de l'évolution de l'idée du Noir et de sa culture dans les lettres françaises du début du siècle à l'entre-deux-guerres*. Neuchâtel: Messeiller. 147 pp.

Ladner, J.A., ed. 1973. *The Death of White Sociology*. New York: Random House. 476 pp.

Leab, D.J. 1975. *From Sambo to Superspade: The Black Experience in Motion Pictures*. Boston: Houghton Mifflin. 301 pp.

Meier, A. and E. Rudnick. 1986. *Black History and the Historical Profession, 1915–1980*. University of Illinois Press. 448 pp.

Morrison, T. 1992. *Playing in the Dark. Whiteness and the Literary Imagination*. Cambridge (Mass.): Harvard University Press.

Newby, I.A. 1967. *Challenge to the Court. Social Scientists and the Defense of Segregation, 1954–1966*. Baton Rouge: Louisiana State University Press. 381 pp.

Nous les nègres: entretiens (de) James Baldwin, Malcolm X (et de) Martin Luther

King, avec Kenneth B. Clark. 1965. Introduced by A. Memmi. Paris. Maspero. 101 pp.

Sartre, J.P. 1948. "Orphée noir", introduction to *Anthologie de la poésie noire* by Léopold Sédar Senghor. Paris: PUF.

Schuman, H. and S. Hatchett. 1974. *Black Racial Attitudes: Trends and Complexities*. Ann Arbor: University of Michigan. 157 pp.

JEWS

Abella, I. and H. Troper. 1982. *None is Too Many: Canada and the Jews of Europe 1933–1948*. Toronto: Lester & Orpen Dennys. 336 pp.

Aris, S. 1970. *But There Are No Jews in England*. New York: Stein & Day.

Belth, N.C. 1979. *A Promise to Keep: a Narrative of the American Encounter with Anti-Semitism*. New York: Times Books.

Dreyfus, A. 1901. *Cinq années de ma vie*. Paris: E. Fasquelle. 360 pp.

Erens, P. 1984. *The Jew in American Cinema*. Bloomington: Indiana University Press. 455 pp.

Finkielkraut, A. 1982. *L'avenir d'une négation: réflexion sur la question du génocide*. Paris: Le Seuil. 180 pp.

Friedman, L.D. 1982. *Hollywood's Image of the Jew*. New York: Frederick Ungar Pub. Co. 390 pp.

Gerber, D.A., ed. 1986. *Anti-Semitism in American History*. Urbana: University of Illinois Press. 428 pp.

Harap, L. 1974. *The Image of the Jew in American Literature: from Early Republic to Mass Immigration*. Philadelphia: The Jewish Publication Society of America. 586 pp.

Isaac, J. 1956. *Genèse de l'antisémitisme: essai historique*. Paris: Calmann-Lévy. 352 pp.

Lehrmann, C. 1960. *L'élément juif dans la littérature française*. 2nd edition. Paris: A. Michel.

Memmi. A. 1972. *La libération du Juif*. Paris: Payot. 262 pp.

Memmi, A. 1962–1966. *Portrait d'un Juif*. Paris: Gallimard. 2 vol.

Paris, E. 1980. *Jews. An Account of their Experience in Canada*. Toronto: Macmillan. 304 pp.

Poliakov, L. 1955–1977. *Histoire de l'antisémitisme*. Paris: Calmann-Lévy. 4 vol.

Rosenberg, E. 1960. *From Shylock to Svengali. Jewish Stereotypes in English Fiction*. Stanford University Press. 388 pp.

Sartre, J.P. 1954. *Réflexions sur la question juive*. Paris: Gallimard. 185 pp.

Savona, J.L. 1974. *Le Juif dans le roman américain contemporain*. Ottawa: M. Didier, 243 pp.

Teboul, V. 1977. *Mythe et images du Juif au Québec: essai d'analyse critique*. Montreal: Lagrave. 234 pp.

Wardi, C. 1973. *Le juif dans le roman français, 1933–1948*. Paris: A.-G. Nizet. 285 pp.

FOREIGN WORKERS, IMMIGRANTS, AND REFUGEES

Ben Jelloun, T. 1977. *La plus haute des solitudes. Misère sexuelle d'immigrés nord-africains.* Paris: Le Seuil. 176 pp.

Bernard, Ph., ed. 1976. *Les travailleurs étrangers en Europe occidentale.* Paris, La Haye: Mouton. 416 pp.

Castles, S. and G. Kosak. 1973. *Immigrant Workers and Class Structure in Western Europe.* London, Toronto: Oxford University Press. 514 pp.

Charon, M., ed. 1983. *Between Two Worlds: The Canadian Immigrant Experience.* Montreal: Quadrant. 326 pp.

Cinémas de l'émigration/Cinémaction. 1983. Paris: L'Harmattan.

Cintrat, I. 1983. *Le migrant: sa représentation dans les manuels de lecture de l'école primaire.* Paris: Didier. 154 pp.

Cogswell, J.A. 1983. *No Place Left Called Home.* New York: Friendship Press. 132 pp.

Emigrer. Immigrer/Le genre humain. 1988. Paris: Le Seuil. 192 pp.

Granotier, B. 1979. *Les travailleurs immigrés en France.* 5th edition. Paris: Maspero. 300 pp.

Jacques, A. 1985. *Les déracinés. Réfugiés et migrants dans le monde.* Paris: La Découverte. 241 pp.

Labelle, M., C. Lemay, and C. Painchaud. 1980. *Notes sur l'histoire et les conditions de vie des travailleurs immigrés au Québec.* Québec: CEQ. 61 pp.

Priore, M.J. 1979. *Birds of Passage: Migrant Labor and Industrial Societies.* Cambridge, New York: Cambridge University Press. 229 pp.

Power, J. 1979. *Migrant Workers in Western Europe and the United States.* Oxford, Toronto: Pergamon Press. 167 pp.

Schnapper, D. 1991. *La France de l'intégration: sociologie de la nation en 1990.* Paris: Gallimard. 374 pp.

Tardos, T. 1982. *Transitville: étranges émigrants de l'Est.* Paris: Maspero. 188 pp.

REGIONAL POPULATIONS

Berthet, C. et al. 1982. *Langue dominante, langues dominées.* Paris: Edilig. 178 pp.

Bidart, P., ed. 1991. *Régions, nations, états. Composition et recomposition de l'espace national.* Paris: Publisud. 209 pp.

Cinémas des régions/Cinémaction. 1980. Paris: Papyrus.

Clout, H.D. 1976. *The Regional Problem in Western Europe.* Cambridge: Cambridge University Press. 59 pp.

Gibbins, R. 1982. *Regionalism: Territorial Politics in Canada and the United States.* Toronto: Butterworths. 217 pp.

Giles, H. and P.F. Powesland. 1975. *Speech Style and Social Evaluation.* London: Academic Press. 218 pp.

Gras, C. and G. Livet, eds. 1977. *Régions et régionalisme en France du 18e siècle à nos jours.* Paris: PUF. 594 pp.

Gras, S. and C. Gras. 1982. *La révolte des régions d'Europe occidentale: de 1916 à nos jours*. Paris: PUF. 263 pp.
Hechter, M. 1977. *Internal Colonialism: the Celtic Fringe in British National Development 1536–1966*. Berkeley: University of California Press. 361 pp.
Lafont, R. 1971. *Décoloniser en France: les régions face à l'Europe*. Paris: Gallimard. 308 pp.
Lebesque, M. 1970. *Comment peut-on être Breton?* Paris: Le Seuil. 240 pp.
Petrella, R. 1978. *La renaissance des cultures régionales en Europe*. Paris: Éditions Entente. 317 pp.
Philipponneau, M. 1967. *La gauche et les régions*. Paris: Calmann-Lévy. 254 pp.
Les régions culturelles. 1983. (Questions de culture, 5). Québec: IQRC. 188 pp.
Touraine, A. et al. 1981. *Le Pays contre l'État: luttes occitanes*. Paris: Le Seuil. 318 pp.

COLONIZED PEOPLES

Arnold, D., ed. 1988. *Imperial Medicine and Indigenous Societies*. Manchester: Manchester University Press. 231 pp.
Astier Loutfi, M. 1971. *Littérature et colonialisme: l'expansion coloniale vue dans la littérature romanesque française, 1871–1914*. Paris: Mouton. 147 pp.
Baudet, H. 1965. *Paradise on Earth: Some Thoughts on European Images of Non-European Man*. New Haven: Yale University Press.
Bouillon, A. 1981. *Madagascar. Le colonisé et son "âme". Essai sur le discours psychologique colonial*. Paris: L'Harmattan. 423 pp.
Calvet, L.J. 1974. *Linguistique et colonialisme*. Paris: Payot. 272 pp.
Césaire, A. 1955. *Discours sur le colonialisme*. Paris: Présence africaine. 59 pp.
Charra, A. 1975. *L'image du colonialisme espagnol dans le roman américain de 1898 à 1950*. Paris: Didier. 198 pp.
Écrans colonisés/Cinémaction. Non-series. Dossier compiled by Guy Hennebelle. Paris.
Fanon, F. 1974. *Les damnés de la terre*. Paris: Maspero. 232 pp.
Girardet, R. 1986. *Histoire de l'idée coloniale en France*. Paris: Hachette.
Grimal, H. 1965. *La décolonisation 1919–1963*. 2nd edition. Paris: A. Colin. 408 pp.
Guillaume, P. 1974. *Le monde colonial XIXe-XXe siècles*. Paris: A. Colin. 296 pp.
Magdoff, H. 1979. *L'impérialisme de l'époque coloniale à nos jours*. Paris: Maspero. 312 pp.
Mannoni, O. 1950. *Psychologie de la colonisation*. Paris: Le Seuil.
Memmi, A. 1972. *Portrait du colonisé*, followed by *Les Canadiens français sont-ils des colonisés?* Montreal: L'Étincelle. 146 pp.
Merle, M., ed. 1969. *L'anticolonialisme européen de Las Casas à Marx*. Paris: A. Colin. 400 pp.
Nordman, D. and J.P. Raison, eds. 1980. *Sciences de l'homme et conquête*

coloniale. Constitution et usages des sciences humaines en Afrique (19e et 20e siècles). Paris: Presses de l'École normale supérieure. 238 pp.

Ryckmans, P. 1931. *Dominer pour servir*. Brussels: Dewitt. 225 pp.

Street, B.V. 1975. *The Savage in Literature. Representations of "Primitive" Society in English Fiction 1858–1920*. London, Boston: Routledge & Kegan Paul. 207 pp.

Vallières, P. 1968. *Nègres blancs d'Amérique*. Montreal: Parti-pris.

Weston, R.F. 1972. *Racism in U.S. Imperialism: the Influence of Racial Assumptions on American Foreign Policy, 1893–1946*. New York.

THIRD WORLD PEOPLES

Amin, S. 1973. *Le développement inégal: essai sur les formations sociales du capitalisme périphérique*. Paris: Éditions de Minuit. 365 pp.

Amin, S. et al. 1979. *Le Tiers Monde et la gauche*. Paris: Le Seuil. 190 pp.

Bruckner, P. 1983. *Le sanglot et l'homme blanc: tiers monde, culpabilité, haine de soi*. Paris: Le Seuil. 309 pp.

Carfantan, J.Y. and C. Condomines. 1980. *Qui a peur du Tiers Monde?* Paris: Le Seuil. 298 pp.

Chaliand, G. 1984. *Les faubourgs de l'histoire. Tiers-Mondisme et tiers-mondes*. Paris: Calmann-Lévy. 270 pp.

Dumont, R. 1973. *L'utopie ou la mort*. Paris: Le Seuil. 192 pp.

L'état du Tiers Monde. 1989. Paris and Montreal: La Découverte/Boréal. 321 pp.

Guernier, M. 1980. *Tiers Monde: trois quarts du monde*. Paris: Dunod. 153 pp.

Harrington, M. 1977. *The Vast Majority: a Journey to the World's Poor*. New York: Simon & Schuster. 281 pp.

Labbens, J. 1978. *Sociologie de la pauvreté: le tiers monde et le quart monde*. Paris: Gallimard. 312 pp.

Lacoste, Y. 1985. *Contre les anti-tiers-mondistes et contre certains tiers-mondistes*. Paris: La Découverte. 143 pp.

Liauzu, C. 1982. *Aux origines des tiers-mondismes: colonisés et anti-colonialistes en France (1919–1939)*. Paris: L'Harmattan. 274 pp.

Mason, P. 1970. *Patterns of Dominance*. London, Toronto: Oxford University Press. 377 pp.

Mattelart, A., X. Delcourt, and M. Mattelart. 1983. *La culture contre la démocratie? L'audio-visuel à l'heure transnationale*. Paris: La Découverte. 223 pp.

Mattelart, A. and A. Dorfman. 1976. *Donald l'imposteur ou l'impérialisme raconté aux enfants*. Paris: A. Moreau. 202 pp.

Association Québécoise des Organismes de Coopération Internationale. *Le Monde à l'envers/Le tiers monde et l'école*. 1983 (May), I, 1–2. Montreal.

Senghor, L.S. 1964–1977. *Liberté*. Paris: Le Seuil. 1: *Négritude et humanisme*. 448 pp. 2: *Négritude et civilisation de l'universel*. 576 pp.

Le Tiers Monde en films/Tricontinental-Cinémaction. 1981. Paris: Maspero.
Tricontinental/Famines et pénuries. La faim dans le monde et les idées reçues. 1982. Paris: Maspero.

Sexual Preference

Adams, S.D. 1980. *The Homosexual as Hero in Contemporary Fiction*. New York: Barnes & Noble. 208 pp.
Altman, D. 1976. *Homosexuel(le). Oppression et libération*. Paris: Fayard. 230 pp.
Bach, G. 1982. *Homosexualités: expression-répression*. Paris: Le Sycomore. 119 pp.
Bailey, D.S. 1955. *Homosexuality and the Western Christian Tradition*. London, New York: Longmans. 181 pp.
Bell, A.P., M.S. Weinberg, and S.K. Hammersmith. 1979. *Homosexualities: a Study in Diversity among Men and Women*. New York: Simon and Schuster. 505 pp.
Bell, A.P., M.S. Weinberg, and S.K. Hammersmith. 1981. *Sexual Preference. Its Development in Men and Women*. Bloomington: Indiana University Press. 242 pp.
Bergler, E. 1967. *Homosexuality. Disease or Way of Life?* New York: Collier Books. 282 pp.
Bertrand, L. 1984. *Le rapport Bertrand sur le vécu de 1000 femmes lesbiennes*. Montreal: Primeur. 396 pp.
Bieber, I. et al. 1962. *Homosexuality: a Psychoanalytic Study*. New York: Basic Books. 358 pp.
Bonnet, M.J. 1981. *Un choix sans équivoque. Recherches historiques sur les relations amoureuses entre les femmes XVIe-XXe siècle*. Paris: Denoël-Gonthier. 293 pp.
Bory, J.L. 1977. *Comment nous appelez-vous déjà?: ces hommes que l'on dit homosexuels*. Paris: Calmann-Lévy. 237 pp.
Brooks, V.R. 1981. *Minority Stress and Lesbian Women*. Lexington (Mass.), Toronto: Lexington Books. 219 pp.
Brown, H. 1976. *Familiar Faces, Hidden Lives: the Story of Homosexual Men in America Today*. New York: Harcourt Brace Jovanovitch. 246 pp.
Bullough, V.L. 1979. *Homosexuality: a History from Ancient Greece to Gay Liberation*. New York: New American Library. 196 pp.
Bullough, V.L. 1976. *Sexual Variance in Society and History*. New York: New American Library. 715 pp.
Caprio, F. 1962. *Female Homosexuality. A Modern Study of Lesbianism*. New York: Grove Press. 334 pp.
Caprio, F. 1970. *L'homosexualité de la femme*. Paris: Payot. 337 pp.
Churchill, W. 1971. *Homosexual Behavior Among Males: a Cross-Cultural and Cross-Species Investigation*. Englewood Cliffs (N.J.): Prentice-Hall. 347 pp.
Cinémas homosexuels/Cinémaction. 1981. Dossier compiled by Jean-François Garsi. Éditions Papyrus. 347 pp.

Cory, D.W. 1951. *The Homosexual in America*. New York: Greenberg
Courouve, C. 1985. *Vocabulaire de l'homosexualité masculine*. Paris: Payot. 252 pp.
De Jongh, N. 1991. *Not in Front of the Audience. Homosexuality on Stage*. London, New York: Routledge. 224 pp.
D'Emilio, J. 1983. *Sexual Politics. Sexual Communities: the Making of a Homosexual Minority in the United States. 1904-1970*. Chicago University Press. 272 pp.
Dorais, M. 1982. *La sexualité plurielle*. Montreal: Éditions Prétexte. 101 pp.
Dyer, R., ed. 1980. *Gays and Film*. London: British Film Institute. 78 pp.
Eck, M. 1966. *Sodome: essai sur l'homosexualité*. Paris: Fayard. 352 pp.
Ettore, E. 1980. *Lesbians, Women and Society*. London: Routledge & Kegan Paul. 208 pp.
Faderman, L. 1981. *Surpassing the Love of Men. Romantic Friendship* and *Love Between Women from the Renaissance to the Present*. New York: William Morrow & Co. 496 pp.
Fisher, P. 1972. *The Gay Mystique: the Myth and Reality of Male Homosexuality*. New York: Stein and Day. 258 pp.
Foster, J.H. 1975. *Sex Variant Women in Literature*. Baltimore: Diana Press. 420 pp.
Foucault, M. 1976. *Histoire de la sexualité, vol. I: La volonté de savoir*. Paris: Gallimard.
Girard, J. 1981. *Le mouvement homosexuel en France, 1945-1980*. Paris: Syros. 206 pp.
Greenberg, D.F. 1988. *The Construction of Homosexuality*. Chicago: University of Chicago Press. 635 pp.
Grier, B. 1981. *The Lesbian in Literature*. 3rd edition. Tallahassee (Fla.): Naiad Press. 168 pp.
Heger, H. 1981. *Les hommes au triangle rose. Journal d'un déporté homosexuel 1939-1945*. Paris: Persona. 160 pp.
Hoffman, M. 1969. *The Gay World. Male Homosexuality and the Social Creation of Evil*. 2nd edition. New York, Toronto: Bantam Books. 212 pp.
Hooker, E., ed. 1969. *Final Report of the Task Force on Homosexuality*. Bethesda (Ind.): National Institute of Mental Health.
Humphreys, L. 1972. *Out of the Closet: the Sociology of Homosexual Liberation*. Englewood Cliffs (N.J.): Prentice-Hall. 176 pp.
Hyde, H.M. 1970. *The Other Love: an Historical and Contemporary Survey of Homosexuality in Britain*. London: Heinemann. 323 pp.
Jacques, J.P. 1981. *Les malheurs de Sappho*. Paris: Grasset.
Johnston, J. 1973. *Lesbian Nation. The Feminist Solution*. New York: Touchtone Book. 279 pp.
Katz, J. 1976. *Gay American History: Lesbians and Gay Men in the U.S.A.: a Documentary*. New York: Harper & Row. 690 pp.

Kinsey, A.C. et al. 1953. *Sexual Behavior in the Human Female*. Philadelphia: Saunders. 863 pp.

Kinsey, A.C. et al. 1948. *Sexual Behavior in the Human Male*. Philadelphia: Saunders. 804 pp.

Kinsman, G. 1987. *The Regulation of Desire. Sexuality in Canada*. Montreal, New York: Black Rose Books. 233 pp.

Kleich, D. 1976. *Femme et femme: attitudes envers l'homosexualité féminine*. Paris: Édition des femmes. 315 pp.

Krich, A.M. 1954. *The Homosexuals, as Seen by Themselves and Thirty Authorities*. New York: Citadel Press. 346 pp.

Kronemeyer, R. 1980. *Overcoming Homosexuality*. New York, London: Macmillan. 220 pp.

Lanteri-Laura, G. 1979. *Lecture des perversions. Histoire de leur appropriation médicale*. Paris: Masson. 160 pp.

Marmor, J., ed. 1980. *Homosexual Behavior: a Modern Reappraisal*. New York: Basic Books. 416 pp.

Martin, D. and P. Lyon. 1980. *Lesbian/Woman*. 5th edition. New York, London, Toronto: Bantam Books. 310 pp.

Masters, W.H. and V.E. Johnson. 1979. *Homosexuality in Perspective*. Boston: Little Brown. 450 pp.

McNeill, J.J. 1976. *The Church and the Homosexual*. Kansas City: Sheed Andrews & McMeel Press Inc. 211 pp.

Ménard, G. 1982. *De Sodome à l'Exode. Jalons pour une théologie de la libération gaie*. Montreal: Éditions Guy Saint-Jean. 262 pp.

Meyers, J. 1977. *Homosexuality and Literature, 1890–1930* Montreal: McGill-Queen's University Press. 183 pp.

Nobili, N. and E. Zha. 1979. *Les femmes et l'amour homosexuel*. Paris: Hachette. 317 pp.

Not a Passing Phase: Reclaiming Lesbians in History 1840–1985. 1989. London: The Women's Press. 264 pp.

Oraison, M. 1975. *La question homosexuelle*. Paris: Le Seuil.

Pastre, G. 1980. *De l'amour lesbien*. Paris: Éditions Pierre Horay. 291 pp.

Plummer, K. 1975. *Sexual Stigma: en Interactionist Account*. London: Routledge and Kegan Paul. 258 pp.

Raymond, J. 1981. *L'empire transsexuel*. Paris: Le Seuil. 255 pp.

Rofes, E.E. 1983. *"I Thought People Like That Killed Themselves": Lesbians, Gay Men, and Suicide*. San Francisco: Grey Fox Press. 162 pp.

Rowse, A.L. 1977. *Homosexuals in History: a Study of Ambivalence in Society, Literature and the Arts*. London: Weidenfeld and Nicolson. 346 pp.

Roy, C. 1985. *Les lesbiennes et le féminisme*. Montreal: Éditions Saint-Martin. 142 pp.

Rule, J. 1975. *Lesbian Images*. New York: Doubleday & Co. 216 pp.

Russo, V. 1981. *The Celluloid Closet: Homosexuality in the Movies*. New York: Harper & Row. 276 pp.

Sarotte, G.M. 1976. *Comme un frère, comme un amant: l'homosexualité masculine dans le roman et le théâtre américains de Herman Melville à James Baldwin*. Paris: Flammarion. 353 pp.

Scacco, A.M., ed. 1982. *Male Rape: a Casebook of Sexual Aggressions*. New York: AMS Press. 326 pp.

Schofield, M. 1965. *Sociological Aspects of Homosexuality*. London: Longmans. 244 pp.

Sortir. 1978. Montreal: Éditions de l'Aurore. 303 pp.

Stambolian, G. and E. Marks, eds. 1979. *Homosexualities and French Literature: Cultural Contests, Critical Texts*. Ithaca (N.Y.): Cornell University Press. 387 pp.

Sylvestre, P.F. 1976. *Propos pour une libération homosexuelle*. Montreal: Éditions de l'Aurore. 154 pp.

Tripp, C.A. 1975. *The Homosexual Matrix*. New York, Toronto: McGraw-Hill. 314 pp.

Weeks, J. 1983. *Coming Out: Homosexual Politics in Britain from the Nineteenth Century to the Present*. London: Quartet Books. 278 pp.

Weinberg, G.H. 1973. *Society and the Healthy Homosexual*. New York: St. Martin's Press. 150 pp.

Wolff, C. 1979. *Bisexualty. A Study*. 2nd edition. London: Quartet Books. 262 pp.

Gender

Aebischer, V. 1985. *Les femmes et le langage*. Paris: PUF. 200 pp.

Anderson, B.S. and J.P. Zinsser. 1988. *A History of their Own. Women in Europe from Prehistory to the Present*. New York: Harper & Row. 2 vol.

Atkinson, T. 1975. *Odyssée d'une Amazone*. Paris: Éditions des femmes. 280 pp.

Aubert, J.M. 1975. *La femme. Antiféminisme et christianisme*. Paris: Cerf/Desclée. 226 pp.

Audé, F. 1981. *Ciné-modèles, cinéma d'elles. Situation des femmes dans le cinéma français 1956–1979*. Lausanne: l'Âge d'homme. 233 pp.

Backhouse, C. and L. Cohen. 1979. *The Secret Oppression. Sexual Harassment of Working Women*. Toronto: Macmillan. 208 pp.

Badinter, E. 1980. *L'amour en plus: histoire de l'amour maternel (17e–20e siècle)*. Paris: Flammarion. 472 pp.

Beauchamp, C. 1987. *Le silence des médias: les femmes, les hommes et l'information*. Montreal: Ed. du Remue-ménage. 281 pp.

Bédrines, N. et al. 1978. *Idées reçues sur les femmes*. 4th edition. Paris: Éditions Hier et demain. 189 pp.

Benjamin, M., ed. 1991. *Science and Sensibility: Gender and Scientific Enquiry, 1780–1945*. Cambridge (Mass.): Basil Blackwell. 295 pp.

Bessiere, J. ed. 1982. *Figures féminines et roman*. Paris: PUF. 191 pp.

Boucher, J. and A. Morel, eds. 1970. *Le droit dans la vie familiale*. Montreal: PUM. 302 pp.

Boynard-Frot, J. 1982. *Un matriarcat en procès: analyse systématique de romans canadiens-français, 1860–1960*. Montreal: PUM. 231 pp.

Branca, P. 1978. *Women in Europe since 1750*. New York: St. Martin's Press. 233 pp.

Bridenthal, R. and C. Koontz. 1977. *Becoming Visible. Women in European History*. Boston: Houghton Mifflin. 510 pp.

Brownmiller, S. 1975. *Against our Will. Men, Women and Rape*. New York: Bantam Books. 541 pp.

Callu, M.F. 1978. *Le nouveau droit de la femme: essai sur la condition juridique de la femme*. Lyon: L'Hermès. 429 pp.

Carmody, D.L. 1979. *Women and World Religions*. Nashville (Tn.): Abingdon. 172 pp.

Carrier, M. 1983. *La pornographie, base idéologique de l'oppression des femmes*. Québec: Apostrophe. 77 pp.

Carrière, L. et al. 1983. *Femmes et cinéma québécois*. Montreal: Boréal Express. 282 pp.

Ceulemans, M. and G. Fauconnier. 1979. *Image, rôle et condition sociale de la femme dans les médias: recueil et analyse de documents de recherche*. Paris: UNESCO. 87 pp.

Champagne-Gilbert, M. 1980. *La famille et l'homme à délivrer du pouvoir*. Montreal: Leméac. 415 pp.

Collectif Clio. 1982. *L'histoire des femmes au Québec depuis quatre siècles*. Montreal: Quinze. 521 pp.

Coquillat, M. 1982: *La poétique du mâle*. Paris: Gallimard. 472 pp.

Corbeil, C. et al. 1983. *L'intervention féministe: l'alternative des femmes au sexisme en thérapie*. Montreal: Saint-Martin. 188 pp.

Cott, N.F. and E.H. Pleck, ed. 1979. *A Heritage of her Own. Toward a New Social History of American Women*. New York: Simon and Schuster. 608 pp.

Dardigna, A.M. 1980. *Les châteaux d'Eros ou les infortunes du sexe des femmes*. Paris: Maspero. 334 pp.

D'Eaubonne, F. 1977: *Histoire de l'art et lutte des sexes*. Paris: Éditions de la différence. 182 pp.

De Beauvoir, S. 1949. *Le deuxième sexe*. Paris: Gallimard. 2 vol.

Delamont, S. 1980. *The Sociology of Women*. London: Allen and Unwin. 244 pp.

Descaries-Bélanger, F. 1980. *L'école rose ... et les cols roses: la reproduction de la division sociale des sexes*. Laval: Albert St. Martin. 128 pp.

Duby, G. and M. Perrot, eds. 1991–1992. *Histoire des femmes en Occident*. Paris: Plon. 5 vol.

Dufrancatel, C. et al. 1979. *L'histoire sans qualités*. Paris: Galilée. 223 pp.

Dunnigan, L. 1975. *Analyse des stéréotypes masculins et féminins dans les manuels scolaires au Québec*. Québec: Conseil du statut de la femme. 188 pp.

Ehrenreich, B. and D. English. 1979. *For HER Own Good. 150 Years of the Experts Advice to Women*. New York: Anchor Press/Doubleday. 369 pp.

Erens, P. ed. 1979. *Sexual Stratagems: The World of Women in Film*. New York: Horizon Press. 336 pp.

Evans, M. and C. Ungerson, ed. 1983. *Sexual Divisions, Patterns and Processes*. London, New York: Tavistock. 213 pp.

Faludi, S. 1991. *Backlash. The Undeclared War on American Women*. New York: Crown Publishers. 542 pp.

Fargier, M.O. 1976. *Le viol, Enquête*. Montreal: L'Étincelle. 221 pp.

Les femmes dans la sociologie/Sociologie et sociétés. 1981 (October), XIII, 2. Montreal: PUM.

Finn, G. and A. Miles, ed. 1982. *Feminism in Canada: From Pressure to Politics*. Montreal: Black Rose Books. 315 pp.

Firestone, S. 1979. *The Dialectic of Sex, the Case for Feminist Reaction*. 9th edition. New York: Bantam Books. 242 pp.

Fitzgerald, M. et al. 1982. *Still Ain't Satisfied. Canadian Feminism Today*. Toronto: The Women's Press. 318 pp.

Foreman, A. 1977. *Feminity as Alienation: Women and the Family in Marxism and Psychoanalysis*. London: Pluto. 168 pp.

Franz, M.L. von. 1979. *La femme dans les contes de fée*. Paris: La Fontaine de Pierre. 316 pp.

Friedan, B. 1963. *The Feminine Mystique*. New York: Dell Pub. Co. 384 pp.

Friedan, B. 1981. *The Second Stage*. New York: Summit Books. 346 pp.

Gallant, C. 1984. *La philosophie au féminin*. Moncton (N.B.): Éditions d'Acadie. 279 pp.

Gelles, R.J. and C.P. Cornell, eds. 1983. *International Pespectives on Family Violence*. Toronto: Lexington Books. 171 pp.

Gilligan, C. 1983. *In a Different Voice. Psychological Theory and Women's Development*. Cambridge (Mass.): London: Harvard University Press. 184 pp.

Greer, G. 1971. *La femme eunuque*. Paris: "J'ai lu." R. Laffont. 437 pp.

Groult, B. 1977. *Le féminisme au masculin*. Paris: Denoël-Gonthier. 195 pp.

Guillaumin, C. 1978. "Pratique du pouvoir et idée de Nature. 1) L'appropriation des femmes. 2) Le discours de la nature." *Questions féministes*: 2-3.

Hans, M.-F. and G. Lapouge. 1978. *Les femmes, la pornographie, l'érotisme*. Paris: Le Seuil. 400 pp.

Haskell, M. 1974. *From Reverence to Rape: the Treatment of Women in the Movies*. New York: Penguin Books. 388 pp.

Hellerstein, E.O., L.P. Hume, and K.M. Offen, eds. 1981. *Victorian Women. A Documentary Account of Women's Lives in Nineteenth Century England, France and the United States*. Stanford University Press. 534 pp.

Hess, T.B. and E.C. Baker, eds. 1973. *Art and Sexual Politics*. New York: Collier Books. 150 pp.

Hubbard, R., M.S. Henifin, and B. Fried. ed. 1979. *Women Look at Biology*

Looking at Women: a Collection of Feminist Critiques. Boston: G.K. Hall. 268 pp.

Hymovitz, C. and M. Weissman. 1978. *A History of Women in America*. New York: Bantam Books. 400 pp.

Irigaray, L. 1977. *Ce sexe qui n'en est pas un*. Paris: Éditions de Minuit. 224 pp.

Irigaray, L. 1974. *Speculum. De l'autre femme*. Paris: Éditions de Minuit. 468 pp.

Janssen-Jurreit, M.L. 1982. *Sexism: the Male Monopoly on History and Thought*. New York: Farrar, Straus & Giroux. 376 pp.

Keller, E.F. 1985. *Reflections on Gender and Science*. New Haven: Yale University Press. 193 pp.

Knibiehler, Y. and C. Fouquet. 1983. *La femme et les médecins: analyse historique*. Paris: Hachette. 333 pp.

Kramarae, C. 1981. *Women and Men Speaking: Frameworks for Analysis*. London: Newbury House Publishers, Rowley. 194 pp.

Lakoff, R. 1975. *Language and Women's Place*. New York: Harper and Row. 83 pp.

Lascault, G. 1977. *Figurées, défigurées: petit vocabulaire de la féminité représentée*. Paris: Union générale d'éditions. 222 pp.

Lederer, L., ed. 1982. *Take Back the Night. Women on Pornography*. Toronto, New York, London, Sydney: Bantam Books. 365 pp.

Lemieux, D. and L. Mercier. 1982. *La recherche sur les femmes au Québec*. Québec: IQRC. 336 pp.

Lemonde, A. 1984. *Les femmes et le roman policier. Anatomie d'un paradoxe*. Montreal: Québec/Amérique. 261 pp.

MacKinnon, C.A. 1979. *Sexual Harassment of Working Women: a Case of Sex Discrimination*. New Haven, London: Yale University Press. 312 pp.

Martin, D. 1983. *Battered Wives*. 2nd edition. New York: Pocket Books. 292 pp.

Mathieu, N.C. 1971. "Notes pour une définition sociologique des catégories de sexe," *Épistémologie sociologique*, 11. pp. 19–39.

Mazey, M.E. and D.R. Lee. 1983. *Her Space, her Place: a Geography of Women*. Washington (D.C.): Association of American Geographers. 83 pp.

McConnell-Ginet, S., R. Borker, and N. Furman, eds. 1980. *Women and Language in Literature and Society*. New York: Praeger. 352 pp.

Michard-Marchal, C. 1982. *Sexisme et sciences humaines: pratique linguistique du rapport de sexage*. Presses universitaires de Lille. 200 pp.

Millett, K. 1984. *Sexual Politics*. 5th edition. New York: Ballantine Books. 543 pp.

Mitchell, J. 1974. *Psychoanalysis and Feminism. Freud, Reich, Laing and Women*. New York: Pantheon Books. 456 pp.

Monaghan, P. 1981. *Women in Myth and Legend*. London: Junction Books. 318 pp.

Morgan, R. 1984. *Sisterhood is Global: the International Women's Movement Anthology*. New York: Anchor: 815 pp.

Murray, J.A., ed. 1982. *Strong-Minded Women and Other Lost Voices from Nineteenth-Century England*. New York: Pantheon Books. 453 pp.

Neuls-Bates, C., ed. 1982. *Women and Music. An Anthology of Source Readings from the Middle Ages to the Present*. New York: Harper and Row. 351 pp.

Olivier, C. 1980. *Les enfants de Jocaste. L'empreinte de la mère*. Paris: Denoël/Gonthier. 192 pp.

Ouellette-Michalska, M. 1981. *L'échappée des discours de l'oeil*. Montreal: Nouvelle Optique. 327 pp.

Paquot, E., ed. 1982. *Terre des femmes: Panorama de la situation des femmes dans le monde*. Paris and Montreal: Maspero/Boréal Express. 448 pp.

Paradis, S. 1966. *Femme fictive, femme réelle: le personnage féminin dans le roman féminin candien-français, 1884–1966*. Québec: Garneau. 330 pp.

Parker, R. and G. Pollock, 1981. *Old Mistresses: Women, Art and Ideology*. New York: Pantheon Books. 184 pp.

Pearson, C. and K. Pope. 1981. *The Female Hero in American and British Literature*. New York, London: Bowker. 314 pp.

Peterson, K. and J.J. Wilson. 1976. *Women Artists: Recognition and Reappraisal from the Early Middle Ages to the Twentieth Century*. New York: Harper and Row. 212 pp.

Pottker, J. and A. Fishel, eds. 1977. *Sex Bias in the Schools: the Research Evidence*. Cranberry (N.J.): Associated University Press. 571 pp.

Price, B.R. and N.J. Sokoloff, eds. 1982. *The Criminal Justice System and Women: Women Offenders, Victims, Workers*. New York: Clark Boardman. 490 pp.

Rafter, N.H. and E.A. Stanko, eds. 1982. *Judge, Lawyer, Victim, Thief: Women, Gender Roles and Criminal Justice*. Boston: Northeastern University Press. 383 pp.

Reed, E. 1979. *Féminisme et anthropologie*. Paris: Denoël/Gonthier. 271 pp.

Rich, A. 1976. *Of Woman Born: Motherhood as Experience and Institution*. New York: Norton. 318 pp.

Riemer, E.S. and J.C. Fout, eds. 1983. *European Women: a Documentary History, 1789–1945*. Brighton: Harvester Press. 258 pp.

Rosaldo, M.Z. and L. Lamphere, eds. 1974. *Women, Culture and Society*. Stanford University Press. 352 pp.

Rosen, M. 1973. *Popcorn Venus: Women, Movies, and the American Dream*. New York: Coward, McCann & Geoghegan.

Rossi, A.S., ed. 1973. *The Feminist Papers: from Adams to de Beauvoir*. New York, London: Columbia University Press. 716 pp.

Rowbotham, S. 1974. *Hidden from History. 300 Years of Women's Oppression and the Fight against it*. 2nd edition. London: Pluto Press. 181 pp.

Ruether, R.R. and R.S. Keller, eds. 1981–1986. *Women and Religion in America: A Documentary History*. San Francisco: Harper and Row. 3 vol.

Russ, J. 1984. *How to Suppress Women's Writing*. London: The Women's Press. 160 pp.

Sacks. A. and J.H. Wilson. 1979. *Sexism and the Law: a Study of Male Beliefs and Legal Bias in Britain and the United States*. New York: Free Press. 257 pp.

Sarde, M. 1983. *Regard sur les Françaises: Xe siècle-XXe siècle*. Paris: Stock. 667 pp.

Le sexisme ordinaire. 1979. Paris: Le Seuil. 384 pp. Preface by Simone de Beauvoir.

Siclier, J. 1957. *La femme dans le cinéma français*. Paris: Le Cerf. 196 pp.

Spender, D. 1983. *Women of Ideas (and what Men Have Done to Them)*. London, Boston, Melbourne: Ark Paperbacks. 800 pp.

Stone, M. 1979. *Quand Dieu était femme: à la découverte de la Grande Déesse, source du pouvoir des femmes*. Montreal: L'Étincelle. 350 pp.

Strauss, S. 1982. *Traitors to the Masculine Cause: the Men's Campaigns for Women's Rights*. Westpoint (Conn.): Greenwood Press. 290 pp.

Sullerot, E., ed. 1978. *Le fait féminin*. Paris: Fayard. 520 pp.

Trofimenkoff, S.M. and A. Prentice, eds. 1977. *The Neglected Majority. Essays in Canadian Women's History*. Toronto: McClelland & Stewart. 192 pp.

Weigle, M. 1982. *Spiders and Spinsters: Women and Mythology*. Albuquerque: University of New Mexico Press. 340 pp.

Wolf, N. 1991. *The Beauty Myth: How Images of Beauty Are Used Against Women*. New York: William Morrow. 348 pp.

Woolf, V. 1975. *A Room of One's Own*. Harmondsworth (Middlesex): Penguin Books. 112 pp.

Yaguello, M. 1978. *Les mots et les femmes*. Paris: Payot. 202 pp.

Multiple Parameters

Amott, T.L. and J.A. Matthai. 1991. *Race, Gender and Work: A Multicultural Economic History of Women in the United States*. Boston: South End Press. 433 pp.

À nous la parole: les femmes autochtones du Canada. 1975. Ottawa: Secretary of State. 125 pp.

Balandier, G. 1985. *Anthropo-logiques*. Paris: Livre de poche. 320 pp.

Berger, R.M. 1982. *Gay and Gray: The Older Homosexual Man*. Boston: Alyson Pub. 233 pp.

Brody, E.B. *et al.* 1968. *Minority Group Adolescents in the United States*. Baltimore: Williams and Wilkins. 243 pp.

Butler, R.N. and M.I. Lewis. 1977. *Aging and Mental Health: Positive Psychological Approaches*. 2nd edition. St. Louis: Mosby. 365 pp.

Chesler, P. 1983. *Women and Madness*. New York: Avon. 359 pp.

Cohen, L. 1984. *Small Expectations: Society's Betrayal of Older Women*. Toronto: McClelland & Stewart. 228 pp.

Cornwell, A. 1983. *Black Lesbian in White America*. Minneapolis: Naiad Press. 129 pp.

Davies, M., ed. 1983. *Third World, Second Sex: Women's Struggles and National Liberation. Third World Women Speak Out.* London: Zed Books. 257 pp.

Davis, A.Y. 1983. *Women, Race and Class.* New York: Vintage Books. 271 pp.

Derenski, A. and S.B. Landsburg. 1981. *The Age Taboo: Older Women-Younger Men Relationships.* Boston, Toronto: Little Brown. 262 pp.

Devereux, G. 1969. *Reality and Dream: Psychotherapy of a Plains Indian.* 2nd edition. New York: New York University Press. 615 pp.

Etienne, M. and E. Leacock, eds. 1980. *Women and Colonization: Anthropological Perspectives.* New York: Praeger. 339 pp.

Forer, L.G. 1991. *Unequal Protection: Women, Children and the Elderly in Court.* New York: W.W. Norton. 256 pp.

Gelfand, D.E. 1982. *Aging: the Ethnic Factor.* Boston, Toronto: Little Brown. 113 pp.

Glazer, N.Y. and C.F. Creedon, eds. 1969. *Children and Poverty. Some Sociological and Psychological Perspectives.* 2nd edition. Chicago: Rand McNally. 328 pp.

Guyon-Bourbonnais, L. 1981. *Va te faire soigner, t'es malade.* Montreal: Stanké. 158 pp.

Les handicapés mentaux vieillissent. 1986. Paris: PUF. 281 pp.

Harry, J. 1982. *Gay Children Grown Up: Gender Culture and Gender Deviance.* New York: Praeger. 270 pp.

Hernton, C.C. 1965. *Sex and Racism in America.* New York: Grove Press. 180 pp.

Herron, A., ed. 1986. *One Teenager in Ten: Testimony by Gay and Lesbian Youth.* 2nd edition. New York: Warner Books. 104 pp.

Hollingshead, A.B. 1975. *Elmtown's Youth and Elmtown Revisited.* New York. Wiley & Sons. 395 pp. (Reprint of *Elmtown's Youth: Impact of Social Class on Adolescents,* 1967).

Hollingshead, A.B. and F.C. Redlich. 1958. *Social Class and Mental Illness.* New York: Wiley & Sons. 442 pp.

Kergoat, D. 1982. *Les ouvrières.* Paris: Le Sycomore. 142 pp.

Labelle, M. *et al.* 1987. *Histoires d'immigrées.* Montreal: Boréal. 276 pp.

Lerner, G., ed. 1972. *Black Women in White America: a Documentary History.* New York: Pantheon Books.

Lloyd, P.C. 1982. *A Third World's Proletariat?* London, Boston: G. Allen & Unwin. 139 pp.

Lutte de classes ou conflit de générations? 1969. Paris: Pavillon. 189 pp.

MacDonald, B. and C. Rich. 1984. *Look Me in the Eye: Old Women, Aging and Ageism.* San Francisco: Spinsters Ink. 115 pp.

Matthews, G.F. 1983. *Voices from the Shadows. Women with Disabilities Speak Out.* Toronto: The Women's Press. 192 pp.

Mouvement nationaux d'indépendance et classes populaires aux 19e et 20e siècles en Occident et en Orient. 1971. Paris: A. Colin. 2 vol.

Myers, J.K. and L.L. Bean. 1968. *A Decade Later: a Follow-up of Social Class and Mental Illness*. New York: Wiley & Sons. 250 pp.

Osborne, R.T., C.E. Noble, and N. Weyl, eds. 1978. *Human Variation: the Biopsychology of Age, Race and Sex*. New York: Academic Press. 392 pp.

Polenberg, R. 1980. *One Nation Divisible: Class, Race, and Ethnicity in the U.S. Since 1938*. Harmondsworth (Middlesex): Penguin Books. 363 pp.

Scott, H. 1984. *Working your Way to the Bottom. The Feminization of Poverty*. London, Boston: Pandora Press. 192 pp.

Storper-Perez, D. 1974. *La folie colonisée*. Paris: Maspero. 156 pp.

Toth, E., ed. 1984. *Regionalism and the Female Imagination. A Collection of Essays*. New York: Human Sciences Press. 205 pp.

Vinet, A. et al. 1982. *La condition féminine en milieu ouvrier. Une enquête*. Québec: IQRC.

Willie, C.V., B.M. Kramer, and B.S. Brown, eds. 1973. *Racism and Mental Health: Essays*. University of Pittsburgh Press. 604 pp.

Wilson, J.P. 1978. *The Rights of Adolescents in the Mental Health System*. Boston, Toronto: Lexington Books. 321 pp.